POSITIVE SUM

POSITIVE SUM

Improving North-South Negotiations

Edited by

I. WILLIAM ZARTMAN

Routledge
Taylor & Francis Group

LONDON AND NEW YORK

To
Virgilio Barco
for success in
negotiations from asymmetry

First published 1987 by Transaction Publishers

2 Park Square, Milton Park, Abingdon, Oxfordshire OX14 4RN
605 Third Avenue, New York, NY 10017

Routledge is an imprint of the Taylor and Francis Group, an informa business

First issued in paperback 2020

Copyright © 1987 Taylor & Francis

Library of Congress Catalog Number: 86-11401

Library of Congress Cataloging in Publication Data

Positive sum.

   Includes bibliographies.
   1. Developing countries—Foreign economic relations.
2. International economic relations. 3. Diplomacy.
I. Zartman, I. William.
K3820.P67   1986   341.7′5   86-11401
ISBN 0-88738-107-3
ISBN 0-88738-650-4 (pbk.)

ISBN 13: 978-0-88738-650-3 (pbk)
ISBN 13: 978-0-88738-107-2 (hbk)

Contents

1. Introduction: Explaining North-South Negotiations   1
   I. William Zartman
2. Commodity Bargaining: The Political Economy
   of Regime Creation   15
   Robert L. Rothstein
3. The United Nations Committee of the Whole: Initiative
   and Impasse in North-South Negotiations   48
   Ronald I. Meltzer
4. The Third United Nations Conference on the Law of the
   Sea: North-South Bargaining on Ocean Issues   73
   Robert L. Friedheim
5. The Wheat Negotiations: Loss or Gain in North-South
   Relations?   115
   Raymond F. Hopkins
6. The Multifiber Arrangement: The Third Reincarnation   149
   Joseph Pelzman
7. The World Administrative Radio Conference 1979
   Negotiations: Toward More Equitable Sharing of the
   Global Radio Resources   171
   Barbara A. Fliess
8. Negotiating the Lomé Conventions: A Little Is Preferable
   to Nothing   213
   John Ravenhill
9. Debt Negotiations and the North-South Dialogue,
   1974-1980   259
   Chandra Hardy
10. Conclusions: Importance of North-South Negotiations   278
    I. William Zartman
    Index   302

1

Introduction: Explaining North-South Negotiations

I. William Zartman

North-South encounters are full of exhortation. Much of the literature is occupied by one side's telling the other, in beguiling or condemning tones, how it should behave for the greater good of humankind, while the other side spends a somewhat smaller portion of the debate telling how it is not so. From the bastions of their interest, the two sides throw bolts of righteousness at each other and are dismayed when the walls do not fall. The situation is one of conflict, unmitigated by any convincingly conveyed perceptions of common interest in a shared fate. The two sides are admonished to negotiate the future, but they currently argue like parties to a negotiation between those in a full lifeboat and those afloat outside. There is therefore not only conflict but disparity of power: those outside keep going under; they have not convinced those inside that there is room for both; and when they have threatened to tip the lifeboat and take the others' place, their failure to do so has discredited the threat. The problem is even worse than the metaphor, however, because it will not even go away. The weak states keep on clamoring outside the boat, fitfully struggling but never sinking, while the strong states throw them bread, discuss philosophy, and consider their fate.

It is no wonder that North-South relations have been at a low point during the 1980s. For half a decade in the 1970s, the countries of the poor, raw-material-producing, underdeveloped Third World of the South brought their case against the affluent, industrial, developed countries of the First World of the West in many different arenas, trying to produce a global wave of change in the international economic order. On the broadest level, emboldened by the appearance of power in the oil price rises and embargoes of 1973-74, the South tried to launch global negotiations for the inauguration of a New International Economic Order (NIEO). Beginning with the VI Special Session of the

1

United Nations General Assembly in 1974, it mobilized UN agencies and forums in an effort to effect sweeping change. At nearly the same time, before the total failure of global negotiations had become evident, it found inspiration in the appearance of the Organization of Petroleum Exporting Countries (OPEC) as a commodity cartel to seek both broad 'and commodity-specific reforms in trade relations around primary exports. In addition to attempting to change the terms of trade on export commodities, the South also asked procedural alterations in the decision-making institutions that governed the established order, seeking a greater participation or total changes in the bodies set up at Bretton Woods, notably the World Bank and the International Monetary Fund (IMF). For the most part, these assaults on the substance and procedures of the world economic order were turned back by a Northern response that combined delays, token measures, and partial remedies with outright stonewalling. Oil prices, which increased fourfold in constant dollars in the half-decade since 1969 and sixfold in the subsequent half-decade (and much more in current prices), were seen by both sides as a threatening weapon in the middle of the decade but as only a paper tiger by the end. The old order remained essentially unshaken because the Southerners did not have the power to shake it and the North was unshaken by their needs.

Greater progress was registered in other arenas. New international law or regulations were necessitated by technological advances in other subject areas, requiring global conferences on specific subjects such as maritime relations or telecommunications. Other attempts at specialized negotiations were inaugurated—to some extent by the North—to define trade and aid relations between parts of the two halves of the world such as Europe and Africa, or the United States and Latin America, with varying degrees of success. Finally, negotiations continued throughout the period and beyond on financial relations when Third World debts accumulated faster than repayment possibilities, either on the part of individual countries or categories of them.

Such partial measures may be variously interpreted as the arenas of real success, the fig leaves of real failure, or the signs of a waning wave of pressure for change. No doubt all three are correct, and the period that followed the half-decade of assault was a distinct lull in the conflict. Even the slight eruptions of the issue after 1979 were only symbolic demonstrations to show that the question of North-South relations was still alive. The advent of the world recession and the Reagan administration kept the conflict muted. Selected leaders of North and South met at Cancún in 1981 and, in the style of the Reagan administration, agreed to keep in touch. Negotiations on specific issues pattered on, sometimes arriving at renewal agreements that were more favorable to the North than to the South. After the strident United Nations Conference on Trade and Development (UNCTAD) at Manila and the Non-Aligned Movement (NAM) in Havana in 1979, the next "event" of the Group of 77 was the NAM in New Delhi in 1983 that postponed its usual call for global negotiations. There was a two-year lapse before a special conference was scheduled by members of the World Bank and Monetary Fund for April 1985. That too was a non-event and the two halves of the world now await the results of the eighth GATT negotiations opening in late 1986 and probably lasting the decade.

Yet the conflict between North and South remains, and beneath it an ongoing and perhaps worsening problem. The essence of the problem is that the two parts of the world are at different stages of development, so that the South only produces the ingredients for the industry of the North, and it sells them at uncertain and fluctuating rates to buy the more expensive finished products. There is an interdependence that locks the two parties into their unequal roles, and when the South seeks to share in the industrial role of the North it enters an arena where both the conditions of technology and the rules of competition put it at a disadvantage. Thus, there is neither equality of present status nor equality of opportunity for the future, and the inequality of condition is mirrored and magnified by the inequality of capability to change it. Not only have the norms and practices of postcolonial international relations trained the new nations to expect something different from their status of economic inferiority, after having emerged from a status of political subjugation, but the problems of economic inferiority within the international economic order keep coming back to the doorstep of the rich, who must keep their debtors alive enough to continue to service their debt, stable enough to continue to export their raw materials, and even prosperous enough to continue to buy the exports of the rich. But kept alive to that degree, the South calls for more, demanding the equality that humanitarian norms promise to human beings and that the norms of the United Nations—as part of the current international political order—promise to states. Hence, it is a conflict not only of relations but also of perspectives, for it is primarily seen by both sides in zero-sum terms.

What is it, then, other than the obstinate refusal of the problem to go away, that makes it appropriate to address it now, in the second half of the 1980s? The indicators are necessarily many, not predictive assurances but straws in the wind that suggest that it is time to start positioning and preparing for a new approach to the problem. For one, the period of solidarity–making has been played out, preparatory to a period of problem solving. Weak and disparate parties need an initial time of consciousness–raising and solidarity–making before they can turn to more detailed and pragmatic solutions. Aspects such as identity, awareness of interests, and sense of confidence are all aspects of the solidarity phase of activity, and are best built through confrontation. The half-decade of the 1970s was that time of confrontation, but now the stridency has disappeared from the language of the 1980s, the confrontationalist leaders such as Algeria's Boumedienne, Pakistan's Bhutto, Mexico's Echeverria, and others have been replaced, and some of the important forums for Third World solidarity such as the Organisation of African Unity, the League of Arab States, and even the NAM have been momentarily split and disabled. Although these may be signs of weakness, they may also give rise to more pragmatic approaches to problems now that the initial solidarity has been established, as the 1986 Priority Program of the OAU has shown.

The crisis dimension also had negative effects in the first half of the 1980s, pushing the parties to the bottom line of "each one for itself." The forms of this reaction are many, including protectionism, the lowering of expectations, more realistic stocktaking about domestic efforts, and others. Although it is possible to continue and intensify these efforts, this can be done only separately by each state; together, the efforts would move in the opposite direction, to seek common cooperative measures. The world recession of the late 1970s pushed rich and poor alike to separate measures in the early 1980s, but as the decade moves on, the possibilities of coordination and common attention to North-South relations become more evident. The Reagan proposal for a global economic conference is not the end but possibly the beginning of such a turn.

There is another side of this same effect, the domestic dimension. It is not clear whether parties make greater concessions when they are weak and therefore vulnerable, when they are strong and therefore cushioned, or whether both conditions obtain under the differentiating impact of some yet-unknown intervening variable. Politically, the effect seems to be the third: beleagured parties do not concede if the implications are immediately costly, if the concession is touted as a defeat, if zero-sum perceptions are high, but beleaguered parties do concede if concession raises the siege, if concession can be recast as victory, if positive-sum perceptions can be made dominant. Obviously, much is in the packaging. It might be expected that North and South may have learned something about packaging and presentation in the past decade. Even if they have not on their own, the time is ripe for a discussion of the process of packaging, presentation, and negotiation that builds on the lessons learned from the ups and downs of the past experience.

The Negotiation Process

In a situation of conflict and stalemate, where a problem cannot be gotten rid of even by the stronger side in the conflict, negotiation is an appropriate means of handling the problem. Studies of its potential for usefulness in the North-South conflict are sorely lacking. With exhortation as the main mode of discourse on North-South relations, little attention has been devoted to exploring ways of conflict management, conciliation, and cooperation. The rights and wrongs of the problem have been endlessly debated, with both sides talking primarily to themselves and their home audiences and with little attempt either to persuade the other party through appeal to its own interests in its own terms or to join forces in seeking a mutually satisfactory solution. What is needed is not only a return to the North-South problem but a new focus in terms of the process of problem solving. If inequality is the characteristic of the problem, negotiation is the appropriate means of changing the structure of relations on the margins and of providing new positions that are more satisfactory to both sides.

The lack of attention to process is perplexing. War is studied and taught as a process, as are many other things such as cooking, tennis, and expository writing. Why, then, is it so rare to see discussions of the process of North-South negotiations, learning from past performance rather than getting stuck on substantive positioning and debating? The question is more than only intellectually interesting, for it can bring some insights with its answer. Negotiation is not usually studied because it is caught among three more common deterministic explanations—economic, political, and moral. Much of the discussion on North-South matters is carried on (primarily by the North) in terms of established economic mechanisms with determinate outcomes—comparative advantage, supply and demand, pricing, and so on. The rest of the discussion in the North is in terms of simple power determinacies, in which the stronger parties decide and the weaker have not even the choice of rejection. On the part of the South, discussion is usually in equally determinate terms of morality, according to which what must happen is what should happen.

Determinacy does not kill debate, as any economist, political scientist, or philosopher knows, but it does deflect attention from process.

Outcomes, rather than the business of getting to them, are the subject of debate. Yet, as every baseball player knows, how you play the game has much to do with whether you win or lose. Process dominates—even if it does not determine—outcome. And because the economic, political, and moral determinates of outcomes are less sure than their advocates would have us believe, and are in any case mutually contradictory, it is worthwhile focusing on the process of negotiation, where economic, political, and moral factors all have a rightful but limited place.

There is no single approach to the study of the negotiation process. Instead, a recent surge of scholarship has produced a number of different approaches, all agreeing on roughly the same essence of the process but each focusing on a different aspect for its analysis. Each then produces different insights into the best ways of conducting negotiations and reaching an optimal result, and each produces different explanations of outcomes, i.e. hypotheses and propositions about why particular outcomes are reached. Without giving a full exposition of each school, a concise summary of their basic parameters and implications can be presented so as to identify the elements that may be useful for analysis of North-South negotiations. All of the approaches currently in use to explain outcomes start from a common appreciation of the essential nature of negotiation as a process of joint decision making that combines conflicting positions into a common outcome, a process in which each party is required to give something from its initial positions to attain an outcome that is mutually (although usually unequally) beneficial and is preferable to nonagreement, i.e. to unilateral attempts at a solution. The analytical question remains, How are such outcomes obtained? Its practical corollary is, How can each party deploy its own efforts to obtain an outcome favorable enough to be acceptable but attractive enough to the other party to draw it away from its own attempts at a unilateral solution and win its acceptance of an agreement?

The *structural* explanation is given in terms of power, either as relative positions of the parties at the outset of negotiations or as the relative ability of the parties to make their options prevail (or to counter the other's efforts to make the other's options prevail).[1] Structural analysis tells us that effective negotiations begin when the parties have a veto over each other's ability to solve the problem and/or when the parties can inflict pain on each other. The ability to inflict deprivations, such as threats or warnings, or provide gratifications in the form of promises or predictions, determines the outcome, and the appropriateness of one or another means is related to the power position (structural imbalance) of the parties. Shifts in the power position of the parties toward balance (strengthening of the weaker, weakening of the stronger) create conditions favorable to negotiation. From the structural point of view, North-South negotiations take place in face of an obvious imbalance that needs to await signs of redressment before they can occur fruitfully. Even without greater equality, however, negotiations can occur in those areas where mutual veto exists, and certain tactics (toughness for the weaker, softness for the stronger) are indicated and to be expected if a productive outcome is to be reached.

The *strategic* explanation is given in terms of the structure of value attached to the various outcomes produced by the actions of both parties.[2] Strategic analysis tells us that rational (value-maximizing) parties will (and should) frequently choose a less favorable noncooperative outcome to avoid being tricked in the search for a more favorable outcome through lack of trust. The party for whom concession is less acceptable than stalemate will do less well in negotiation than the party with a reverse value preference, and the relative ability of a party to do without an agreement determines the other's ability to obtain a more favorable outcome. From the strategic point of view, then, North-South negotiations suffer from the absence of both trust and balance. Attempts by the South to reverse the Northern preference for stalemate over concession undermine the attractiveness of an otherwise-indicated Northern policy for establishing trust.

The *tactical* explanation is based on the choice of the right move at the right moment, defined in terms of the evolution of the problem.[3] Tactical analysis indicates that a problem is ripe for resolution when the parties are caught in an intolerable stalemate that neither can break and that is marked by a looming or recent catastrophe, and that parties in negotiation come to terms only in the face of a deadline (a time when outcomes become predictably worse in the absence of an agreement). During negotiations, moments of agreement come from proper levels of openers, proper timing of toughness and softness, and proper disarticulation of the issues into exchangeable items on agreed terms of trade. From the tactical point of view, therefore, North-South relations are not ripe for negotiation and even if negotiated do not operate under any terminal time constraint, two points that explain why there have been so few successful outcomes. On lesser intermediate points, however, there may be occasions for agreement if a conscious effort is made to "buy" an agreement with equivalent concessions on related issues through the establishment of appropriate terms of trade.

The *incremental* process explanation uses a critical-risk or cost calculation based either on the benefits of the outcome or on the other party's cost calculations, or a mutual benefit calculation based either on each party's evaluation of outcomes or on each party's rates of movement toward them. These various calculations determine which party should make how much concession as the parties either move away from costs of nonagreement or move toward benefits of agreement.[4]

Incremental process analysis sees outcomes as determined by momentary cost-benefit calculations at each step of the negotiations, without any room for power or tactics (although some of these considerations are inherent in the contexts on which the calculations are based). It is essentially an economic analysis and assumes fixed values and defined agendas, and frequently even inevitable outcomes. For North-South negotiations, many such theories would indicate an outcome favorable to the North, although not all, and careful analyses remain to be done before conclusions can be indicated.

The *phased* process explanation is based on an understanding of a process that has to meet certain procedural imperatives in order to arrive at substantive goals. The three major phases are identified as diagnosis (the development of an information base for both parties' aims and needs), formulation (the need to find a formula that defines the area of agreement and provides a conceptual referent from which the details of the agreement can be deduced), and implementation (the application of the formula to the determination of details of agreement).[5]

We learn from phased analysis of process that agreement is best achieved through a conscious formula rather than merely concessions on details. Packaging issues is important to their resolution, and a problem-solving attitude that regards the problem, not the other party, as the "enemy" is helpful in achieving an outcome that maximizes one's own payoffs while providing the other party with reasons for holding to the agreement. From this angle, North-South negotiations thus far have never gotten beyond the incompatibility of competing formulas, and even agreements in smaller areas do not add up to a clear picture of new (or renewed) relations.

To date, most of the study of North-South relations has remained quite separate from the creative work being pursued on such analytical approaches, but some has generated hypotheses that purport to explain the North-South encounter in negotiatory terms.[6] Such provisional conclusions and others that appear in general discussions of North-South relations need to be tested against a range of experiences to establish their validity. In addition to the hypotheses already noted in each approach to negotiations, others that are currently available for testing are the following:

1. New international orders are negotiated only after a cataclysmic collapse of the old order, correcting the causes of the past collapse and using the defeated parties of the old order to provide the payoffs for those constructing the new.
2. Northern (or specifically U.S.) obstructionism has become an assumption or excuse for Southern inability to propose mutually agreeable outcomes.
3. Confrontationism is necessary for solidarity to produce change and dare not be relaxed until full change has resulted.
4. Southern collective self-reliance is necessary to establish a separate-but-equal basis for later North-South negotiations.
5. Negotiation is bound to fail when the parties' definitions of the problem diverge.
6. When one side possesses primarily negative power (i.e. only veto power but no positive incentives or trade-offs for the other party), a mutually favorable outcome is unlikely and an unfavorable atmosphere prevails, making matters worse.
7. Global forums keep results low because of the need to pace the slowest member and combine all interests.
8. Specific functional negotiations are fruitful and mutually productive; global negotiations are not, because of the broad demands and the complex agenda.
9. Unity within sides reduces the incentive to look for alternative solutions and strengthens commitment to a single choice.
10. In the absence of an ability to negotiate substantive change, North-South negotiations can fruitfully focus only on rule change for systemic relations.
11. Maximum demands as an opener lead to stalemate because of the inability to concede; "camel's-nose" openers lead to incremental changes.
12. Negotiations fail where demands of one side and the concessions of the other are imbalanced, and succeed only where equal trade-offs are possible.
13. Concessions are made by the party with the lowest tolerance for breakdown or conflict (critical-risk factor), which lies permanently on the Southern side.
14. North-South negotiations are more successful in a context that allows for crosscutting interests than in one that allows for only two (North and South) groups.
15. In the absence of an ability to produce constraints (sticks), only rewards (carrots) or moral obligations can produce results for the South.
16. Agreements are made when moderates from both sides find a

common ground and isolate their own extremes; or, agreements are made when the extremes of both sides discover or invent a new common ground and bypass their moderates; or, agreements are made when members of the extreme join the moderates after new discoveries or new circumstances.

Although other hypotheses might be found, the above hypotheses seem to contain the major points of interpretation of North-South negotiations. The purpose here is to test these notions, while at the same time looking for other possible explanations of success and failure. Presumably, when such explanations are found, they can be used to increase the incidence of success and reduce the probability of failure by guiding negotiation conditions and behavior.

The question of success is more complex than may first appear. The nature of negotiation is to arrive at a satisfactory agreement for the two or more sides, with satisfaction judged by the willingness of the sides to sign. By its very nature, it is not a process of winning and losing, so that success must be evaluated against the problem, not against the adversary. This point is frequently missed, particularly in public and media debates, and even among experts. But this nature of negotiations makes evaluation of successes a matter of degree, and judgment and ultimately of debate. To produce a useful judgment, a number of elements must be taken into account. First, as suggested, *signature* of an agreement is a prima facie or nominal sign of success because it indicates a judgment of the parties that they expect to be better off with the agreement as formulated than without and that they can do no better, either by continuing negotiations or by finding an alternative solution. Second, this conclusion must be verified by the observer, by checking the calculations of the participants and thereby ascertaining that indeed the parties are *better off* with this agreement than without (or than they were before). Nothing says that the parties must be equally better off. Pareto optimal criteria do indicate that the parties should be able to improve their position, with or without depriving the other parties of their advantages, but to insist that the parties benefit equally from the outcome may be imposing too stringent a condition for success. Third, the results should be evaluated against the *demands* or opening positions of the parties, with all the caveats about initial exaggeration that are necessary to an understanding of the process. Some might suggest—as indeed does one of the following chapters— that the judgment must also be taken in a historic context because parties may succeed in the longer run by forgoing an agreement now that would foreclose future progress. That is usually an iffy judgment to make, although all judgments of negotiated outcomes are based on contingent benefits and are therefore iffy. There is no way to wring the iffiness out of the matter of evaluation; these three criteria help make the process of judging success more explicit, which is all that can be expected. The criteria for success also help in selecting the cases for examination.

One can learn from failure as well as success, on condition that the two be separated and then the reasons for either be adduced. The cases chosen include three successful cases, two failures, and three cases of mixed success where an agreement was reached (criterion one) but the benefits remain under dispute. Furthermore, cases were sought where participants were the world community of nations (global negotiations), alongside others where the participants were limited by region or subject. Finally, cases were also chosen to enable a comparison between limited subject matter and a broader range of issues allowing different degrees of trade-offs. As a result, the following cases will be used as the basis for comparison.

The broadest and longest case is the Third Conference on the Law of the Sea (UNCLOS), which involved all the members of the United Nations in a series of meetings from Caracas in 1974 to the signatory meeting in Jamaica in December 1982. UNCLOS as a negotiation covered hundreds of issues but the broadest one was the principled conflict between the notion of the deep seabed as "Global Common," the property of the world community whose mining would be controlled by an administrative authority, and the idea of the seabed as an open nonstate area, available to private "homesteading" free of supranational controls. Broad issues such as the deep-sea mining provisions divided the negotiating states into North and South, but many other issues broke up the polarized confrontation into smaller and often crosscutting interest groups where trade-offs were possible. UNCLOS was a success in producing a signed and workable agreement, even though the U.S. government of Ronald Reagan is not among the signatories, the only major exception to an otherwise universal agreement.

Another case of global negotiations concerned the Integrated Program for Commodities (IPC) debated in the United Nations Conference on Trade and Development (UNCTAD) between 1974, just after the first oil shock, and 1979, when an agreement on the Common Fund was signed. The basic issue has been one of guaranteeing income and equalizing available resources for the poorer, commodity-producing countries of the South by means of a program that integrates various commodity measures. Despite the apparent success of the negotiations in setting up the Common Fund, the compromise was such that few are satisfied with its effectiveness and few have ratified the agreement.

One more global attempt was made in the Committee of the Whole (COW) of the United Nations General Assembly, established to prepare the XI Special Session of the United Nations General Assembly in 1980. This the COW did, but its own agenda since 1977 foundered on the rigidity of each side in anticipatory response to the rigidity of the other. The COW could never agree whether it was a negotiating forum or not, and so never reached any specific agreement.

Other narrower negotiations are part of the North-South encounters as well. Some are narrow in geographic terms, as in the negotiations every five or six years since 1962 between the European Communities and a growing number of African (and latterly, also Caribbean and Pacific) states, resulting in 1963 in the Yaoundé I Convention (named after the African capital where it was signed); in 1969, in Yaoundé II; in 1975, in Lomé I; in 1980, in Lomé II; and in 1985, Lomé III. The conventions provide for European aid to Africa to stabilize export earnings funds (STABEX and SYSMIN) for certain commodities, trade preferences for African products, special treatment for nationals in another member country, and other matters. Each round of negotiations has resulted in a successful agreement, marking an improvement over its predecessor, although still less than the South has demanded. The parties entered the negotiations with a prior commitment to success and lived up to their commitments.

Another set of negotiations, narrowed by subject but diffuse in its venue, concerns Southern countries' debt to Northern creditors, including both governments and commercial banks. Although single-country cases continue, an across-the-board effort at UNCTAD and the Conference on International Economic Cooperation (CIEC) in 1974-78 resulted in a conversion of some loans to grants for poorest countries. The latter negotiations succeeded only by being narrowly restricted in scope, whereas single-country negotiations have always been successful by dealing with the symptoms but never the cause, for the weaker country can turn its weakness into threat against the strong.

Two commodity agreements typify the spectrum of this sort of narrowing. Negotiations that began in 1974 for an International Wheat Agreement collapsed in 1979. Conflicting interests and a lack of power kept the parties from negotiating the creation of wheat reserves for market and food security. Negotiations for a second Multifiber Agreement from the end of 1980 to the end of 1981 were successful, but at the cost of providing a somewhat protectionist regime that restricted Southern textile exports and penalized the South for industrialization.

Finally, the World Administrative Radio Conference (WARC) of 1979 was a periodic negotiating event to update and redesign the International Telecommunication Union (ITU) radio regulations, including assignment of frequencies. At stake was the more populous but poorer countries' future access to frequencies now largely occupied by the more affluent countries of the North. Nonetheless, an agreement was reached to the satisfaction of the world community represented at the meeting, partly by compromise and partly by postponing tough decisions.

Many other cases could be cited; these will be used for reference in the following discussion. If they are not fully representative (a quality that would be difficult to attain), they are at least typical of the broad span of North-South negotiations. Their record is not good, and even those that can be counted successful were so often only at a major cost to their substantive value. *What can studies of the cases and theories of the process tell to practitioners about ways of improving North-South negotiations?* This study proposes to find answers to this question under particularly difficult conditions. It would be easy (and not irrelevant) to return to notions of morality, to urge parties to lay down their antagonisms and their zero-sum perceptions, and to seek the common good in interdependence. Such an approach is important, but it is already adopted by much of the goodwilled, pro-South literature on the topic. Necessary though it is, it has not worked. Therefore, prescriptions based on a precondition of conversion are not realistic. This study will adopt a more restrictive assumption, that parties from North or South will pursue their own aims and seek their own benefits first, with only secondary concern for common benefits, but that even from that perspective there are things a party can do to improve the chances of agreement beneficial to both sides, to build a positive-sum outcome.

Notes

1. See Thomas Schelling, *The Strategy of Conflict* (Cambridge; Harvard University Press, 1960); Samuel B. Bacharach and Edward Lawler (San Francisco: Jossey-Bass, 1981); W. Howard Wriggins, "Up for Auction," in *The 50% Solution,* ed. I. William Zartman (New York: Doubleday, 1974); Morton Deutsch, *The Resolution of Conflict* (New Haven: Yale University Press, 1973).
2. See Oran Young, ed., *Bargaining* (Urbana: University of Illinois Press, 1975); John Harsanyi, *Rational Behavior and Bargaining Equilibrium in*

Games and Social Situations (New York: Cambridge University Press, 1977); Steven Brams, *Game Theory and Politics* (New York: Free Press, 1975); Robert Axelrod, "Prisoner's Dilemma Strategies," *Journal of Conflict Resolution* 24, no. 1 (1980): 3-26; Glenn Snyder and Paul Diesing, *Conflict Among Nations* (Princeton: Princeton University Press, 1977).

3. See Fred Ikle, *How Nations Negotiate* (New York: Harper & Row, 1964); Roger Fisher and William Urey, *Getting to Yes* (Boston: Houghton Mifflin, 1981); Howard Raiffa, *The Art and Science of Negotiations* (Cambridge: Harvard University Press, 1983); Richard Walton and Robert McKersie, *Behavioral Theory of Labor Negotiations* (New York: McGraw-Hill, 1965).

4. See John Cross, *The Economics of Bargaining* (New York: Basic Books, 1969); Otomar Bartos, *The Process and Outcome of Negotiations* (New York: Columbia University Press, 1974); Young, *Bargaining;* Paul Pillar, *Negotiating Peace* (Princeton: Princeton University Press, 1983); Alan Coddington, *Theories of Negotiation Process* (Chicago: Aldine, 1968).

5. See Charles Lockhart, *Bargaining in International Conflict* (New York: Columbia University Press, 1979); I. William Zartman and Maureen Berman, *The Practical Negotiator* (New Haven: Yale University Press, 1981); I. William Zartman, ed., *The Negotiation Process* (Beverly Hills: Sage, 1978).

6. Propositions come in part from such works on North-South negotiations as Robert Rothstein, *Global Bargaining* (Princeton: Princeton University Press, 1979); Philippe LePrestre, "The North-South Conflict—From Game to Debate," *World Affairs* 142, no. 2 (1980): 99-117; Roger Hansen, *The "Global Negotiation" and Beyond* (Austin: University of Texas Press, 1981); Gerald Helleiner, ed., *For Good or Evil* (Toronto: University of Toronto Press, 1982); Harald Malmgren, *International Economic Peacekeeping in Phase II* (New York: Quadrangle, 1973); Jagdish Bhagwati and John Gerard Ruggie, eds., *Power, Passions and Purpose* (Cambridge: MIT Press, 1984); Robert Olson, *U.S. Foreign Policy and the New International Economic Order* (Boulder: Westview, 1981); Norman Graham et al., *A Handbook for U.S. Participants in Multilateral Diplomacy,* Report 520-34-04 (Glastonbury, Conn.: Futures Group, 1981); Commonwealth Group of Experts, *The North-South Dialogue: Making It Work* (London: Commonwealth Secretariat, 1982).

2

Commodity Bargaining: The Political Economy of Regime Creation

Robert L. Rothstein

The attempt to create a new regime in commodities was the central issue on the North-South agenda from 1974 to 1979. The terms of the debate were set by the United Nations Conference on Trade and Development's (UNCTAD) Integrated Program for Commodities (IPC), a strikingly ambitious attempt to restructure the entire commodity order so that the developing countries would earn a greater share of the income and wealth derived from commodity production and trade. The most contentious part of the IPC was the Common Fund, a financing mechanism (for buffer stocks and, later, for "other measures") designed to link—or integrate—a series of individual commodity agreements.

Each of the individual commodity agreements was also to incorporate a common set of objectives, principles, and techniques. The negotiations to establish the IPC and the Common Fund were widely perceived as the cutting edge of the Third World's effort to construct a New International Economic Order (NIEO). In any case, they were the first major attempt to deal with the resource universe in a multilateral setting in the aftermath of the Organization of Petroleum Exporting Countries (OPEC) "shock."

Negotiations over the IPC and the Common Fund are far from over. Nevertheless, this is a reasonable time to look back at the record because a Common Fund agreement has been signed by many countries, although ratification is still short of the minimum necessary. If the necessary countries ratify, "a" Common Fund institution might become part of the international economic order. In addition, although negotiations on individual commodities are far behind schedule (originally they were to conclude two years after UNCTAD-IV in May 1976), what has happened thus far provides some very persuasive evidence to judge the conflicting claims of North and South about why commodity agreements have been so difficult to negotiate.

Gamani Corea, the secretary-general of UNCTAD, has recently declared the Common Fund negotiations a success. This success, he argued, must be attributed to the fact that the Common Fund negotiations were always seen as part of the wider North-South dialogue—in effect, as a political and not an economic issue. Conversely, he attributes the relative failure of the individual commodity negotiations to the fact that they have been dominated by producers and consumers and accordingly have been essentially economic or technical in nature.[1] These judgments are eminently challengeable, for it is far from clear that the Common Fund negotiations could or should be described as a "success" and it is equally unclear that the individual commodity negotiations have faltered because they have been dominated by the economic interests of producers and consumers. Indeed, some critics have been very harsh in their judgments about what the IPC and the Common Fund negotiations have accomplished. Lance Taylor, a professor of economics at MIT, has recently called the negotiations a "fiasco" and "a resounding failure that had much to do with dragging other, more sensible NIEO proposals down."[2] Moreover, it is clear that Corea's judgments are not even widely shared within the Third World: diminished enthusiasm is evident in the slow pace of ratifications of the Common Fund agreement and growing doubts that some key Third World countries (e.g. Brazil, Malaysia, Colombia) will ever ratify; in the revival of discussion about a producer fund to finance buffer stocks and measures to raise prices (a discussion now considerably muted by OPEC's problems); and by a shift in focus from price stabilization (the ostensible purpose of the Common Fund and buffer stocks) to vastly increased funds for compensatory finance (i.e. *ex post facto* stabilization of export earnings rather than market intervention to achieve price stabilization).

The disagreements about what has been accomplished are worth noting in that they reflect the inherent uncertainties about criteria of success and failure in ongoing negotiations that might look considerably different in historical retrospect and that anyway involve very different calculations of gain and loss for individual countries on both sides of the "great divide." Nevertheless, we need more than an entirely nominal conception of success or failure (that is, the negotiations were successful merely because "a" Common Fund agreement was achieved), even if such a conception must inevitably be bound by relatively short-term considerations. Otherwise, we have no means to make judgments about either the process itself or its substantive outcome.

What we shall seek to do is to assess the gap not only between original aims and current outcomes but also, to the extent possible, between what was sought and what was actually achievable in the period of concern (roughly 1974-81). The latter obviously requires some degree of subjective judgment by that mythical person, the impartial (and analytical) observer. We might also employ another criterion, weighing the respective needs of each side for an early agreement—in effect, asking who gains or loses most from not reaching agreement or who has the best alternative to agreement. But this criterion has at least two problems in current circumstances. In the first place, the focus is essentially short-run, which makes the outcome foregone: the richer and more powerful side can always "win" merely by adopting a policy of passive resistance. In the second place, the short-run focus is especially doubtful in the present case because one side, albeit inconsistently, deliberately sacrificed short-run incremental gains in the hope of achieving major, long-run gains. Thus the criterion is at least partially misleading.

A third criterion may be even more ambiguous but nonetheless is of great significance. This is the shape of the learning curve. I do not mean by this the process of modifying expectations in response to particular moves during a bargaining game. Rather, I refer to a broader set of considerations: learning about the need to rethink the terms of the existing game—its goals, procedures, values—and to consider new alternatives. This is especially important in the present case because the existing game has generated only stalemate and the opposition of "hard" versus "hard" positions, whereas more successful outcomes seem likely to require a different kind of bargaining game. In addition, this criterion is also more long-run in focus, a shift in perspective that is imperative in the North-South arena because progress will probably occur only if the North lowers its discount rate on the future and the South accepts the need to approach its goals by moderate means.

In making these evaluative judgments it helps greatly to remember to ask, success or failure for whom? And here the response North and South is necessary but not sufficient. We need also to think about different countries within each coalition, although this can be done only in a very sketchy fashion in this context. Above all, it must be emphasized that the secretary-general and UNCTAD itself were independent actors in these negotiations with interests of their own that were not always identical with interests of the other players (especially, of course, the Group of 77). Put another way, there is something more at stake in these negotiations than the political economy of commodities: the power and role of international institutions in setting the agenda and resolving such conflicts is very much at issue.

This multiple perspective provides some insight into why judgments about the results of the IPC negotiations have been so diverse. Thus, on the surface, the United States and the other "conservative" developed countries (West Germany, Japan, the United Kingdom) have been the clear winners: the gap between what they wanted and what has ensued is surely smallest. The Common Fund is a weak (and acceptable) copy of "the" Common Fund originally sought (it has much less money and much less power); the individual commodity negotiations are being dealt with de facto on a case-by-case basis; only one new commodity agreement with buffer stocks has emerged (rubber); the other commodities seem likely to end only with producer-consumer forums; and there has been increased concern with measures that do not seem likely to require direct market intervention (compensatory finance, diversification, improvements in market functioning).[3] Conversely, the Group of 77, which sought a powerful Common Fund, large resource transfers (indexation and so on), direct market intervention, many buffer stocks, and a rapid reconstruction of the commodity order, has been the clear loser. The developing countries also lost in terms of the other criteria of success. They achieved neither quick agreement nor much movement toward any of their long-term goals. Nor has either side apparently learned to question the wisdom of a process that seems to generate only rigidity and rhetoric.[4]

The case is much more mixed for the secretary-general and UNCTAD. The reputation of both has surely suffered substantial damage, for developed-country doubts about UNCTAD impartiality and competence have grown even more profound and many developing countries have expressed bitterness, both privately and publicly, about the secretary-general's negotiating strategy, about the weaknesses of UNCTAD technical analyses, and about the excessive expectations of substantial benefits that were generated and encouraged by the UNCTAD leadership—and, of course, about the meager results that have ensued. But these negative judgements could be balanced against the facts that the secretary-general has survived a difficult period of leadership, UNCTAD has been granted increased resources and continues to make a case for a much greater role in North-South negotiations, and the Common Fund might eventually be established and might even slowly accumulate more power and influence than now seems likely. In any case, efforts of UNCTAD to enhance its own role in commodities have always been a central part of these negotiations and the efforts have not been conclusively thwarted. (Perhaps a final comment on potential winners would not be inappropriate: As the humorists in Geneva would have it, the only certain gainers from these negotiations will be the bureaucrats who staff the Common Fund and the country that wins the battle to become its residence.)

Recent forecasts of the world economy have been dominated by expectations of slower growth if not stagnation, retrenchment, increased self-centeredness and nationalism, rising difficulties in implementing collective efforts at reform, and political instability. In addition, the factors that generated ambitions of radical restructuring of the international system among the Group of 77 have diminished in force: OPEC is powerless; euphoria about commodity power has dissipated; pressures have risen on the developing countries because of trends in food, energy, trade, and debt; and the unity of the Group of 77 has seemed more and more precarious and artificial.[5] This unfortunate combination of circumstances might seem to imply that the North-South arena will be dominated during much of this decade by a new pattern of relationships in which bilateral ties with the developed countries dominate any concern for Third World solidarity, a *sauve qui peut* emphasis on extracting short-run gains dominates any commitment to long-term restructuring, and the North-South dialogue becomes—even more—an empty rhetorical shell dominated by expatriate elites with few ties to their own countries and those countries' immediate needs. Still, one might argue in response either that this picture is much too pessimistic or, if accurate, that the very policies and actions that it generated would soon make clear the need to make a serious effort to restructure the system and to create a more stable basis for North-South relations. Perhaps also some of the lessons that can be derived from the IPC negotiations might be powerful enough to retain a degree of relevance even in, or in spite of, the new negotiating context.

The relevance of this case study might also be increased if it is understood not only as an illustration of bargaining between North and South but also in a broader sense as an illustration of a deliberate attempt at regime creation. Ernst Haas, in an especially stimulating article, has defined a regime as the "norms, rules, and procedures agreed to in order to regulate an issue-area."[6] And UNCTAD, especially in the early years, was definitely intent on establishing just such a regime. Note, for example, Corea's statement that the IPC "implied the establishment of some kind of regulatory regime to govern world commodity trade."[7] Certainly there are few clearer examples of an attempt at regime creation by the weaker and poorer participants in a particular issue area. The central point is that a group of poor and weak states sought not only a greater share of existing gains but also a large, if not decisive, say in writing the rules for an entirely new regime—of which they would be the primary beneficiaries. This challenge was unprecedented, it was inevitably resisted, and it gradually grew less forceful as economic circumstances worsened. Nevertheless, for a few years at least it had an important impact on bargaining strategy and tactics and it may once again influence events should conditions improve.

Adopting this perspective is useful because it provides a wider framework within which to assess the bargaining strategies of the major actors. We may also get a better sense of the difficulties confronting the strategists of UNCTAD and the Group of 77. Thus, Haas notes that new regimes may be more likely to emerge when there are changes in goals that facilitate a convergence or congruence of interests, when there are changes in consensual knowledge, and when there is a change in the underlying configuration of power.[8] But if there were new goals for the participants in these negotiations, most of the goals increased conflict, rather than congruence, of interests: the developing countries wanted a greater share of the benefits of commodity trade even if at the expense of developed-country producers and consumers. There was also little new knowledge, at least during 1974-77, about the nature of the commodity order. And when new knowledge did begin to appear in the later years, it seemed to confirm developed-country criticisms—and was not very consensual. There was also sharp disagreement about whether the configuration of power had altered and about whether any changes were transitory or reflected underlying structural weaknesses. The latter point seems to imply that, in a challenge to the status quo by the weak, shared perceptions about the implications of changes in power may be as important as the changes themselves. At any rate, taken together, these factors suggest that the effort to impose the IPC on the developed countries was quixotic and doomed to failure. In short, the Group of 77 and the UNCTAD leadership should have been more aware of their own limitations and more willing to accept the incremental gains implicit in following a more prudent strategy.

But an additional perspective needs to be applied to any effort by the poor and the weak to change the rules (and the rule makers). External conditions, especially disarray among the strong and persistence of instability and turbulence in the system itself, might seem to make such a challenge relatively more reasonable; the challenge remains a long shot, but the odds nevertheless might seem as short as they were likely to get. In these circumstances, given the needs of the challengers, taking the gamble cannot be dismissed as necessarily naive, foolish, or irrational.

There are, however, major qualifications to this argument. For any reasonable chance of success—if not in actually changing the rules, then at least in gaining more than might be gotten through prudent, incremental tactics—the coalition of the weak needs to make a major effort to choose the issue on which to take a stand very carefully and to devise a coherent negotiating strategy that seems likely to be able to stand the inevitable strains of the negotiating process. It is perhaps at this level that criticism of the Group of 77 and the UNCTAD leadership is most justified. As we shall see, although choosing commodities was not incorrect, the wrong sectors within commodities were emphasized. And tactically, because maintenance of group unity and prior agreement to sacrifice short-run gains were necessary to thwart, divide-and-conquer tactics by the rich, there were also serious failures. Perceptions of commodity power were not entirely illusory, but the degree and scope of that power were vastly overestimated. Apart from this, unity on goals was never really achieved: some members of the coalition wanted only a larger share of the gains in the existing system, some wanted only a new system, and many wanted both. This ambivalence may be a persisting characteristic of a coalition of the weak, but it undermines credibility and it means vast amounts of time and effort must be expended on maintaining group unity—at a cost to intergroup bargaining. In addition, leadership of the coalition was weak, lacking both power and authority. This too may be an intrinsic weakness for any large coalition of poor and weak countries, especially when the countries are under intense domestic pressures and very jealous of any threats to sovereignty. These comments obviously imply that systemic challenges by the weak can succeed—and should be attempted—only under unusual circumstances. They also imply the need to think about fall-back strategies when such challenges are resisted, a point to which we shall return.

The Commodity Debate: Themes and Variations

This chapter will not cover commodity economics or the details of the IPC except as they arise in the context of the negotiations.[9] This section, however, will discuss a number of issues that were not part of the negotiations themselves but nevertheless had a significant impact on the perceptions and behavior of the major actors.

One needs to begin with the obvious: commodity production and trade is extraordinarily complex. Producers and consumers and exporters and importers cannot be neatly divided between developed and developing countries; the objectives of both producers and consumers are very diverse, thus complicating the problem of achieving consensus within and between the two groups; conditions and prospective trends for individual commodities vary greatly, creating very different attitudes and expectations among producers of "strong" and "weak" commodities; and negotiations over commodities, which stretch back to the 1920s, have been generally unsuccessful, usually because of disagreements over price ranges or export quotas among the producers. These factors, among others, made the task of constructing a common program to help developing country producers and exporters very difficult.

Nevertheless, the need to "do something" about commodities was very clear to the developing countries. Commodity trade, excluding fuels, still accounted for almost 60 percent of export earnings for these countries (even though it has been a lagging sector in the past two decades), and that trade has suffered from a number of familiar problems: sharp fluctuations in both prices and earnings; heavy concentration on a few commodity exports to a small number of buyers for many LDCs; market imperfections; the dominance of a few multinational corporations over production and/or distribution and marketing; a small share for producers of the final consumer price for many commodities; a declining trend in the real value of export earnings for some critical commodities; and so on. In short, the need to do something conflicted with the complexities that made it so difficult to devise common policies. Moreover, the complexities of commodities combined with an unstable international environment to create another problem: uncertainty. No one was certain about what would work or about how reliable projections from past experience might be. In effect, an unusual degree of structural uncertainty prevailed because there was indecision and ambiguity about both ends and means.

The developing countries, more fearful about the implications of current trends in commodities and more convinced of the need to take advantage of the disarray in the post-1974 environment, were more willing to face the risks of gambling on a bold, new approach; the developed countries, less convinced that such an approach was either necessary or wise, were much more averse to risk. There was also an issue of time valuation here: the developed countries did not feel under great pressure to act quickly, for they were not convinced time was working against them; the developing countries not only needed quick results but also feared increasing marginalization in the world economy.[10]

Other aspects of the structure of commodity production and trade should also be kept in mind. It does not take much reflection to recognize the vast disparity in what is at stake in these negotiations. The developing countries are very dependent on the foreign exchange earned by commodity exports, and many lack the resources and the flexibility domestically to adjust to market changes; conversely, the import bill for commodities (except for oil) is small for most developed countries—Japan is an exception—and there is usually no great difficulty in adjusting to market problems by domestic means. One important implication of this is that the developing countries inevitably have a larger view of what can or should be done by international means and indeed in many cases can make the legitimate claim that an international solution to commodity problems is imperative—in the double sense that sometimes the problems of individual commodities cannot be ameliorated without concurrent actions on other commodities (e.g. where they substitute for each other) and even wise domestic policies by developing country producers can be undermined by external forces that they are too small or poor to counter. Put another way, rich and poor countries have a divergent bias about the need for international solutions or policies.

There is another side to the argument about developing-country dependence on commodities. The countries were weak, but they were not powerless. A condition of asymmetrical interdependence surely prevailed—unequal sensitivity and vulnerability to external trends— but it was less pronounced and less one-sided in commodities than it was in many other North-South areas of contention (say, the international monetary system).[11] We shall discuss in the next section some of the factors responsible for the shift or apparent shift in the bargaining terms of trade in commodities, but it suffices here to emphasize that it meant that the challenge was taken seriously—at least for several years—and that both sides recognized that more was at stake than the economics of commodities.

Although there were important debates and conflicts over technical issues like price stabilization and the viability of various buffer stocks, *neither* side ever really believed that these were the only or even the most important conflicts. These virtually subterranean conflicts (over issues like increased prices or market interventions by the Common Fund or the real intentions of the Group of 77) meant that trust, or rather the absence of trust, was an important variable in both process and outcome. The absence of trust suggests that we should think about the role of potential "honest brokers" in facilitating the development of trust—and why that role was not played by obvious candidates like the secretary-general or the representatives of the Nordic countries and the Netherlands. It is also worth emphasizing that the developing countries sought to use what leverage they had in commodities to pursue a large variety of goals—price stabilization, a transfer of resources, industrialization, intergroup equity, and efficiency to the extent that it did not undermine other goals. This made compromise difficult, not merely because the developed countries were pursuing fewer and narrower goals but also because all of the developing-country goals could never be satisfied and any likely agreement always seemed insufficient.

Finally, neither these nor any other North-South negotiations are completely autonomous. Outcomes are generally more decisively affected by what happens elsewhere—usually in the domestic political economy of the developed countries or in the international economy itself—than they are by anything that happens in the negotiating process. Sometimes diplomats and civil servants in Geneva seem so wrapped up in their own concerns that they ignore these wider considerations.

The Origins of the IPC

The factors that provoked the IPC negotiations were obvious enough in the circumstances of the time. Indeed, the much more interesting question is not why the negotiations began but why they took the form that they did.

UNCTAD had been dealing with the commodity issue since 1964, although without any substantive results. Giving fresh impetus to the effort to restructure the whole commodity order, however, were the events of 1973-74: the OPEC phenomenon and the euphoria it induced in much of the Third World (despite the damage OPEC inflicted on the Third World); the evident disarray among the developed countries; and the new perceptions of the resource universe that were emerging in response to the "limits-to-growth" debate. An end to the post-1972 commodity boom was also of some significance in energizing commodity producers. UNCTAD and the Group of 77 clearly hoped that these factors, particularly rising fears of resource scarcities, would change developed-country attitudes toward commodity agreements (and international regulation).

UNCTAD itself, as an institution, also had key interests at stake in the effort to begin the restructuring process. Its recent conferences had not been successes. Moreover, it needed a rallying point for the 1976 conference in Nairobi, and commodities were an obvious choice in the circumstances. Finally, a psychic factor is worth noting. Underlying the Third World demands was a widely shared belief in the basic unfairness of the international economic system, a belief that was especially strong in regard to commodities (because of the terms-of-trade issue and Prebisch's "center"-versus-"periphery" arguments). A felt sense of dependence and exploitation, and shared resentments against the center, not only helped to contain centrifugal pressures within the Group of 77 but also predisposed the coalition toward grand schemes that promised to reverse the existing distribution of benefits and to provide substantial gains for as many developing countries as possible.

An initiative in commodities thus seems virtually inevitable in the context of the time, but an initiative centered on the IPC and the Common Fund was not. After all, existing conditions might also have seemed to increase the chances that the traditional, case-by-case approach might have a much greater likelihood of success. Perhaps also a more modest and narrowly focused scheme, in which only commodities that were linked together (copper-aluminum, coffee-tea-cocoa, oilseeds-oils and fats-butter-sugar-grains, and so on) as substitutes or in terms of alternative land uses were treated according to the same principles and objectives and in a common arena, might have had some chance of success, but this was never even discussed during the negotiations. Instead, a decision was made to seek "global resource management in the interests of the development process" using means that were "to encompass the totality of the commodity problem from production to consumption." Stabilizing prices via buffer stocks (for those commodities of interest to the developing countries for which stocking was feasible) was the initial objective, but efforts to strengthen prices, to restructure the economies of the developing countries (diversification, increased domestic processing, a greater role in distribution and marketing), to improve market access to the developed countries, to intervene to control the "unfettered operation of markets," and to create an institution to guide and control this vast process of change (an institution that reflected the new commodity power of the developing countries) were also contemplated. It should also be emphasized that the Group of 77 demanded an initial agreement in principle to the whole IPC, after which the details could be negotiated—principle first, feasibility later.[12] In short, a decision was made to shoot for revolution, not reform, to aim for a new regime with a different distribution of power, income, and wealth, not incremental adjustments in the old regime.

Why was such a decision made? Apart from the circumstances of the time, there were a number of specific factors that were responsible for the decision. One of the most important was the fear that individual commodity negotiations, in which weak producers confronted powerful buyers, would dissipate or fragment the new bargaining power of the Third World. A central forum, acting according to common principles and techniques and grouping together all the producers (perhaps as a majority), would thus optimize the bargaining power of the whole group. Moreover, the unity of the group could be more easily maintained through a comprehensive program that promised something to everybody.

UNCTAD itself also had an institutional interest in a comprehensive program. It lacked the staffing and the expertise to control individual commodity negotiations. Its influence had to come through the creation and establishment of a common program that would be applied in particular cases. And UNCTAD would presumably dominate or at least strongly influence the central forum—the Common Fund—that was to be negotiated. At any rate, success in the IPC negotiations would enhance its prospects of becoming the central negotiating forum for all North-South issues, a role it desperately coveted.

A third factor concerned the financing issue. Gamani Corea consistently maintained that previous commodity agreements had failed because of insufficient financing for buffer stocks.[13] Consequently, he argued, the *prior* creation of a central financing mechanism with contributions from both producers and consumers would serve as a necessary catalyst for buffer-stock agreements. Thus, acceptance of a Common Fund with significant power and large resources was the necessary first step, from this perspective, to ensure that the rest of the program could unfold. It should also be noted that the secretary-general had to keep a large and disparate coalition unified. Something had to be promised to nearly everyone, and that something had to be produced quickly. Only the Common Fund, and the presumed power within it of developing-country producers, might produce the necessary benefits, although exactly how was never made clear—and perhaps could not have been without derailing the whole negotiating process. Still, ambiguities about the role of the fund (would it do more than finance stabilization via buffer stocks?) were not accidental. The ambiguities also fueled the suspicions of the developed countries, one need hardly add.

The developed countries were opposed to commodity agreements (and especially buffer stocks) for "weak" commodities like tea, jute, and hard fibers, but perhaps they might be willing to accept such agreements in exchange for agreements on stronger commodities like copper, tin, and rubber. From this perspective, grouping together many commodities in a comprehensive program (the ten core commodities were coffee, cocoa, tea, sugar, cotton, rubber, jute, hard fibers, copper, tin) seemed the only way of reversing the decline of weak commodities—provided, of course, that the producers of strong commodities were willing to make some sacrifices for the benefit of producers of weak commodities. Taken together, these factors account for the emphasis on a comprehensive program and for the decision to make the negotiation of the Common Fund the determinant—and symbol—of success or failure.

There are a number of points about the decision to seek a fundamental restructuring of commodity production and trade that need special emphasis because they had a significant effect on the ensuing negotiations or because they illustrate aspects of North-South bargaining that recur in other settings. We can begin by asking who actually made the decision. In fact, the decision seems to have been largely made by the secretary-general himself after limited consultations with a small number of advisers and diplomats from key Third World countries. Most developed and developing countries, as well as officials of existing commodity organizations, were apparently not consulted beforehand and would have objected if they had been—which may be why they were not consulted. This was, in effect, a decision made at the top and then communicated to the members of UNCTAD. The majority of the developing countries responded enthusiastically, although there were great but unpublicized doubts about some of the more technically sophisticated countries; the majority of the developed countries responded unenthusiastically, but again there were some small countries that were generally supportive, if largely on political grounds. Insofar as this interpretation of responsibility is true—and it must be emphasized that there are always uncertainties about such essentially private matters—it raises profound questions about the power of a handful of civil servants to set the international agenda and to influence strongly the course of eight years of negotiation.

Another aspect of this initial decision is also crucial. The same small group of UNCTAD officials decided to treat the negotiations from the start as if they were largely political—as if only a mystical "political will" in the developed countries was necessary to overcome all the complexities of commodities and more than fifty years of negotiating failures. And this decision was made before the analysis that might have supported (or refuted) it was done. Thus Christopher Brown, a former member of the UNCTAD Commodities Division, argues that this meant that the staff was forced into "fueling a self-fulfilling prophecy" by selectively "proving" the value of the IPC and selectively repressing work that might have raised doubts on both sides.[14] This had many consequences: oversimplification, dissension within the staff and with some outside economists, a loss of credibility with the developed countries, and perhaps most important, a loss of credibility with the Group of 77 as time passed and as other analyses indicated the doubtful nature of some UNCTAD judgments and promises.

The decision to politicize the debate and to underemphasize economic issues also had other consequences. It meant, for example, that the negotiations could be regarded, and came to be regarded by many, as essentially a zero-sum game: what was at issue was power and influence, a direct challenge to the basic value position of the developed countries, not more manageable (though not completely manageable) questions of mutual interest in an area of the international economy that both sides agreed was malfunctioning. As one illustration, price stabilization could be clearly seen as a joint interest, but the distrust exacerbated by politicization (and the weakness of some UNCTAD studies about the benefits of stabilization) meant that *stabilization* was regarded as a euphemism for raising prices arbitrarily— which was definitely not in the interest of the developed countries and not even clearly in the interest of the developing countries over any period of time. The point at issue here is the relationship between the technical and the political in this and other North-South issues. The politicization of technical issues does not mean that they are no longer technical; there is an addition to the debate, not a substitution of one for the other. In the IPC negotiations, bargaining did not rest on any prior analytical consensus at all, what was at stake was not clarified, and the process of reaching agreement was stalemated by the presentation of divergent statements of faith. Excessive politicization also enforced a short-run perspective and a commitment to essentially nominal rhetorical "victories" at the expense of slow but genuine progress. Unfortunately, it is not really clear that the secretary-general had much of a choice if he was required to satisfy all of his constituency, a point to which we shall return.

A third point of importance about the original decision to seek radical change is that it tended to set the framework for the entire negotiating process. The terms of the debate that were being negotiated in the summer of 1974 were virtually the same as the terms being negotiated three years later. Even in the period from 1978 to the present, the issues at stake really shifted only marginally. Where the negotiations end thus has a very close connection to where they begin. This raises a number of tactical questions about the need to take seriously the initial period in which issues are being framed. Neither side can afford to ignore this period in the hopes of intervening to great effect at a later date because what one will be compromising at that date will already have been determined. But there are also other questions of significance here. Why was the learning process so flawed and so weak that it is difficult to determine whether any learning at all occurred? And what effect did the structure of the bargaining process have on the inability or reluctance of the various parties—but especially the secretary-general and the leadership of the Group of 77—to alter the terms of the debate as it became increasingly clear that the negotiations were foundering? We shall seek answers to these questions in the next section.[15]

Structure and Process: From Confrontation to Stalemate to Indifference

Because the structure of the game was so closely related to the process, both will be treated in this section. I intend also to discuss briefly two things that did not happen: a mediatory role for the secretary-general, and the creation of trade-offs on the issues.

The structure of the commodity debate was largely set by the group bargaining system that prevailed in UNCTAD. The driving force behind the group system has been the Third World's intense desire to maintain unity. As President Nyerere has said, "Unity is our instrument—our only instrument—of liberation."[16] Although this is unassailable in the abstract, it begs an important question: Is the kind of unity that over a hundred very different countries, under great political and economic pressure, can achieve ever likely to be more than procedural and rhetorical, and ever likely to produce more than stalemate in the negotiating process? The discussion will concentrate primarily on the Group of 77 because it is the process of demand formation within that group that largely sets the terms of the debate.[17] The role of the UNCTAD staff in demand formation will also be considered.

What usually emerges from the deliberations of the Group of 77 (after prior caucuses among its various subgroups) is an exceedingly complex package proposal, for agreement can be achieved only at a broad level of generality. The operating principle in the quest for agreement is, as Nyerere noted, that successful packages must provide "equal benefit for all the participating Third World countries in each package of cooperation."[18] Because this is virtually impossible without sleight of hand, each agreement is burdened with promises of side payments or compensation, none of which have been accurately calculated. Moreover, because consensus can be blocked by any country or subgroup, each set of demands is simply added to the others, not genuinely compromised. This also means that negotiations with Group B (the developed countries) are exceedingly difficult in that the package is always threatening to come apart, especially when the discussion moves from grand generalities to the specifics of who gets what and when. The achievement of consensus within the Group of 77 takes so much time and effort (and usually requires promises that dangerously inflate expectations) and the commitment to Third World unity is so powerful—effectively prevailing over the need to reach agreement by detailed bargaining with Group B—that a number of consequences ensue: the bargaining process tends to get encapsulated within each group; the Group of 77 is prone to establishing and maintaining broad negotiating positions ("blue-sky" proposals) that are difficult to compromise; and intergroup bargaining largely becomes an exercise in the exchange of rhetoric (hopefully compromised, but usually only by an agreement to disagree or deliberate ambiguity that allows everyone to claim "victory" at a grand conference). Over time, a sense of futility corrodes attention and concern, a counterfeit agreement is achieved— as with the Common Fund—and the development dialogue moves on to other matters.

The group system has usually been defended on two grounds. The first is that it is the only alternative to chaos. However, the substitution of immobility and counterfeit agreement for chaos may not be a very sensible exchange. The second ground is that the process of consensus formation within the Group of 77 is democratic. There is less here than meets the eye. In fact, the process—setting the agenda, forming proposals, determining strategy and tactics—is dominated by a small oligarchy of key Third World delegates and key staff members of a few international institutions. In the commodities case, the leadership and staff of UNCTAD were indispensable. Many Third World governments need external expertise to establish positions on complex issues. The explosion of meetings, conferences, special sessions, and the like also overwhelms the capacity of poor governments to cope; policy at these meetings in many cases must come, virtually by default, from external experts. In addition, only the staff of an institution like UNCTAD—in the absence of a Third World "OECD"—has the competence, the staffing, the resources, and the time to put together a technically (and to some extent politically) acceptable program for the whole Group of

77. The staff and the secretary-general play both a technical role in developing proposals and a political role in packaging the elements, in selling them to both groups, and in indicating the boundaries of acceptable compromise (a role played badly or ineptly). Two further points are worth noting. The first is that this dual role puts great strain on the morale of a staff caught between professional and advocacy functions; it also helps to explain both internal staff discontent and external discontent by the Group of 77 (when the staff emphasizes its professional tasks). The second is that the secretary-general and the staff are very influential, especially in the early stages of the process when the agenda is set and proposals are formed, but they are not omnipotent; they have been overruled, especially at the grand conferences when higher-level delegates appear (but note that haggling by ministers in the late stages is over proposals created many months before by the staff).

A third aspect of the bargaining structure in Geneva, the significance of which is not well understood, concerns the separation between what is going on in Geneva and what is going on in Lima, Lomé, or Kuala Lumpur.[19] Interviews and other research material clearly indicate that the elites in the capital know little about the issues being debated in Geneva, and that they tend to interpret the meaning of these multilateral negotiations as essentially political and symbolic—talking on equal terms symbolizes the new status of the South. But for tangible economic benefits and for the solution of pressing economic problems, the elites "at home" put primary emphasis on bilateral relationships with various developed countries. UNCTAD itself has taken note of this discrepancy between diplomatic support in Geneva and the indifference or ignorance of ministers in the capital.[20] One should note, of course, that there are great variations in individual cases. In particular, the advanced developing countries (Brazil, India, and the like) are well able to understand what interests they have at stake in Geneva, although they also still emphasize bilateral ties.

One thing that this separation means is that the bargaining process in Geneva becomes even more politicized, for the elites at home tend to be less ideological and more concerned with programs that promise real benefits relatively quickly. Moreover, for the most part, the elites at home simply instruct their representatives in Geneva to support the Group of 77 position, which at least partially explains why unity has been preserved even though some proposals (including the IPC) involve losses for some developing countries. The governments at home apparently assume little of substantive consequence will occur in such global negotiations but maintain rhetorical support so as to remain in good standing with the rest of the Third World. And, of course, this also bolsters the power and influence of the secretary-general and the staff because it is they who establish the Group of 77 position. The result is a largely two-track process: rhetorical confrontation in Geneva, dominated by a small oligarchy of diplomats and civil servants; and a bilateral or occasionally regional track that is reserved for what are perceived as genuine national interests. This separation does harm to both tracks. Poor and weak states can develop successfully only if both tracks are integrated, so that the international system provides enhanced opportunities for development, and domestic policy is designed to take advantage of international opportunities.

In sum, the proposals that emerge from the group system tend to be excessively ambitious, perhaps beyond the state of the art in either politics or economics, for they must promise too much to too many. They are also difficult to compromise. The proposals are frequently badly designed because they seek primarily a single goal, restructuring to facilitate development, usually by a rapid transfer of resources. This ignores the interests and needs of the developed countries and is excessively simplistic for a world that is no longer clearly divided into North and South, in which each side contains rich and poor, and in which winners and losers on each issue rarely follow group lines. Finally, most of the proposals require large increases in central control or direction of international economic activity; wholly apart from ideological considerations, it is reasonable to ask whether we know enough to run such a system equitably or efficiently. There is very little experience with such ventures to suggest we do.

The bargaining process itself, from the presentation of the original set of proposals in late 1974, was remarkably uneventful. The most surprising thing about it was how little genuine bargaining occurred, either in terms of marking mutual concessions or in seeking a common formula or framework of agreement. The Group of 77 and the UNCTAD leadership, energized by the circumstances of the time, demanded a fundamental reform of commodity production and trade, insisted that commitment to the principles, the objectives, and the techniques of this program must precede resolution of any of the detailed questions that any such program was bound to engender, and maintained that only the absence of "political will" prevented the developed countries from acceptance of the entire program. This "hard" bargaining position was maintained unchanged for three years, despite the fact that it became increasingly clear that the whole package—a powerful Common Fund, many buffer stocks, stabilized and strengthened prices—never had the slightest chance of acceptance. But the hard position was maintained anyway, initially perhaps because there was a genuine belief that UNCTAD could really succeed in creating a new commodity regime for the benefit of the developing countries, and over time because personal reputations had been staked on the outcome and because any retreat from the whole package would have threatened to wreck the unity of the Group of 77. In a real sense, the leadership of UNCTAD and the Group of 77 had become prisoners of the bargaining structure in which they operated, for unity was the primary value; compromise threatened unity—as would any clear statement of how much would be gained and by whom through changes in the existing commodity regime—and thus the only choice was to "hang tough" and pray that the other side would suddenly adopt a "soft" strategy.[21]

In retrospect, the original decision to seek a new regime and to challenge directly the ideology and interests of the developed countries was probably a mistake, reflecting both a misestimation of power and an oversimplified interpretation of commodity problems, but it was an *understandable* mistake. Frustration and opportunity had seemed to come together to justify an unprecedented challenge by the weak, a challenge that, even if it failed, might still achieve more gains than conventional incremental bargaining and might at least lead to reconsideration of prevailing patterns of thought and action. From this perspective perhaps the more critical mistake was not in launching the challenge but, rather, in being unable to adjust to new circumstances— the unwillingness of the developed countries to accept the program, the change in external economic conditions, the realization that OPEC would not help much, the gradual loss of support within the Group of 77—and to prepare to fight at a new level. In the new context, flexibility and feasibility should have superseded innovation and reconstruction, but the nature of the bargaining system and the personal and institutional resources invested in the grand challenge made this adaptation to circumstances especially difficult.

The position of the United States tended to determine the position assumed by all of Group B. At any rate, as long as the United States, West Germany, Great Britain, and Japan (the weakest link, as all recognized) were in general agreement, the power of the potential dissenters was very limited. The United States has followed a fairly consistent policy through three administrations, although there was some change during the Carter years. The Carter administration was more sympathetic to Third World concerns, less opposed to commodity agreements, and less ideological in its objections to the Common Fund (and other matters). Nevertheless, on the crucial technical issues—how many buffer stocks made sense, what kind of powers and resources the Common Fund might have—the Carter administration did not differ greatly from its predecessors. Its successor, of course, was more broadly indifferent to Third World concerns, with a more deeply hostile position than that shown in the IPC negotiations.

The United States throughout these years did not want to stand in isolation during the negotiations, not least because of some initial fears about how OPEC would respond if the negotiations broke down completely, and thus sought to oppose UNCTAD proposals but to keep the game going; the tactics of nonsettlement and the disguise of fundamental disagreement were as much in play as the tactics of settlement. Basically the United States followed a strategy of delay (more studies, questions about the accuracy of existing documentation), damage limitation, and what one U.S. official called "passive opposition." This largely succeeded because the available technical material raised more questions than it resolved and because there were no more external "shocks" to compel reconsideration of the conventional wisdom. (The McCracken Report for the OECD had concluded that the problems of the international economic system were essentially cyclical, not structural.[22])

The negotiations persisted in complete stalemate until UNCTAD-IV in Nairobi in May 1976. Something of a compromise appeared to emerge in the last two days of the conference, in that a resolution was agreed to that requested the secretary-general to convene preparatory meetings and then a negotiating conference on "a" (not "the") Common Fund in the following year. But how much had really changed was unclear, for the United States stated that the "preparatory meetings were consultations prior to a decision on *whether* to embark on negotiations" (my italics) and the Group of 77 insisted that "nothing other than *the* Common Fund" (my italics) was to be negotiated. In the event, it became clear that the compromise was merely a device to prevent complete (public) failure at Nairobi because the subsequent meetings ended in failure and merely repeated the same arguments that had dominated in Geneva.

A "compromise" did emerge in early 1979 at the last commodity meeting before UNCTAD-V in Manila. This was a compromise that surprised the developed countries and angered some of the staunchest supporters of "the" Common Fund, for it essentially accepted the concept of a very limited Common Fund—without large resources or powers—that had been supported by the United States and most other developed countries. Why this compromise was accepted has never been very clear, although an UNCTAD official argued that it was accepted because it had become clear that the developed countries would accept no more (that had been clear to others for several years) and because several developing countries had indicated that they would not contribute to the fund unless they could see how their contributions were being used in specific commodity agreements (which meant the fund could not be the sole source of, and dominant factor in, allocation of financing).[23] Others attributed the decision, less charitably, to the secretary-general's need to have an agreement of some kind that could be trumpeted at Manila as a vindication of his negotiating strategy.

I have said nothing about any of the technical issues in dispute primarily because UNCTAD and the Group of 77 chose to treat the conflict in political terms and because the technical exchanges that did go on—and that formed a kind of subgame between professional economists—were in their early stages (a comment on how prepared UNCTAD was) and were quite inconclusive. The econometric studies that each side produced tended to rely on very different assumptions about the reliability of extrapolations from the past and about likely future developments, thus inevitably ending with very disparate conclusions. There were major disputes about how harmful price instability had been and about how beneficial stabilization would be. Because the benefits from stabilization were not likely to be massive, there was also a debate about price "strengthening" (by indexation or other means) that tended to degenerate into an insoluble conflict about fair or just prices for producers.[24] On buffer stocks, the major means of stabilization, the debate centered on how many commodities were reasonable candidates for stocking and how costly (interest and storage costs) such stocks would be.

Only one new commodity agreement on buffer stocks has been negotiated—rubber—so it appears that at least part of the UNCTAD argument for stocks has been rejected.

Many of the arguments about the Common Fund itself appear to be provisionally resolved, for the fund, should it come into existence, will be only a pale copy of the original model. The inconclusive nature of these comments (and remember a political compromise on "a" Common Fund does not necessarily mean much technically) reflects not only the complexities of the technical issues but also a deliberate decision not to resolve as many technical issues as possible before seeking a political solution. For UNCTAD in particular the reduction in uncertainty was perceived as potentially dangerous to the unity of the Group of 77; it might have revealed that all the promises about "something for everyone" could not be kept.

The structure of the bargaining game, which was largely a result of the strategies each side chose and the nature of the group bargaining system, thus dominated and determined the bargaining process itself. Each side adopted a "hard" strategy, the Group of 77 because of the need for unity (and initially because, perhaps, it seemed to have a chance of success) and the developed countries because they believed that the Group of 77 would not remain unified (and because the proposals in contention were one-sided and technically uncertain), and then each waited for the other to crack. The process essentially froze around initial positions, and the few cosmetic concessions each side was willing to make—and neither ever offered or considered major concessions—were held back until UNCTAD-IV itself or one of the later, ministerial-level meetings. The very limited and barren nature of the process—few concessions, little movement, very limited contact across group lines, no evidence of genuine learning—probably accounts for the fact that much of the literature on bargaining is not very helpful. A linear exchange of concessions never developed, there was no common search for a formula or framework for the negotiations (in part because the formula itself was at stake and in part because values and perspectives were too divergent), and there was certainly no attempt to move toward a new kind of bargaining game in which the choice between "hard" and "soft" strategies was not the only option.

The primary characteristics of this bargaining process on the technical side were complexity and uncertainty; on the political side, distrust. This was a situation that cried out for an impartial and respected mediator who might have suggested a few ways to diminish the technical conflicts and to build some political bridges across group lines—there were, after all, in all the developed countries at least some influential groups that saw mutual interests in commodity agreements and that were not ideologically hostile to the Third World. The mediator might especially have been useful in suggesting certain points at which the negotiating process could be suspended while whatever changes that had been made were digested. This would have been particularly useful because one of the factors that inhibited U.S. concessions was the fear that any concession would only immediately generate a new set of demands, a not unreasonable fear, especially if expectations about what concessions would produce were too high. In addition, there were one or two occasions when a particular compromise appeared to have great prominence or salience[25] but was difficult to approach because of mutual distrust and unwillingness to make the first offer. Thus, a mediator with a commitment to the process itself—to reaching agreement and nurturing a means of settlement, as distinct from supporting a particular settlement—would have been a useful addition to a process that was too frequently manipulated for parochial short-term gains.

The secretary-general was the obvious candidate to fill this role, but he apparently never made the effort—and would probably have failed if he had. One needs compassion for his difficulties in confronting conflicting pressures without much substantive power of his own. He was caught between rising demands and needs from his major constituency and insufficient responsiveness, if not hostility, from his other constituency. He was advised in textbook fashion that, above all, he should not become prisoner of any constituency, but unless he becomes prisoner of his major constituency, he cannot get or hold his position. What power he has in setting the agenda, directing his staff, and so on consequently must be used to maintain and sustain his key supporters. This is hardly surprising or unusual, but it does have an unfortunate result: he cannot act as a genuine mediator.

Mediation does not necessarily require complete independence or a position equidistant between the parties, but it does require some independent power over both sides, even if there is more power and influence toward one side.[26] But Corea lacked any power vis-à-vis the developed countries, and even his power with the Group of 77 was constrained. Even if he were to seek, for example, to indicate or suggest certain salient points of potential compromise, his efforts would probably be unavailing. That is largely because salience is not the only quality necessary for agreement. At a minimum, one would also probably need implicit agreement that the salient compromise was also fair. But with so much distrust and without any consensus on values or goals, or even the nature of the problem, it is very unlikely that agreement on what is fair could even be approximated. This leaves the negotiating process without an effective mediator, a condition that is not necessarily decisive but nonetheless does not help the quest for settlement.

Another weakness of the bargaining process was the absence of any effort to establish trade-offs between the issues. Trading concessions on one issue for more or less reciprocal concessions on other issues is, after all, a very familiar aspect of the politics of bargaining, and in some circumstances—especially complex negotiations with many issues and many actors—may be more efficient than treating each issue on its merits and negotiating each outcome separately.[27] Trade-offs or linkages between issues may facilitate the achievement of agreement by adding more areas of potential compensation to the game. Moreover, as Tollison and Willett have argued, this may be most important where the distribution of benefits on any single issue is heavily skewed: one needs then to add other issues with offsetting patterns of distribution.[28]

As already indicated, a major reason that UNCTAD and the Group of 77 made no effort to investigate the possibility of trade-offs was that compromise might undermine group unity—procedure dominating substance. A second reason was that complexity and uncertainty were so great that it was difficult to determine who were winners on any single issue, let alone across several issues. There were also ambiguities about whether to seek trade-offs within one large issue (like commodities), or between different issues, or between short-run or long-run returns.[29] And, of course, the absence of real bargaining, as distinct from the persistent exchange of divergent manifestoes, made the issues of trade-offs largely redundant. However, the major perceptual reason that no trade-offs were sought was, I believe, that both sides, but especially the developed countries, tended to believe that the developing countries had nothing to trade. That is an issue worth a brief comment, for a lack of items to trade means a lack of power to bring the other party to an agreement.

The conventional response is to point out the growing importance of the South to the North as a trading partner, a source for profitable investment, and a provider of critical resources. In a broad sense this is certainly true, but in a narrower, short-run perspective three qualifications must be noted. In the first place, power in most of these cases rests largely with a relatively small number of developing countries, not the Third World at large. In the second place, there is very little persuasive evidence that individual developing countries will forgo potentially profitable agreements with the developed countries because the latter adopt negative or hostile positions toward proposals developed in the North-South dialogue. Finally, the growing economic ties of North and South do not intersect with Northern political systems in a fashion that encourages support for meaningful substantive concessions in the dialogue, largely because each issue has different patterns of winners and losers. In short, the growing importance of some developing countries can be, and has been, used to justify a focus on individual countries, not the North-South dialogue.

There were, however, some specific gains that the developed countries desired in the commodity negotiations. For example, there was general agreement that price stabilization could bring mutual gains (although not on the order foreseen by UNCTAD), provided that achieving the goal did not entail commitment to all of the demands in the IPC. In addition, the developed countries were worried about potential resource scarcities, especially if investment in Third World resources continued to decline, and about growing degrees of unpredictability and uncertainty in the resource economy. Consequently, the developing countries could have achieved some bargaining leverage by offering some kind of agreement on investment policies for the development of raw materials, perhaps through a revised version of the resource bank proposed by Secretary of State Kissinger at UNCTAD-IV, which was rejected at the time for largely extraneous reasons. The developed countries also placed a good deal of value on maintaining the negotiating process and avoiding a breakdown in North-South relations. The inevitable controversy over responsibility for the breakdown, the potential costs, and the increase in unpredictability all suggested that some concessions would be made merely to keep the game going. As a result, the developing countries might have made some gains by offering procedural and institutional concessions that eased fears that the dialogue was about to disintegrate—for example, by giving up the rhetorical challenges to GATT and the IMF, by demanding fewer resources for the immediate expansion of UNC-TAD's role, and by recognizing the futility of manipulations based on numerical superiority in a context where results required consensus.

These suggestions are obviously tenuous, which may always be the case, but they are not completely irrelevant. It makes sense for the North to accept some short-run sacrifices in exchange for potential long-run benefits and an increased chance of long-run stability. Unfortunately, this kind of trade-off has become even more problematic in the context of systemwide economic difficulties. This suggests that the Group of 77, if it seeks to achieve genuine gains in the negotiating process, will have to think about establishing reciprocal—but not equal—patterns of concession, for otherwise the perception of a one-sided game in which the North always loses will persist. This perception prevailed in the commodity case because the Group of 77 offered little of significance in return for accepting the IPC, perhaps because it could not do so within the negotiating context that it had established.

Reasoning Why: Explanations and Alternatives

It should be clear from the foregoing discussion that there is no simple explanation, no single factor, responsible for the outcome of the IPC negotiations. In fact, there are layers and phases of explanations, all of which are eminently challengeable. After all, there is as yet far from complete agreement about how to characterize the outcome. But if judgment is based on which side achieved more of its original aims, the answer seems reasonably clear: the negotiations were a failure for the Group of 77 and UNCTAD, thinly disguised by a few cosmetic concessions, all of which were probably well within reach without eight years of costly negotiation. Persistent description of these negotiations (and other North-South negotiations) as a "stalemate" perhaps helps in confusing judgments. In reality, although the negotiations were indeed immobile, the lack of movement clearly reflected and incorporated the goals of the conservative developed countries: damage limitation and the retention of control. The use of a different criterion of success, such as the shape of the learning curve, does not generate more hopeful judgments. From this perspective, one can conclude only that both sides lost.

The original decision to seek an entirely new regime in commodities may have been a mistake, for it reflected misperceptions of power, insufficient technical preparation, an oversimplified view of commodity problems and solutions, and excessive hopes about what could be accomplished internationally. But these mistakes were understandable, though not completely excusable, because euphoria and need were great in much of the Third World and because it was unclear that a better opportunity to strike for major change would appear. It is in this context that one must evaluate the strategy and tactics of the leadership of UNCTAD and the Group of 77. The emphasis on unity, the spurning of short-run incremental gains in the hope of achieving long-run structural gains, and the indifference to many of the tactical suggestions from conventional bargaining theorists about how successful negotiators should behave all reflected the decision to seek a new order.[30] Presumably the unique nature of an effort at regime creation by the weak in a period of great uncertainty—when the conventional wisdom was not producing anticipated results—justified a new approach to negotiations.

But as the negotiations settled in during 1975 and 1976, several things became apparent. In the first place, the United States and the other large developed countries did not share the view that the existing crisis was structural, did not believe that UNCTAD's program was either politically or economically feasible, and did not intend to do much beyond wait for the unity of the developing countries to crack. In the second place, euphoria in the Third World was dissipating, needs were rising, external trends were unpropitious (in trade, aid, debt, food, energy), and the assertion of national interests over group interests was becoming more pronounced. Consequently the strategy and tactics of UNCTAD and the Group of 77 should have changed: a dignified retreat to more feasible goals should have been attempted, pragmatism should have prevailed over ideology, and attentions should have been diverted from virtually metaphysical debates about the Common Fund to other reforms in commodity production and trade.

The developing countries and UNCTAD were not, however, able to adjust. The emphasis on unity and on gains for all in each package of proposals meant that any move toward compromise threatened to unravel the whole package; standing fast behind very broad principles of change was, or seemed, the only alternative. This was reinforced by UNCTAD's own desire to become the central forum in commodities and by its intention to prove that it should or could become the major international forum for all North-South issues. The secretary-general's inability to play a mediating role reinforced the stalemate. In the last few years, when external conditions worsened and when a more hostile administration came to power in the United States, ambitions were obviously scaled down and attention turned elsewhere. Nevertheless, even in this period, UNCTAD's ambitions and the desire of the secretary-general to proclaim a success continued to play some role in delaying adjustment and compromise.

Were alternative outcomes possible? A more resounding failure was always possible, for the negotiations were constantly threatening to break down completely. Perhaps this would have been useful if it had turned Third World attentions away from the quest for external salvation, but it is probably more likely that attentions would simply have been diverted to another quest for a mechanism to transfer resources rapidly (as happened more recently in UNCTAD with a new emphasis on a vast compensatory finance program—up to $20 billion a year). This simply adds failures together and increases cynicism on both sides.

Were more positive outcomes possible? If the Group of 77 persists in its negotiating strategy, the answer is probably no; failure is built into the negotiating process. I think, however, that *some* movement was in fact possible because there were influential dissidents on both sides (most of whom remained silent, for their dissent seemed futile) and because dissatisfaction grew as the negotiations dragged on without results. The United States, had it been committed to reforming commodity trade, might have been able to break the stalemate by guaranteeing that no commodity agreement for which a buffer stock had been mutually agreed would fail because of a lack of sufficient finance. This would have removed the major rationale for a *prior* commitment to the Common Fund. Also, a proposal to start the individual commodity negotiations immediately probably would have attracted some Third World support and added some movement to a process that was stuck.

Perhaps being somewhat more forthcoming about the other aspects of the IPC would also have helped. All of this presumes, however, that the United States would or could shift its attitudes toward these kinds of negotiations—away from damage limitation and passive resistance—and that it also reorganizes bureaucratically so that coherent positions can be adopted before a minicrisis looms. Both are doubtful; also they might not make much difference unless the Group of 77 also adjusts.

There were several key countries in the Group of 77 that had substantial technical and political doubts about the IPC but nonetheless remained silent. If these countries had expressed their doubts within Group of 77 (or subgroup) meetings, a shift in approach might have been possible. For example, in the negotiations before UNCTAD's special session on debt (March 1978), several of the advanced developing countries, with interests and needs clearly different from those of their poorer allies in the group, sharply disagreed with UNCTAD's proposed position for the Group of 77 and indicated that they would not support it. As a result, demands were moderated and the debt meeting ended as a small, but useful, success. If the dissidents in commodities had done this, the result might have been a shift in emphasis toward more negotiable areas: trade liberalization, increased domestic processing, compensatory finance, and improvements in marketing and distribution. Among other things, these were areas of change that were acceptable to market enthusiasts and might even have forced some of the developed countries to live up to their own rhetoric.[31] These measures were hardly panaceas but they probably reflect what could be gotten—and gotten much quicker if the terms of the debate had shifted. The problem with these proposals is that most have only long-term impact (except for compensatory finance, which does not stop price fluctuations or alter production structures) and do not provide quick returns for all; it was thus easy to denounce them as "too little, too late." Unfortunately, however, there are no "quick fixes" in commodities and it would have been better for most of the Group of 77 to learn this sooner rather than later.

Prescriptions for Reform

Procedural reforms of the bargaining process are necessary but not sufficient; a change in attitudes toward the bargaining process and a broad agreement about what is at stake and how the game will be played are also necessary.[32] In fact, this is the only way to reach the point where both sides are playing the same game. The result would be a bargain about how to bargain, an agreement separate from, but providing general guidance for, the specific negotiations on the issues. For example, one such general agreement would involve a trade-off in which the developed countries accepted the need to institute a process of reform, thus abandoning strategies of damage limitation and passive opposition, in return for a commitment by the developing countries to abandon the demand for immediate and massive global restructuring. The partially shared goal would be the creation of a more liberal system (albeit with continued preferential and differentiated treatment for different groups of developing countries) to be produced by moderate means. Neither the current political and economic situation nor the limited state of our knowledge about the consequences of present actions permits more. The point here is not really whether one agrees or disagrees with this trade-off; it is that only such an agreement makes the discussion of procedural reforms worthwhile.

Specific reforms, which respond explicitly to the failures of the bargaining system already noted, might include the following:

1. The quest for a new principle of representation to replace the current group-versus-group confrontations. Smaller negotiating groups are obviously imperative, probably reflecting a defined interest in an issue, but one point needs emphasis: there must also be an explicit tie between the small-group negotiations and the need for collective legitimization by larger forums. This offers some protection to those not included in the small group, and it ensures that agreements will be evaluated to avoid negative externalities.
2. The creation of a small expert group to provide a map of the technical terrain: what is agreed or not agreed, what needs further research, and what cannot be agreed. The experts would meet before formal negotiations began, would not be bound by prior group positions, and would be asked to suggest a variety of approaches (and not a single grand design) to deal with the technical issues. In addition to diminishing inflated expectations, the expert group could make an important contribution toward the creation of consensual knowledge (knowledge *both* sides accept as true), the absence of which is likely to destabilize any agreement reached.[33]
3. The creation of a Third World "OECD," which is problematic in terms of providing analyses that are superior to UNCTAD's (unless it is genuinely independent and very well staffed), might nonetheless be very useful in terms of allowing institutions like UNCTAD to perform a mediatory role, rather than a confrontational role.

A final word about regime creation may be useful. The IPC case could be called an illustration of premature regime creation. However, it might also be described as a case in which a mistaken strategy of regime creation was followed by the Group of 77. The latter point implies two things. First, the quest for a new regime was not itself foolish or irrational, given the malfunctioning of the existing regime and given the existence of some common interests in the commodities arena. But second, this also implies that a better strategy of regime creation was indeed available. It seems that there was, so long as we recognize that some incremental systems are different from others—in effect, that a system of directed incrementalism, prefaced by the kind of agreement on the bargaining game already noted, can produce consistent and cumulative gains in a desired direction. This is regime creation by indirection, which may be the only kind available.

This strategy will be possible only if the developing countries recognize the need for a conscious strategy of regime creation that is appropriate to prevailing conditions.[34] The elements of such a strategy might include three rules of thumb. (1) Better analytical preparation is imperative because the issues are not completely political. (2) Proposals that require a jump into the unknown will always be resisted, perhaps justifiably, so global solutions can only be approached step by step. (3) Proposals that take as their only operating principle Third World development are too narrow, for the developed countries have interests and needs on these issues that will always be defended, and both developed and developing countries share an interest in a just and stable system—which cannot be achieved without some commitment by *both* sides to longer-term and broader sets of values.

Notes

1. Corea's comments are in an interview in "North-South Dialogue," *Third World Quarterly* 3 (October 1981): 608, 613.
2. Lance Taylor, "Back to Basics: Theory for the Rhetoric in the North-South Round," *World Development* 10 (April 1982): 328.
3. The fact that several of the existing commodity organizations probably will not join the Common Fund also weakens its significance. Some reports, unconfirmed, suggest that coffee, cocoa, tin, and bauxite intend to stay out.
4. It is worth noting that speculators have gained by not losing many opportunities to speculate, and that some commodity importers have probably gained in the short run; exporters of weak commodities have lost unless they have learned not to rely on external salvation.
5. For discussion of recent trends in food, energy, and trade, and their implications both for Third World unity and U.S. foreign policy, see Robert L. Rothstein, *The Third World and U.S. Foreign Policy—Conflict and Cooperation in the 1980s* (Boulder, Colo.: Westview Press, 1981).

6. Ernst B. Haas, "Why Collaborate? Issue Linkage and International Regimes," *World Politics* 32 (April 1980): 358; italics deleted.
7. Quoted in L.N. Rangarajan, *Commodity Conflict* (Ithaca: Cornell University Press, 1978), p. 295.
8. Haas, "Why Collaborate?" especially p. 371.
9. Most, but not all, of the comments on the IPC and the Common Fund rely on my *Global Bargaining—UNCTAD and the Quest for a New International Economic Order* (Princeton: Princeton University Press, 1979). Further noting of it seems unnecessary, except where specific quotations are at issue.
10. Perhaps the latter statement needs qualification: the remark refers primarily to the non-OPEC, non-NIC (non-New Industrial Countries) part of the Third World, although even within these favored groups some fall closer to the rest of the Third World than to the developed countries.
11. There is a discussion of asymmetrical interdependence, and the meaning of sensitivity and vulnerability, in Haas, "Why Collaborate?" p. 363. These ideas were, of course, originally developed in a variety of well-known studies by Professors Robert O. Keohane and Joseph S. Nye.
12. See Rothstein, *Global Bargaining*, pp. 49-50.
13. There is a very valuable discussion of this and other commodity issues in Jere R. Behrman, *International Commodity Agreements* (Washington, D.C.: Overseas Development Council, 1977). Behrman notes that "successful agreements broke down most often due to competition among the members, with competition from non-members being the second most common cause" (p. 33). Most other economists also disagree with Corea's argument, which has never been cited with evidence.
14. Christopher P. Brown, *The Political and Social Economy of Commodity Control* (New York: Praeger, 1980), p. 80.
15. Another issue that might be raised at this point concerns the obvious conflict between global solutions (costly and unstable as the range of values that have to be satisfied increases) and incrementalism (which is prudent but insufficient), but I shall delay further comment about the relation between the desirable and the possible until the last section.
16. Quoted in Rothstein, *The Third World and U.S. Foreign Policy*, p. 20.
17. In the comments that follow, I have borrowed various sentences and phrases, not to mention arguments, from my *The Third World and U.S. Foreign Policy*, pp. 20-25. In *Global Bargaining* I discuss the group system in the UNCTAD context at some length.
18. Rothstein, *The Third World and U.S. Foreign Policy*, p. 22. Nyerere's views are widely shared in the Third World. For example, both the editor and a high UNCTAD official argue the same "something-for-everyone" view in Arjun Sengupta, ed., *Commodities, Finance, and Trade—Issues in North-South Negotiations* (Westport, Conn.: Greenwood Press, 1980), pp. xvi, 309.
19. I discuss this issue at greater length in *The Third World and U.S. Foreign Policy*, pp. 24-25.
20. See Corea's comments in "North-South Dialogue," pp. 606-7. In essence, there are four Third World or pro-Third World groups that influence the process of policy formation in the Group of 77: officials at home, most of whom are pragmatic; officials and staff members of international institu-

tions, most of whom support extreme Third World demands but also protect their own interests; free-floating intellectuals and experts who range over a wide spectrum but generally support radical proposals; and diplomats in Geneva and elsewhere who may or may not be pragmatic but lack the expertise or the information from home to challenge the substantive content of various technical proposals. The last, virtually by default, thus become prisoners of "grand designs" propounded in Geneva.

21. Thus UNCTAD and Group of 77 officials were always awaiting deus ex machina, for example, defection by a few Group B countries or a new administration in the United States. They could never believe that neither would really make much difference, the first because the likely candidates (the Dutch, especially when Jan Pronk was development minister) were not important enough in the debate, and the second because the new administration would have the same problems and doubts (as those of the Carter administration). This strategy also necessitated papering over conflicts in the Group of 77 (potential defectors included countries already doing well in a commodity agreement, net import losers, countries with commodities that could not be stocked, and OPEC if too much was said about the problems of importers of commodities whose prices increased). The dissidents were kept in line by peer pressure, institutionalization of the Group of 77, and lack of a good offer from the developed countries— and a belief that the developed countries would not accept the IPC. The distinction between "hard" and "soft" strategies is discussed in Richard E. Walton and Robert B. McKersie, *A Behavioral Theory of Labor Negotiations* (New York: McGraw-Hill, 1965), pp. 6f. See *OECD Observer* 77 (September-October 1975): pp. 4-5 on the formation of the McCracken group.

22. Note also that the fact that a variety of developing countries were telling the United States privately not to take the commodity debate seriously, that their support was essentially rhetorical, helped to confirm a policy of passive resistance.

23. See the comments by I. S. Chadha in Sengupta, *Commodities, Finance and Trade*, p. 330.

24. Basically the argument revolved around the case when instability originated on the supply side, as it does for many agricultural products. In such circumstances, stabilization might actually decrease average earnings. On prices, the problem centered on the fact that UNCTAD wanted "prices" consistent with development objectives," an objective that had little to do with the long-run equilibrium price (which some said was as mythical as the UNCTAD objective). The fact that stabilization would produce limited benefits (and mostly for the developed countries) raised suspicions about what the price objectives really were, an issue that UNCTAD deliberately fudged. Finally, I should note that the other elements of the IPC (beyond stocks and the fund) were multilateral long-term contracts, domestic processing, and (sometimes) indexation of prices.

25. The idea of prominence or salience comes from Thomas C. Schelling, *The Strategy of Conflict* (Cambridge: Harvard University Press, 1960).

26. I. W. Zartman and Saadia Touval, eds., *The Man in the Middle: The Theory and Practice of International Mediation* (Boulder, Colo.: Westview Press, 1985).

27. For a discussion, see Lewis A. Froman, Jr., and Michael D. Cohen, "Compromise and Logroll: Comparing the Efficiency of Two Bargaining Processes," *Behavioral Science* 15 (March 1970): 180-83.

28. Robert D. Tollison and Thomas D. Willett, "An Economic Theory of Mutually Advantageous Issue Linkages in International Negotiations," *International Organization* 33 (Autumn 1979): 427.

29. One would hazard the guess that it would be preferable to make trade-offs on the same issue and in the same time-frame, if only to be better able to show domestic losers where compensating gains would be achieved. This is probably impossible in the North-South arena because on this level of reciprocal concessions (as in the trade area) the South has little to give and most of the Northern gains must come in the long term.

30. Thus negotiators are urged to act on their expectations of how the other side will respond, to seek solutions consistent with the other side's principles, to build on shared interests, to avoid excessive initial demands, to fractionate problems so that momentum can be built behind a series of small agreements, and so forth. But such precepts seem to assume a settled universe, a conflict in which bargaining over shares is central, and the absence of conflict over the nature and rules of the game itself. None of this was generally true in this encounter, although the developing countries were ambivalent and ambiguous about mixing a quest for larger shares in the existing game and establishing a new game, particularly as time passed.

31. I have made such an argument in *Global Bargaining*, pp. 73-74, and it is also made by G. K. Helleiner in Sengupta, *Commodities, Finance and Trade*, pp. 268-69. The debt negotiations are analyzed in chapter 9.

32. See "Is the North-South Dialogue Worth Saving?" *Third World Quarterly*, 6 January 1984. pp. 155-81.

33. The issue of consensual knowledge has been developed and discussed in a number of works by Ernst B. Haas. I have applied the idea directly to the IPC negotiations in "Consensual Knowledge and International Collaboration," *International Organization* 38 (Autumn 1984): 4: 733-62.

34. It may be that the greatest utility of the regime focus is not in its conceptual advances—which do not as yet seem very great—but rather in its utility to decision makers trying to discover a framework and a strategy for dealing with a rapidly changing universe. In any event, I argue this in greater detail in an article on the NIEO and the IPC from a regime perspective: "Regime Creation by a Coalition of the Weak," *International Studies Quarterly* 28 (September 1984) 3: 307-28.

3

The Committee of the Whole: Initiative and Impasse in North-South Negotiations

Ronald I. Meltzer

Institutional issues, particularly regarding the locus and character of international economic negotiations, have long been at the center of North-South relations. Indeed, questions about institutional venue, jurisdictional authority, decision-making processes, the nature of agreements, and relationships between sets of deliberations frequently preoccupy negotiators within North-South discussions. In recent times, these institutional matters have become especially problematic, reflecting the underlying turbulence of current North-South relations as well as widespread recognition that the format and results of past encounters often have proved inadequate. As a result, the Group of 77 has coupled its quest for "a new international economic order" (NIEO) with an institutional corollary. Just as NIEO is seen to require a restructuring of international economic relations, the developing countries argue that international economic institutions and decision making similarly must be restructured to realize and sustain such a transformation.

The creation and proceedings of the United Nations Committee of the Whole (COW) during the 1977-80 period represent an important example of how institutional and substantive issues have been approached—and linked—within North-South relations. Clearly, relationships between structure, process, and policy can be handled in different ways. On the one hand, focusing upon institutional issues can be a vital step toward insuring that effective policy deliberations are mounted and eventually completed. On the other hand, as negotiations in the COW revealed, discussions about institutional questions can drift into a time-consuming and draining sideshow, which precludes any movement on substantive issues.

The COW also reflects a legacy of UN institutional arrangements and difficulties. For the most part, the UN system has grown more from institutional inheritance and proliferation than it did from design. In this uncoordinated and decentralized structure, UN members frequently respond to new or persistent problems by creating further machinery—even if these additional bodies are not accompanied by any new policy initiatives. In addition, UN institutions have become increasingly brittle as a result of strong symbolic associations or political attachments that different groups of member states assign to various UN bodies. This feature has limited the adaptability and usefulness of many UN arenas. Thus, when new deliberations are considered, there often is pressure to establish additional entities to house them—not so much to create greater negotiating or administrative capacities as to avoid raising political objections or distractions tied to the use of existing settings.

In recent years a great deal of attention has been given to the effectiveness of UN forums of negotiations, especially in connection with the roles and activities of the General Assembly. The Group of 77 has long pressed for greater General Assembly authority and jurisdiction in the area of international economic negotiations. Western governments prefer a much more restricted and recommendatory position for the General Assembly, with actual deliberations conducted within existing specialized forums.[1] This issue about the General Assembly's role and authority in international negotiations has gained prominence in North-South relations, because "all negotiations of a global nature relating to the establishment of a new international economic order" are expected to take place within the framework of the UN system.[2]

The COW represented a key phase of a continuing process to resolve such institutional issues about the conduct of North-South negotiations. It explicitly grew out the perceived failure of a previous encounter (the Paris Conference on International Economic Cooperation) and became drawn into the preparations for the launching of a future round ("global negotiations relating to international economic cooperation for development"). Accordingly, the COW displayed important negotiating dynamics involving processes of both initiative and impasse. This study will analyze the creation and proceedings of this committee, seeking to explain the conduct of these negotiations and their outcomes. It will conclude with several propositions about the conduct of effective negotiations in North-South relations, drawing upon the experiences of the UN Committee of the Whole from 1977 to 1980.

The Creation of the Committee of the Whole

In December 1977 the General Assembly created the Committee of the Whole, which under resolution 32/174 would have the following responsibilities:

A) Overseeing and monitoring the implementation of decisions and arrangements reached in the negotiations on the establishment of the New International Economic Order in the appropriate bodies of the United Nations system;

B) Providing impetus for resolving difficulties in negotiations and for encouraging the continuous work in those bodies;

C) Serving, where appropriate, as a forum for facilitating and expediting agreement on the resolution of outstanding issues;

D) Exploring and exchanging views on global economic problems and priorities.[3]

The COW was intended to have to have special characteristics and roles within North-South relations. First, it was to meet on an intersessional and pluriannual basis, reporting directly to the General Assembly. By COW's creation, the General Assembly was seeking to demonstrate its strong and preeminent involvement in negotiating NIEO matters. Second, the committee was established to fulfill a high-level "political mission" and was given priority attention in UN activities concerning international economic cooperation and development. In this matter, it presumably would be capable of achieving results that were not possible in other UN forums of negotiations.[4]

These characteristics sought for and attributed to the COW were rooted in important background conditions leading to its establishment. During the 1973-75 period discussions on NIEO gained growing definition and impetus. The sixth special session of the General Assembly produced codified statements about NIEO's desired contents, as well as heightened political sensitivities about North-South matters. The actions of the OPEC states in this period also introduced a new tone and set of issues within international economic relations. One major response to these events was the convening of the Paris Conference on International Economic Cooperation (CIEC) in 1975—a North-South encounter that entailed several distinctive features, including its location outside the UN framework, its limited membership, and its inclusion of energy as a prominent agenda item.[5]

CIEC, however, quickly became bogged down by the very factors that separated it from past interactions. It confronted many political and institutional problems, notably issues concerning representation and methods for implementing its results. The difficulties produced a strong reaction of frustration and dismay on the part of many countries, particularly because the conference came in the wake of rising expectations generated by the seventh special session of the General Assembly.[6]

Despite these problems industrialized countries were not prepared to discount CIEC's work nor disregard its outcomes. At the resumed thirty-first session of the General Assembly, the U.S. delegation and others sought a favorable resolution on the Paris conference. But the Group of 77 firmly resisted such a move and opposed further consideration of CIEC's work.[7] In effect, an institutional and political vacuum was created, triggering efforts to seek a new venue for the continuation of the North-South dialogue. The desire for maintaining discussions was heightened by the fact that energy issues might now be incorporated into future negotiating agendas. Developed and developing countries alike did not want to pass up potential opportunities that this inclusion might present.

Several important factors motivated the Group of 77 to establish the Committee of the Whole. As noted, the group's members sought a more prominent role for the General Assembly in centralizing and conducting North-South negotiations. The desire grew out of their majority position within the Assembly, as well as their growing discontent with the current dialogue and its likely course within specialized forums such as the General Agreement on Tariffs and Trade (GATT) and the International Monetary Fund (IMF). In addition, there was increasing recognition on the part of many countries that negotiating agendas were becoming more and more interrelated, limiting the usefulness of sectorial approaches to North-South deliberations.

The creation of a body like the Committee of the Whole also was perceived as an important opportunity to improve the functioning of the UN system in international economic relations. As the director-general for international economic cooperation and development stated, the establishment and work of the COW "would be the first major test of the efficacy of the process of UN restructuring, generally regarded as an integral part of the establishment of the new international economic order."[8] The Group of 77 shared this sentiment about the committee's potential importance as an "architect of change" in future international economic relations.[9] In the words of one UN official, "The Group of 77 initially looked upon the creation of the Committee with highly ambitious plans and expectations."[10]

In addition, attempts to centralize North-South negotiations within a General Assembly forum were tied to two important tactical considerations for the Group of 77. First, managing North-South deliberations through a single arena would be advantageous to the developing countries to the extent that their staffs and quality of representation could be maximized. Second, the creation of a committee of the whole would alleviate a persistent problem of "forum tactics." This negotiating dynamic, often used by the developed countries, involved changing or questioning institutional venues so as to avoid granting concessions or resolving substantive issues. As one UN official stated, "The 77 had a great deal of difficulty developing and coordinating common strategies across different forums. By seeking a central arena, they would finally be able to pin down the B group within a single forum."[11]

The industrialized countries greeted the prospect of establishing a new UN forum on North-South matters with varying degrees of interest, but clearly without the intensity displayed by the Group of 77. Generally, the Western governments were willing to consider the committee's formation, in large part to avoid an interruption or breakdown in North-South talks after CIEC.[12] Beyond this common position, however, were several different shades of response to the creation of the COW. On one end of the spectrum were the Nordic states, which expressed strong enthusiasm for such a body and its potential role as an agent of change in North-South relations. The European Community members and Japan also were interested in the establishment of the committee, particularly because energy might become a key agenda item. Indeed, in the early discussions about the creation of the COW, the Group of 77 dangled the energy issue as an enticement for Western participation in this initiative.[13]

The United States first regarded the COW as a mixed bag of problems and prospects. U.S. officials were not pleased about another new body on North-South matters, particularly as an organ of the General Assembly. But the U.S. government wanted to continue discussions from CIEC, and it was increasingly apparent that these talks could be held only within the context of the United Nations. Several intended features of the committee also held special appeal, particularly its operation as an intersessional and high-level arena. A former U.S. official commented, "The United States took the idea of high-level representation very seriously. But we are very disappointed after the initial meetings, since no one was sending their top people."[14] The failure to maintain high-level representation jaundiced U.S. officials very early in the committee's deliberations.

Other factors also limited U.S. interest in the COW. First, the United States did not attribute any great priority or urgency to North-South matters at this time. In one U.S. official's words, "CIEC was tried and went nowhere, plus it didn't put any special responsibility on American door-steps. Besides, the seventh special session was seen as the cat's meow within the U.S. government—the end-all and be-all of successful North-South deliberations. There was no strong feeling that we needed to move ahead."[15]

Second, U.S. officials had no clear sense about where the proposed committee might lead in terms of potential impacts or obligations. The prevailing U.S. approach to North-South matters was predicated upon a series of small steps in specialized forums. The committee was being established along dramatically different lines, indeed in large part to counteract and overcome past practices within North-South deliberations. As one U.S. official indicated, "The Group of 77 was hinting towards some impending, all-inclusive global trade-off involving such vital areas as energy and money and finance. We certainly did not have anything we wanted to put on the table, nor did we want to be pressed into a negotiating situation of that kind."[16] Thus, when the COW first was proposed, the United States was willing to entertain its creation, but the U.S. government and the Group of 77 had very different starting points and horizons about the COW's intended purpose and likely impacts.

The different expectations and interests surrounding the creation of the COW were highlighted when the General Assembly was considering resolution 32/174.[17] As noted, the Group of 77 originally adopted very ambitious plans for the COW, particularly as a negotiating body with wide jurisdiction in terms of issues within its domain and authority vis-à-vis other forums of negotiation. However, this position was moderated considerably as a result of extensive consultations with Western governments prior to the formal resolution. The United States and other developed countries strongly opposed language that would empower the COW to conduct negotiations or to usurp such authority within specialized agencies such as the GATT and the IMF. More specifically, the U.S. government held fast to two key contentions. First, the authority and decisions of the General Assembly and its organs were recommendatory under the Charter, not binding. Second, the General Assembly's relationships to other forums of negotiations were to be guided by the principle that actual decision-making power in international economic relations resided independently within these agencies, rather than as a derivative of the General Assembly. Therefore, they would not be subject to its direction and authority.[18]

When resolution 32/174 finally was adopted by the General Assembly in December 1977, its language regarding the identity and functions of the COW was vaguely worded in compromise. For example, the resolution stated that the COW should serve as a "forum for facilitating and expediting agreement on the resolution of outstanding issues" rather than designating it as a negotiating forum with respect to any particular matters. In addition, the resolution stated that the COW should "provide impetus" and "encourage" negotiations in other forums rather than clarifying any specific relationship to them. In the words of one UN official, "The Western countries managed to take the

teeth and specificity out of the Group of 77's initiative on the COW."[19]
But the compromises about the basic purview of the committee—
whether it could undertake negotiations or simply act as a reviewing
body—eventually came to haunt the COW. The consensus that had
permitted adoption of resolution 32/174 left these issues unresolved
and hence only carried them forward into the future proceedings of the
committee.

In explaining the onset of negotiations in this case, two basic types of
initiating factors came into play. The creation of the Committee of the
Whole reflected a general recognition that a "necessary moment" had
been reached in North-South discussions, particularly because the
perceived failure of CIEC left an institutional and political vacuum
concerning the future of the dialogue. Neither side wanted an interruption or breakdown in the process that had begun in 1974, or at the very
least wanted to be held responsible for its demise.

It was also a "ripe moment" to the extent that the past frustrations
of North-South discussions and changing background conditions (the
energy issue and interdependent economic difficulties) now created the
basis for a new departure in structuring international economic negotiations. This viewpoint, however, clearly was held much more strongly
within the Group of 77 than among Western delegations. In large part,
their lack of responsiveness to the Group of 77's initiative in creating
the COW was tied to the scope of change envisioned, as well as to the
centrality of considerations (the locus of decision making in North-
South negotiations and the integrity of the specialized agencies) directly affected by such proposed changes in structuring future North-
South encounters.

Committee Deliberations, 1978–1979: Impasse and Attempted Reinvigoration

In February 1978 the Committee of the Whole took up its work, with
organizational meetings on its agenda.[20] Shortly after, the issue of
decision making within the COW brought the proceedings to a halt.
Informal negotiations between representatives of the Group of 77 and
Western countries led to a suspension of the committee's first session
and to renewed efforts to convene in September, but given the continuing disagreements over this important aspect of interpreting its competence, the committee was unable to proceed with its work. The
committee chairman submitted an interim report to the General Assembly at its thirty-third session and asked for a clarification of the
COW mandate.

Following extensive informal discussions during the course of the summer ECOSOC sessions, the chairman proposed new compromise language on the mandate of the committee:

> to negotiate with a view to its adopting guidelines on central policy issues, as well as achieving agreement on the resolution of fundamental or crucial issues underlying problems related to international economic cooperation. The results of the negotiations will be expressed in the form of action-oriented agreed conclusions of the Committee addressed through the General Assembly to States and international organizations concerned. . . .[21]

In this statement the chairman was seeking to take account of concerns of the United States and other Western countries about the COW's possible interference with ongoing negotiations in other forums. In addition, he was trying to accommodate their concerns about how committee actions would be addressed to states and other international organizations. But attempts at bridging viewpoints about the mandate, competence, and decision-making processes of the COW broke down over efforts by the United States to insure that the committee's work and actions "do not overlap with other agreements that might be achieved in other forums or bodies." The U.S. delegation was insistent on this point, despite the understanding that the committee would operate on the basis of "agreed conclusions" involving the consent of all the parties.

The Group of 77, however, did not want to limit the purview and decision-making authority of the COW simply because similar problems were being discussed elsewhere. Moreover, after preliminary agreements were reached about the committee's ability to act, the U.S. delegation later proposed that another "formulation" be used regarding the outcomes of COW deliberations. The Group of 77 objected that this would negate the purpose and process of committee negotiations, and an impasse ensued.[22] Thus, fundamental disagreements continued over the committee's right to negotiate and adopt decisions, issues that were critical to an interpretation of its mandate and competence.

In reviewing this situation, the Group of 77 indicated that its members were committed firmly to the committee's essential "function of negotiation" and ability to reach agreements. Its position was based upon "the need for an unambiguous statement which would remove the possibility of a future challenge to the competence of the Committee and another serious delay in its work." The objectives behind the Group of 77's position was not "to preempt the functions of other United Nations bodies, but . . . [to] supplement and complement their work in positive ways and seek to exercise a responsible influence on the whole process." In its view, the committee reached an impasse because of a "lack of political will on the part of some delegations to engage in meaningful negotiations and to take fundamental decisions." Spokesman for the Group of 77 argued that the position taken by developed countries reflected a long-standing "refusal to achieve movement towards the establishment of the new international economic order," a perspective evident in their unwillingness to accept the real "purpose" of the committee, and, not incidentally, to confer a more explicit name on the committee.[23]

For the United States, the breakdown of discussions within the committee was an unfortunate development, especially because it isolated and stigmatized the U.S. delegation in a rather graphic manner. But as one U.S. official stated,

> We came prepared to talk, not to negotiate. Our strategy was to select a limited number of priority areas on which discussions could then proceed. We didn't want decisions being made in the Committee. The U.S. has long felt that decision-making resided in the specialized agencies, not the GA. But the issue of decision-making within the COW increasingly became a problem, since a number of far-reaching matters would be on the agenda. So for the first year, we just stone-walled it.[24]

When the matter was brought before the thirty-third session of the General Assembly, consultations among the member-states continued regarding the mandate and competence of the committee. Similar to the creation of the COW with resolution 32/174, the General Assembly reached consensus about the committee's purpose and ability to act. It was agreed that the committee "would negotiate with a view to its adopting guidelines on central policy issues underlying problems related to international economic cooperation." The results of such negotiations would be expressed in the form of "action-oriented agreed conclusions addressed through the Assembly to States and international organizations concerned. Additionally, the rules of procedure of the Assembly would continue to apply to the Committee."[25]

The consensus, in the words of a former U.S. official, was the result of a "tortuous diplomatic word-game, involving a watering down process in which it became hard to recognize what was being adopted."[26] In addition, the tactic used to present this consensus was a statement read by the president of the General Assembly, which even further distanced the agreed formulations from the governments involved, thereby making the level of consensus and its effects even more tenuous. One UN official remarked, "By resorting to this tactic, no one had to sponsor it formally, or felt compelled to challenge it. It was represented only as an understanding. As such, no one is responsible for it."[27] On 19 October, 1978 the Assembly formally adopted resolution 33/2, which included the consensus agreement as submitted by the president; the COW was called upon to renew its deliberations and make "a determined effort . . . to achieve real progress."[28]

When the committee resumed its sessions in January 1979, the Group of 77 proposed a "selective approach" to prospective negotiations within the COW. Its preferred items would include increasing the flow and quality of overseas development assistance; strengthening the financial resources of multilateral financial institutions and their aid to developing countries; improving the terms imposed by the International Monetary Fund for developing countries; and providing easier access to capital markets for developing countries.[29] Clearly, these topics reflected the Group of 77's strategic interest in money and finance matters—both as bastions of industrialized countries' power and control in international economic relations, as well as areas in which desired concessions might be gained in the negotiating process.

The United States emerged from the thirty-third session of the General Assembly with quite another perspective about the committee's future course. U.S. officials argued that the committee's "crowded calendar" in relation to other international meetings and agendas "made it difficult to put forward concrete proposals." In this context, then, the U.S. government believed that the most appropriate role and action of the COW should be "identifying for future attention the most urgent developmental objectives and their relationship to proposals for structural and institutional change." From the standpoint of the U.S. delegation, the most important objectives along these lines included agricultural and human development; rational use of the world's natural resources; and smooth adjustment to changing economic conditions and reduced economic uncertainty.[30]

These views about the manner and level at which the committee would function again reflected a U.S. negotiating posture aimed at limiting the COW's actual impacts and involvement in specific negotiations. A former U.S. official said, "We wanted to talk about things like agricultural and human development to get the discussions moving again without running into the previous conflicts. Substantively, it was expected that each side would go back to past texts and positions in these areas and resubmit them to the Committee. This would get the talks going, but on a safe-track of treading water for a while."[31]

During this 1979 session the committee produced "agreed conclusions" on four agenda items: transfer of resources; food and agricultural development; a reaffirmation of the United Nations Industrial Development Organization (UNIDO) as a specialized agency; and problems of island developing countries. No agreements could be reached on broader questions of industrial development or matters pertaining to other types of least developed countries.[32] During this session, the committee followed a routine course, especially in comparison to its originally envisioned mandate and role within North-South relations. The description of one UN official: "The delegations went through a standard sector-by-sector review they had undertaken many times in the past. The developed countries obviously favored this process, since it didn't raise critical issues about negotiating within the COW or the GA's relationship to the specialized agencies."[33] But this process and its outcomes proved increasingly dissatisfying to the Group of 77.

One clear measure of the extent to which the COW had lost its standing and perceived usefulness was the developing countries' inclination to seek yet another initiative for dealing with North-South issues. At the Havana Conference of the Non-Aligned States in September 1979, the Group of 77 called for the launching of "global negotiations relating to international economic cooperation for development." Its purpose was to "give impetus to the North-South dialogue." The Group of 77 brought this proposal before the committee to recommend that this "important initiative" be considered by the General Assembly at its 34th session "as a matter of priority."[34] In effect, the COW was presented with a proposal to recreate itself, but this time in a manner that would realize its intended dimensions and objectives.

Two major factors led to this new initiative on global negotiations. First, the economic situation facing many developing countries had deteriorated to crisis proportions, in part because of major oil price increases instituted during this period. The actions of the Organization of Petroleum Exporting Countries (OPEC) created greater hardships for developing countries at this point than they had in 1973. Moreover, they were no longer cushioned by expectations about OPEC's potential benefits in changing the course of North-South relations. Indeed, many developing countries greeted these new energy developments with open criticism of OPEC. One UN official recalled,

> The tensions within the Group of 77 over oil and its impacts grew increasingly evident at UNCTAD V and elsewhere. Many members insisted that energy problems had to be addressed. But the OPEC states did not want these matters considered in isolation, or as bald producer-consumer problems. Thus, Venezuela, Algeria, and others sought to

situate energy within the North-South framework to avoid an impending split within the ranks.[35]

However, one key result of this effort was a change in the underlying negotiating posture of the Group of 77. A greater potential bargaining tool was added to the developing countries' arsenal as a result of bringing OPEC and oil so explicitly into North-South discussions, but considerable negotiating flexibility was lost in the process, given the difficulties of maintaining agreement among oil-producing and other developing countries.

A second reason for this initiative on global negotiations was the quickly fading horizons of the Committee of the Whole and the Group of 77's growing discontent with its proceedings. According to one UN official, "Well before Havana, people were looking around for some other avenue to pursue, given the weak performance of the COW."[36] The prospect of a new round of global negotiations also would solve another problem within North-South discussions: what to do next in the COW, given its diminished stature and capabilities. A former U.S. official recalled, "The 77's initiative on global negotiations cleared the deck within the COW, allowing its members to start fresh with a new focus. It reinvigorated the Committee just when it had lost much of its steam and purpose."[37]

The Committee of the Whole in Preparation for Global Negotiations

The Group of 77's proposal for global negotiations became the central focus and eventual *raison d'etre* of the Committee of the Whole after 1979. Emphasizing that all NIEO negotiations must take place within the UN system under the direction of the General Assembly, this initiative called for the launching of a "round of global and sustained negotiations" at the 1980 special session. The developing countries proposed that the negotiations should be "action-oriented" and adopt an integrated approach to the main issues of raw materials, energy, trade, development, and money and finance. These matters should be addressed simultaneously within a specified time frame and involve the full participation of all states and relevant bodies of the UN system. It was expected that the negotiations would contribute to the implementation of a new international development strategy and "should not involve any interruption of the negotiations in other United Nations forums, but should reinforce and draw upon them."[38]

Although there were variations in tone, most Western delegations expressed considerable doubt and hesitancy about the Group of 77's proposal. The Canadian representative declared that North-South negotiations were "at a crossroads" in attempting to move from generalized principles to practical agreements. Deliberations, therefore, should focus upon the specific costs and benefits of North-South issues from the standpoint of "particular national economic experiences and needs" rather than attempt "global solutions through comprehensive strategies."[39] The British representative similarly questioned the viability of this approach, particularly because the previous Paris conference "gave no reason to believe that a major institutional project of this sort would be the way to make genuine progress in the vital enterprise to which the Committee was dedicated."[40]

The representatives of both the European Community (EC) and the United States greeted the idea of global negotiations with detailed sets of questions about actual arrangements and implications. The EC spokesman noted that the proposal raised numerous institutional issues and had far-reaching potential impacts requiring that "definitive decisions" on the matter be delayed beyond the current session of the COW.[41] The U.S. representative also referred to a long list of questions that needed clarification before the initiatives' merit would be addressed directly. The questions dealt with the relationships between a global forum and specialized arenas; the priorities of issues and their placement within different forums; the decision-making procedures; the distinctiveness of global negotiations from existing deliberations within the COW; the order of consideration of issues within forums; and the character and consistency of representation.[42]

The General Assembly adopted resolutions 34/138 and 34/139 in late 1979, officially launching global negotiations as proposed by the Group of 77. The key task before the COW was to recommend to the General Assembly an agenda, procedures, and time frame for the negotiations.[43] Over the course of its 1980 session the committee received numerous working papers and proposals from different groups of countries to guide its work. The Groups of 77 submitted a further elaboration of its designs for global negotiations. The developing countries emphasized the need to convene a high-level UN conference at the headquarters, which should be the forum for conducting negotiations to insure a coherent and integrated approach to its agenda. The conference outcome should be a "package agreement" relating all five issue areas within a prescribed time frame, January to September 1981.[44]

Norway also submitted its suggestions about the procedures and time frame for global negotiations. The deliberations should be organized as a UN conference, proceeding in three phases: conceptual, negotiating, and concluding. The earlier phases should draw upon various bodies within the UN system, as well as the central confer-ence, which would have negotiating and coordinating powers of its own. The concluding phase, which should produce a package of comprehensive, agreed conclusions that were more binding than past UN resolutions, should be completed by early 1982.[45]

The European Community's position differed considerably on the role and authority of a central body within any global negotiations. The EC representative noted that the central forum could examine ques-tions considered within specialized agencies and provide any neces-sary impetus to resolve outstanding differences. But the European states did not wish to grant specific negotiating authority to this central body, adding as well that any results of global negotiations should be adopted by means of consensus. The U.S. delegation provided the clearest and most stringent limitations regarding the centralization of global negotiations. The U.S. government favored the extension of the Committee of the Whole as an "oversight body," with actual negotia-tions occurring in a decentralized manner within the specialized fo-rums. The central forum would determine the objectives for such negotiations and receive their results, operating on the basis of consen-sus decision making. It was expected that these negotiations would be completed by September 1981.[46]

The various proposals clearly highlighted the differences that existed over the preferred locus and character of global negotiations, disparate viewpoints that had long been apparent within earlier deliberations of the COW. For the Group of 77, the global negotiations should encom-pass concrete, comprehensive, and global solutions to major issues in the five issue areas, with negotiations proceeding in a simultaneous and integrated manner at a centralized arena. According to the developing countries' representative, these notions "were an essential prelude" to further discussions about global negotiations.[47] At the other end of the spectrum was the United States, which also had its "bottom-line" considerations. First, U.S. officials sought to protect the specialized agencies' integrity and role as negotiating forums. Second, the United States wanted the adoption of consensus procedures for any discus-sions on the process and content of global negotiations within the COW.[48] This call for consensus decision making had previously been accepted by all the parties, but its practice had yet to be fully resolved or firmly established in North-South negotiations.

In addition to wide divergences about the character of global negoti-ations, the committee became embroiled in subsidiary disputes about the order in which topics were to be addressed. The Group of 77 spokesman stressed the importance of devising a provisional agenda for global negotiations as the first step toward preparing for this round. The Norwegian representative, who played important broker and bridging roles in the committee, supported this view, arguing that both logically and politically it made sense to proceed in this manner—especially given the past problems of the COW.[49]

But both the European Community and the U.S. delegations preferred to discuss procedures first because significant institutional changes were being proposed that had important bearing upon the treatment of substantive issues. One U.S. official noted, "Our position was that you needed to know what the process was first, before you get into the substance. If you could agree on how you would proceed, then it makes life easier when you discuss the agenda. You can be more flexible."[50] Yet as a former U.S. official indicated, adopting this approach also kept the subject and reality of global negotiations at a greater distance: "When you have a negotiating strategy based upon procedure before agenda, you're really talking about how things might be set up, without indicating you're ready to do anything about the issues. It keeps things at a level of principle and abstraction, safely removed from real actions and commitments."[51]

Similar to earlier deliberations of the COW, discussions about the procedures and timetable for convening global negotiations brought the committee to an impasse. The United States and other Western countries effectively held to their position through a variety of tactics. The spokesman for the Group of 77 complained,

> When, after intense private consultations, a formulation was arrived at and presented in the negotiating group, they [the developed countries] invariably suggested further changes to weaken the text even more. At the same time, their own concerns were presented with varying degrees of vagueness, even dissimulation. When they were asked to concretize their suggestions, the burden of doing so was invariably transferred back to us, the Group of 77. We were left with the impression of trying to punch holes through smoke.[52]

Thus, the committee prepared its final document to the General Assembly much like it began, indicating that "it regretted having to report . . . that it had been unable to agree on proposals for the agenda, procedures, and time-frame for the global negotiations under Assembly resolutions 34/138 and 34/139." It could pass on to the Assembly, as an "annex," only the proposals submitted within the committee, as well as texts of statements made by various delegations.[53]

Although the Committee of the Whole could not complete its work on the agenda, procedures, and time frame for global negotiations, these matters were pursued further at the eleventh special session of the UN General Assembly. As expected, the dynamics and cleavages that left the COW in stalemate continued during the special session. Toward the end of the session, elaborate efforts were made to devise acceptable terms to launch global negotiations. Indeed, all of the developed countries were willing to accept compromise proposals put forward by the chairman of an ad hoc committee—except the United States, the United Kingdom, and the Federal Republic of Germany. The basic reason for their continued opposition in the face of strong conference pressures and extraordinary attempts to reach agreement involved lingering concern that a central UN forum might be able to "renegotiate agreements reached in the specialized agencies without any further involvement of those agencies." As the U.S. representative further noted, this could "adversely affect the functioning of the specialized agencies" and compromise their integrity and authority.[54] Thus, these three delegations effectively vetoed the launching of global negotiations.

Additional efforts in regard to global negotiations were made at the thirty-fifth session of the General Assembly. The discussions focused almost exclusively on ways to resolve U.S. objections. But despite the fact that almost all of the provisions relating to the launching of global negotiations were agreed upon, the outstanding issues about how to deal with the rolè and authority of the central UN forum vis-à-vis the specialized agencies could not be resolved.[55] Successive summit meetings since that time that have involved the Organization for Economic Cooperation and Development (OECD) states, as well as North-South participants, also have not produced much progress on global negotiations. If anything, subsequent international economic developments have reduced both the salience and prospects of global negotiations. This change in priority and emphasis, even among the developing countries, could be seen, for example, at the 1983 Fifth Ministerial Meeting of the Group of 77 in Buenos Aires, Argentina. Almost ritualistically, the members called for global negotiations, but much greater attention was given to measures relating to international debt problems of developing countries and to trade protectionism—items that would have to be addressed within the very same specialized agencies, such as the IMF and the GATT, which the United States sought to preserve vis-à-vis UN global negotiations.[56]

Overall Negotiating Dynamics

The UN Committee of the Whole represented an important phase of a continuing, even if beleaguered, process aimed at resolving institutional issues about the conduct of North-South negotiations. It wrestled with fundamental questions concerning the most appropriate venue for conducting negotiations; the nature of decision making within these bodies; the character of agreements reached; and the relationships between different arenas and items of negotiation. Of particular importance was the prescribed role and authority of the General Assembly vis-à-vis specialized forums in which past international economic negotiations have been held and decision making power resided. The history of the COW, however, was one of alternating periods of initiative and impasse, reflecting the asymmetry of interest, commitment, power, and purpose behind the participation of its major actors, the Group of 77 and the governments of the industrialized West.

The Group of 77 and the Western countries had very different starting points and horizons for the Committee of the Whole—differences that were carried forward throughout various sessions of the COW. The Western governments looked upon the COW as a way to avoid any breakdown in North-South discussions and to explore their possible implications for dealing with international energy policies. They did not, however, share the Group of 77's expectations and ambitions regarding the eventual role and authority of the committee as a negotiating body. Given these differences, the process of encounter within the COW took the shape of a search for a framework of agreement. In the process the interactions between the Group of 77 and leading Western countries evidenced some movement toward mutual concession, but each side still sought to preserve critical aspects of its own position. For example, the Western nations showed increased willingness to structure talks within the COW, so long as the Group of 77 did not force the key issue of contention: the negotiating and decision making authority of the General Assembly vis-à-vis the specialized forums of negotiation. In later stages of the COW, this same posture was adopted toward the global negotiations initiative. Many Western governments appeared increasingly willing to concede the convening of such negotiations so long as they would not affect the prevailing structure of international economic negotiations and decision making.

The Group of 77's moves were aimed primarily at gaining recognition for some specified negotiating authority—however residual or circumscribed—to be vested in the General Assembly, ceding in the process the specialized agencies' distinctive domains and decision making power. Once this authority was established for the General Assembly in international economic negotiations, then presumably later deliberations could deal with its possible expansion in terms of other policy realms or particular tasks.

The movement toward mutual concession did not proceed very far in the COW's deliberations. Two factors accounted for this very slow-moving, partial process of encounter. First, looming over the various consensus efforts and attempts to salvage what became of the COW were core priorities and differences that each side held regarding the conduct of North-South negotiations. Throughout the COW's deliberations, representatives from both sides repeatedly referred to the potentially far-reaching implications of the committee's actions, a factor that constrained efforts to find agreeable formulations to get beyond the stalemate. Issues concerning the integrity of long-revered international economic institutions (for the West) and a restructuring of international economic decision making (for the Group of 77) were not matters easily accommodated by traditional negotiating techniques, such as splitting the difference.

In addition to the centrality of matters affected by the COW mandate, the committee represented a major departure in negotiating arrangements and objectives, a factor again militating against easy accommodation. In one UN official's words, "Throughout most of the COW's discussions, the U.S. and other developed countries seemed to distill everything down to what it would mean in terms of change. This preoccupation naturally led to their determination to leave as much as possible intact."[57] These frustrations also were tied to the disjointed manner in which the committee approached questions of power in North-South relations. In effect, the COW became involved in attempts to negotiate a redistribution of power by designing new institutional arrangements. Most negotiations, however, *reflect* underlying power capabilities rather than *restructure* them. Thus, the normal relationship between negotiation and power was turned on its head in the COW deliberations, and predictably the committee experienced an impasse.[58]

A second major factor slowing down the process of encounter within the COW was an element found more generally in North-South discussions—the group system of negotiations. However, in this case, the usual difficulties of the Group of 77 were exacerbated by the direct stakes of the OPEC states in the negotiations. The development of the group's negotiating positions normally reflects the compilation of maximum packages to sustain internal agreement and cohesion. Thus, these positions frequently are difficult to reduce or reformulate as a result of intragroup pressures and constraints. Within the COW's proceedings, the margin of leeway was restricted even further as a result of delicate relations between the OPEC states and other group members. The OPEC states actively opposed any arrangements that would situate energy issues within a strictly producers-consumers framework. They similarly resisted any format for global negotiations that singled out energy, or left it unconnected to deliberations within the specialized forums, especially the IMF.

The OPEC-related difficulties of group negotiations for the developing countries could be seen in two important ways. First, the positions of the seventy-seven members often reflect bilateral ties and interests, as well as multilateral considerations. But the prominence given to OPEC interests within the Group of 77 position highlighted this bilateral dimension. As one UN official indicated, "During these meetings of the COW, governments took positions not only on the basis of what might be gained within the UN system, but also what could be gained from OPEC as a side deal. This reduced the Group of 77's flexibility and incentives for accommodation with the B group."[59]

Second, the Group of 77 representative is often a vital component of the negotiating process. His bargaining skills, reputation, delegated authority, and relationships with key delegations can shape the process and outcomes of negotiation. In the case of the COW, the relationship of the group's representatives to the OPEC states was critical, but at several points during the negotiations, in the words of one UN official, "it was clear that you couldn't count them to deliver the OPEC states when it was necessary. This caused many difficulties in the negotiating process."[60]

Despite the problems introduced by the inclusion of the OPEC states in the Group of 77's negotiating posture, the committee's impasses could not be explained simply on the basis of the developing countries' negotiating behavior. As seen, throughout the virtual life span of the COW, Western countries resisted major changes in the structure of international economic negotiations and decision making. They furthered their positions by various tactics of delay and avoidance. This pattern could be seen early in the COW's deliberations when a review and assessment of world economic factors was undertaken. The tactic also was apparent when global negotiations were proposed. Question after question was raised, in effect putting off substantive matters and keeping the discussions at a safe distance.

Throughout the COW, the Group of 77 reacted to this negotiating behavior with increased frustration and eventually with proposals for new institutional arrangements. In addition, the Group of 77 sought to further its positions by holding out the prospects for negotiating international energy matters and by placing the blame for any possible breakdowns in North-South discussions squarely upon the developed countries' shoulders. But these tactics were incapable of producing major Western concessions on items of important principle, such as the integrity of the specialized agencies.

It is difficult to measure precisely the negotiating success of each party in the Committee of the Whole. If the actual results of the committee itself are evaluated, then clearly the COW did not go very far before differences over its definition and purpose led to an impasse. Similarly, the committee could not attain its objectives as a preparatory body for the convening of global negotiations. From this standpoint the ability of Western countries to hold off unwanted initiatives on North-South negotiations prevailed over the efforts of the Group of 77.

If the COW is evaluated as part of a continuing interaction in North-South relations, however, determinations about success take on different terms. For example, irrespective of its concrete results, the Committee of the Whole can be seen as a reaffirmation of a core principle for the Group of 77: the UN system should be the framework within which North-South negotiations take place. But recent international economic conditions, particularly involving debt problems of developing countries, have affected the relative importance of global negotiations as a priority issue in North-South relations. As noted, many countries within the Group of 77 require immediate actions in specialized forums to deal with their international debt positions and related economic situations. For the most part, activities undertaken in the IMF, the World Bank, and elsewhere to deal with these short-term exigencies have reinforced the existing authority and decision making patterns of these bodies and have forestalled consideration of any long-term restructuring of international economic relations. For example, at the 1983 Conference of the Non-Aligned Countries in New Delhi, India, member states called for a 1984 United Nations conference to take up the launching of global negotiations once again, but the thrust of their efforts centered on a "programme of immediate measures" to be adopted within the specialized agencies.[61]

In concluding this study, it is useful to draw lessons about effective North-South negotiations from the experience of the UN Committee of the Whole. First, although it is vital symbolically to situate North-South negotiations within the UN system, prevailing negotiating processes within the United Nations do not lend themselves well to effective agreements. As one UN official stated, "The whole practice of UN negotiations has been oriented to the achievement of consensus, even beyond having practical meaning. There are often desperate attempts to find agreeable language amidst glaring substantive differences. Preoccupation with consensus in these circumstances only sows the seeds of future problems."[62] This dynamic and its debilitating effects were apparent throughout much of the COW's early sessions, and unresolved issues about its mandate and competence came back to haunt subsequent negotiations.

In addition, the process of getting negotiations started in the United Nations may prove counterproductive to the achievement of effective final results. As a UN official suggested, the initiation of talks frequently requires highly generalized terms for negotiations. "But paradoxically, after you have gotten the negotiations rolling by providing this vague language that each side can live with, you create additional obstacles to realizing effective agreements. You still have to go back to the issues you've avoided and undo the generalizations. Quickly you find yourself at the same starting point of disagreement, only now worse off."[63] Making the transition from elaborating principles to realizing practical agreements remains a difficult task for UN negotiations. The experience of the COW did little to advance this process. Indeed, the beleaguered attempts to launch global negotiations during this period may have convinced all the parties that NIEO issues cannot be effectively approached by means of convening comprehensive international conferences.

A second proposition drawn from this case deals with the impact of international energy issues on the negotiating posture of the Group of 77. The high visibility of OPEC interests within the 77's negotiating posture did add a potential lure and basis for trade-offs to the group's bargaining position. But the reduced negotiating flexibility, along with other distractions and liabilities associated with OPEC's prominence, outweighed the benefits to the Group of 77—especially because the enticement of energy never became translated into a meaningful bargaining factor. In future North-South encounters, the participation of the OPEC states in the Group of 77 may be an important element in the negotiating process, but the experience of the COW demonstrated that the character and impact of this involvement are not as clear-cut, nor as positive, as originally expected.

A third proposition drawn from this case deals with the long-term viability and benefits of the prevailing negotiating stance taken by the United States and other Western countries. Like other encounters in North-South relations, Western participation in the COW was based upon a strategy of resistance and damage limitation, applying tactics of delay and avoidance in response to various initiatives posed by the Group of 77. Although this posture can be effective in the short term, its value and efficacy in the long term remains questionable—particularly in the absence of any *positive* steps or new directions taken by

Western countries in North-South relations. As seen, discussions between developed and developing countries can take place over a series of meetings, and a damage-limitation strategy, when applied within an incremental process, tends to lose its effectiveness. Because there is no clear end point in the negotiating process, gradually a damage-limitation posture gives way to increasing erosion or futility as indicated in the evolution of global negotiations from the COW to the present.

A fourth proposition drawn from this case deals with the importance of individuals within the negotiating process—this despite the elaborate group system of negotiations characterizing North-South encounters. The relative capabilities and authority of the representative of the Group of 77 and the chairman of a committee are especially significant factors, given the former's role as a mobilizer and decision maker within the negotiating process and the latter's role as a broker toward agreement. In light of the importance of individuals in the negotiating process, it is useful to have higher-level representatives participating in discussions. They have greater political standing and can be less bound by fixed instructions. This added flexibility is a significant factor in North-South encounters because the group system of negotiations has many built-in rigidities. One former U.S. official recalled, "Discussions in the COW became increasingly straight-jacketed by lower levels of representation. Obviously, this trend dampened the prospects for agreement, since there were times when high-level impetus could have broken through areas of impasse."[64] But generally it has been very difficult to sustain high-level involvement in North-South negotiations, given their extended duration, level of frustration, and—within the West—relative lack of priority. Furthermore, the processes and outcomes of the Committee of the Whole were troubled by another basic fact underlying North-South relations: continued Western unwillingness to adopt NIEO objectives and policies.

Finally, it is instructive to juxtapose the experience of the Committee of the Whole with several propositions frequently made about North-South negotiations.[65] First, crosscutting interactions in North-South encounters are said to facilitate agreement because they offer greater negotiating flexibility and potential for bargaining. In the case of the Committee of the Whole, the major crosscutting element involved energy issues as presented by the participation of the OPEC states. However, as noted, the high visibility of OPEC interests and energy matters in these negotiations only complicated the search for a framework of agreement and reduced negotiating leeway, especially on the part of the Group of 77.

Second, specific functional negotiations are thought to be more fruitful than global negotiations. Clearly, this issue was what the Committee of the Whole was all about. If the COW is considered an example of global negotiations, then the efficacy of this approach is truly questionable. However, the deliberations in the committee also fell subject to a self-fulfilling prophecy fueled by Western opposition to undertaking this mode of negotiations.

Third, confrontation in North-South negotiations is seen as necessary for Southern solidarity. In the case of the COW, the level of hostility directed toward the West had more to do with the frustration of the Group of 77 with the West's dilatory responses than it did with holding its own membership together.

Fourth, it is thought that the South must rely on rewards and moral obligations to produce negotiating results because it lacks the ability to compel action by the North. In this instance, the powerlessness of the South to force Western compliance was clearly evident. In addition, the tactics of reward and obligation were also largely ineffective. These types of levers were incapable of gaining concessions on the key issues at stake within the COW because matters such as the locus and character of international economic negotiations and the integrity of the specialized agencies touched upon fundamental Western interests not easily accommodated or willingly conceded.

Fifth, it is said that North-South negotiations can focus fruitfully only on rule change because they are unable to produce substantive policy changes. In the case of the COW, rule change was the essence of the encounter. However, not only were deliberations on the terms for North-South negotiations unfruitful but their linkage to substantive outcomes was never very far from the surface.

Sixth, it is thought that negotiations succeed only when trade-offs are possible so that demands and concessions can be offset in the encounter. In the case of the COW and global negotiations, the trade-off presumably behind the encounter—putting energy on the table in return for possible changes in international decision making on money and finance—was never pulled off, nor even seriously considered. In actuality, none of the sides was prepared to deal with such sweeping matters in the Committee of the Whole or any other forum. Broad intersectorial trade-offs pose too many uncertainties and incommensurate considerations, especially in a negotiating context involving multiple parties (i.e. the West, OPEC states, and oil-importing developing countries).

Seventh, it is said that U.S. obstructionism has become an assumption of North-South negotiations. Within the COW and global negotiations, this U.S. stance was very much a reality, although initially it was not assumed nor expected to be so steadfast. Despite the questionable value of this posture as a long-term strategy for North-South negotiations, U.S. obstructionism did succeed in holding off unwanted initiatives by the Group of 77 and remains the most central factor conditioning the outcomes of the future encounters.

Notes

1. See my "Restructuring the UN System: Institutional Reform Efforts in the Context of North-South Relations," *International Organization* 32 (Autumn 1978): 993-1018.
2. See UN document A/32/PV.109, p. 13.
3. See UN document A/33/34, pt. 1, p. 2.
4. See opening statements by the COW's chairman, ibid., pp. 11-12, as well as his statement in UN document A/33/34, vol. 2, pp. 1-2.
5. For a discussion of the major characteristics and results of CIEC, see Jahingir Amuzegar, "Requiem for the North-South Conference," *Foreign Affairs* 56 (October 1977): 136-59.
6. Personal interview, UN official.
7. Personal interview, former U.S. official.
8. See UN document A/133/34, vol. 2, p. 91.
9. See ibid., pp. 57-58.
10. Personal interview, UN official.
11. Ibid.
12. Ibid. The B group members do not have as much cohesion in New York as they do in Geneva, and this difference was apparent in dealing with the COW.
13. Ibid.
14. Personal interview, former U.S. official.
15. Personal interview, U.S. State Department official.
16. Ibid.
17. See UN document A/33/34, pt. 1, pp. 17-19.
18. Personal interview, former U.S. government official.
19. Personal interview, UN official.
20. See UN document A/33/34, pt. 1, pp. 8-12, 25-27, for remarks made by the secretary-general and the committee chairman at the opening of the COW deliberations.
21. See ibid., pp. 23-24.
22. See ibid., p. 26.
23. See ibid., pp. 27-31.
24. Personal interview, former U.S. government official.
25. See *Yearbook of the United Nations, 1978* (New York, United Nations, 1982), p. 408.
26. Personal interview, former U.S. government official.
27. Personal interview, UN official.
28. *Yearbook of the United Nations, 1978*, p. 408.
29. See UN document A/AC.191/SR.17, p. 2.
30. See UN document A/AC.191/SR.18, pp. 3-6.

31. Personal interview, former U.S. government official.
32. See UN document A/34/34, pp. 3-34.
33. Personal interview, UN official.
34. See UN document A/34/34, p. 32.
35. Personal interview, UN official.
36. Ibid.
37. Personal interview, former U.S. government official.
38. See UN document A/34/34, pp. 35-34, for text of this proposal.
39. See UN document A/AC.191/SR.31, pp. 14-15.
40. See UN document A/AC.191/SR.32, p. 11.
41. See UN document A/AC.191/SR.34, pp. 2-3.
42. See ibid., p. 3-4.
43. See UN document A/AC.191/47, p. 4.
44. See UN Press Release GA/EC/62, 16 May 1980, pp. 8-9.
45. See UN document A/AC.191/SR.40, pp. 4-5, and UN Press Release GA/
    EC/62, 16 May 1980, p. 5.
46. See UN Press Release GA/EC/62, 16 May 1980, p. 6.
47. See UN document A/AC.191/SR.40, p. 2.
48. Personal interview, U.S. State Department official.
49. See UN document A/AC.191/SR.40, p. 5.
50. Personal interview, U.S. State Department official.
51. Personal interview, former U.S. government official.
52. See UN document A/S-11/1 (Part IV), pp. 36-37.
53. Ibid.
54. See John P. Renninger with James Zech, "The 11th Special Session and
    the Future of Global Negotiations," *Policy and Efficacy Studies*, No. 5,
    United Nations Institute for Training and Research, p. 17. It should be
    noted that U.S. consideration of global negotiations at this time was
    affected by the impending 1980 presidential election and a desire by the
    Carter administration to avoid acting on matters that could be politically
    troublesome in the campaign.
55. See ibid., pp. 18-22.
56. See *Final Document of the Fifth Ministerial Meeting of the Group of 77*
    (Buenos Aires, Argentina), Document 77/mm(v)/13, 10 April 1983, p. 4.
57. Personal interview, UN official.
58. I am indebted to Catherine Gwin for this observation.
59. Personal interview, UN official.
60. Ibid.
61. See UN document A/38/132,S/15675, pp. 72-80, for the Non-Aligned
    Countries' statements on these matters.
62. Personal interview, UN official.
63. Ibid.
64. Personal interview, former U.S. official.
65. These propositions draw from I. William Zartman, chapter 1.

4

The Third United Nations Conference on the Law of the Sea: North-South Bargaining on Ocean Issues

Robert L. Friedheim

On 30 April 1982 delegates to the Third United Nations Law of the Sea Conference (UNCLOS) voted 130 to 4 (with 17 abstentions) to accept the Law of the Sea Treaty. It had been under negotiation since 1967, when Dr. Arvid Pardo, then ambassador of Malta, introduced the subject of ocean resource management before the First Committee of the United Nations General Assembly. On 6 December 1982, the treaty was signed in Jamaica, where an International Seabed Authority will be located. It will go into effect when 70 of the 117 adhering states have ratified it.

UNCLOS represents the largest continuous and most technically demanding set of large-scale negotiations ever attempted. Its participants spanned the entire membership of the United Nations, and the issues covered nearly the entire range of ocean use topics.[1] Moreover, the conference has also been characterized as one of the premier arenas for confrontation between North and South on a wide range of economic and security-related issues. Because of the breadth of the issues,[2] UNCLOS was not strictly a North-South clash. Nevertheless, in terms of the issues on which consensus was not reached, the underlying problem was North-South in that the focus of the dispute involved a conceptual framework for management of deep ocean mineral resources. The "winning" framework could be characterized as inspired by New International Economic Order (NIEO) considerations in that (1) it does not allow first-come, first-served access; (2) it sets up a rival (to private enterprises and state corporations) international agency, "The Enterprise," that could also exploit the resource; (3) it features production controls and mandatory technology transfer

73

(favorite themes in NIEO rhetoric); and (4) it sets up the possibility that within twenty years after implementation, new private and/or national rights may be eliminated.[3]

Indeed, as early as 1975 it had become clear that if statements made by the various states reflected their "true" interests, it would be very difficult to reach consensus on a treaty that contained these features.[4] The treaty did include these features, albeit with a number of last-minute concessions that true believers may characterize as vitiating the purity of NIEO principles. Among the major developed states—both East and West—only Japan and France voted for the treaty; all of the others abstained (except for the United States, which voted against it), thereby reserving their positions. The United States did not hesitate or reserve anything; its representatives opposed the treaty and voted against it. The U.S. government indicated not only that it would not support efforts to reopen the negotiations even after the vote but that it would do its best to persuade others not to sign the treaty. At least at the time of the signing ceremony, the United States seemed to have deterred a significant number of developed states: Belgium, Italy, Spain, Switzerland, the United Kingdom, the Federal Republic of Germany, and South Korea, as well as Japan. At the time the treaty was voted on, all of these states, except Japan, had elected to show their displeasure with the treaty by abstaining, but it had been expected that they would sign it. Japan, as noted, had voted for the treaty, but later opted not to sign it. Whether or not these states will consider it in their long-term interest to remain outside the treaty framework is a matter that remains to be seen.

Because of the complexities of UNCLOS, one paper cannot do justice to an analysis of even one subset of UNCLOS—the North-South issues. Obviously, the deep-sea mineral issues were suffused with North-South considerations, but so were other issues, although perhaps more obliquely. In addition, UNCLOS, over the fifteen-year period, involved many different types of negotiation, not just one. In addition to the overall "parliamentary" type of negotiation, there were innumerable bilateral negotiations, small-group negotiations, drafting sessions, coalition and intercoalition meetings, and so on. There were many substages.[5]

Here, a macroanalysis of the main thrust of the Law of the Sea negotiations is provided in the hope that it will contribute to an understanding of the nature of large-scale multilateral negotiations, particularly because it is one of the major arenas for the negotiation of North-South issues.

Characteristics of the Case—Parliamentary Diplomacy

If the essential nature of negotiation is joint decision making by participants with mixed motives[6] who are trying to anticipate each other's moves (a process characterized by Young as an "outguessing regress"[7]), then multiplying significantly the number of parties whom the negotiator must anticipate creates staggering problems of bargaining management. Even at the most superficial level, wherein we assume that one of the participants in UNCLOS wished to understand the participant's nation-state's own position and those of each of the other participating nation-states on the 320 articles of the UNCLOS Treaty and the 118 articles of the six annexes to the treaty, the resultant decision matrix would have 66,138 cells. The "real world" with many large-scale sessions, smaller committees, informal bargaining groups, and inter- and intracoalition meetings is much more complex. *Parliamentary diplomacy* as a descriptor for this type of negotiations only hints at the range of complexity.

The literature describing behavior in multilateral organizations is voluminous, but remarkably few works deal explicitly with multilateral negotiations within large organizations.[8] A number of special characteristics dominate our case: (1) large numbers of participants; (2) numerous agenda items; (3) the technical nature of many of the issues; (4) a skewing of real-world "power" or influence among the negotiating states; (5) the assumption of sovereign equality; and (6) the continuity of the bargaining arena over time. These characteristics have led to the development of a negotiating system with a number of distinct attributes.

First, parliamentary diplomacy is parliamentary in structure. To reduce the confusion that would result if all of the participants were to try to negotiate simultaneously on a large number of issues, there must be organization, leadership, rules of procedure, and rules for formal decision making. All of the major trappings of a domestic legislature are present: formal debate, committees of the whole, substantive committees, working parties, informal negotiating groups, and posts of honor such as president, vice-presidents, committee chairpersons, and members of general or drafting committees. These honorary posts are the objects of vigorous competition, not only because of the prestige and honor such appointments bring but because those who hold such posts are assumed to have a disproportionate role in effecting outcomes. UNCLOS is no exception. The first president of the conference, Hamilton Shirley Amersinghe of Sri Lanka, seized the moment to develop the procedures by which the first draft of the treaty—the Single Negotiating Text—would be assembled. His successor, Tommy Koh of Singapore, tried to weave his way through the complexities of the final negotiations to achieve a concensus outcome. The chairpersons of the main committees were largely responsible for the general character of the texts that were produced by their committees.

Some observers of the UNCLOS process believe that the outcomes were shaped largely by the personalities of a number of prominant participants. They point to the polish and experience of Amersinghe; the shared sense of trust in such persons as Tommy Koh, John Stevenson (the first U.S. senior representative), and Elliot Richardson; the erratic, flamboyant, and stubborn behavior of Paul Engo of the Cameroon, chairman of the First Committee; and the steadiness, deviousness, and/or technical competence of a number of other personalities. Indeed, many participants or observers believe that a different person in a key position at a critical point might have effected a different outcome.[9] However, major posts in UNCLOS are assigned using a formula similar to that used in the General Assembly, that is, seats are distributed to represent major permanent regional geographic groups. This resulted in limited representation of developed states in major posts, although they were represented on general and drafting committees. Except for Ambassador Yankov of Bulgaria (chairman of the Third Committee, which is considered by many to have dealt with lesser issues), all major posts were held by representatives of Third World states—the presidency by an Asian, the First Committee by an African, and the Second Committee by a Latin American.

Formal equal representation of nation-states created two other characteristics of UNCLOS as a bargaining arena: formal debate and formal decision making. Formal debate gave states and groups the opportunity to put their positions on record; it was often used for this purpose. This had the usual consequence of casting opening positions in concrete, making movement from them difficult, particularly in the case of positions announced as representative of bargaining-group positions. Speeches also took an inordinate amount of time, thus reducing the time available for direct interactions of interested parties.

A second consequence of parliamentary organization was a set of formal rules concerning decisions. Decisions in the formal sense had to be made by vote. Since the usual two-thirds-present-and-voting formula, if invoked, would most likely lead to an automatic majority for any position espoused by the Group of 77 on issues of importance to that group, it was assumed that the conference would fail early if the formal rules were invoked routinely. At the first substantive session in

Caracas 1974, a modified two-thirds rule was adopted for the conference. If it had been used, it would have made no difference in the two-thirds-present-and-voting formula unless there had been massive abstentions.[10] More important was a gentlemen's agreement on voting and "cooling-off" procedures before a vote was invoked. The situation was "cooled off" for nine years, and only a final overall vote on the package was called in 1982. It was assumed from the beginning that a viable treaty would result only if it emerged as part of a consensus or, at worst, a near consensus. How to arrange it, and what represented near consensus was left to informal developments.

The notion of working toward a package outcome as the only viable way of conducting the negotiations was also widely shared early among the assembled negotiators. Although probably few knew of Arrow's paradox or could define strategic or sophisticated voting,[11] most of the experienced participants understood that if the usual rules of procedure were invoked (vote first on the amendment to the amendment, then the amendment, then the amended article, then the section, and finally the treaty as a whole), there was a substantial probability of failure. They feared that if the delegations split into a large number of small common-interest groups, the set of group preferences would be intransitive (Arrow's paradox) or, conversely, if larger groups (such as the Group of 77) remained disciplined there would be a majoritarian outcome unacceptable to a significant minority.

A package outcome implies a number of attributes. First, the agenda issues are interrelated,[12] and therefore a large number of issues may be decided simultaneously. Early in the negotiations the United States, claiming to foresee technical difficulties in dealing with so many issues simultaneously, proposed to split the issues into "separate packets." The Group of 77 would have no part of it. Its members correctly understood that a large agenda would help create a willingness among states to accept trade-offs. In particular, they feared that if the developed countries got an acceptable outcome on issues of great salience[13] to themselves, they would be unwilling to make concessions on issues of importance to the developing countries. Thus, the second attribute was the notion that a package would be a mixed bag with enough favorable outcomes on issues of importance to the vast majority of participants so that they would be willing to accept an overall outcome that included less than favorable results on issues of presumed lesser importance to themselves. This proved difficult to arrange: (1) for many delegations, the necessary trade-offs were unpalatable to strong domestic interests; (2) the sheer size of the package and the technical complexity of the issues made the sorting-out process long and cumbersome; and (3) the inclusion of favorable outcomes on all or most issues of importance to all major states and groups was not possible. Some parties had to give way not only on unimportant issues but on important issues as well so as to complete a large package. Moreover, the degree of importance of issues varied over time and with regime changes.

Although the formal decision rules of parliamentary diplomacy are based on the notion of equality of participants, the actual rule of decision presupposes inequality. But measuring the degree of inequality accepted by members of the conference and thereby stating a precise decision rule is extremely difficult. What is obvious is that most major states expected that they would not be treated as mere equals. Although they were aware of the formal one-state, one-vote rule, they expected that their influence would be roughly commensurate with their own feelings of prowess in the international economic-political system. Hence, they insisted upon a consensus or near-consensus decision rule. On the other hand, they were aware that the major weapon of the majority (often composed mostly but usually not exclusively of developing states) was their numbers if the formal decision process was invoked. Therefore, they were constrained to accept more nonoptimal outcomes within a parliamentary diplomatic setting than they would in the absence of a threat of being outvoted. Conversely, the majority were constrained to accept less than they might formally achieve if they merely voted for what was optimal to the majority—but to what degree is impossible to say. However, all understood that the underlying theme of parliamentary diplomatic interactions is numbers versus real-world capability.

Consensus or near consensus can be achieved in a parliamentary diplomatic setting only by the formation of coalitions. Much of the activity in parliamentary diplomacy is the formation and maintenance of such coalitions. In the case of UNCLOS, these coalitions came in a bewildering variety.[14] It is difficult to sort out the process; on the one hand, existing coalition theory does not help much, and on the other hand most observers of the details of the negotiations have described the interactions at UNCLOS as if they were sui generis.

There are two thrusts to the conventional explanation of coalition building: size and ideology. The belief that a "minimum winning coalition" or a coalition with a slightly safer margin of victory would make good predictors of probable coalition formation proved false in parliamentary diplomacy.[15] Because the actual decision rule was consensus or near consensus, the winning coalition must be the maximum winning coalition or almost maximum winning coalition. The steps that were used to develop this coalition can be found in the history of the entire conference, hence the atheoretical nature of the observation data. It is extremely difficult to sort out even the more visible steps, much less answer the question of whether the steps are typical or necessary in consensus building with this one case.

The notions of "ideological similarity" or "minimization of policy distance" of Axelrod and De Swaan have more relevance.[16] As we shall see, on a number of the major issues of the conference we can trace the cohesiveness of groups as well as the stability or movement of their positions over time.[17] On most major issues, as I will define them, the Group of 77 and its component groups, Asia, Africa, and Latin America, held together by ideology as well as geography, were quite cohesive, and usually when movement was involved, they moved in a coherent direction. However, because I constructed the conflict "issues" to reflect conflict problems that were more general and not of parochial concern to one or a limited number of states, undoubtedly I may have glossed over some high-salience idiosyncratic positions of group members on broader issues. Moreover, because I did not construct conflict variables on parochial issues, I may have missed entirely the positions of states on these types of issues. That a number of issues were parochial does not mean they were unimportant. Indeed, in universal bargaining, the fear of being overwhelmed if isolated has led to the formation of groups that coalesced to protect their less widely shared interests. These special groups included a coastal states group, the landlocked and geographically disadvantaged states (LL/GDS), the territorial group, the margineers (a group of broad-shelf states), the straits states group, the group of archipelago states, the median-line group, the equitable-principle group, island states, the group of fourteen maritime states, and various secret groups and "mafias." Two inside observers, Ambassador Jayakumar and President Koh, believe that the coalitions that were more broadly based ideologically or geographically were not as influential in UNCLOS as were the special interest groups that sprang up for UNCLOS bargaining only. However, they do admit that the Group of 77 "did take a united stand on Committee I [deep seabed minerals] matters."[18]

Some groups promoted a package; others, a single limited group of issues. Some had formal internal structures with internal decision rules (e.g. the unanimity rule of the Group of 77). All were concerned with maintaining their discipline to enhance their bargaining strength with other groups or key negotiators.

Interactions across group lines were critically important in building the grand coalition necessary to get a consensus document adopted.

The steps in building broader coalitions took up many of the sessions of UNCLOS bargaining. Much of the interaction on building large coalitions took place in informal private negotiating groups such as the Evanson Group of Juridical Experts, the Private Group on Straits cochaired by the United Kingdom and Fiji, the Nandan Group on the rights of the LL/GDS in the economic zone, and others. Much bargaining was also done bilaterally as well as in secret negotiating sessions within and between groups. It is the interaction between the representatives of the special interest groups, the ideologically and geographically broad-based coalitions, the representatives of the key states, and the formal and informal leaders that attempted to build the maximum winning coalition in support of "the" package that are the key steps in parliamentary diplomacy. It is still too little known for an adequate theory to be developed.

Observers have pointed out other important attributes that resulted from the size and complexity of UNCLOS. First, a number of states, particularly smaller developing states, had difficulty understanding the legal, scientific, and engineering complexities of a variety of issues. Efforts were made to hold information seminars and to do studies to help provide necessary information.[19] Sometimes these were looked upon (correctly at times) as efforts by the developed countries to exert influence. Related to this is the tendency of many developing countries to fear complex issues as a result of lack of technical expertise at home.[20] More of the delegations from the developing countries were composed of political generalists than was the case with delegations from the developed countries.

A third characteristic related to complexity was that there was a great deal of variability in the number of issues on the agenda in which states had important interests. Some small states were either not interested at all in certain issues or were intensely interested in other issues. For larger countries, particularly developed ones, the problem was quite the opposite. They were interested in finding favorable outcomes on most issues on the agenda. For them, the problem was often making internal trade-offs among interests that were roughly equal in salience. Even when decisions were made, it was difficult to make them stick. If ever a demonstration was needed that the state is not a unitary actor, the behavior of a number of major developed states at UNCLOS would serve nicely, particularly the United States. Internal struggles and bargaining took up much of the time of the U.S. delegation. Often, representatives of substantive departments or observers on the delegation represented their positions separately or undercut the supposedly agreed-to position. Moreover, the sheer size and diversity of the delegation and its advisers compounded the problem. Often these internal quarrels were well known to foreign delegations and made it easy for other delegations to understand the difficulties of the United States and to manipulate its position. The outguessing regress and various forms of strategic behavior were made easy for non-U.S. delegates with even a modicum of bargaining skill. These problems—according to rumors—plagued other developed delegations as well. In any case, the chairman of the U.S. delegation faced an unenviable task in trying to control his delegation.

Another related characteristic was the difficulty in establishing what was the national interest on most of the major issues, making it commensurately difficult to establish opening positions, fallback positions, and settlement points. These were questions of both "what" and "how much." As we saw, developing states often had difficulties because too few issues were salient. On the less-salient issues, particularly during the early negotiations, the range in statements on what was in their national interests was very large. For developed states the problem was different, and it relates to the nature of the benefits associated with the internal trade-offs. On many issues it can be quickly established that a particular position has a potential benefit to one party while the opposite would have little or no benefit. Decisions in these situations are obvious. For example, for the United States, freedom of science provides benefits to the U.S. ocean science community and to those branches of the U.S. government that use scientific data, while its opposite does not. If scientists were required to obtain permission for scientific expeditions near foreign coastal states, the predictable results would be increased costs, administrative delays, and the danger of being turned down. The U.S. government could benefit from increased control under a consent regime, but because there are relatively few foreign nonfishery scientific expeditions near the U.S. coasts, it was believed that greater control was not needed.

The real decision difficulty arises on issues where the opposing poles represent one type of benefit versus another, rather than no benefit. Again, we present an example from the United States. At the beginning of UNCLOS a choice had to be made on the basic jurisdiction question. The United States could espouse as its national interest the acceptance of a 200-meter depth of water delimitation principle, thereby ending "creeping jurisdiction," and protecting movement and other rights, or it could espouse extended resource jurisdiction by accepting a 200-mile exclusive economic zone. Both would be simultaneously desirable, if possible. The United States would like to have as much near-shore resource jurisdiction as it wished and as many distant water rights as its citizens could use, but at a universal bargaining conference, it was forced into a trade-off. This was not only the source of a fierce internal battle but a source of confusion to others when the United States at the Caracas session in early 1974 did a 180-degree turn on the issue. Indeed, although the extension of resource jurisdiction was ardently espoused by the coastal state members of the Group of 77 (especially Latin Americans), the chief beneficiary (by comparative standards) was the United States. As a way of specifying its rights, about a year after it rejected the UNCLOS treaty, the United States adopted a 200-mile economic zone over waters adjacent to the continental United States, Alaska, Hawaii, the Commonwealth of Puerto Rico, the Commonwealth of the Northern Marianas, and the Trust Territory of the Pacific Islands. This presidential proclamation enclosed six million square nautical miles of ocean space—the largest ocean resource area under the national jurisdiction of any country in the world.[21] There were many issues at UNCLOS on which large, complex, developed states had to evaluate the alternatives as one benefit versus another rather than as a benefit versus no benefit.

Two other observations especially drawn from particular characteristics of UNCLOS may not affect other parliamentary diplomatic negotiations. First, UNCLOS was a plenipotentiary conference that was expected to produce a definite outcome. As a result of the outcome's being a treaty rather than, say, a resolution of the General Assembly that was not binding on its members, it was assumed that because the outcome was meaningful, this would give leverage to whoever was in control of the process. Second, UNCLOS III was very poorly prepared. The previous comprehensive conference, UNCLOS I, had been aided by a draft convention prepared by the International Law Commission. Not only was no such draft prepared by experts for the subsequent multi-issue conference, UNCLOS III; there was no agenda for the work of the Seabed Committee, merely a list of issues. The learning process was long and arduous, but the lack of formal preparation was deliberate. It effectively reduced the importance of the technical aspects of the work of the conference and emphasized the political or allocation aspects of the work of the conference. This, too, was a choice forced by the developing states' majority in the United Nations.

Although most observers have conceded a strong North-South dimension in some parts of UNCLOS III, there is skepticism about how central the considerations of North-South or New International Economic Order elements have been to the overall treaty. The degree of North-South polarization has varied among issues; themes characteristic of the debate can be found throughout the negotiations.[22]

We have previously demonstrated a strong North-South dimension in the issues relating to the creation of an International Seabed Authority and the enterprise to manage deep-ocean mineral resource exploitation; less North-South polarization concerning most issues dealing with extension of national jurisdiction to 200 nautical miles;[23] substantial North-South polarization concerning control or freedom of ocean science in the economic zone;[24] and less polarization concerning matters of ocean pollution. As a result of events in the bargaining history that have occurred between the single Negotiating Texts of 1975 and the treaty of 1982, I see no reason for changing these assessments. To a substantial degree, UNCLOS III was one of the most important North-South confrontations of our time.

In contrast, many observers point to the roles played by the varied special interest groups in influencing the outcome of UNCLOS III. For them, this was a demonstration of the fact that states devoted more attention to protecting their own special interest(s) regardless of "ideological distance." I believe this view to be shortsighted because many of the participants frequently experienced what Axelrod called "overlapping cleavages."[25] They participated simultaneously in several of the major ideologically based and interest-based groups. What occurred here was that the drives of each group reinforced one another. For example, members of the coastal states group were motivated to extend national jurisdiction off their shores, including coastal states who dominated the Group of 77. Being poor and suspicious of the designs of developed states on their coastal resources, they specifically insisted on pushing the developed states away from their shores. Therefore, being coastal overlapped to a considerable degree with being poor. Being rich and coastal, however, caused what Axelrod called cross-pressures for countries such as the United States, who had difficulty in reconciling their distant-water interests and their coastal interests.[26]

An evaluation of the bargaining in UNCLOS III also hinges on its North-South context. Virtually all of Group of 77 members stated their positions in terms of the New International Economic Order. They demanded a redistribution of benefits from North to South. The implication of the language was that if redistributive measures were successfully negotiated, the benefits would be equally shared by all members of the Group of 77. For the most part, this did not occur at UNCLOS III. Rather, the benefits were somewhat skewed in favor of those states with either ocean capability or an advantageous geographic position. Obviously, the means of forcing a real redistribution were unequally shared not only between North and South but also among members of the groups that represented the South position.

Southern states with ocean capability or geographic position took advantage of their assets to the detriment of members of the group who did not have such assets. Because the former perceived their bargaining victories in the most part as being directed against potential intruders from the developed countries, these Southern states believed that their gains were contributing to rather than moving away from a New International Economic Order. Overlapping cleavages do that. Therefore, I believe we must look at a wider range of issues at UNCLOS III as being suffused with North-South considerations, particularly the matter of an extension of national jurisdiction. This is often overlooked by observers of the UNCLOS bargaining process because the basic delimitation decision was made in the first substantive UNCLOS session in 1974.

There is another reason that UNCLOS as a whole should be looked at primarily as a North-South negotiation: UNCLOS III is an example of what Krasner calls plan B of the Third World to deal with its vulnerability in the international system. "Their [Third World nations'] fundamental objective has been to enhance their influence in international organizations that can alter the rules and norms governing the international economic regime."[27] I believe that despite last-minute compromises accepted by the leadership of the Group of 77 so as to try to make the seabed mineral provisions of the treaty palatable to the United States, the structure of the proposed International Seabed Authority and the Enterprise preserves the ability of the developing states to control a new organization that will establish norms for a set of potentially important economic interactions between North and South.

What Provoked the Negotiations?

A shared sense of unresolved problems provoked the convocation of a Third United Nations Conference on the Law of the Sea. When Arvid Pardo made his four-and-a-half hour speech in 1967, he exposed a set of issues that various states thought should be taken up at that time. But although the moment was ripe for entering into negotiations, it was not necessarily ripe for settlement. Most major parties wanted negotiations for quite different and often opposing reasons. Nevertheless, the desire to negotiate on the issues (but not necessarily in the arena chosen) was widely shared, and no overt pressure was necessary to bring any of the participants to the table.

Most of the developed states each had a variety of reasons for wanting negotiations on ocean issues. In the United States, for example, the impetus for reopening negotiations on ocean issues was clear. The United States and the USSR had been discussing ways to "perfect" the results of the treaties promulgated by the First and Second Law of the Sea Conferences in the mid-1960s. In particular, the superpowers wished to resolve the question of the delimitation of the territorial sea and the continental shelf. Efforts in 1958 and in 1960 to delimit the territorial sea failed, but in the meantime the ocean capability of the USSR increased and its ocean interests changed. It was now—along with the United States—more interested in preserving the ocean status quo via formal acceptance of key features of the doctrine of freedom of the seas.[28] The Legal Advisor's Office of the U.S. Department of State informed other departments of its intention to reopen these issues, and this triggered a series of studies and plans.[29]

The reopening of issues suited a number of internal U.S. interest groups, most of whom believed that it was now or never. That is, the twentieth-century trend toward expansion of national jurisdiction by creation of, at best, functional zones or, at worst, sovereign zones was obvious. The newly independent nations that had emerged, especially after 1955, were eager to protect their own resources, and this accelerated the trend. Many interest groups that preferred the status quo feared what had been called "creeping jurisdiction." They shared the concern that if relatively narrow bands of national jurisdiction were not recognized within the foreseeable future, it would become impossible to prevent "Balkanization" of the oceans—carving them up into national lakes. This helped create an odd coalition: the U.S. Department of Defense with U.S. political and religious liberals. Both wished to prevent further nationalization of the oceans.[30] The commonality of position still exists today.[31] A third group of allies included a sizeable proportion of professional international lawyers who saw the trends in ocean space as leading to a law of "exclusion" rather than toward a law of inclusion.[32] All wanted to negotiate.

A very different motivation influenced some of the newer users of the ocean, particularly those who were actual or potential exploiters of nonliving resources from ocean space. For them, legal uncertainty about where they could exploit and with what rights was most important. Uncertainty over the extent of national jurisdiction created uncertainty among the bankers whose support was necessary to provide capital to prospective ocean exploiters. For the most part, advisers from the oil industry, accustomed to working under U.S. law (the Truman Proclamation and the Outer Continental Shelf Lands Act) preferred a definitive boundary delimitation, but one established well offshore. The nascent manganese nodule industry, hoping to exploit ores found on deep seabeds often thousands of miles from shore was more internationally minded. Exploiters were willing to pay for the privilege of being given legal title to the resource by paying royalties and purchasing licenses. But both groups were aware that the certainty they sought could be gained only in one of two ways—a unilateral claim by the United States backed by a willingness to use force to enforce rights, or consent of the "international community." They were willing to try the latter.

What united all of these groups in their willingness to negotiate was that confusion and its concomitant costs would result if a number of coastal states continued to act unilaterally. The desire to avoid the Tower of Babel of unilateral claims united most ocean users and gave them a momentum in favor of negotiations. Naturally, they preferred an arena in which they either exercised some control or which was at least neutral. Thus, there was considerable trepidation in putting all of the issues in the pot of a single universal negotiation associated with the United Nations. But when the "separate packets" proposal failed, they participated vigorously in the alternative.

When Arvid Pardo called for a common heritage of mankind for the ocean, not many developing states knew very much about the problems of ocean space or had strong opinions about what the solutions to those problems should be, but the notion of common heritage sounded egalitarian enough to attract their attention. Among them, however, was a minority that was strongly motivated to try to stage a universal negotiation with ocean subjects on the agenda, in particular, the states of the west coast of Latin America—Chile, Ecuador, and Peru—who espoused a 200-mile territorial sea, and other Latin American states who were developing the notion of the "patrimonial sea."[33] Under the guise of sovereignty, they could and did make 200-mile claims of varying exclusiveness, but they could not get many other states, particularly developed ocean-using states, to recognize those claims. In particular, the United States government disputed their authority to deny U.S. fishing vessels or merchant vessels the right to fish or transit freely in the outer 197 miles of their claimed zones. These states, who were members of the Group of 77, perceived in mid-1960s the possibility that a universal conference could be a useful alternative in their effort to get ocean users from developed countries to recognize their claims. After all, if they could hope to lead the Group of 77, they would control a substantial bloc of votes. That was not an unreasonable expectation at the time. The fact that the control of deep-sea manganese nodules could provide a test case for the New International Economic Order probably did not strike many of the Group of 77 as a major reason for going to the universal bargaining table in the mid-1960s because so little was known about the resource at that time. But delegates from the Group of 77 learned fast in the meetings of the ad hoc and permanent committees. Although it quickly became the dominant North-South issue after 1974, I believe the seabed minerals issue was coequal with the question of extended jurisdiction over resources within 200 miles rather than being the sole issue. The fact that the developing nations "won" over the developed nations early when the United States and the USSR endorsed the idea of an economic zone has led observers to overlook the importance of extended jurisdiction as a North-South issue. In sum, many of the developing countries wanted to go to a plenipotentiary conference.

It is important to recognize that most major parties assumed that they could reach their objectives only with the consent of others. None believed that the status quo was an attractive alternative. To be sure, the status quo of unilateral behavior was a possible fallback, and most participants recognized that if they pushed their opponents too far at UNCLOS, there remained the unilateral alternative. However, it was not a preferred one. I believe that one reason the Reagan administration rejected the draft treaty was a genuine change in its (if not the U.S.) perception of the importance of gaining the consent of others. For it, the status quo is better, and it assumes that it can get along without the consent of other ocean states on ocean issues. For many years, civilian and uniformed representatives of the Department of Defense insisted upon having the right to transit straits freely embodied in a formal treaty provision. They were willing to trade off other rights. The Reagan administration is not willing to make those trade-offs and does not highly value a formal recognition of the right to transit international straits. Although John Lehman, secretary of the navy, denies that he claimed the United States would shoot its way through straits if necessary,[34] nevertheless he must believe that the U.S. has the right to continue to use transit rights as it pleases even if others withdraw their consent. He is betting that other states, particularly straits states, will not withdraw their consent because of an implied threat of U.S. forceful resistance.

Structure of the Encounter

The structure of the encounter of Third United Nations Law of the Sea Conference was parliamentary diplomatic. All parties were to some degree aware that once ocean issues were raised in the First Committee of the General Assembly the rules of the game would resemble procedures associated with operating within the United Nations system. What was not well understood at the beginning was whether or not the rule that would be followed would resemble normal parliamentary process used in UNCLOS I and II, with a target document and decision by formal voting process, or some modification. Many delegates from the developed countries came to the early sessions expecting the normal rules to prevail; however, when they perceived the hostility of a substantial majority to traditional international law, they quickly embraced the notion of decision by consensus or near consensus.

The structure of the encounter, as perceived by the parties, was quite different from committee to committee and from issue to issue. In the First Committee, where deep-sea mining was negotiated, the structure was voting strength of a majority of poor states versus the ocean-capable states. I am not sure whether any official participant articulated this feeling, but to this semioutside observer, it appeared that the delegates from the developing countries at least instinctively understood that they could afford to "lose" in the sense that they might not, with their majority, force the developed countries to conform to their outcome preferences at the conference, but that the onus of failure would be on the developed states. Moreover, one of the bargaining strengths of the developing states was their real-world weakness. They did not need definitive rules for most ocean uses because their ocean capability was limited. In other words, they could afford to be tough and unyielding on issues that had high moral or ideological salience but that were not really important to the immediate economic or political well-being of a significant number of their members.

The developed countries were, for the most part, the ocean users who needed outcomes with which they could work. Failure meant operational confusion or lack of title to resources. Thus, the developed nations had an incentive to negotiate incrementally—to move from their opening positions to accept modifications to their ideal if an offered deal was a variant of the maximum preferred position. Underlying the situation was the assumption by the developed countries that the framework was fixed or did not need change. As long as the matter was primarily technical-legal, the developed countries were flexible, but when the basic structure was threatened, they were often more obdurate. In general the developed states needed definitive outcomes. It was initially assumed that these outcomes could be gained only by a treaty achieved by consensus, but the very length of the conference eventually undermined some of the value of a formal treaty. Today some parties believe they can have most of the benefits of the treaty without adhering to the treaty because the provisions they value most have already, they claim, been incorporated into customary international law.

From the beginning of the conference virtually all of the participants knew that it would be necessary to form coalitions in order to achieve any recognizable outcome other than confusion. Others, among them Miles, Buzan, Oxman, and Ambassadors Jayakumar and Koh, have described the formation, membership, and patterns of behavior of the groups that played a role at UNCLOS III.[35] It is not necessary to replicate their findings here; instead, I would like to comment on one major possibility for coalition formation that was explored but never really came to fruition. If the major developed ocean users (East as well as West) had really been willing to commit themselves to a set of solutions for ocean use that allowed only a moderate expansion of national jurisdiction, they would have found themselves in a natural coalition with the group of landlocked and geographically disadvantaged states. The only subject about which any area of disagreement would remain would have been deep-ocean minerals, for many landlocked countries are developing states. But this, too, could have been worked out by a side payment because the issue of deep ocean minerals was not the most salient issue to the landlocked and geographically disadvantaged states.

Using the data and models we developed, it is possible to demonstrate in a "what-if" mode that if a coalition for a moderate enclosure outcome had been able to maintain discipline (1) it commanded more than a blocking one-third and therefore could have prevented unacceptable outcomes; and (2) it could have been the nucleus of a winning majority package but possibly not a consensus package. As it happens, both major constituents of such a potential grand coalition were cross-pressured and such a coalition was never realized. As a result, the landlocked, and, to a lesser extent, other geographically disadvantaged states were the major losers in the treaty that was eventually passed. They gained few valuable rights. Few concessions were made to them on issues of high salience, such as transit to the sea and other rights that would have been obtained at the expense of their coastal neighbors, such as control of mineral rights in extended offshore areas. Their coastal neighbors became better off by seizing valuable rights that increased the economic disparities between the two groups.

Process of the Encounter

As befitting a negotiation that went on for more than fifteen years and eventuated in a draft treaty with 320 articles and 8 annexes, UNCLOS III had a most complex process of encounters. It went through numerous stages where there was a recognizable principal type of encounter, but within these stages other means of interaction were often used simultaneously. The general stages are shown in table 1.[36]

In stage 1, there was little concern among the parties for movement toward an outcome. The issues were new and technically demanding, and many of the participants needed time not only to become acquainted with these issues but to determine where they should stand on the issues. Debate and putting on record what various states thought their positions should be was the basic function of the process of interaction.

Of the three parts of the phased process of negotiation, stage 1 is most like the search for a framework for agreement or formula. On the

Table 1
Stages of the Law of the Sea Negotiations

Stage	Process	Outcome
1. 1967-70	Stating basic orientations; exploring others' positions; looking for coalition partners	Better understanding of issues and alignments
2. 1970-73	First statement of formal proposals; firming up of coalitions	Realization of basic trade-offs necessary for a treaty
3. 1973-74	Formal negotiations; beginning of informal negotiating groups' drafts showing patterns of agreement on some issues	Announcement of basic trade-offs being accepted
4. 1975-80	Formal drafts of committee chairpersons; informal single negotiating text, revised single negotiating text; informal composite negotiating text, etc.	Basic outline of the full treaty; resolution of many issues in disagreement by refinement of language, drafting improvements
5. 1981-82	Crisis: U.S. reviews draft after a year and insists upon major revisions; compromises offered but not enough; U.S. calls the question	Treaty adopted with most industrial countries either abstaining or opposing

issues assigned to Committees II and III, the formulas were found, but not without years of effort toward their refinement. Alas, the framework for resolution on Committee I issues, the quintessential North-South deep-scabed resource issues that could have been managed under free-market principles, New International Economic Order principles, or perhaps some blend, was not found. The parties came close, according to some observers,[37] but not close enough for the Reagan administration. In any case, much of the damage may have begun in stage 1 because of the tendency of a number of states to put themselves on record on the basis of general principles rather than a specific assessment of their national needs, often before the facts of the situation became clear. For the most part, these principles were free market and NIEO. Although there was little unity on these archetypal positions, they became the poles around which the various camps gathered later in the negotiation. Further complications arose later because in stage 1 much nonsense was put on record that vastly exaggerated the nature of the resource in dispute, making it difficult to evaluate whether or not the game was worth the candle. Because the economic rents are likely to be small for a number of years, the candle was not worth very much in the short run to either the developing or the developed states. But the game on this issue became, through all of the phases of the negotiation, a search for mutually agreeable referents, a search for the "principles of justice on which both parties [could] agree."[38] It was largely a search for acceptable symbols.

In the first two phases, it became obvious that the only method by which a successful outcome could be reached (one that represented consensus or near consensus) was by adoption of a package. It was apparent that all of the major groups would have to have positive outcomes within the package on issues of high salience to themselves if the package had any chance of adoption. Thus, by the time of the first full conference session at Caracas in 1974, the shape of the package was understood and the trade-offs were announced, even though formal treaty language had not yet been worked out. Both of the superpowers had expressed their willingness to accept extensions of national resource jurisdiction in return for the establishment of a relatively moderate 12-mile territorial sea and a formal affirmation of rights of movement through straits and archipelagos. Almost implicitly, opposition to a narrow territorial sea and rights of movement melted away. It is difficult to say precisely whether or not statements by the United States and Soviet Union that acceptable territorial sea limits and rights of movement were fundamental to their participation in a package outcome were perceived by others as a threat or as a signal that on these issues it would be profitless to push hard; it was a fairly obvious signal that the superpowers had to be willing to accept a trade-off elsewhere. As mentioned earlier, it was difficult to arrange trade-offs only on lower salience issues in return for favorable outcomes on higher salience issues. By 1975 the trade-offs were alleged to be part of the fundamental package. According to Edward Miles, radicals among the Group of 77 claimed that a NIEO-type solution on deep-sea minerals should be demanded from the United States as the price for its preferred solution on straits transit.[39] Not even in the most optimistic days of U.S. participation in the negotiations was this ever publicly conceded.

Getting to the next stage of developing a single proposal that could be modified into a formal agreement presented one of the most difficult problems in the UNCLOS process. Essentially, a solution was found in stage 4 with the development of the Informal Single Negotiating Text and its subsequent modifications that were eventually refined into a treaty.

Even though the general shape of the agreed-to trade-offs and the outline of the package issues on which there was general agreement were known, it would have been difficult to hammer these out in face-to-face bilateral meetings or even in meetings of the informal negotiating groups, although some of the individual issues or subsets of related issues were worked out by these means. Rather, in a very parliamentary manner, the task of assembling the text was entrusted to the three committee chairmen. They were expected to reflect the understandings reached on issues on which there was general agreement and to suggest on their own where they thought consensus might lie on issues on which general agreement had not been reached. Even Ambassadors Koh and Jayakumar were somewhat nonplussed that the delegates were willing to trust this task to persons, whatever their personal reputations for integrity, who "were themselves representatives of states having clear national interests."[40] They speculated that perhaps most delegations were frustrated by the slowness of progress toward agreement in the previous stage. In any case the chairmen's texts were to be negotiating—not negotiated—texts, but in fact they became a guide for the remainder of the negotiations. If a state did not agree with the chairman's formulation of the issue, it could not simply ignore his text; instead, the text became the base point for further negotiations.

Stage 4, which encompassed the several iterations of the negotiating text, was primarily a process of refinement.[41] Refinement in the general process of negotiation means working toward making marginal improvements on a general outcome that the parties essentially have decided upon. It presupposes the acceptance by the parties, willingly or unwillingly, of a conceptual framework.

The stuff of day-to-day activities of the negotiator is the process of working toward improving the principal's utility marginally. The negotiator pushes and probes to get a bit more than is being given. The negotiator seeks to sharpen or to make vague the language describing what is agreed to; to increase or decrease the exceptions to the general rule that supposedly all parties will accept. The negotiator seeks a different way to express the agreement being negotiated to make the language more palatable to the principals. The negotiator seeks a face-saving gesture or tries to arrange a side payment (a payoff on a nonagenda item for a concession on an agenda item).

The process and consequences of working on making marginal improvements differ significantly, depending upon whether the general principle is agreed to willingly or unwillingly. If it is agreed to willingly, then the task of the negotiator is essentially technical—to perfect the document to which all parties are likely to agree. The outcome should be at, or somewhere near, the classic 50 percent solution. What conflict is present is largely personal or professional; it does matter whose formula proves acceptable.

The process and consequences are quite different if the underlying framework is still under dispute. Any negotiator in the position of trying to make marginal improvements to a conceptual framework with which the negotiator or the state represented disagrees, but cannot avoid accepting, has one or two (or both) purposes in mind. The first is to make sufficient marginal improvements to make the agreement minimally acceptable to the principal. The second is to undermine the general principle in the detail provisions. This can be done by working for piecemeal improvements, changes in language, a multiplication of details provisions that allow the principal an escape hatch, time limits to provisions, conditional requirements, and so on. In this latter purpose a negotiator will often have difficulties demonstrating to skeptics in his or her own government that the national interest is really being protected. In operating at the margin, the negotiator risks having clients judge that they may be better off with the status quo.

In stage 4 of the UNCLOS negotiations, much of what occurred when NIEO-related issues were being resolved was marginal negotiation of the above-mentioned type, where negotiators from the developed states tried to make the provisions under negotiation minimally acceptable so as to undermine them. There were three subtypes, each with hard-fought interactions occurring over a relatively narrow range of possible outcomes. The most critical was where the conceptual framework was in dispute even though it was clear that if put to a vote that a majority, indeed a substantial majority, would have voted for a particular version of the formula. Many of the key issues in the First Committee that were viewed as essentially North-South issues were of this nature. Figure 1 shows one such critical issue—the nature of the deep-sea minerals management system.

The potential positions ranged from a registry system only (the Soviet opening position), which would put the least restrictions on states' access to the minerals of the international common, all the way to the other end of the spectrum, where no access by national or private entities would be allowed. If the policy position represented at rank 16-17 came to fruition, the deep sea would be a monopoly zone for the exclusive exploitation by the Enterprise. According to content analysis data, the U.S. opening position was at rank 4, and the opening position of the Group of 77 was 11 (the mean of the positions of its members). Thus, the spread between the states that carried the banner for private access and those searching for what they claimed was a more equitable solution was seven ranks, a substantial policy distance. To measure change, we divided our content analysis data into two time periods: 1967-73 (T1) and 1974-75 (T2). As figure 1 shows, the median or central tendency for T1 was at rank 10 or a dual system. This demonstrated that if the Group of 77 had a specific plan at that time it was close to a winning position. But the distribution was relatively flat across the spectrum and the standard deviation was rather high (2.85), indicating lack of unity as they searched for a common position. 'But as members explored the types of measures they wished to impose that they thought would exemplify a new international economic order they became more extreme. In 1974-75, the Group of 77 mean moved to 14.7 (with a standard deviation of 0.18 demonstrating great unity), and the median of all states consequently moved to rank 14. The developing nations were increasing the substantive distance between themselves and their opponents. The first version of the negotiating text, the Informal Single Negotiating Text (ISNT) was judged to fall out at rank 15, reflecting accurately where the overwhelming majority preferred to be. In the meantime the United States made further incremental adjustments and moved toward its opponents by introducing the banking proposal (rank 8). Although the negotiations were not stalemated, they proceeded slowly.

It was only after the Reagan administration indicated in March 1981 that it insisted upon reviewing U.S. participation in the negotiations that the leadership of the conference was able to persuade the more radical members of the Group of 77 to accept significant modifications

FIGURE 1
Bargaining on the Deep-Sea Minerals Management Issue

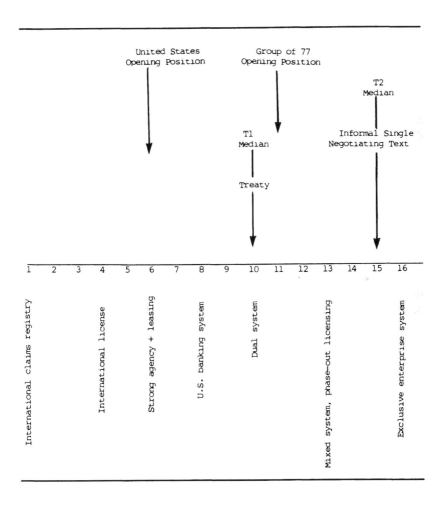

of the demand for an immediate imposition of a NIEO system. By including pioneer status, an assured seat for the United States on the Seabed Authority's Council and the operation of the dual system whereby two areas for exploitation would be nominated and one granted to the national claimant and one banked away for the Enterprise, a genuine mixed system would be created. The question of converting the system to an exclusive monopoly of the Enterprise, a favorite NIEO idea, was shelved, perhaps permanently, perhaps temporarily. That subject can be raised at a review conference twenty years after the first commercial production commences. The relatively rapid movement in the last sessions toward compromise (a fallback of 5 ranks to a dual system at rank 10) engineered by the conference leadership and accepted by the Group of 77, was also not enough. The Reagan administration was also moving but away from the developing states, perhaps to a position less forthcoming than the opening position of the United States. The shell of the New International Economic Order concept is still embodied in treaty provisions, but agreement proved elusive.[42]

Refinement of issues of importance to North and South also occurred in other ways. The second typical pattern was the establishment of a NIEO framework and sticking rather firmly to it, forcing the developed states to accept it. What made it minimally acceptable to the developed states was the developing states' acceptance of some exceptions to the general rule. What was negotiable at the margin narrows in this second case. As we can see in figure 2, this happened on the issue of conducting scientific research in the economic zone.

The positions range from freedom of scientific research to complete and unfettered coastal control of the right to conduct scientific work in the economic zone. In the 1967-73 time period, science was looked upon widely as a benefit to mankind, and the freedom of science was ardently supported by both the United States (1.5) and the USSR (2.4). Because the median in that time period was at 5, it seems that most states would have preferred some restrictions on gathering data in the coastal zone, albeit modest. But the beginning of a shift toward control of science could be seen. What was emerging was the feeling that knowledge in the hands of the developed states might be a potential threat to the resource control of the developing states. In particular, the radicals among the Latin American group (rank 8.9 in T1) and, to a lesser extent, among the coastal African states (rank 7.5) were helping to move the Group of 77 toward further control measures. But these groups were by no means united on the issue at that time. By 1974-75, opinion moved solidly to a consent regime (rank 12) that made rela-

FIGURE 2
Ocean Science in the Economic Zone; Articles 246, 248, 252

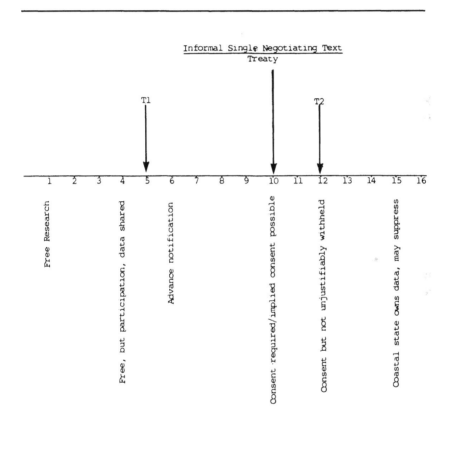

tively few concessions to the preferences of the developed states. Not only had the median increased drastically but the distribution shows a single peak (support) with a small flat tail (opposition). In other words, a substantial majority had formed, although not a consensus. Moreover, the Group of 77 and all its major components now were solidly in the consent camp (rank 12). If we gauged preferences correctly, control of science became a cornerstone of the NIEO approach. Although some marginal movement was necessary to gain consensus, there was little reason for the Group of 77 to move far. By accepting some limitations, we judged, they did move to rank 10 on the consent regime. One limitation was the requirement of a six-month lead time for permit requests (Article 248 of the treaty), with consent implied if a reply is not received after six months from the coastal state (Article 252). Although the science community bitterly protested that its interests were being traded off,[43] most of the developed states accepted this slight compromise by the Group of 77 as protecting their minimum national interests, and accepted consent as part of the package deal. (As my scientist friends now lament, few scientists vote.) In other words, the national salience of their preferred outcome on this issue was not high, and the U.S. negotiators prior to the Reagan administration team judged that the incremental improvements made by the bargaining at the margin were sufficient to make the science provision minimally acceptable. The Reagan judgment was, however, quite different.

The third pattern in the process of refining the negotiating texts into a draft treaty shows a confident majority seemingly moving almost not at all in order to make a key portion of the text acceptable to a recalcitrant minority; however, it was willing to juggle the technical details of its winning formula. The bargaining range in this case of incremental adjustment was the narrowest of the three cases under examination.

Among the important features of the arrangements to manage deep-ocean mineral resources were the measures taken to protect the economies of the major land producers of the constituent minerals from competition from ocean producers of the same minerals. The favored method was production controls. As we can see in figure 3, there was never any question of what type of provision would be placed in the various drafts.

From the beginning, there was no question of what the majority wanted. During the first time period (T1), when, on many other issues, most states were feeling their way (as shown by the high standard deviations on group positions), they were certain on production con-

FIGURE 3
Production Controls; Articles 150(e) (G), 151

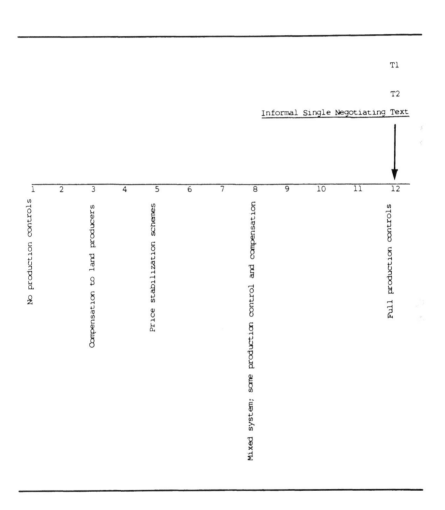

trols. Not only was the median at rank 12 but the Group of 77 as a whole also was at rank 12. All of the constituent subgroups (Latin America, Africa, and Asia) also were at approximately rank 12, and only Asia had a standard deviation of more than 1.0 (1.4). There was no change in the pattern at T2. As in T1, the United States, the European Economic Community, and other groups representing the developed countries opposed the imposition of production controls on the still-aborning ocean mining industry. Indeed, the opposition to production controls seems to have grown on the part of the United States. Our data show a U.S. retreat from price stabilization schemes at ranks 5-6 in T1 to support for compensation-only schemes shown at rank 2.4 in T2. This was a good tip-off to the actual position the United States took after it reviewed its continued participation in the negotiations. But so was the stability of the developing states position a tip-off that they did not consider this item renegotiable. Despite the fact that it should have had little real hope for success, when the United States published its "Green Book" of preferred revisions of the draft treaty, its redraft of Article 151 allowed only for adjustment assistance or compensation during a fifteen-year period.[44] As figure 3 shows, the informal negotiating text and the treaty showed production control measures written into the documents.

The formula for calculating the levels of production allowed did change over time. The composite negotiating text specifies that production for the first seven years not exceed the "projected cumulative growth . . . of the world nickel demand." After seven years of production, output should not exceed 60 percent of cumulative growth. The rate of increase is to be calculated for a twenty-year period by the least-squares method.[45] The treaty shows production controls to be enforced during a twenty-five-year interim period. They are to be based upon the sum of trend line values for annual nickel consumption and 60 percent of the difference between the trend line values for nickel consumption. The rate is to be calculated by the linear regression of the logarithms of actual nickel consumption.[46] Perhaps there is a difference, but it is one only an econometrician could appreciate. In my less flippant moments, I must admit that the so-called Archer Group made a valiant effort to find a technical fix. If found, that technical fix might have made a marginal improvement sufficient to mask the lack of agreement on a conceptual framework.

In any case, critics of the U.S. position claim that the quota is so generous that it would not inhibit the pioneer producers, therefore making an objectionable framework meaningless, at least for the first generation of miners.[47] Moreover, with whatever "learning" occurred concerning ocean mining among the developing nations about the "real" world of ocean mining, perhaps that framework will melt away over time. Obviously, the United States and other mineral producers were not willing to take the risk concerning a change in Third World perceptions. They wanted guarantees of access under significantly better conditions now,[48] but the majority forming the near consensus saw no reason to make any changes other than technical ones.

Distribution of the Benefits

As we have seen by the manner in which the major issues were assembled into a package, it was assumed through much of the long, arduous negotiations that the outcome should provide a balance of benefits to all of the major parties. Only if all major states and groups were satisfied would the resulting treaty be widely adopted and ratified, the stated goal of negotiators willing to operate under a consensus or near-consensus decision rule. Concessions were sought on that basis. By 1974 the basic outline of a treaty had emerged. At Caracas the developed states—East as well as West—openly traded off coastal control over living and nonliving resources in the guise of a 200-mile exclusive economic zone (EEZ) and acceptance of a modified archipelago concept for a formal ratification and perhaps strengthening of transit rights through straits and archipelagic waters and acceptance of a 12-nautical-mile territorial sea. Once the basic shift had taken place, many developed coastal states moved to the coastal camp with a vengeance. They soon became supporters of the claims of coastal states with extensive seabeds to a right to control out to at least 350 nautical miles, 60 miles beyond the foot of the slope or 100 nautical miles beyond 2,500 meters depth of water. As we are aware, a number of developing states also claimed that the developed states should also have been forced to throw in support for a NIEO-influenced deep-seabed regime in return for navigation rights. This became the major sticking point in reaching agreement.

The lineup of states supporting the emerging package was remarkably robust over time. Based on data gathered in T2 (1974-75), we ran many iterations of our packaging model. The model compares one set of packages of preferred outcomes (we used seventeen) with another set of packages of preferred outcomes. What forced states to "make a choice" in the model was not only how close a state's preferences are to one of the two packages posited in the model but how salient each of the issues in each package is to each deciding state.

In most of the runs that reflected known real packages or that were incremental modifications of real packages, the lineups consistently were in the range of 115-120 states on one side and 20-34 states on the other. (There were 149 states participating by 1975; more joined later.) The vote taken seven years after the last data were gathered was quite similar, showing a winning majority of 130 for, 4 against, and 17 abstaining. The opposition and abstention votes were recorded by the same states that the model showed clustered together—the United States, the USSR, and the other industrial states of the Communist Bloc and European Economic Community with the other negative voters, Israel and Turkey, folded or clustered nearby.

The problem during the last seven years of the UNCLOS III negotiations was obviously to satisfy the last remaining 20 to 35 states that their essential interests would be taken care of in the treaty. If we were to plot the preferred positions of states on most of the issues within the overall package, we would see that on most issues there would be a single peaked distribution with a tail. The tail, of course, would be composed of the 20 to 35 mostly developed states who were disturbed by the NIEO features of the draft treaty. There was never any possibility that those 20 to 35 objectors could have reversed the trends established throughout the history of the negotiations. The tail was not going to wag the dog. The developed states could only hold out as stubbornly as possible in the hope that the majority wanted a consensus treaty badly enough to modify some important features of the widely preferred package. This is essentially what went on in terms of bargaining efforts during much of the long period of perfecting and polishing the negotiating texts into a draft treaty.

I believe they came fairly close. We did find one model treaty that did achieve consensus support as compared to the rivals we tested it against. In figure 4, we show the model package and compare it to the provisions of the treaty on the same issues. What we did was play a "what-if" game. In this instance, we asked, "If this set of outcomes were packaged together to form a draft treaty, would it beat a rival set of preferred outcomes?" In other words, we were trying to forecast what it would take to achieve consensus.[49] I believe we show how close the conference came to satisfying the minority. To achieve consensus, the overwhelming majority would have had to be more forthcoming on the general deep-seabed minerals system, a bit more flexible on foreign rights in the economic zone, and perhaps might have provided more rights to the developed ocean science community—all issues with important economic implications to the developed states. In all of these areas, there were attempts to accommodate, but not enough to achieve consensus.

FIGURE 4
Consensus Package and Treaty Outcome

Issue	Model	Treaty
Committee I		
Deep mineral management system*	Limited mixed machinery	More powerful mixed machinery
Production controls	Full production controls	Full production controls
Distribution of ISRA revenues	Equitable but LDC priority	Equitable but LDC priority
Decision-making in Council	3/4 majority	3/4 majority
Committee II		
Territorial sea delimitation	12 nautical miles	12 nautical miles
Straits transit	Transit passage	Transit passage
Economic zone	200 n.m. EEZ	200 n.m. EEZ
EEZ Powers*	Foreign rights preserved	Coastal state exclusive rights
Navigation in EEZ	Free navigation	Free navigation
Foreign fishing in EEZ*	Some foreign rights under full utilization	Coastal allow access only to surplus
Migratory fish	Coastal management/international regulations	Coastal management/international regulations
Disadvantaged fishing in EEZ	Disadvantaged right after coastal use	Disadvantaged after coastal use
Continental shelf*	200 n.m. plus edge of shelf	200 n.m. beyond 350, 60 miles to foot or slope; 100 miles beyond 2500 meter isobath
Committee III		
Vessel pollution standards	Coastal law in harmony with international law	Coastal law in harmony with international law
Vessel pollution enforcement	Flag state/port state	Flag state/port state
Science in ISRA area	Free science but ISRA rights	Free science but ISRA rights
Science in EEZ*	Notification	Consent, but implied after 6 months

*Issues on which there is a discrepancy between the model and the treaty outcome.

To achieve further redistribution of benefits would have required acquiescence in the United States effort as assault and battery. Clearly, the United States signaled when it withdrew from the negotiations in 1981 that it demanded the majority give concessions that were quite fundamental. The only way to achieve such concessions was by a gesture as dramatic as the one attempted. In other words, the United States made it clear that it was not interested in marginal improvements, but the United Stated dissipated its tactical advantage by not having a concrete set of demands ready when it threatened to withdraw. If the United States had done its homework, it might have been able to play a game of chicken successfully. In 1981 many participants did not believe a treaty without U.S. participation would work effectively. Rumor at the time had it that significant movement by the majority might have been supported by the conference leadership and acquiesced to by the developing majority. But the full year it took for the United States to study the issue and to get its domestic house in order (the year's delay was basically designed to do this) vitiated its advantage.[50] The panic that the United States might remain out was over. The value of U.S. participation was reappraised, and all participants were one year older and even more desirous of finishing the job. If what the United States wished to achieve was a moral victory—a justification of its unswerving loyalty to capitalist principles—it succeeded. If what it really hoped to do was achieve a tactical victory by forcing the majority to compromise further, its effort was a miserable failure.

The UNCLOS Treaty—Is It a Success?

In the most formal sense UNCLOS III was a success. After fifteen years of total work and nine years of official conference deliberations, a long, complex treaty was produced. It spanned a broad range of ocean-use problems and promulgated a number of policy measures that will be a fundamental impact upon the way in which the oceans will be used and managed for a number of generations to come. Thus, the treaty (or perhaps the outcome measured in terms of the issue on which there was broad agreement) also may be judged a success in terms of the degree to which it transformed the status quo ante.

Ocean management post-UNCLOS III is already very different from what it was prior to the convocation of the conference. The most notable change was the broad acceptance of the trend toward expanded national jurisdiction—or enclosure, if you will. Most coastal states are already enforcing their versions of a 200-mile zone. Many are already exercising much tighter control of fishing, minerals exploitation, science, and pollution activities. The right to make these management decisions in the 200-mile zone is now less frequently challenged by states whose citizens have been disaccommodated. Perhaps there will be a broad acceptance of a uniform territorial sea of twelve miles, and straits states will accept the right of transit passage, thereby reducing the number of ocean issues that might threaten the peace. In any case on a broad range of issues covered by UNCLOS III, there will be no going back to the status quo ante. For the most part, the Latin American group that drove (and pulled along) most of its landlocked and shelflocked members into the negotiations in order to get expanded coastal jurisdiction ratified and that engineered the exclusive economic zone (EEZ) for straits and territorial sea trade-off, should be pleased. They achieved what they set out to do. Ironically, by a standard of comparative square miles coming under their jurisdiction, the developed states did far better than the developing states. The rich get richer. . . . Ironically, for such reasons as the vagueness in language forced by the necessary compromises, the threat to the original common heritage principles implied by acceptance of broad zones of national enclosure, and the failure to solve some critical problems such as finding an adequate delimitation principle for settling the claims of adjacent and opposite states, the "father" of the Law of the Sea Conference, Arvid Pardo, has denounced the legitimacy of his offspring.[51]

The answer to the question of whether the treaty will alter the way in which the states of the world attempt to gain access and manage the process of exploiting deep ocean mineral resources must await the outcome of the ratification processes. Japan and France were the only major industrial countries to vote for the treaty draft, and France was the only non-Eastern bloc developed state to adhere to the treaty when it was first opened to signature in December 1982. The interesting question will be whether the industrial North, other than the United States (at least during the Reagan administration), will ultimately accept in an extended signature stage and the ratification stage the imposition of a management system it deemed unacceptable.

Seventeen states chose to sit on the fence in the voting. The United States conducted an intensive lobbying campaign to try to induce its industrialized friends neither to sign nor ratify the draft treaty. The United States has been promoting a "Reciprocal States Agreement" in which ocean-mining states exercising their rights under the traditional law of capture would recognize one another's claims to mining sites without involving the International Seabed Resources Agency (ISRA).

Some parts of an acceptable arrangement have been adopted, but all parties approached have resisted signing a reciprocal states agreement in lieu of the UNCLOS draft treaty.[52] Japan, which did vote for treaty, has protested these negotiations and its exclusion therefrom.[53] Japan, which recently passed a domestic ocean mining law, has indicated lately that it would be interested in reciprocal rights if certain features of the reciprocal states approach were altered. Japan's overtures were refused, but its behavior is probably typical of most developed states—it will try to cover its bets. Although some states may sign, I suspect that even they will try not to commit themselves exclusively to either the UNCLOS treaty or the reciprocal states agreement until it becomes clear whether or not ISRA will function according to the treaty and whether the United States shows effective efforts to gain access to seabed minerals outside the treaty. What it probably means is a long slow ratification process on the part of the developed states because only ratification will bind them. In any case there is time. Industry says that seabed mining could start within three years but that no one within the industry expects it actually to begin before the 1990s. My own hunch is that it will not begin much before the twenty-first century. Certainly no one needs seabed mineral production very soon, for the noncommunist world's nickel consumption has fallen steadily for three years.[54]

Explaining the Outcome

There is no single explanation of the outcome of an effort as large as UNCLOS III. Nevertheless, I will offer some factors that I believe should be examined if we are to evaluate parliamentary diplomacy as a mechanism for dealing with global problems.

The immediate cause of the passage of the draft UNCLOS treaty in its final form was, I believe, exhaustion and the feeling that no further incremental improvements of the draft would satisfy the United States. In other words, all reasonable efforts had been made, and therefore it was time to end fifteen years of work. No one wished to tear apart and reweave the complex web of trade-offs. The U.S. threat not to participate had suffered entropy between the last two sessions. Although some improvements were offered, they were incremental in nature, not conceptual. What the United States wanted was surrender—and it did not get it.

If we step back from the turmoil of the last several sessions, we can better view the general nature of the final treaty document. In my judgment it was a least-common-denominator document that represented what the major forces in world politics will tolerate and where the main trends in ocean politics over the years show we have been going. Despite the complexity of the document, there are only three major themes that run through it.

The first theme is a reaffirmation of movement rights in straits, archipelagoes, economic zones, and territorial seas. Although each of the specific rights to move freely have been altered—expanded in a few cases, and slightly restricted in others—nevertheless there has been no substantial alteration of the rights of major blue-water naval and merchant marine states to move at will. Strategic mobility has been preserved. The movement rights of merchant ships were also essentially preserved. I would argue that whatever serious threats to these rights existed were substantially independent of the multilateral bargaining process and related to the policy needs of a limited number of straits states. The world community shared an interest in the preservation of these rights. As a result, the threat to these rights at UNCLOS was tactical in nature. Because of the sensitivity of the superpowers on this theme, it was a useful ploy—seemingly to threaten these movements so as to get the superpowers to the bargaining arena—but only a handful of states had any real incentives to impose serious restrictions. For most states, a reaffirmation of movement rights would protect their future ocean-use interests. Finally, virtually all of the participants understood that this issue was not really negotiable because the major ocean users would never have agreed to severe restrictions, and that while no one before Secretary Lehman threatened to shoot his way through the straits, the capability to do so was available and therefore the implied threat was credible. The cost of imposing major restrictions is likely to be very high, as virtually all participants were aware.

The second theme that is embodied in the treaty is a reaffirmation of the trend toward the enclosure of ocean space. It has become obvious that the underlying assumptions of the freedom of the seas are no longer valid in the twentieth century as they relate to ocean resources. We can overutilize the resources and we can damage the ecosystem. We might have enclosed the oceans centrally, as Pardo suggested in his original formulation of the common heritage of mankind, but that was never probable. Coastal states had the advantage of possessing government structures that could easily extend their jurisdictional reach. Moreover, it is the coastal states who have had to face the problems that heavier patterns of near-shore use bring. UNCLOS III consolidates the hold of the members of our decentralized world political system. Both those whom I have called elsewhere the functional and normative nationalists should be pleased.[55]

The final theme that runs through the UNCLOS III draft treaty is the need for international equity. On this issue the developing states stood firm, and because they controlled the process, they could dominate the outcome. I believe that the negotiations over the fate of manganese nodules on the sea floor had more to do with whether the developed states could be persuaded or coerced into accepting a different approach to North-South economic relations than it did with whether the new seabed mining industry needed to be managed. Indeed, it is a good probability that even if most of the features obnoxious to the United States on nodule exploitation were removed from the treaty, size alone of the contemplated ISRA bureaucracy would deal a mortal blow to the establishment of an ocean mining industry. At the end the developing states compromised, I believe significantly. What is in the treaty is a mixed system. It is fascinating to speculate about the system as a test bed of two economic theories. For the initial period, both licensees and the Enterprise would coexist, demonstrating whether economic exploitation based upon NIEO principles could work or whether the use of free enterprise principles would make its license operation so efficient that the Enterprise's activities would look shabby by comparison.

   In sum, some observers, and especially participants, may think that if an opportunity had been seized at a key moment, the outcome could have been altered. Perhaps. Perhaps with a different regime the United States would be in rather than outside the treaty. But I believe that even if the lost tactical opportunities had been taken, essentially the same treaty would have been produced by the parliamentary diplomatic process. Size may be the main "explanatory" variable in explaining the outcome. It necessitates a slow, laborious process, and perhaps dictates a least-common-denominator outcome, and eventually, exhaustion.

Methodological Appendix

   My involvement in the study of negotiations concerning the Law of the Sea goes back many years. The substance and process of the first (1958) and second (1960) UN conferences on the Law of the Sea were the subjects of my doctoral dissertation. While on the staff of the Center for Naval Analyses at the University of Rochester during the mid-1960s, I dealt with ocean policy issues; I developed preparatory materials for the prospective third conference and did position studies on seabed arms control. After the UN Seabed Committee activities appeared to be developing into the first stage of the conference, I collaborated with Professor Joseph Kadane, now chairman of the

Statistics Department at Carnegie-Mellon University, in developing a large-scale forecasting model of the conference process. Initially, the project that I directed was under contract with the U.S. Navy and later under contract jointly with the Navy and the Department of State. Until 1975 the results were provided the U.S. delegation to the UNCLOS, sometimes reluctantly, by the original sponsors.[56]

Since returning to teaching and academic administration, I have had no resources with which to bring the data I had gathered up to date (and because, after 1975, the mode of bargaining changed to more private negotiations, there is a serious question of whether it was feasible to keep current the type of data I had collected). I have continued to follow the negotiations closely but less systematically, reading both the documents generated and the voluminous secondary literature. But the models we developed have molded the way I go about analyzing the negotiations. As we shall see subsequently, it is possible to place the bargaining that took place from 1975 to 1982, and particularly the results, into the modeling framework developed earlier.

The basis of the modeling effort was a thematic content analysis performed on the records of the conference. This allowed us to capture systematically where states said they stood on the issues. Moreover, we could also record and use conditional statements of support by states. Using a regression model, we were able to generate estimates concerning probable positions for states for which we did not have information. This raw material was turned into data by developing a series of conflict-issues variables created by scaling. Later those "issues" were converted at UNCLOS into treaty articles. In fact, our issues often became multiple articles because the issue was usually a broad-scale problem with a number of interrelated parts that required resolution.

Our conflict issues models were developed in one-dimensional space. We assumed that we could discover the array of issues and order them on the basis of some underlying dimension. They were first scaled ordinally and then, in an attempt to replicate the perceived world of the negotiator, were transformed into an interval scale. The initial ordering was done by the principal investigator and fine tuned by a panel of U.S. negotiators. Figure 1 is an example of a conflict issue. It is more than a sample of the method because it deals with *the* key contentious North-South issue of UNCLOS III. We will build on it later in this discussion. The "preferred positions" of states, composed of data and/or estimates from each state, can be displayed on this spectrum. The median of these preferred positions will show the central tendency of the collective opinion, and the distribution, if strongly single peaked, will show if there is consensus or movement toward consensus. Because we can divide the data into two or four time periods, we can show change over time for individual states or groups. We also have a measure of the discipline shown by the groups, by calculating the mean and standard deviation of the preferred position of their members. We can also display on the same spectrum, the opening positions of states and the fallbacks, as well as the outcome of various draft texts and the final treaty on the conflict issue in question.

The LOS forecasting project also developed more sophisticated tools. A model built on the individual issues model calculates the probable package and trade-off outcomes. Finally, a "maximization" model was developed. The problem it helps illuminate is in what direction and how far must one push a package to achieve the best chance of consensus or near consensus.[57]

Notes

1. Robert L. Friedheim and Robert E. Bowen, "Neglected Issues at the Third United Nations Law of the Sea Conference," in *Law of the Sea: Neglected Issues,* ed. J. K. Gamble, (Honolulu: Law of the Sea Institute, 1979), pp. 2-39.
2. Robert Axelrod, *Conflict of Interest* (Chicago: Markham, 1970), pp. 158-63.
3. Draft Treaty on the Law of the Sea, Articles 144, 151, 153, 155, and 170.
4. Robert L. Friedheim and William J. Durch, "The International Seabed Resource Agenda Negotiations and the New International Economic Order," *International Organizations* 31 (Spring 1977): 343-84.
5. Knut Midgaard and Arild Underdahl, "Multiparty Conferences," in *Negotiation: Social-Psychological Perspectives,* ed. Daniel Druckman, (Beverly Hills: Sage Publications, 1977), p. 334.
6. I. William Zartman, ed., *The 50% Solution* (Garden City, N.Y.: Doubleday, 1976), p. 9.
7. Oran R. Young, *Bargaining: Formal Theories of Negotiation* (Urbana: University of Illinois Press, 1975), p. 13.
8. For example, both Midgaard and Underdahl, and Druckman cite more from the coalition literature than from major works on parliamentary diplomacy. For a descriptive work of a number of its major characteristics, see my "Parliamentary Diplomacy," Memorandum 71-0046.10 (Washington, D.C.: Center for Naval Analysis, April 1971).
9. Leigh S. Ratiner, "The Law of the Sea: A Crossroads for American Foreign Policy," *Foreign Affairs* 70 (Summer 1982): 1006-21; and S. Jayakumar and T. T. Koh, "The Negotiating Process of the Third United Nations Law of the Sea," First Preliminary Draft, March 1980.
10. Joseph B. Kadane, "Analysis of Voting Rule Possibilities of Law of the Sea," Memorandum 9013-74 (Washington, D.C.: Center for Naval Analysis 18 June 1974).

11. Kenneth J. Arrow, *Social Choice and Individual Values*, 2d ed. (New Haven: Yale University Press, 1963), p. 203; Robert Abrams, *Foundations of Political Analysis: An Introduction to the Theory of Collective Choice* (New York: Columbia University Press, 1980), pp. 28-39.
12. The term is that of Jayakumar and Koh.
13. Salience is the comparative importance of the preferred outcome on two or more choices.
14. See Jayakumar and Koh, "The Negotiating Process of the Third United Nations Law of the Sea"; Edward Miles, "The Structure and Effects of the Decision Process in the Seabed Committee and the Third United Nations Conference on the Law of the Sea," *International Organizations* 31 (Spring 1977): 159-234; Barry Buzan, "Informal Negotiating Groups and UNCLOS III," *Marine Policy* 4 (July 1980): 183-204.
15. For a review of coalition theory, see Abrams, *Foundations of Political Analysis* pp. 235-79; Eric C. Browne, "Coalition Theories: A Logical and Empirical Critique," Sage Professional Paper, vol. 4 (1973).
16. Axelrod, *Conflict of Interest*, pp. 168-87; Abram De Swaan, *Coalition Theories and Cabinet Formations* (San Francisco: Jossey-Bass, 1970).
17. See, in particular, Friedheim and Durch, "The New International Seabed Resources Agency," on deep seabed issues.
18. Jayakumar and Koh, "The Negotiating Process of the Third United Nations Law of the Sea," p. 52.
19. For an account of some of these efforts, see Jonathan I. Charney, "Technology and International Negotiations," *American Journal of International Law* 76 (January 1982): 97; James Sebenius, *Negotiating the Law of the Sea* (Cambridge: Harvard University Press, 1984); Howard Raiffa, *The Art and Science of Negotiation* (Cambridge: Harvard University Press, 1982; J. D. Nyhart and M. S. Triantafyllou, *A Pioneer Deep Ocean Mining Venture* (Cambridge: Massachusetts Institute of Technology Sea Grant College Program report 83-14, June 1983).
20. Robert L. Friedheim, "The 'Satisfied' and 'Dissatisfied' States Negotiate International Law: A Case Study," *World Politics* 18 (October 1965): 20-41.
21. For the 200-mile zone proclamation and its official interpretation, see "Exclusive Economic Zone of the United States of America: A Proclamation by the President of the United States of America," *Fact Sheet: United States Ocean Policy* (Washington, D.C.: The White House, Office of the Press Secretary, 10 March 1983).
22. These themes relate to claims of past injustice, redistribution, and NIEO.
23. Friedheim and Durch, "The International Seabed Resources Agency."
24. Robert L. Friedheim and Joseph B. Kadane, "Ocean Science in the UN Political Arena," *Journal of Maritime Law and Commerce* 3 (April 1972): 473-502.
25. Axelrod, *Conflict of Interest*, pp. 160-63.
26. The major exception of a state that was rich and coastal and did not act cross-pressured but, rather, was an ardent proponent of the expansion of natural jurisdiction was Canada. Canada's overlapping cleavage was that it was rich but had no distant-water interests.
27. Stephen D. Krasner, "North-South Economic Relations: The Quests for Economic Well-Being and Political Autonomy," in *Eagle Entangled: U.S.*

Foreign Policy in a Complex World, ed. K. A. Oye, D. Rothchild, and R. J. Lieber (New York: Longman, 1979), p. 124.

28. Robert L. Friedheim and Mary E. Jehn, "The Soviet Position at the Third U.N. Law of the Sea Conference," in *Soviet Naval Policy: Objectives and Constraints,* ed. M. MacGuire, K. Booth, and J. McDonnel (New York: Praeger, 1975), pp. 341-62.
29. N. Breckner, R. Friedheim, L. Heselton, Jr., L. Mason, S. Schmid, and R. Simmons, *The Navy and the Common Sea* (Washington, D.C.: Government Printing Office, for the Office of Naval Research, 1972), pp. 135-225.
30. Robert L. Friedheim, *Understanding the Debate on Ocean Resources,* Monograph Series on World Affairs (University of Denver) 6y:3 (1968-69).
31. See any issue of *Soundings: Law of the Sea News and Comment,* joint publication of the United Methodist Law of the Sea Project and the Ocean Education Project (Society of Friends).
32. Myres S. McDougal and William T. Burke, *The Public Order of the Oceans* (New Haven: Yale University Press, 1962).
33. For a description of the "patrimonialist" group, see Anne L. Hollick, *U.S. Foreign Policy and the Law of the Sea* (Princeton: Princeton University Press, 1981), pp. 252-53.
34. Mary McGrory, "Sailing the Sea Treaty Shoals without the Lighthouse of Facts," *Washington Post,* 22 July 1982; John Lehman, "Letter to the Editor," *Washington Post,* 30 July 1982. For another attempt to explain the Reagan shift, see Sebenius, *Negotiating the Law of the Sea,* ch. iv.
35. For these works, see notes 9, 12, and 14.
36. For an attempt to show general stages of negotiations that are compatible with this case, see: I. William Zartman and Maureen R. Berman, *The Practical Negotiator* (New Haven: Yale University Press, 1982), chs. 3-5.
37. Elliot Richardson has written a number of articles indicating how close he thought agreement had come under his leadership. See, for example, "Sea Bed Mining and the Law of the Sea," *Department of State Bulletin* 80: 60-64.
38. I. William Zartman, "Negotiations: Theory and Reality," *Journal of International Affairs* 9 (1975): 71.
39. Miles, "The Structure and Effects of the Decision Process in the Seabed Committee," p. 211.
40. Jayakumar and Koh, "The Negotiating Process of the Third United Nations Law of the Sea," p. 103.
41. To keep the discussion manageable, only the first of these, the ISNT, will be discussed.
42. The opening positions and the medians displayed were derived from the data of the forecasting project. The placement of the ISNT and the treaty on the scale are the personal estimates of the author.
43. Warren S. Wooster, "Ocean Research Under Foreign Jurisdiction," *Science* 212 (May 1981): 754-55; David A. Ross and John A. Knauss, "How the Law of the Sea Treaty Will Affect U.S. Marine Science," *Science* 217 (September 1982): 1003-8.
44. The U.S. Proposals for Amendment to the Draft Convention of the Law of the Sea (the "Green Book").
45. Article 150, 1(g)B(i), *Composite Single Negotiating Text* (A/CONF. 62/WP.10/Corr. 1, 15 July 1977).

46. Article 151, 2(b)(i)(ii)(iii), *Draft Convention on the Law of the Sea* A/ CONF. 62/L. 78, 28 August 1981.

47. Richardson, "Seabed Mining and the Law of the Sea," p. 62; Ronald S. Katz, "Are There Workable Principles for Managing the Resources of the Deep Seabed?" Ocean Studies Symposium, Asilomar Conference Center, November 1982; Jennifer S. Whittaker, "Outside the Mainstream," *Atlantic*, October 1982, p. 22.

48. F. G. Adams asserted, based upon a model of future seabed mining efforts, that seabed mining would transfer producer interests to consumer interests. For developed market economies that are both producers and consumers, the net transfer is positive, but for developing producer countries the transfer would result in a loss of $1.5 billion per year. Cited in Per Magnus Wijkman, "UNCLOS and the Redistribution of Ocean Wealth," *Journal of World Trade Law* 16 (January/February 1982): 40.

49. Our packaging model assumes an equal willingness of participants to negotiate on all issues simultaneously. If that condition holds, then it provides a useful set of clues to the negotiator on what are the most important substantive issues to work on and how far to move in altering the substance of a proposal, but it does not provide answers to specific tactical questions. It was not designed to help the negotiator answer the question as to what the next move should be in a diplomatic interaction. Such a model, which helps forecast the appropriate moves in the outguessing regress, perhaps based upon game theoretic principles, might be possible, albeit difficult. Although U.S. negotiators often requested that we also develop such a model, we did not have the time, resources, or appropriate circumstances to do so.

50. For an interesting account of the internal U.S. interplay in the process of deciding to go along with or drop out of the UNCLOS negotiations, see Daniel S. Nossiter, "Underwater Treaty: The Fascinating Study of How the Law of the Sea Treaty Was Sunk," *Barrons*, 26 July 1982, pp. 10-12.

51. Arvid Pardo, "Law of the Sea Conference—What Went Wrong," *Managing Ocean Resources: A Primer*, ed. Robert L. Friedheim (Boulder, Colo.: Westview Press, 1979), pp. 137-48; Arvid Pardo, "The Symbolic and Practical Import of the Negotiations," *Center Magazine* 15 (March/April 1982): 26.

52. "U. S., 3 Nations Sign Sea-Mine Pact," *Los Angeles Times*, pt. IV, 7 September 1982.

53. *Nihon Keizai Shimbun*, 3 February 1982, p. 1.

54. "World's Nickel Prices Continue to Plunge, Ending Bid by Firms to Maintain Quotes," *Wall Street Journal*, 19 August 1982, p. 26.

55. Friedheim, *Understanding the Debate on Ocean Resources*, pp. 2-27.

56. Robert L. Friedheim, "Research Utilization Problems in Forecasting the U.N. Law of the Sea Conference, Or, the Perils of the Persian Messenger," in *Formulating Marine Policy: Limits to Rational Decision-Making*, ed. T. M. Hennessey (Kingston, R.I.: Center for Ocean Management Studies, 1978), pp. 144-67.

57. For an exposition of the forecasting methods developed in the LOS project, see: Robert L. Friedheim, Karen G. Goudreau, and William J. Durch, *Forecasting Out-comes of Multilateral Negotiations: Methodology Techniques and Models*, CRC 291, vol. 1; Karen W. Goudreau,

William J. Durch, *Forecasting Outcomes of Multilateral Negotiations: Methodology Code Book,* CRC 291, vol. 2; Karen W. Goudreau, *Forecasting Outcomes of Multilateral Negotiations: Computer Programs, Guide for Users,* CRC 290, vol. 1; Karen W. Goudreau, *Forecasting Outcomes of Multilateral Negotiations: Computer Programs, Guide for Programmers,* CRC 290, vol. 2—all Center for Naval Analysis, Washington, D.C., January 1977.

5

The Wheat Negotiations: Loss or Gain in North-South Relations?

Raymond F. Hopkins

In February 1979 negotiations to establish an international system for reserve stocks of wheat collapsed.[1] This effectively ended the search, launched by the World Food Conference in Rome in 1974, for improved world food security through grain reserves. Although talks sputtered on for two more years, there was little basis after the February collapse for the food security interests of developing countries to be met through a revised International Wheat Agreement.

The failure of the South, or more concretely the Group of 77, to secure demands sunk the talks. The wheat talks, however, may never have been a realistic arena for North-South bargaining. The hope for LDC food security through reserves may have been a chimera but nevertheless had strong inertia set in motion by the 1974 World Food Conference endorsement of the Food and Agriculture Organization's (FAO) International Undertaking on World Food Security. The basic premise for this scheme, developed in 1973, was that many LDCs had been harmed by the sharp rise in their food import bills in 1973, and that such harm could be avoided in the future through a coordination of national policies in regard to the holding of grain stocks. Public grain reserves is an old idea whose time seems to come and go with each major shift in food supplies.

This paper tells the story of the negotiations over one such reserve system, a story beginning in London in February 1975 under the aegis of the International Wheat Council (IWC) and ending four years later in Geneva at a United Nations conference. The story is then analyzed in a second section of the paper where I try to identify and evaluate what shaped the negotiations and led to their breakdown. The paper concludes with an assessment of the outcomes of the talks. Was the failure to create an international reserve system during the 1970s a gain or a loss for the South?

The Story

Of all the world's foods, wheat has become the most important. Wheat is the preferred cereal for direct consumption among more affluent populations. It can be stored and shipped more efficiently than other foods, that is, with less energy spent and less waste. For its price, it delivers more nutrition than most traded foods. With these advantages, wheat not surprisingly accounted for nearly half the world cereal trade in 1981. Twenty-one percent of wheat production moved in international trade, compared with 13 percent of coarse grains and 4 percent of rice.[2] Its suitability for trade and fungibility in meeting food needs make wheat politically and economically the most central crop in the world's food supply.

There has been a general expansion of the world wheat market since World War II. In 1949-50 world production was 166 million tons, and 14 percent was traded. In 1962-63 production was 256 million tons, and 17 percent was traded. By 1972-73 production was 337 million tons, and 20 percent was traded; by 1981-82, 461 million tons, and 21 percent traded. By the early 1970s the United States and Canada had become the dominant suppliers, accounting for 60 to 70 percent compared with 30 percent in the 1930s. Prices were stable or declining during the 1950s and 1960s. Large reserve stocks existed, largely held in Canada and the United States.[3] Grain reserves were of little interest internationally, certainly not in developing countries, even though imports of these countries were growing. When the price shock of 1972-73 occurred and wheat prices tripled, the value of reserves became apparent. The major exporting countries released their reserves, the Soviet Union became a major importer, and the world price of wheat shot up from $60 a ton in 1970 to over $200 a ton in 1974. Other grain prices rose also, though less sharply. In this panic market many LDCs experienced food crop shortfalls in either 1973 or 1974, and in addition found food aid less available. As a result, their food import bills rose dramatically, wiping out foreign reserves and leading to delays or cancellations of imputs for development projects. The rise in food costs along with the dramatic rise in oil import costs for nonoil exporters slowed the economic growth and vastly increased the debt of most LDCs. Secure access to food, especially wheat, at stable prices became one of the demands of Third World countries as they sought sweeping reforms in the international economic order. One means they identified to realize this end was by commodity stabilization using reserve stocks.

Historically grain reserves have been sought for two purposes: market stability and food security. The purposes are similar but not identical. Market stability has been sought by grain producers, exporters, and importers to reduce economic risk. Low or falling grain prices in the twentieth century have triggered considerable interest in international action to prevent a market glut and to provide a fair return to producers. For instance, price cooperation on wheat was discussed at the 1927 Geneva International Economic Conference. Prices rose and the topic was dropped. When the worldwide recession of the 1930s hit, efforts to collaborate were renewed. After twenty conferences on wheat problems, the first International Agreement on Wheat was reached by twenty-two countries in London in August 1933. It failed almost immediately when the signing countries neglected their obligations. Subsequent efforts to draft and sign agreements occurred in 1938, 1942, and 1948; in 1949 the first "successful" agreement was reached and eventually signed by forty-six countries. Every few years since then wheat agreements have been renewed, sometimes with substantial changes. Negotiations have been facilitated by the International Wheat Council, established during the war as a successor to the Wheat Advisory Committee of the original 1933 agreement. In 1967 the International Grains Agreement (IGA) was pursued in the context of the broader Kennedy Round of GATT trade negotiations. Its successor, the International Wheat Agreement of 1971, was negotiated under the auspices of the United Nations Conference on Trade and Development (UNCTAD). All these agreements were basically arrangements for policy coordination to improve supply assurance and price stabilization among major traders.

The second basic purpose of reserves is food security. Here the emphasis is not income guarantees for farmers or stability of prices to facilitate trade but rather the availability of minimum physical quantities for nutritional needs. At the extreme such security would buy time against a Malthusian situation. Security against global shortages has rarely been a factor in establishing reserves. The purpose to be achieved is too far in the future to arouse much support and the benefit of security reserves can be seen as a palliative at best, merely postponing shortages for a brief time. The principal security purpose, then, is distributional. The aim is to provide a hedge for poor consumers during periods of temporary scarcity and high prices. Reserves for this purpose, however, would be most effective if they were dedicated for release only to those most physically vulnerable during shortfalls. Food aid channels would be the most appropriate existing institution for such dedicated release.[4]

The international community's alarm during the panic market of 1973-74 tended to see these two purposes—stability and security—as one. A reserve that stabilized prices, it was argued, would help rich and poor commercial importers alike. Furthermore, a reserve would also stabilize food aid programs. In the United States in 1973 food aid had been sharply reduced for both fiscal reasons (the same dollar allocation bought far less tonnage) and policy reasons (consumer opposition to exports arose in reaction to high prices). Thus, the various schemes and proposals discussed in preparation for the November 1974 World Food Conference all assumed a collective undertaking on reserves. The policy envisaged would be principally undertaken by the major exporters and importers—excluding the Soviet Union most likely—but would benefit rich and poor trading nations alike. Officials in the U.S. Department of Agriculture (USDA), for example, estimated that a reserve of 60 million tons (30 of wheat, 25 of corn, and 5 of rice) would provide stable grain supplies for nineteen of twenty years. Edwin Martin, chief coordinator of the U.S. preparations for the conference, asserted that such a reserve, based on international agreement for managing national reserves in many states, would distribute the costs of reserves and secure benefits for both LDCs and the major traders.[5] Thus, as understood in the United States and supported in various international meetings, the task was to create one system of reserves to serve several purposes.

The Problem, 1974-1977

The proposal to create a system of international grain reserves, though resisted by developed countries, was never controlled by the South. It was first promoted in the FAO by its director-general, Addeke H. Boerma, a European. After 1974 the secretariat task was assigned to the International Wheat Council, largely a developed-country institution based in London. The leadership for the undertaking was left to the United States as the world's largest exporter and self-declared food power. The LDC efforts at the World Food Conference to create a stronger world food authority were led by the Egyptian Sayed Marei, the conference secretary-general. His proposal for a world food authority was modified and new jurisdiction over food affairs was diffused in the formation of several new institutions: the World Food Council (WFC), the Committee on Food Aid Policies and Programs (CFA), and the International Fund for Agricultural Development (IFAD). The CFA was the successor of the Inter-Governmental Committee of the World Food Program (WFP). None of these organizations is governed by a universal, one-state, one-vote system. The result is that the power of the South, embodied in the LDC coalition of the Group of 77, is attenuated in most food organizations.

With the election of a Lebanese, Edward Saouma, as director-general of the FAO in 1975, the Group of 77 asserted its control in that institution. The FAO after 1975, however, never had the lead over the idea, design, or working negotiations for international reserves. Nor did UNCTAD play a role. In the first Program of Action for a New International Economic Order (NIEO) tabled by UNCTAD in 1973, eighteen commodities, including wheat and rice, were included in the Integrated Program for Commodities (IPC). A $10 billion fund for buffer stocks was estimated to be needed to manage these commodities, the largest amount of this for grains. UNCTAD and the Group of 77 soon dropped eight commodities, including grains, from the proposed IPC. The reasons were economic and political. Grains, especially wheat, constitued net imports, and it was not sensible to push for price stabilization at high prices for imported commodities. UNCTAD had little commodity analysis competence in wheat. Moreover, the existing commodity organization, the IWC, and the International Wheat Agreement that it served, were already the focus of demands from the FAO to take steps that would improve food security for LDCs. Thus, the 1975 IPC dropped grains but did call for an assured access to foodstuffs and improved quantity and reliability of food aid; soon even these concerns were relegated to other forums.

Politically, the South wanted lower stable prices and compensatory financing of imports of grain but just the opposite for the commodities it exported. The South quickly accepted, therefore, that wheat negotiations would not be part of the major NIEO negotiations. At the *ad hoc* Conference on International Economic Cooperation (CIEC), which met from December 1975 to June 1977, wheat and grains were on the agenda, but this issue was relegated at an early date to the discussions already under way at the IWC. In 1975-76, therefore, in UNCTAD and the CIEC, the South agreed to delete food security, as obtained through wheat stockholding, as an item for general North-South talks.

The security issue was delegated to a preparatory group of the IWC. The group, made up basically of major grain traders invited to a London meeting in February 1975 at the instigation of the United States, monopolized international discussion. Even the FAO Committee on World Food Security, the only international organization in which there was both significant Group of 77 influence and technical competence, agreed in April 1977 that "the objectives and main elements of . . . [food security] should be appropriately reflected in the provisions of a new International Grains Agreement" negotiated by the International Wheat Council members to replace the old International Wheat Agreement. The World Food Council also called on the IWC to negotiate a reserve system rapidly (as part of the WFC's program for eradicating hunger and malnutrition).[6] The South in essence transferred the security issue to an existing Western-led commodity organization.

The IWC task thus became formally defined as improving food security (lessening the risk of hunger) and reducing price instability (lessening the risk of erratic, inefficient markets) through a common solution: international rules for coordinating national reserve stocks. As noted, many believed in 1974-76 that the same reserve stock could simultaneously guarantee stability to food aid and commercial trade. Furthermore, distributing stocks around the world would further promote security, provided LDCs received financial aid for the stockholding. Reserves, it was argued, provided a collective good of security and stability. The United States, Canada, and Australia had largely provided this good to the world community in the 1950s and 1960s. Its benefits needed to be restored. Because the exporters' domestic policies had changed, however, the burden of stockholding would now have to be shared more widely. What remained to be decided were the important "technical" details: how should stocks be acquired and released, how large should stocks become, and who should pay for them. The negotiations were essentially over these three issues.

The Negotiations

The negotiations to replace the International Wheat Agreement with an international reserve arrangement had three distinct phases. The first ended in a stalemate between Europe and the United States over the question of price versus quantity triggers. The second ended in a United States-European Community accord on major issues, and the third in a North-South impasse.

The 1975-76 period ended in disagreement on key issues. The United States-European Community disagreement was so basic that it over-shadowed other points of dispute, such as the absence of progress on Group of 77 concerns over the size and reliability of food aid or how exporters might help LDCs hold stocks. The disagreement also displaced other developed-country differences.

The Europeans, in principle, favored managing markets through government intervention prices, a system they had developed in their Common Agricultural Policy (CAP). Their proposals were largely aimed at undertaking nothing that would require revising the CAP. The European Economic Community (EEC) introduced a proposal at the GATT Tokyo Round discussions in January 1976 for stabilizing international trade between maximum and minimum prices. It was in many respects a projection of CAP operations onto the world economy and was a direct contradiction of the U.S. view that markets not governments should set prices. The quantitative trigger proposal of the United States had been tabled a year earlier at the IWC. The proposal for a 30-million-ton reserve (25 of wheat, 5 of rice) was itself a compromise between the USDA under Earl Butz, who preferred no reserve scheme, and the State Department, which supported a 60-million-ton reserve. Quantity triggers would be an advantage to the United States, which had the best information on shortfalls and the largest ability to expand or contract production through policy. This would allow exporters to take advantage of the lag between price shifts, which can come quickly when a supply shift occurs, and official quantity estimates. Even with several months of checking, official production and stock numbers may be suspect. In short, quantitative triggers would be slower, less trustworthy, and more debatable than prices, but they would intervene less to depress prices or export earnings.[7]

The views of other participants in this period were more opaque. The Soviet Union as the world's largest and most erratic wheat producer took no position, waiting for the implications for the USSR to become clear. The Soviets had joined the International Wheat Agreement in 1964 as an exporting country, but by the mid-1970s were the world's leading importer, and more important, the largest single source of unpredictability in the world wheat market. The Group of 77, having abandoned a plan to incorporate wheat in the IPC, voiced criticism of the 1975-76 proposals, largely for their failure to provide for the special interests of developing countries.

In many respects the first phase of the negotiations ended in October 1975 with the conclusion of the U.S.-USSR bilateral agreement on grain trade, which reduced the major source of uncertainty for U.S. exports. This was coupled with forecasts of growing wheat stocks during 1975-76. By the fall of 1975, prices had begun to drop and the fears and concerns of the "crisis" period in 1973-74 were abating. Following the Moscow negotiations, U.S. Undersecretary of Agriculture Richard Bell stopped in London to participate in the discussions of the IWC Preparatory Group. He later reported that the effect of the U.S.-Soviet bilateral agreement was to kill high-level U.S. and Soviet interest in an international grain reserve agreement from the very moment of its signing.[8] Discussions continued during 1976 but by September even the group of experts working under the Preparatory Group concluded that the limits of profitable technical work had been reached.

Two factors revived the talks and brought on a second phase. In 1977 the Carter administration came to Washington with a greater commitment to LDC food security concerns. Second, grain prices declined, a drop in real terms by the summer of 1977 to near depression prices. The United States instituted mandatory acreage set-aside requirements for wheat and corn to reduce production. Domestic opposition to reserves melted, and the United States accepted the European position of using prices to dictate stock purchases and sales, a position now favored in Washington.

Protecting domestic farm income was the major political concern among developed countries, however. The 1977 farm bill in the United States established a farmer-owned reserve scheme to reduce pressure from large supplies of U.S. grain on the market. Once the bill was passed, the Carter administration turned full attention toward the wheat negotiations as a means to reduce Treasury costs in supporting this domestic reserve scheme. By the fall of 1977 basic agreements were being reached, and the IWC in November asked UNCTAD to convene a conference to negotiate a new grains agreement to replace the existing International Wheat Agreement.

Since 1971 (or effectively 1969), the International Wheat Agreement (IWA) had consisted of the Wheat Trade Convention governing consultations over wheat trade and the Food Aid Convention (FAC), setting minimum tonnages of grain aid pledged by donors. The FAC had originated in the 1967 agreement, known as an International Grains Agreement. At that time, as the Kennedy Round of GATT tariff negotiations was drawing to a close, a compromise between the United States and Europe was worked out whereby trade rules for coarse grains were developed and a price range for multilateral wheat trade agreed upon. The United States had argued that because European countries benefited from exporters' stockholding and food aid, they should supply a portion of the food aid. In exchange the Europeans wanted rules for wheat trade extended to other grains, with maximum prices guaranteed for wheat. Because prices were moving up at the time, and because a deal on agriculture was needed to conclude the Kennedy Round under the terms of the U.S. legislative mandate, the formula for the 1967 Grains Agreement was worked out by the March deadline for GATT negotiations and the details were finalized later that year. By the time the agreement took effect in July 1968, prices were falling; by 1969 the price provisions were broken for all the various grains. Although the IGA did not expire until 1971, only the Food Aid Convention seemed to have much effect after 1969. Signatories to the FAC generally adhered to their commitments, supplying at least the minimum of 4.2 million tons of wheat (or wheat equivalences). In 1971 a Wheat Trade Convention without substantive economic provisions and a Food Aid Convention constituted the IWA; the IWA has been periodically extended for one and two years ever since.

In February 1978 negotiations opened at Geneva under UNCTAD auspices to replace the 1971 IWA with three new conventions dealing with wheat, grains, and aid. The revised draft of the Food Aid Convention called for a target of 10 million tons minimum of food aid and expected donors to increase the size of their 1967 pledges. The Wheat Trade Convention draft had a system of six price triggers, three "falling" and three "rising points" at which action was to be taken. The grains agreement was to be consultative in nature because the United States firmly opposed a price system for coarse grains whereby the United States supplied nearly 70 percent of the exports.

During the 1978 negotiations differences among the major groups were clarified. Except for increased food aid pledges, food security was sidestepped by the developed countries. Group of 77 countries were prepared to participate in stockholding for price stabilization, but only if special provisions were made for them. They demanded that the Wheat Trade Convention generate funds to pay the costs for LDC acquisition and holding of stocks, and also permit them to release stocks in case of domestic need, even if this did not coincide with world conditions. The LDCs wanted more than to be merely "free riders" on a collective good. They wanted stocks given to them, the cost of holding them paid for, and then the right to sell them independently of the rules for developed countries. For a long time such LDC demands were not taken very seriously. It was assumed that every participant understood the shift in mood and purpose from stabilizing supplies (the U.S. proposal) to stabilizing prices (the EC approach). The Wheat Trade Convention was primarily to be a developed country commercial trade agreement. At the GATT talks, agricultural trade restrictions were being discussed, but grains had been delegated to the IWC forum. Because the LDCs would benefit from an agreement that reduced the risk of rapid price rises, as in 1973-74, the North believed the South should be content. Even if the agreement also put a floor under wheat prices, that should have no serious negative effects for possible LDC food crises.

In July 1978 the deadline for a new agreement proposed by the WFC and FAO passed. The old Wheat Agreement was renewed for a year. The United States and the EC, meeting in a twelve-member "interim committee" of the negotiating conference, narrowed their differences. Trade would not be guaranteed within fixed prices, as with the CAP, but a price band for buying and selling stocks so as to smooth prices was agreed upon, one that would allow accumulation of stocks to begin soon. Some compromise on the size of the reserve between the United States' 25 million tons—lowered from 30—the 15 million of the European Communities (EC), and Japan's 12 million would be reached. An assistance evaluation committee of the IWC would be established that would facilitate bilaterial and multilateral financing from existing agencies, e.g. the World Bank and the International Monetary Fund, for LDC stockholding needs. In November the conference resumed to seek final compromises. With the death of Rabot, the director-general of agriculture in the EC Commission and a key figure shaping the EC position, greater flexibility in the EC position was perceived, at least by U.S. negotiators. Claude Villain, his successor, genuinely seemed to prefer some agreement to none. Moreover, a new deadline imposed by the need to close the Tokyo Round of GATT talks loomed in March 1979. The second session of the conference narrowed differences. The Food Aid Convention was essentially ready, with higher pledges decided but not announced.[9] The grain accord was also agreed. When the second session broke up, only a breakthrough to agreement on wheat prices and the size of the reserve was needed.

The stage was set for a third and final act. In January of 1979 Dale Hathaway, the U.S. undersecretary of agriculture, met in Europe with Villain and Gundelach (the EC agriculture commissioner). A price band and a target for stocks that vaguely split the difference between the EC and U.S. numbers were agreed upon. The third session of the UNCTAD-hosted negotiating conference began on 22 January 1979, and an agreement was expected. Even the Soviets, who initially preferred more rigid prices and no stockholding obligations, declared a willingness to participate. Serious doubt existed, however, as to how their stockholding claims could be verified and hence be taken seriously. Arthur Dunkel, the Swiss chairman of the conference gathered pledges (some made privately) for stocks countries were prepared to hold. By 1979 these were below the Group of 77 figure of 30 million tons or the U.S. compromise of 25 million. A generous total was 21 million tons, but this included 3 million by the Soviets and 2 million by some twenty-two LDC participants. The lower figure would be accepted. For some time the "inner six"—the United States, Canada, Australia, Argentina, Japan, and the EC—assumed that if they agreed, the other countries would go along. By February 1979 they had resolved all their major differences. The resolution, however, offered fewer benefits to each than initially sought, especially for their domestic farm programs.

In early February the conference began to unravel. After a week's extension it was indefinitely adjourned and has never been recalled.

Informal consultations have been held, but these never uncovered serious prospects for an agreement, even one among the group of six.

The apparent reason for the failure of the talks was LDC intransigence. After the basic drafts had been prepared in 1978, the LDCs warned through the Bangladesh spokesmen on the Interim Committee that "in the absence of firm assurances . . . of assistance within the Convention and the acceptance of special measures in their favor, as proposed," the LDCs might not participate.[10] Because the LDCs were perceived to have something to gain and nothing to lose from any agreement the inner six could agree upon, their threat was not taken seriously. Moreover, some major LDC wheat producers, such as India, displayed flexibility privately and were respected as technically competent. It was something of a surprise, then, that at the culminating session delegates from countries such as Yugoslavia, Pakistan, Iraq, and Tunisia emerged as vigorous proponents of relatively inflexible Group of 77 demands. Generously, these delegates were perceived by Northern delegations as inexperienced, naive, and myopic in their demands and intervention. Considerable hostility toward them developed.

There was substance as well as symbolism to the South's disagreements, however. On price, the Group of 77 wanted a lower band, buying at $125 a ton and selling at $160, compared to the $140 buying trigger (or second falling point) so painfully worked out between Europe and the major exporters, and the $200/$210 release price.[11] A compromise of $140-$180 floated by the Indian delegation was rejected by other LDCs as tactically unsound and was never put forward.

The quantity issue attracted less attention. To satisfy the LDCs and the United States, a "target" of 30 million tons was mentioned in the agreement. The LDCs spent little time pressing for actual substantive commitments to meet it. The U.S. delegation had developed some "objective" criteria (based on consumption) that showed the EEC well below its implied obligation, but the LDCs did not push this issue.

The LDCs did push on special conditions; these would have allowed LDCs to accumulate at lower prices, the $125 third falling point, and release earlier, at the $185 first rising point. Their effect on world markets was expected to be so small that these concessions were not difficult. Still, the United States at the last meeting believed that such release from the general obligations of the convention should not be automatic upon declaration of a country but, rather, reflect a "deserving case." Clearly, it would be politically and economically difficult for an LDC to sit on reserves while its domestic prices were rising substantially. The LDCs rejected any prior approval by the Executive

Committee for initiating "special conditions." They also opposed Australia's view that countries could not join by making a pledge that was "automatically" relieved if their storage facilities were inadequate. Finally, they insisted that there be some financial obligations for assistance in the convention—something more than existed without an agreement. Despite last-minute efforts to find a compromise, led by international-organization executives,[12] an impasse was declared and the conference adjourned. In the last days the United States declared "flexibility" in order to reach an agreement, but offered no new proposals. The WFC thought it would find a $50 million fund to help LDCs with storage costs, but the United States rejected that idea.

One interpretation of the closing drama is that the Group of 77 wrecked a Western traders' commercial deal that offered them little, thus demonstrating their power and depth of commitment to redistributive principles. Another, more cynical version holds the LDCs were deluded into taking the blame for failure to reach an objective that only they really wanted. In the major countries, domestic political and internal bureaucratic support for the final compromise was thin. Perhaps only the long investment in the negotiations themselves, the subjective value of fulfilling, however superficially, the World Food Conference commitment, and the personal attraction of the reserve concept to some of the main negotiators can account for the U.S.-EC compromise. The time for an agreement was ripe, but the value of seizing the opportunity was ambiguous.

There is a postscript. What happened in 1979-82 is important in evaluating the negotiations and their outcome. The old consultative International Wheat Agreement has been extended three times: 1979, 1981, and 1983. The Food Aid Convention as negotiated in 1979 was adopted a year later. Beginning in July 1980 minimum pledges of cereal aid rose from 4.2 to 7.6 million tons. Signing a new FAC was delayed largely so the major donors could use it as a carrot to encourage LDC agreement in preparatory talks. The plan failed. So in 1980 the enlarged FAC agreement was reached without success in finding a new wheat or grains reserve arrangement.

Initiatives to improve food security have shifted. The FAO five-point plan, tabled in 1979, has been pushed as the major food security agenda. In doing so the FAO seeks to be the exclusive champion of food security, often in conflict with other food and UN agencies. The WFC in 1982 gave priority to a proposal for an LDC reserve system. The World Bank has increased its willingness to support LDC food system improvements, including stock facilities. The IMF in 1981 created a special compensatory financing category to finance food imports; however, it has been used by only a handful of countries in the three years following its creation. Meanwhile, the IMF has also brought pressure on poor-country food subsidy and entitlement pro grams, encouraging austerity measures because of their debt burden. The United States created a 4-million-ton wheat reserve to back up its food aid system in 1981.

Interest in internationally coordinated and nationally held stocks, however, was virtually dead in 1984. The African food crisis, while not a global shortage, does bring up issues of food security and supply. Would the IWC reserves have enabled an earlier and more adequate response to the two dozen African emergency cases? Probably not. The use of the reserve for the crisis would have depended on rising prices. Until 1984 however, prices had not been rising. They had not been affected by the African shortages. Therefore the crisis may show more the need for larger international emergency aid commitments than for internationally held wheat stocks.

In any event in 1984 separate domestic policies are the mechanisms for adjusting production and regulating prices. Perhaps some new period of food shortages and panic buying on a global scale will again bring the reserve issue to the agenda. Currently, however, the issue is of low priority to both the North and the South.

The Analysis

Like many events, the failures of the wheat negotiations present analysts with too many explanations. We can better sort out and evaluate various explanations by separating three questions: (1) Why in 1979 did a general deal emerge between the United States and Europe, one acceptable to most other major wheat traders? (2) Why did the Group of 77 refuse to accept this deal? (3) Why did the deal not materialize anyway? The last question is germane because non-Group of 77 countries spent two more years (1979-81) trying to reach an agreement for coordination of wheat stocks. Even if all discussions had ended in February 1979, we would still have to look beyond the North-South standoff for explanations of failure. Otherwise, it would be like believing that a bride and groom called off their announced wedding simply because the bridesmaids and ushers refused to attend. That might explain why a ceremony is canceled, but hardly accounts for why the principal partners fail to go through with their match.

Three explanations account for the near completion of a deal: the congruence of power balances and concessions among the "inner six"; tactical considerations related to GATT negotiations and to trends in world prices; and the development of formulas that offered all parties symbolic rewards as well as guarantees against risk. The very search for an agreement, of course, was premised on the assumption that greater stability in the world wheat market was a collective good for all participants and that the costs of securing this benefit should be shared. Two explanations, separately or together, account for the South's bargaining stance in the failure: international bureaucratic politics and strategic calculation. Finally, five explanations account for the general failure: bad timing, leadership problems, misperceptions, technical barriers to operation, and uncertainty as to benefits.

The Near Agreement

In January 1979 an agreement seemed at hand. Were these expectations merely illusions? I think not. The bargaining process had arrived at a point where deals are finalized and, once made, stay made. The Europeans had extracted major concessions from the United States and other exporters. They had kept grain negotiations out of GATT, an issue that previously had been extremely contentious among Organization for Economic Cooperation and Development (OECD) countries. They had secured an agreement that prices, not quantities, would be used as triggers for coordinating national stock accumulation and release, and the prices to be used were below the community's internal prices. Finally, the EC had held the effective tonnage of the agreement close to the relatively small number it preferred. The EC would be obligated to hold only 3 million tons of wheat—half a million of which would be dedicated to release in food aid channels. The United States and other exporters, however, also achieved some of their goals. They had a guarantee that importers would help them prevent low prices through acquiring stocks. They also gained a favorable climate for trade expansion. All the largest exporters, producers, and importers except India, Egypt, and China[13] indicated general acceptance. Even the Soviets were seeking to participate.

There were tactical reasons that an agreement seemed imminent. The exporters, most importantly the United States with its nearly 50 percent share of the market, expected to reap immediate benefits through higher prices (and thus reduced cost for their farm programs). Classically, commodity agreements in wheat, and in coffee and sugar, have been reached only when prices were low or expected to decline, as was the case. Stock accumulation under the convention could be an immediate value, especially because it was expected to be additional to other stockholding; the U.S. farmer-held reserve, for example, would not count toward this goal, but neither would private stocks in other countries. This may have been an illusory expectation or hope, of course. Importers tactically faced no real domestic costs. The Europeans and Japanese would not have to alter their domestic farm policies, which had prices above the "ceiling." They also could anticipate benefits from surer supplies and lower import prices. Even if these expected future benefits were uncertain and would be available to all importers, not just stockholders, these major U.S. trading partners still would enjoy the immediate benefit of a "successful" conclusion to the general trade negotiations without having to lower their agricultural trade barriers. In general, the principle of stockholding to reduce price variability was accepted and price triggers were found that fit the requirements of both the current Common Agriculture Policy (CAP) and U.S. farm loan rates. The major participants in the wheat market, including the Soviet Union, had made the right moves. The moment had arrived. An agreement was drafted that reflected a balance among the respective countries' power and differing initial preferences. These conditions conform roughly to the requirements for agreement proposed by structural and tactical theories of negotiation.

Not only were these "necessary" conditions met but there was also an additional element present in the bargaining that created a sufficient condition for agreement. This was the symbolic element that arose in the process and was attached to signing an agreement itself. The process aspects of negotiation that Zartman has described emphasize the need for a common formula and a favorable climate for negotiations to reach an accord. These I take to be symbolic rather than economic (material) benefits derived from negotiations. For the wheat negotiators memories of the 1973-74 "crisis" period were still strong. This episode had created personal and governmental commitments to improve world food security. The responsibility was taken seriously by many involved in the negotiations. Technical analysis indicated that the substance of the draft convention was of marginal benefit to the goal of world food security.[14] The stocks were too small, there was no special help for LDCs, and there were no requirements for change in European, Japanese, or Soviet domestic policies or trading actions that had been major contributors to the 1973-74 panic market that so disadvantaged LDCs.[15] As long as even minor obligations for both LDCs and the developed states were created, however, the security goal of the reserves formula remained plausible.

Food security was a major symbolic, and hence political force motivating OECD countries. True, the draft Wheat Trade Convention (WTC), and to a lesser extent the companion Grains and Food Aid Conventions, were basically West-West and East-West deals. Nevertheless, the North-South food security issue was the initial motivating force that brought the negotiating parties together. The issue became increasingly symbolic as the substantive effects of the proposed convention changed and as the East-West trade talks took on greater contextual importance. Still the Wheat Trade Convention, as proposed, was a new approach, one quite different from the economic provisions of the earlier Wheat Trade Conventions, which were essentially multilateral trade contracts with prices but no requirements that participating countries undertake adjustments, e.g. production controls or stockholding. As such it was a formula that corresponded to the system of coordinated national reserves called for by the World Food Conference (WFC) and repeatedly urged by the FAO and WFC. There were substantial domestic audiences and even lobbies inside some of the developed countries, certainly the United States, pushing governments to accept and implement this principle of international reserves.[16] Commitment was substantial, then, to the reserves formula and to the security goal, at least by the United States and some other developed countries. Unlike other North-South negotiations, WTC disagreements were over details, e.g. the price band, not principles or formulas. The issue was how much substantive help for LDC food security must a price stabilization agreement contain. There were real benefits expected by the United States and others in improving, at least symbolically, the goal of food security, benefits in the form of approbation for meeting moral and humanitarian responsibilities. Such responsibilities were especially incumbent upon the United States as the world's major exporter. This moral prod, both internal and external to the cognitive processes of the negotiators, accounts for the continued search for a "successful" agreement, and explains why the transfer of grain negotiations moved rather easily from the GATT subcommittee on grains to the UNCTAD forum. Security was the icing that made the price stabilization cake look worth the price.

Why the South Balked

The refusal of the Group of 77 to go along with the compromises as worked out in January 1979 may be attributed to stupidity or wisdom. In both cases these collective attributes are intimately associated with the more general confrontational character of Group of 77 strategy and bargaining behavior. The group's action in Geneva in February 1979 was consistent with past actions in other international forums such as the UNCTAD commodity talks and FAO meetings. Unlike other commodity negotiations, however, basic principles or even a Group of 77 package was not at stake. Hence, three major Group of 77 weaknesses pinpointed by others—capricious leadership, inadequate technical preparation, and intransigent bargaining styles—were less in evidence in the wheat negotiations than elsewhere, at least until the final weeks.[17]

The most apt way for understanding Group of 77 behavior as collective stupidity is to see it as reflecting *international bureaucratic politics*. This explanation largely ignores the interests of the states banded together under the group's banner, either as a whole or as representing the few most powerful. It focuses instead on the interests and competencies of the organizations and individuals who concretely have carried the banner. I earlier noted that the preparatory work for the final draft was done largely by the "inner six" and under the IWC aegis. This meant that the staff of UNCTAD and the FAO were not closely involved, nor were their leaders committed through their participation to an outcome. In particular, FAO Director-General Saouma, the most prominent spokesman for Group of 77 interests on food matters, was kept informed only through liaison. There was nothing he could take credit for in the proposed agreements. Indeed, the FAO had been deliberately and publicly kept at arm's length from the negotiations, beginning with the earliest meetings.[18] The FAO and Saouma, therefore, had little institutional or personal investment in the negotiation's "success."

The technical understanding of the Group of 77 was always weak. Although occasionally quite able and knowledgeable representatives from India, Egypt, Bangladesh, and Kenya attended meetings, most of the group's representatives at London or Geneva were people permanently stationed in these cities and with little interest or expertise in wheat trade. Much of the continuity of the group's negotiating position came from a cadre of Third World diplomats stationed in Rome who specialized in food affairs. Some of these formed a kind of personal claque around Saouma, seeking to promote LDC interests through every avenue available.[19] When a large number of these Rome food diplomats moved to head delegations at the full negotiating conference, as especially happened at the final session in 1979, the mood and tone of the Group of 77 changed. It became more strident. Delegates asserted strong views about likely future prices or the effects of different storage rules based on little research. The staff of UNCTAD played almost no role in briefing Group of 77 delegates, explaining political implications, or examining likely economic effects of various proposals. Little agreed upon in the earlier months of negotiations was sacrosanct for Group of 77 leaders. The marginal involvement of the group's diplomats in these earlier behind-the-scenes talks gave them little experience to understand the complex trade-offs involved in the final draft or reasons to feel committed to it. Because such delegates were not well briefed, either by UNCTAD or the FAO, it is quite understandable that they did not acquire negotiating norms peculiar to the wheat talks but tended, rather, to project the attitudes and tactics learned from other North-South bargaining. For some delegates, the negotiations may even have been a license for displacing personal vindictiveness onto public discussions under the cloak of LDC righteousness. Whether the strident and inflexible position taken by Group of 77 spokesmen during final days of the talks resulted from personal or collective frustrations, its effects were to anger the Northern delegates and chill interest in accommodating LDC weaknesses.

Three bureaucratic foibles are identifiable in this account. First, Group of 77 delegates with short experience in the wheat negotiations but long experience in other North-South talks would predictably exhibit learned behavior. They had had a chance to develop little trust in other negotiators, had a thin substantive grasp of the issues, and would naturally fall back upon standard operating procedures for the Group of 77 as it had emerged in other forums. If they saw a common formula agreed upon by North and South, they took less note of it than they did the usual case of insufficient concessions. Aside from this regression to standard procedures by group delegates, a second weakness was the nearly total absence of technical expertise. This led to an "off-the-wall" character to group interpretations and analysis. Northern delegates, often with twenty or thirty years' professional experience in economics of agriculture, were neither persuaded nor attracted by the confident pronouncements of Group of 77 novices. Finally, the lack of commitment by the FAO and Saouma seem important. This may have been a result of institutional interests. Failure in Geneva would allow a new champion for food security and reserves to step forward. From the vantage point of Rome, success in Geneva would allow UNCTAD and the North to claim undeserved credit; failure might bring the issue back to Rome—whence it had departed after the 1974 World Food Conference. The FAO might be a forum for getting a better deal for the Group of 77.

All of these institutional and personal factors seemed to have been at work. They help explain what was for some delegates a major misperception, that the Group of 77 could get further concessions in the new wheat agreement. Beyond misperception, however, they account for why the group seemed to prefer nonagreement to the deal as worked out by 1979, even if it risked sabotaging a truly beneficial collective good.

The second major explanation of why the LDCs balked is *strategic calculation*. The LDC refusal to go along with the final package may be viewed from a strategic bargaining perspective as rational.[20] Whether it truly served LDC interests will be considered later. The point is, given the information and utility calculations available to the leaders of the Group of 77 position at the wheat talks, a strong case can be made that they acted rationally. It is plausible to assume that, for the group, the leaders' refusal to accept the last, best offer of the North amounted to a calculation that a better deal could be secured at less cost than gain. They saw few or no resource transfers being offered that did not already exist. The North rejected the idea of a tax on wheat trade to generate funds to pay for improved LDC storage facilities. If LDCs went to the World Bank or the IMF for funding, as the North proposed, such assistance as they received would only reduce the existing fixed amounts available for a competing set of LDC needs. There was no security for food aid in times of stress. The actual levels of food aid in 1978-79 were higher than the proposed aid convention's new minimum pledges. The U.S. proposal that food aid minimums be raised automatically by 20 percent in any period of global grain shortfall (and rising prices) had been quickly rejected by other developed countries. Finally, the Group of 77 could calculate with some confidence that a new FAC might be achieved even if the Wheat Trade Convention (WTC) was not signed, possibly with even higher pledges if European countries were in a concessionary mood. In the WTC itself, the prices for reserve stock accumulation and release were far higher than the LDCs wanted. Some LDCs, certainly India, were convinced by technical arguments that a $140 floor and $185 ceiling would more realistically contain the average trend price, and therefore such a narrower and lower price band held out a chance for near-term stock accumulation. Accumulation was critical if the WTC was to protect LDCs against exorbitant price rises. This view, however, did not prevail. If it had, and if the U.S.-EC deal was seen as the last, best offer for a reserve, then the LDCs should rationally have accepted it according to bargaining theory.

The LDCs were, of course, the weak party to the negotiation and were being asked to pay little. Indeed, the largest resource they controlled was symbolic: the ability to give or withhold praise, rectitude, and legitimacy for the accords. This was not a trivial resource, nor one without consequences for the Group of 77 as a group. Suppose the LDCs were to construe the accord as satisfying the World Food Conference's mandate on reserves and as a positive first step toward achieving a global bargain on commodity management. Because negotiations on many NIEO proposals were failing to achieve either the principles or the substantive benefits that Group of 77 proponents had envisioned, the Wheat Trade Convention would probably be seen as a counterinstance, perhaps even a model agreement. Such a construction by the group would certainly have improved the otherwise increasingly hostile North-South climate. To do this, however, would have required a rational Group of 77 negotiator to calculate that this was the best deal the group could get, and that its effects on other negotiations or future wheat and food security issues would not be to reduce potential benefits. I think they calculated just the opposite. Accepting the deal could have legitimated North-South contracts that continued to serve principally Northern interests and that offered no special income transfers. This violated the working definition of *equity* held by many Group of 77 negotiators. It could weaken their hand elsewhere by creating the appearance that the group was ready to accept any agreement for mutual benefits whether it was "fair" or not. Symbolic calculations, then, were another reason for the Group of 77 to hold firm for a better deal.

In summary, there are two strategic reasons that the LDCs could rationally choose to opt for no agreement on reserves. First, they could reasonably expect that a better deal on the reserve issue was possible, with little costs for them except those of further bargaining. Given that personal calculations of many LDC officials, furthermore, more time in Geneva may have been a benefit rather than a cost. Bargaining theory suggests that one party frequently chooses a less favorable noncooperative outcome rather than risk being tricked into accepting an agreement that offers less than possible. Second, they saw the deal as inadequate in terms of their broader and largely symbolic NIEO perspective. They could not accept as a North-South bargain a deal that offered no foreign aid to them and primarily facilitated developed countries' trading relationships. Such an acceptance would detract from their general economic negotiations and undercut their reputation as a tough bargainer. To be relatively free riders on a price stabilization agreement may have been enough to secure Soviet acquiescence, but it was not enough for the LDCs. It was symbolically incompatible with their image of preferred solutions.

Explaining the Failure

Given the objective of international coordination of reserve stocks, the 1975-79 international wheat talks clearly failed. The purely consultative agreement was merely extended in 1979 and 1981. Even the Food Aid Convention, which was achieved in 1980, achieved pledges of only 7.6 million toward the target of 10 million tons set in 1974.[21] I find five general explanations for this failure.

Bad timing. Bad timing is the first explanation. In some sense the time was never right for an agreement because one or another party could always see a time in the future when a better agreement would be generally acceptable or more realistic. In 1975-76 world wheat stocks were at their lowest level in twenty years. Although production improvements promised a better supply situation, prices had just begun to fall. Pressure to create a security reserve arising from the food crisis was at its zenith, but it was an inappropriate time to accumulate stocks. Stocking then would surely have driven prices upward again. Importers had little incentives to hold stocks above their "working-level needs" in this situation. Exporters, conversely, were not going to agree to a multilateral contract guaranteeing a maximum price at or below the EC's Common Agricultural Policy (CAP) price simply to help the very European agricultural policies that were the subject of their attack. The U.S.-Soviet trade insecurity had been the most threatening concern, and the five-year, 6-to-8-million-ton bilateral agreement of 1975 resolved that. In short, no one—LDCs, developed importers, developed exporters, or the Soviets—found the time propitious in 1976 for an accord.

By 1977 world grain prices dropped to a point nearly as low in real terms as those during the 1930s depression, and the interest of exporters in a stockholding scheme mounted. Exporting countries, moreover, maintained an incentive for importers to join in holding stocks by turning to acreage controls. This promised to lower production rather than to build stocks, as had occurred earlier. Another factor was the Carter administration. It favored international action to fight hunger, as evidenced in the creation of a World Hunger Commission, and it was not wed to a free market ideology. Reserves were, therefore, philosophically acceptable to major officials of the Department of Agriculture. Thus, in 1977-78, negotiations made progress. When modestly increasing prices leveled off in late 1978, a compromise on a price band with a bottom acceptable to Europe and a top acceptable to the United States was reached. A final timing factor was the desire to conclude an agreement by the end of the Tokyo trade negotiations. For these reasons the time was ripe in the winter-spring of 1978-79 to reach an agreement. This corridor of good timing slipped by when the Group of 77 resisted an accord. After April 1979 prices rose, the GATT round ended, and the moment was lost.

Leadership Problems. Successful negotiations require imagination, goodwill, diligence on the part of negotiators, and a willingness of the more powerful parties to bear a disproportionate share of the costs. Securing the collective good of price stability, as a reserve arrangement purported to provide, was a special responsibility for the United States as the leading exporter.[22] A second explanation for the failure is that negotiating leadership and special U.S. willingness to pay the cost or bear the risk were inadequate.

The United States, along with Canada and occasionally Australia, had provided world reserves in the 1950s and 1960s. Many expected this to continue. However, domestic farm programs changed, and these exporters since 1970 have deliberately sought to avoid such large reserve holdings. In 1975-79, domestic interests lobbied against a return to unilateral reserve holding.[23] The decline in the United States position and relative economic strength in the world economy, manifested through the 1971 devaluation and the negative balance of trade during most of the 1970s, made U.S. foreign policy leaders reluctant to continue paying adjustment burdens for international collective goods.[24] Thus, in both the Ford and Carter administrations, the United States refused to enter into guarantees of the very kind it had provided its trading partners in the early wheat agreements or to provide LDCs food aid at levels equal to the first fifteen years of food aid programs. Under the first Wheat Agreement, signed in 1949, for instance, the United States sold wheat to importing countries for less than the spot market price in compliance with the ceiling figure in the agreement. This was a concession the United States would not make in the 1970s.

U.S. leadership did help break impasses in the wheat negotiations. With reduced U.S. military and economic power, however, U.S. negotiating initiatives were less potent. Furthermore, they were limited by domestic politics. In 1977 the renewal of the four-year farm bill took most of the attention of the top officials in USDA. This delayed talks on reserves. The bill itself, by creating a new system of domestic reserves, also undercut incentives for importers to do more by way of stockholding. As one European asked, "Why should we pay for what the United States will do anyway?"[25]

Among individual negotiators no one proved emotionally committed to reserves, particularly during the final session. Saouma did little to spur compromise and some suspect his leadership was more in the form of sabotage. Villain and Hathaway, while satisfied with the framework for the deal worked out, were also not prepared to make additional concessions for such an ambiguous goal. Maurice Williams, a vigorous sideline proponent of the reserve scheme and head of the World Food Council worked to promote support, but he had few personal or international resources with which to succeed. The food security issue had sharply declined in importance on the international agenda since 1974, and no state or individual emerged to provide leadership toward agreement as had occurred earlier at the World Food Conference or in the establishment of other conference proposals, such as IFAD and the WFC.

Misperception. Three major misperceptions also account for the deadlock that emerged in 1979. First there was a general misconception, one fostered by Western leaders at the Rome conference, that a trade agreement could simultaneously serve food security needs. In fact, the design of security and trade agreements might be similar but would certainly have different rules and dimensions. Second, the "inner six" nations that worked out the major elements of the agreement falsely assumed that the LDCs would eventually accept what concessions were offered; for the sake of efficiency they were not heavily consulted. This, of course, proved to be a misreading of the Group of 77. Finally, the group miscalculated that an agreement wanted by both developed country importers and exporters, and reached only after several years of negotiations, was sufficiently valued by them to be worth saving at the cost of at least some additional concessions. This last misperception was crucial.

The LDC leaders had no authority to offer concessions, but they believed that they were in a position to stand firm in order to extract further concessions. They reasoned that nonagreement was more acceptable to them than to the United States or Europe, hence their price band offer of $125-160 negotiable." They misperceived a willingness on the part of the United States and the EC to negotiate any further on price. To reopen that deal would jeopardize the whole agreement. Strangely enough, Group of 77 leaders did not appreciate that packages worked out among a major bloc in North-South encounters are usually quite inflexible; this in spite of their own experience in creating rather rigid negotiating packages.

Technical Barriers. There were a number of issues of a more technical character that concerned negotiators. The resolution of these in practice would influence the true effects and hence the virtues of the reserve system. These issues, moreover, had not been resolved to general satisfaction. Three are prominent in this regard: wheat equivalences, verification, and displacement. In the Wheat Agreements of the 1950s a Canadian wheat was used as a price reference, although all grades and types of wheat traded were to fit the price band. Eventually, trade in this wheat was judged too thin for it to serve as a reference. In 1967 a complicated system of equilibrating higher- and lower-priced wheat was worked out. Within a year a major flaw in this system appeared. Australian wheat had been pegged below U.S. wheat but had improved in quality. The Australians, by underpricing their wheat without breaking the floor price, were able to win a number of sales away from U.S. exporters. It took high-level bilateral threats from the United States to force the Australians to agree to reduce the differential for their wheat (i.e. raise their price).[26] In 1979 the system returned to a single indicator but was to use an average of seven wheat varieties as a reference. This compromise, still left doubts about problems that could arise from shifts in wheat strains.

Verification was another concern. Participants in the stock reserve arrangement were expected to supply the International Wheat Council with information on their stock operations, first to facilitate consultations and unilateral adjustments, and later to demonstrate faithful performance of buying or selling responsibilities under the Wheat Trade Convention. Skepticism existed as to how the Soviet Union, because of its traditional secrecy, and some LDCs, because of their poor management systems and corruption, would fulfill this task. If countries reported they were holding or releasing stocks, what proof, if any, could be required? What if a government parastatal exchanged stocks with the agency designated as the government stockholder—would that constitute compliance? These questions led some negotiators to discount LDC and Soviet participation.

Displacement posed the most serious intellectual issue. What guarantee was there that private traders or nonsignatory countries would not adjust their own stockholding behavior so as to nullify the effectiveness of the reserve? Might not governments, especially LDCs try to load most of the costs of their existing stockholding operations, i.e. needed domestic working stocks, onto a stockholding pledge? If so, they could maximize the aid they were eligible to receive to assist in meeting their obligations under the proposed convention. Negotiators wondered whether review committees of the IWC would be able to detect violations, whether of the spirit or the letter of the agreement, and whether having done so, they could do anything useful about it. Even if governments did not construe normal stocks and costs as meeting convention obligations, i.e. doing nothing "extra," private reserves held by farmers and traders would probably shrink.[27] Furthermore, if large supplies loomed ahead, speculation might increase as purchases for the reserve were under way. At this point traders with long positions could sell at the floor price, but could sell short in the futures markets, anticipating a price drop once governments reached their stock accumulation limit. A large reserve commitment would be needed to prevent displacement and speculation effects, both of which seemed to have occurred in 1973-75. The actual total of commitments in 1979, however, was too small for this purpose.[28]

Uncertainty. Uncertainty over benefits was a psychological condition confronting negotiators. Once the symbolic benefit of achieving a global bargain with the South for food security was removed, the remaining benefits of the Wheat Trade Convention were too uncertain to make a reserve agreement worthwhile. Technical reservations in regard to effects cast doubt that many alleged benefits would be realized. For the United States and the other countries, the agreement offered little promise to improve trade relations and little help in legitimating or managing domestic farm programs. The reserve was seen by the United States as too small to have much market effect. The government would be carrying financial costs that would outweigh financial gains. Exporters lose from stockholding, according to many analysts. Rationally, then, exporters would hold stocks only to reassure customers or because storage costs, shared by others, were cheapest there. Suppose, however, that holding of public stocks at fixed prices, in fact, would discourage private stockholding as noted earlier. If the decline in private holding turned out to be equal, or even greater, than the stocks held publicly, the reserve would be counterproductive, not stabilizing prices and shifting a stock burden from private to government hands.

Consider these negative arguments. When supply and demand trends were roughly in balance the reserves would merely cost the government money for storage and interest. If there were a shortfall, as in the 1972-74 period, the stocks would be too small to hold prices within the agreed band. If prices rose after all stocks were released, the panic market and price rise might be greater than if releases had been from privately held stocks. Such reasoning raised doubt in the minds of negotiators and made it difficult for negotiators to see unambiguous advantages in the convention. They could, however, see clear financial costs, some loss of future national discretion, and possible domestic political costs to implement obligations at a bad time. In addition, "selling" the agreement to domestic farm interests and national legislatures who frequently opposed government stockholding was an additional cost. This uncertainty as to the agreement's real effects, its possible domestic political repercussions, especially for the United States, and the usual uncertainty about future market conditions eroded much of the commercial trade advantages the convention sought to secure. In contrast, bilateral trade agreements, which all major exporters had found useful in the preceding years, offered a simpler and surer alternative.[29] The trade advantages for the North, then, were too uncertain in the U.S.-EC "deal" of February 1979 for it to be consummated without an LDC blessing.

Perhaps if no food security objective had clouded the 1978 negotiations and the undertaking had been understood as a GATT/IWC trade undertaking, an agreement would have been reached during the favorable time of late 1978 and early 1979.[30] Reasons that this was a real possibility have been reviewed. Even so, it would not have achieved much as a reserve, given the shift in market conditions. Its main benefit would have been symbolic, creating a framework for improved global stock management.

Evaluation and Lessons

Was the failure to achieve international agreement for a system of grain reserves a net loss for the South? Was it a negative outcome for the global community? Most negotiators for the North, as well as officials of the World Food Council, thought it was a loss to the South. The U.S. team's chief negotiator characterized the outcome as "the LDCs snatching defeat from the jaws of victory."[31] The absence of expressions of regret from Group of 77 representatives, however, and their subsequent success in securing improvements in food security through several different, nonstocking strategies provides little evidence that the group shared then or now this interpretation. If it was not a Southern defeat, then, it does not seem to have been a loss for the North either.

Evaluation

I believe the failure of the wheat talks was for the South a net gain, *given* the objectives of the South and the events in 1979-81. From a global perspective, however, it was a real loss, both to the elusive goal of food security and to prospects for North-South collaboration.

The South can still live with its scuttling of the talks. With the relatively low prices and large stocks existing in 1983-84, the Southern importers continue to be well served. If we assume the proposed agreement itself or its failure had no measurable effect on the subsequent behavior of wheat producers or wheat trade, even if agreement had been reached there would have been no stockholding under it. In February 1979 prices were just at the proposed $140/ton purchase price. The forecast was for a slight decline, and indeed in early April prices fell to below $140. By July, however, when stock purchases could have begun if the agreement had been signed, prices had risen. From a low of $112/ton in 1976-77 and $116 in 1977-78, prices rose to

$166 in June of 1979 and to $201 by November 1980.[32] There were no escalators to adjust the real 1979 floor price of $140 to the "inflated" prices of later years; reserve stocks would not have and probably never would be built under the convention as drafted.

There was a second flaw in the agreement with respect to benefits for the South. If stockholding had occurred, some countries, such as India, would have been expected to hold stocks during a period when a domestic production shortfall would have dictated for them to release stocks. Although escape mechanisms were specified to allow LDCs to avoid the most perverse instances of applying international policy to national conditions, such provisions were contradictory to the general purpose of the reserve. It is difficult to find any instance where LDCs individually or collectively would have been better off substantively if the agreement had been signed. Following the collapse of the talks, the food aid convention guarantees were secured anyway, the IMF set up a special facility for compensatory food financing, and reserve stocks were built, including a U.S. 4-million-ton food aid (wheat) reserve. By 1982 the United States had 45 million tons of farmer-held reserves, roughly 15 million tons of wheat and 30 million of corn, and during 1983 U.S. total reserves were projected to surpass 100 million tons.

The first serious challenge to this conclusion as to the low substantive value of the agreement is the "food crisis" that African states faced in 1983-84. Because world prices remained low, the reserve agreement would have provided little relief for this shortage. Emergency food aid and development assistance to aid restructuring of markets, producer incentives, and food relief operations were needed, and to some degree provided. The convention would have guaranteed none of this. The fact that the United States chose *not* to open its 4-million-ton emergency wheat reserve during this period and that many states increased their minimum FAC commitments suggests that reserves would not have been critical in the first place, and that humanitarian concerns may drive policy without formal international commitments made in advance.

Only on subjective factors might the South have lost by its failure to accept the February 1979 deal. It is arguable that the establishment of a wheat reserve agreement itself and the commitments in principle that would have flowed from it were of considerable value to the LDCs. If such an agreement had been achieved (and it must be recalled that it might not have been achieved, even if there had been no LDC opposition), the result would have created a different context and climate within which food security issues could be addressed. Some of the LDC redistribution proposals might have been advanced if they had accepted the proposed reserve scheme. Furthermore, a "positive" outcome in the food arena might have had spillover effects, changing the climate or outcome of other North-South negotiations. In general, perhaps greater amity rather than enmity would have stemmed from the wheat negotiations. Could the commodity management and stock-holding provisions of the convention have been valuable precedents in arguments for commodity agreements by the South, irrespective of their modest near-term substantive benefits? Given the emotion-infused demands of the Group of 77 for agreement in principle on commodity management for its Integrated Program for Commodities/Common Fund proposals, the symbolic aspects of the proposed agreement should have been desirable.

Just the opposite, however, seems to have been the case. For reasons that were simultaneously rational and irrational, the South balked, refusing to accept the draft as a serious North-South deal. For the South it was too much an OECD-designed arrangement. The inference seems clear: the South wants commodity agreements on its terms or prefers none at all. The projection of bureaucratic and private motives by Group of 77 negotiators and their organizations seems to have been behind the intransigence they displayed in February 1979; that this expressive behavior could also be considered rational is an independent, perhaps even coincidental outcome. In summary, the negotiations failed, but the South won. Food security was not to be achieved by commercial marketing agreements. Food security was an LDC issue and will have to be settled in a forum more to their liking, most probably the FAO. Until a major new threat to security arises, however, little will happen. In the meantime the experience and legitimation of a system of reserves, at least in principle, have been lost.

Lessons

In conclusion, I will speculate about lessons to be drawn from this case. I. William Zartman, in his introduction to this book, proposes various hypotheses to explain North-South negotiating outcomes. I will review certain of these hypotheses as a way to highlight the major lessons of the wheat negotiations. After discussing the bargaining lessons, I will also offer some substantive lessons regarding the prospects for future food security negotiations.

The first lesson of the failure is that even agreement upon principles, a factor usually sought by the South, does not guarantee success. In the wheat talks the initial demand was for international coordination of national reserves. This principle was accepted by both North and

South at the World Food Conference as a realistic alternative to an international body actually managing reserves, as in the Integrated Program for Commodities (IPC) proposals. It was not a maximum demand that locked sides into intractable positions. It was too vague and hedged, however, to be perceived as a principle that challenged the existing order. From 1975 to 1979 the negotiations went through considerable incremental change. They failed to achieve their initial principled objective because in the eyes of the Group of 77 the final stock formula, along with the absence of compensating concessions, offered too little of the goal the group understood to be the central concern: LDC food security. Thus the principle of reserves was insufficient without the substance of direct resource transfers.

The second lesson is that compromise packages worked out without full participation will not seem balanced to those excluded from the trade-offs. A deal was reached between the United States and the EC whereby trade-offs occurred. Consequently, the North-South aspect of the negotiations failed because once the U.S.-EC deal was struck, there was no way for the North to compromise to a significant extent. Concessions by the North were hard, in part, because they posed a sizeable threat that the developed country bargain would become unstruck, perhaps as Canada or Australia backed away. At least in this possibility we see in the North what Rothstein observed among the Group of 77 in the IPC negotiations and Ravenhill in the Lomé diplomacy: inflexibility by one group to a negotiation in order to preserve a deal within the group.[33]

A general axiom of political science is that crosscutting cleavages facilitate agreement. Such cleavages reduce zero-sum conflict, and increase incentives for accommodation. Although there were crosscutting cleavages in the wheat case the lesson from this case is that they do not always facilitate agreement. Cleavages within the North and South, as well as the East-West dimension, encouraged compromise, bargaining, and expectations of success. However, these divisions also encouraged a neglect of "Southern interests," and this proved a mistake. The North was divided on concessions: Europe was far more willing to grant special conditions for stockholding obligations; exporters, such as the United States and Australia, were more willing to guarantee higher levels of concessional food aid. Not only were there Western and North-South splits but there were East-West trade differences. Within the South, furthermore, there were special cases, e.g. exporters such as Argentina, large producers, such as India, and large commercial importers, such as Egypt. The three- or four-sided character of the negotiations, however, did not aid agreement. India and

Argentina, natural mediators, had little sway, while the U.S.-EC split allowed the South to be treated as a free rider to the reserve scheme and resulted in its not being taken seriously until the very end.

Do specific functional negotiations and work by small groups tend to be more fruitful than "global" negotiations, as Zartman suggests? In general, yes. Progress on a draft and on major compromises were worked out by small groups. The large forums were more legitimating theaters than negotiating forums. Small-group effectiveness is surely a truism for all negotiations except perhaps in elections.[34] The fourth lesson is, however, that small size alone is no guarantee of success. The Preparatory Group in 1975-77 made little progress. Smaller meetings at the Negotiating Conference did facilitate progress and the subsequent formulation of positions by the major groups. It also allowed the full extent of LDC intransigence to be concealed for some time, perhaps aiding misperception. A fair amount of education occurred in these talks regarding the world wheat and grain markets and how they worked. The prospect of agreement was much closer here on principles. In this respect a functionally specific topic aided negotiations. Still, the fact remains that the Carter administration did reach a more global agreement with the South on a Common Fund (however ineffectual and unfulfilled) and failed to reach one on the Wheat Agreement.

The wheat talks corroborate a fifth lesson: that a party to a negotiation will hold out for concessions when it perceives its willingness to accept nonagreement is greater than the willingness of others. The assumption is that the other party will offer further concessions as a preferred alternative to losing the agreement. This lesson is well illustrated in the two cases of misperception cited earlier. The U.S.-EC deal presupposed an LDC willingness to accept the best offer on reserves and expected to make none but cosmetic concessions. The Group of 77, alternatively, calculated that the developed countries would, at least eventually, offer a better deal because the proposed agreement served its commercial interests. Thanks to the perception by each party that the other was the least willing to forsake an agreement, neither side made concessions in the last round of North-South bargaining. This was an iterative process, however, as the value of the agreement varied in the calculations of the parties with changes in market forecasts. A further lesson seems to be that misperception can mar an opportunity that otherwise offers common benefits.

Confrontation was not a useful Group of 77 tactic, although it was very much in evidence at the last session of the wheat negotiations.

Whether it arose as a conscious tactic to enhance group solidarity or arose spontaneously from frustration is unclear. On balance, the latter seems more the case. There was substantial solidarity without hostility during the earlier stages of the talks. Because the earlier stages produced little change desired by the Group of 77, the shift to confrontation is understandable as a strategy shift and an expression of frustration. It was either ineffective or counterproductive because it led to no concessions and soured other negotiators.

A final lesson is that the South has few resources it can use as sanctions in negotiations. Zartman's point is clearly upheld in this case. Symbolic rewards or punishments for "moral" obligations were the principal negotiating weapons available to Southern negotiators. The South could have offered to share more in stockholding or bear more of the risk, but, in fact, the negotiators in Geneva were not authorized to agree to anything that would amount to a financial obligation on the part of their governments. They were prepared to negotiate redistribution to the South, not burden sharing. With moral authority and symbolic action their only resources, the South had little ability to get what it wanted on the reserves issue, but these resources were of some value in achieving the new Food Aid Convention to the Wheat Agreement. The developed countries were prepared to raise the floor on this institutionalized international welfare mechanism. Moral concern arising from the food vulnerability of LDCs was a negotiating resource the South could and did utilize.

These lessons point to an overall conclusion, one that applies to North-South relations generally. The South needs more resources before it can "succeed." But can the South develop greater resources? "Collective self-reliance," as Zartman suggests, seems a doubtful path. There is little evidence from events since 1979 that greater self-reliance among LDCs can or will occur, except as a rhetorical slogan. Little collective management of food stocks has taken place, although regional food security schemes are under consideration, most notably in Asia, and the 1982 proposal by the World Food Council for LDC reserves is a logical outcome of the failure of the wheat reserve negotiations. In any event, the requirement of more self-reliant strategies by the South is certainly a general lesson from these negotiations. It is the natural option in a world where collective insurance schemes are failing, for now global food security will be at best a by-product of narrower policy measures taken for reasons of commercial trade interests.

Import dependency may be another path to enhanced power for the

South, however. It is possible that by the end of the 1980s China, Egypt, Nigeria, and other LDCs will constitute the bulk of major importers. The EC is importing less each year, and since 1980 has been a net wheat exporter. The Soviet Union is capable of sharply reducing its wheat imports (as in 1977-78). If LDCs become the major importers, surpassing Europe and the Soviet Union and equaling Japan in importance, then the major exporters will be faced with a Group of 77 with potentially far more power, and with far more stake in a shared stockholding scheme. Until such a power shift occurs, food security will continue to be a North-South issue, but not one jointly resolvable.

Notes

1. I want to thank Dale Hathaway, Timothy Josling, Daniel Morrow, and Thomas Saylor for their help in understanding the wheat negotiations.
2. Based on FAO data in *Food Outlook*, no. 5 (Rome: FAO, 1982), p. 2.
3. These figures are taken from "International Wheat Agreements: A Historical and Critical Background," Ex (74/75)2/2) (London: International Wheat Council, 1974); Daniel T. Morrow, "The Economics of the International Stockholding of Wheat" (Ph.D. diss., Harvard University, November 1980).
4. For a discussion of various reserve purposes and schemes see David J. Eaton and W. Scott Steele, eds., *Analyses of Grain Reserves, A Proceedings*, Economic Research Service Report No. 634, (Washington: Department of Agriculture, August 1976).
5. Martin so argued in an address at the Woodrow Wilson International Center for Scholars in December 1974, immediately after the Rome conference, as well as at the September 1975 American Political Science Association Meetings. Martin's views were a good distillation of the U.S. State Department's thinking at the time.
6. See *Annual Report 1976-77* (London: International Wheat Council, 1978), pp. 24-25.
7. On this point, see Alexander H. Sarris and Lance Taylor, "Cereal Stocks, Food Aid and Food Security for the Poor," in *The New International Economic Order: The North-South Debate*, ed. Jagdish N. Bhagwati (Cambridge: MIT Press, 1977), pp. 276-77.
8. Based on a talk by Richard Bell at Swarthmore College, April 1977.
9. Eventually the EC decided to go with its lowest option of 1.65 million tons rather than 2.0, an increase of only 28 percent, compared to the U.S. increase of 137 percent.
10. Report of the Interim Committee, Geneva, November 1978, Appendix B.
11. $200 as the second rising point for the first year, and $210 thereafter.
12. Particularly active were Dunkel, head of the conference; Parrote, the IWC executive secretary; and Maurice Williams, head of the World Food Council.
13. India and Egypt, while often cooperative, remained in the Group of 77. Turkey and Argentina were neither treated nor behaved as members of the

Group of 77. China was not a member of the Wheat Council and did not join in the talks.

14. See, for example, Morrow, "The Economics of the International Stockholding of Wheat."

15. The negative effects on world markets of actions by these countries, including stockholding above their historic averages and artificially maintaining low domestic prices, are discussed in Robert Paarlberg, "Shifting and Sharing Adjustment Burdens," *International Organization* (Summer, 1978); 655-78; and D. Gale Johnson, Introduction to *The Politics of Food,* ed. D. Gale Johnson (Chicago: Chicago Council on Foreign Relations, 1980), pp. 2-4.

16. As evidence of this, see the Senate Foreign Relations Committee Hearings, 8 May 1979. Church World Service representative Larry Minear lamented the failed negotiations, calling the potential International Wheat Agreement "a measure with far-reaching implications for world food security." Maurice Williams, the World Food Council's executive director, told the General Assembly on 19 March 1979: "Governments have so far failed to meet their responsibilities in the area of world food security." Quoted from testimony of Minear (Washington, D.C.: Xerox copy of statement from Church World Service/Lutheran World Relief, May 1979).

17. The Group of 77's bargaining rationale and behavior are well documented in Robert Rothstein, *Global Bargaining* (Princeton: Princeton University Press, 1979); and Christopher Brown, *The Political and Social Economy of Commodity Control* (London: Macmillan, 1980). Both books emphasize the capricious role of key individuals, the weak technical backup available for Group of 77 negotiators, and the occasional inconsistency of positions they took as a result of the need to create proposals that appear attractive to many countries, and then their subsequent inflexibility on these in order not to undermine the solidarity of the group.

18. An FAO request to attend meetings at the IWC called by the United States in 1975, for example, was denied.

19. Some cynical observers of food diplomacy in Rome believe the ties among this group were reinforced by Saouma's interest in being reelected in 1981 (against past FAO precedent) and the interest of several poor country diplomats in landing a "soft" job with the FAO.

20. See I. William Zartman, and Maureen Berman, *The Practical Negotiation* (New Haven: Yale University Press, 1981).; Charles Lockhart, *Bargaining in International Conflict* (New York: Columbia University Press, 1979), pp. 71-87; Glenn Snyder and Paul Diesing, *Conflict among Nations* (Princeton: Princeton University Press, 1977), pp. 361-418.

21. At the 1974 Rome conference a quick analysis of food aid levels over the previous decade revealed a high of over 15 million tons and a low of about 5 million tons. Without further analysis, the prominent, obvious solution of a 10 million ton "need" target was set by the conference in a classic example of Schelling's "prominate solution." See Thomas Schelling, *Strategy of Conflict* (Cambridge: Harvard University Press, 1960).

22. This inequity of burden is classically the case with collective goods. See Marcus Olson, Jr., *The Logic of Collective Action* (Cambridge: Harvard University Press, 1965).

23. The role of the United States in providing a surrogate role to international

reserves is discussed in Jon B. McLin, "Surrogate International Organization and the Case for World Food Security, 1949-1969," *International Organization* 33 (Winter 1979): pp. 35-55. John Schnitken, a former top USDA official, is one of the few agriculture leaders to have favored a return to unilateral U.S. stock building. See his article, "Grain Reserves Now," *Foreign Policy,* no. 22 (Spring 1976).

24. On the effects of a decline in political hegemony on the ability to bear economic burdens by both England and later the United States, see Stephen Krasner, *Defending the National Interest* (Princeton: Princeton University Press, 1978).

25. Interview with the deputy director of the Agricultural Directorate of the EC, Brussels, November 1978.

26. See Raymond F. Hopkins, "Global Management Networks: The Internationalization of Domestic Bureaucracies," *International Social Science Journal* (January 1978): 31-46.

27. Morrow, "The Economics of the International Stockholding of Wheat," pp. 155-62, makes a strong case on this point.

28. Ibid.

29. See Barbara Huddleston, "World Food Security and a New International Wheat Agreement" (Washington, D.C: IFPRI, September 1981, mimeographed).

30. Dale Hathaway, as undersecretary of agriculture, was the chief official overseeing the negotiations. He now believes that a strict trade accord was possible then (conversation, Washington, D.C., 11 August 1982).

31. Based on a conversation with Thomas Saylor, the U.S. head of delegation, 12 August 1982, and reports of the WFC activities, including those of Maurice Williams.

32. *Food Outlook* (Rome: FAO), various issues, including April and September 1979, June and December 1980, and May 1982, using the table for wheat prices, U.S. #2 hard winter wheat.

33. See Rothstein, *Global Bargaining.*

34. See, for example, Robert Dahl, *After the Revolution* (New Haven: Yale University Press, 1970), on the value of small groups for economy-of-decision-making point, as well as work by Dahl and Edward Tufte.

6

The Multifiber Arrangement:
The Third Reincarnation

Joseph Pelzman

In the present environment of North-South relationships, the Arrangement Regarding International Trade in Textiles, or more commonly the Multifiber Arrangement (MFA III), represents the reality of managed trade between the North and the South. This elaborate trade management system was officially born in 1974, although implicitly conceived more than a decade earlier. MFA III represents the culmination of eight years of fine tuning and fourteen years of experimentation with predecessor agreements. It thus differs from other North-South negotiations being discussed in this series in that the negotiations for MFA III did not represent an attempt to create a new agreement in a previously unregulated environment but, rather, represented an exercise whereby a renewal was being negotiated with some major modifications. In fact, some would argue that MFA III was not simply an extension of the original MFA but a very perverse and highly protectionist instrument created anew in Geneva in December 1982.

Given the debate among industry specialists as to the nature of the resulting beast, it is the purpose of this chapter to present and analyze the negotiating process that resulted in MFA III. In the process, the account will show how a trade management system once established and legitimatized as the status quo begets a life of its own and survives despite the fact that throughout the entire negotiating process it appeared that the MFA was finally going to die.

The chapter is organized as follows: the first section will briefly outline the history of the textile trade management system up to MFA II; the next will present the negotiating environment for MFA III; and the third will discuss the negotiating process and its outcome, and present a number of implications arising therefrom.

The International Regulation of Textile Trade

The MFA, like its predecessor agreements, is akin in many respects to a system of orderly marketing agreements (OMAs). As such it has a number of characteristics that apply to all OMAs. First, they are umbrella agreements within which bilateral agreements are negotiated between an importing and an exporting country. Under MFA II the United States had twenty bilateral agreements with its major suppliers, each limiting imports of a specific list of commodities as well as their growth.

Second, OMAs provide for quantitative limits based on product type rather than price. Under MFA II the United States negotiated limits on an aggregate country basis as well as within-country limits, and established group limits and within such limits commodity-specific limits. Within the commodity-specific limits the quota was set as either specific limits or minimum consultation levels, or consultation categories or agreed limits or designated consultation limits. A list of these quantitative restraints for 1981 is provided in Table 1 for the twenty countries. The four major suppliers (Hong Kong, South Korea, Taiwan, and the People's Republic of China) have the largest share of the U.S. market and consequently have a vested interest in maintaining their market shares within the MFA system. Conversely, new entrants are inclined to demand a larger share of the pie, which if restricted from growing, must come from the major suppliers.[1]

The third characteristic of OMAs is that they generally start as selective restrictions applied to only a few dynamic producers. After a prolonged period of bargaining and selectivity, they begin to encompass more players and a wider net of goods. The MFA should therefore be viewed as an extension of the LTA (Long Term Cotton Textile Arrangement), which itself was an extension of the STA (Short Term Cotton Textile Arrangement), which in turn was born of the initial postwar Japanese voluntary export controls (OMAs) on cotton products. Over the past twenty-five years the United States expanded these restrictions from cotton applied only to Japan, to cotton applied to all the major suppliers, to all fibers applied to all LDC (developing countries) and NIC (new industrialized countries) exporters. Thereafter, the MFA took on a life of its own but should not be viewed as an agreement born in 1973. To understand the negotiating process for MFA III better, one must first review the perverse history that led to it, beginning with the first postwar Japanese OMA to the conclusion of MFA II.

Pre-MFA Period

In the early 1950s the U.S. textile industry was faced with market adjustment problems precipitated by excess capacity in cotton textiles, the shift to synthetic fibers, and technological changes, and by increased imports of certain cotton textile products from Japan. As a partial solution to its problems the industry began to seek protection from import competition. The primary exporter targeted was Japan; in 1957 Japanese cotton textile and apparel exports concentrated in cotton ginghams and velveteens, accounted for over 60 percent of total U.S. imports. The U.S. textile industry filed four escape-clause petitions with the U.S. Tariff Commission between January and June of 1956.[2] In response to escape-clause actions and fearing legislation authorizing import restrictions, Japan in 1957 agreed to voluntarily control its exports of cotton textiles and apparel to the United States.

Although this agreement was successful in limiting Japanese exports of cotton products to the United States, it encouraged increased imports from such new entrants as Hong Kong, Portugal, Egypt, and India.[3] It soon became obvious to the United States that a more comprehensive solution was necessary. From the U.S. point of view a global market arrangement that would consider both the long-term problems of expanding textile industries in the LDCs and the contracting textile and apparel industries in the developing countries (DCs) would be appropriate. In particular, the United States desired to avoid legislated import restrictions, preferring instead a legitimized system of trade restrictions whereby the world market would be divided, such that both the LDCs and DCs would share responsibility for an orderly market suitable for LDC expansion and yet minimally damaging to the U.S. market.

Multilateral discussions designed to reorder textile trade in accordance with these objectives were initiated by the United States and held under the auspices of the General Agreement on Tariffs and Trade (GATT) beginning 16 June 1961. The outcome was the first of a series of multilateral arrangements known as the Short Term Cotton Textile Arrangement (STA), which went into effect for one year beginning 1 October 1961. A more comprehensive agreement, known as the Long Term Arrangement on Cotton Textiles (LTA), went into effect for five years on 1 October 1962, and was extended twice through 1973.

The key feature of the LTA and the STA was the so-called market-disruption provision. Under the GATT safeguard clause (Article XIX), emergency protective action such as imposition of quantitative restric-

TABLE 1
U.S. Bilateral Quotas and Fulfillment Levels under MFA II for 1981
(in thousand equivalent square yards)

	Aggregate Limit	Group 1 Limit	Group 2 Limit	Group 3 Limit	Group 4 Limit	Specific Limits	No. of items on Specific List	Total imports restricted by specific limits
Brazil	159890	56102	68725	35063	100845	100845	17	69084
China	–	–	–	–	–	98920	8	111160
Costa Rica	–	–	–	–	–	7892	1	7854
Egypt	–	–	–	–	–	–	–	–
Haiti	–	–	–	–	–	26619	6	10685
Hong Kong	1140630	313719	712647	70839	43422	789572	33	622317
India	228110	184740	–	43370	–	83242	7	33969
Japan	–	–	–	–	–	–	3	–
South Korea	703173	173978	547037	15860	–	470614	30	439513
Macau	45570	44200	1516	–	–	29438	22	37499
Malaysia	–	–	–	–	–	24139	14	19896
Mexico	–	–	–	–	–	80803	14	33307
Pakistan	188038	162966	27579	–	–	153573	3	127798
Philippines	278722	24552	–	–	–	232841	104	133017
Poland	53753	–	41685	2215	802	45594	22	14018
Romania	–	–	32294	28000	–	16947	7	11332
Singapore	278251	62355	213351	3543	–	111203	18	77004
Taiwan	903915	197728	701034	5713	–	561810	24	525008
Thailand	–	–	64927	–	–	66367	20	42946
Yugoslavia	–	–	–	–	–	816	1	4

	Total Imports	Restricted Imports as a Percent of Total Specific Limits	Restricted Imports as a Percent of Total Imports	Country Share Total Imports
Brazil	75963	68.3	90.9	1.65
China	593564	112.4	18.7	12.94
Costa Rica	21769	99.5	36.1	.47
Egypt	56939	–	–	1.24
Haiti	44041	40.1	24.3	.96
Hong Kong	872064	78.8	71.4	19.01
India	76911	40.8	44.2	1.68
Japan	469356	–	–	10.23
South Korea	706440	93.4	62.2	15.40
Macau	43351	127.4	86.5	.95
Malaysia	38185	82.4	52.1	.83
Mexico	127488	41.2	26.1	2.78
Pakistan	206687	83.2	61.8	4.51
Philippines	157617	57.1	84.4	3.44
Poland	14018	30.7	100.0	2.46
Romania	28917	66.9	39.2	.63
Singapore	109857	69.2	70.1	2.39
Taiwan	834688	93.4	62.9	18.20
Thailand	112267	64.7	38.3	2.44
Yugoslavia	4	0.5	100.0	–

Source: U.S. Department of Commerce, Office of Textiles, Expired Restraints, as of June 7, 1982.

"-" designates no limit imposed

Textile groups are normally defined as:

Group 1—Yarns of cotton, wool, and man-made fibers.

Group 2—Fabrics, made-up goods and miscellaneous, non-apparel products of cotton, wool, and man-made fibers.

Group 3—Apparel of cotton, wool, and man-made fibers.

Group 4—Special made-ups and miscellaneous textile and apparel. In case of Hong Kong the categories are:
435, 436, 438, 443, 445/6, 447/8, 633/4, 635, 638/9, 641, 648.

tions or an increase in tariff rates is permitted when imports enter "in such increased quantities or under such conditions as to cause or threaten serious injury to domestic producers". *Market disruption* as defined in the LTA differs from the "serious injury" referred to in Article XIX in that market disruption is attributed specifically to the threat to an industry from low-priced imports from particular sources. Furthermore, under the LTA, relief was permanent, whereas under Article XIX it is confined to a specific time period. Compensation and nondiscrimination (Article I) were also eliminated with the LTA.

By 1967 the United States had restrained the supply of specific cotton textile and apparel products under Article 3 of the LTA for seventeen of its major suppliers. Later that year the same countries accepted bilateral agreements with the United States under Article 4 of the LTA. The usual course by which the United States imposed quotas was first to negotiate specific limits on a limited set of items under Article 3 and then to follow up with a more comprehensive bilateral agreement under Article 4. In this way the LTA could serve as an anticipatory form of protection. By 1972 the United States had concluded similar restraining agreements with thirteen other countries bringing the total to thirty.

Two major events occurred during the 1961-72 period that affected the operation of the LTA. First, there was a very rapid increase in the trade of synthetic fibers, which was covered under the LTA. Second, new entrants into the market were heavily concentrated in apparel, which was not very well protected under the LTA. Imports of fiber textiles and apparel, unlike cotton textiles, which were bilaterally controlled, increased more than tenfold over the life of the LTA. In response to the LDC success in expanding exports of apparel made from synthetic-fiber textiles, the United States attempted to widen the scope of the LTA. In 1971 the United States reached bilateral agreements with its principal suppliers—Japan, Hong Kong, Taiwan, and Korea—that were designed to control the flow of wool and synthetic-fiber textile and apparel products. These restrictions, however, were not justified under the LTA framework and subsequently the United States focused on amending the LTA such that it would cover textile and apparel products of cotton, wool, and synthetic fibers.

The Multifiber Arrangement

A multifiber agreement was reached on 20 December 1973 by some fifty governments. Known as the Arrangement Regarding International Trade in Textiles, or more commonly the Multifiber Arrangement (MFA), it became "the statement of principle and policy" regarding international textile trade.[4] The MFA, which initially covered the period 1 January 1974 to 31 December 1977—later extended, with some major modifications, first through 31 December 1981 and later through 31 July 1986—took as its primary goal the fulfillment of two mutually exclusive objectives: To achieve the expansion of trade, the reduction of barriers to such trade and the progressive liberalization of world trade in textile products while at the same time ensuring the orderly and equitable development of this trade and avoidance of disruptive effects" (Article 1).

Another principal aim of the MFA is "to further the economic and social development of developing countries and secure a substantial increase in their export earnings from textile products and to provide scope for a greater share for them in world trade in these products." Article 1 further states that the safeguards provision of the MFA would be applied in "exceptional circumstances," and would be designed to "assist any process of adjustment which would be required by the changes in the pattern of world trade in textile products."

The extent to which a particular country could impose unilateral control was limited to "market disruption," which was defined rather strictly in Annex A as serious damage to the producing industry. Despite this definition the safeguard provision still differed substantially from GATT Article XIX. Along the general lines of the LTA, initial quotas were to be based on past import levels, with the exception that the quotas were to grow at a minimum of 6 percent per annum (Annex B). Furthermore, within the MFA provisions were made for a large degree of flexibility in the growth rate of the quota.

Although the MFA sets out an annual 6 percent growth in the levels agreed to in the bilaterals, the flexibility provisions in the original MFA could increase the volume of textile imports in excess of the 6 percent mark in any given year. Under the flexibility provisions, countries could transfer unused quotas among categories and between years. A carryover provision allowed allocating an unused portion of the previous year's quota to the current year. A carry-forward provision allowed allocating to the current year a portion of next year's quota. A "swing" feature allowed an exporting country to shift or reallocate a portion of the quota from one product group or category to another.

The MFA in Article 6 provided for special and more favorable treatment of new entrants and small suppliers. It also provided for surveillance procedures by the Textile Surveillance Body (TSB), composed of both DC and LDC members. Further, through its consultation mechanism the MFA had authority to control unilaterally imports of other product categories considered disruptive. By 1 October, 1977 the

United States had bilateral agreements with eighteen countries that limited their principal textile exports.

Although the original MFA provides the framework for an orderly and equitable[5] regulation of trade in textile products, its specific implementation is dependent on a set of bilateral agreements drawn according to Article 4 of the MFA. The United States interpreted Article 4 to imply that bilateral agreements should provide a more liberal treatment of LDC suppliers "on overall terms." Consequently, under most of the bilaterals, within each aggregate limit, specific quota levels for subgroups and specific quotas for items within subgroups were established. In the event that a particular item was perceived to be "very sensitive," specific levels were negotiated for the duration of the agreement that allow less than 6 percent growth. For example, for the very sensitive wool industry, U.S. bilaterials under the MFA have provided for growth of no more than 1 percent annually for group and specific ceilings. At the expiration of MFA I (December 1977) the United States was satisfied with the controls the regulations provided. Textile imports (excluding apparel) over the 1974-77 period increased by 1.5 percent, an annual average rate of .4 percent. Apparel imports, on the other hand, increased by 27 percent, an annual average rate of 6.8 percent.[6]

When the MFA came up for renewal at the end of 1977, member states of the European Economic Community (EEC) pressed for greater control over LDC exports. Unlike the United States, which had actively pursued bilateral agreements during MFA I, the Europeans had no consistent textile trade policy. Consequently, LDC suppliers increased their sales of textile and apparel products to the EEC markets. In large part to satisfy EEC concerns, the extension protocol renewing the MFA contained an amendment that allowed "jointly agreed reasonable departures" from the 6 percent growth rate in quotas and from the agreement's "flexibility provisions," permitting not only growth at less than 6 percent but also zero or negative growth in products considered sensitive by importing countries. The delay in negotiating bilateral agreements by the EEC member states was in part due to their lack of agreement on allocation of imports within the EEC. Additionally, the community debate over comprehensive or selective agreements impeded an EEC trade position in regard to textiles. A similar disarray in the EEC position was to become visible during the negotiations for MFA III.

Under the new protocol providing for jointly agreed "reasonable departures" from the MFA, the EEC negotiated a series of five-year bilateral agreements that cut quotas below previously achieved levels and curtailed still more the growth of imports from certain developing countries. In effect the EEC managed to use this clause to establish "global" quotas for a number of what it considered to be "sensitive products": cotton yarn, cotton fabric, spun synthetic weaves, knit shirts, sweaters, trousers, blouses, and woven shirts.

Although never formally invoking the "reasonable departures" clause, the United States did respond to industry pressure threatening to hinder U.S. participation in the multilateral trade negotiations (MTN) by reducing some of the flexibility in existing agreements. On 15 February, 1979 the United States issued its Administration Textile Program, referred to as the "White Paper."[7] As part of this program, provision was made to limit the flexibility embodied in the original MFA: a "year to year increase . . . should not normally exceed the previous year's shipments plus one-half of the unfilled portion of the previous year's quota but in no event more than the current year's quota." Furthermore, the program promised closer monitoring of import quotas, and a renegotiation of bilaterial agreements to prevent "surges," and provided a "snap back clause," such that tariff concessions negotiated in the MTN would revert to pre-MTN levels unless the MFA was renewed. By preventing "surges" the administration intended to (a) limit the carryover provisions, (b) impose designated consultation levels, and (c) list categories considered to be sensitive as subject to consultation or to an agreed limit.

Under the provisions of MFA II the United States had concluded bilateral quota agreements with twenty-two supplying countries and consultative mechanisms with eleven other countries. The agreements controlled over 80 percent of total U.S. imports of textile and apparel products in 1980, but it is very difficult to ascertain what in fact the quota system has controlled. Although it is true that over 80 percent of total U.S. textile and apparel imports both in 1980 and in 1981 were controlled by the aggregate limit, imports in both years under specific limits represented slightly over 50 percent of total imports. (For 1981, see table 1.)

The Negotiating Environment

The negotiations to determine whether or not the protocol extending the MFA should be extended, modified, or discontinued, began officially on 7 May 1981 at the first of three scheduled GATT Textile Committee meetings. The official positions of the EEC, the United States, and the LDC governments were not stated prior to this date, but the general proclivity of each group was well known. In all of the countries concerned, pressure groups composed of producers and organized labor were making their positions very clear and thus molding the opening positions of their governments.

In the United States the textile and apparel industry's position was outlined by Shelley Appleton, secretary-treasurer of the International Ladies Garment Workers Union (ILGWU), before the Trade Subcommittee of the House Committee on Ways and Means on 21 July 1980. Representing the Textile-Apparel Steering Group, Appleton called for a global quota system instead of the present country- and product-specific quota system. The resulting quotas would in turn be related directly to the growth of the domestic markets. In addition, the Steering Group proposed that quotas should be redistributed from the major suppliers, i.e. Hong Kong, Taiwan, and South Korea, to the "true" LDCs. It also proposed the elimination of the flexibility provisions in the original MFA.

The position of the European textile industry, represented by COMITEXTIL is remarkably similar to the U.S. industry's position. A COMITEXTIL statement on the renewal of the MFA noted that "the EEC textile industry is ready to share the growth in textile consumption on its home market with third world countries, provided that there actually is growth and that these countries in turn accept genuine reciprocity."[8]

More specifically, COMITEXTIL requested global ceilings for sensitive products; a reduction in growth rates; reciprocity in textile and apparel trade; the inclusion of offshore assembly goods as part of the MFA quotas; the inclusion of handloom and handmade products in the quota; a limit of quota flexibility; an addition of a price clause within the bilaterals to limit dumping; and an MFA to last ten years.

The LDCs naturally saw the textile problem in a far different light. Following a series of meetings among the major LDC producers held in Bogotá in November 1980 and in Jakarta in April 1981, it was clear that most of the LDCs were not pleased with the current MFA. In particular, they argued for the removal of the "reasonable-departures" clause. Some manufacturers, in particular those from Hong Kong, Taiwan, and South Korea, believed that one group of LDCs should not be helped at the expense of other LDCs.[9] In fact, they argued that if indeed the new entrants are small suppliers, they should not be restricted at all.

One should note that, as in case of the EEC, where a common opening position was difficult to negotiate, among the LDCs there were multiple interest groups also. For large exporters such as Hong Kong, South Korea, and Taiwan, the MFA, even with the much-hated "reasonable-departures" clause, was preferred to no agreement. No agreement would imply competition with smaller producers with the outcome extremely uncertain. For smaller LDCs like Thailand, Malaysia, Indonesia, and the Philippines, access to DC markets was absolutely crucial. A redistribution of the quota system in their favor was eagerly welcomed.[10]

By the time the official meetings were under way, the starting positions of each of these blocks should have been molded. On the contrary. At the first meeting, no positions were established other than some very general statements about a continued need for a MFA-like instrument. Among the countries present only the United States came out in clear support of a renewal of the MFA with "little change."[11] The EEC representative made an opening statement but it did not represent a united front. The EEC as early as April of that year had attempted to develop a common program. In fact, the EEC Commission proposed a negotiating position for the MFA; a call would be made for the United States and Japan to absorb a greater share of low-cost imports from LDCs. The proposal revolved around two issues: (1) that all DCs and NICs should take a "fair share of LDC trade," and (2) that LDCs agree to a reduction in growth rates for sensitive products entering the EEC.[12]

The EEC Commission proposal, by all accounts, was very flexible. It did not include actual global ceilings, nor did it list products. Moreover, it pointed out that growth in consumption of textiles may be only 1 percent per year but did not suggest that allowable import growth rates should reflect that prognosis. Nor did the commission come out in favor of a so-called recession clause in the new MFA. In large part because this proposal was so flexible, the EEC foreign ministers were unable to agree on a negotiating position as late as 23 June 1981. At the June meeting the ministers shared the same views on only two points: the MFA should be renewed for five years (not ten years, as European industry preferred); and the MFA should be nothing more than a temporary mechanism to allow European industry to continue restructuring.[13]

On other issues, like the global restraints, a recession clause, a price clause, and a cutback in quotas for the NICs, the Europeans were divided. The French, British, and Italian ministers called for global ceilings, lower growth rates, a link between market growth and imports, an automatic trigger mechanism called a "basket extractor," less quota flexibility, and a limit on outward processing. The German, Danish, and Dutch ministers favored the commission's more flexible approach to the negotiations, which did not specify limits.

It was not until the second official meeting (14-21 July) that the opening positions of the EEC and the LDCs were presented. As expected, that of the EEC as presented by Horst Krenzler of West Germany, the chief negotiator for the EEC, and that of the LDCs as presented by Colombia's Ambassador Jaramillo were diametrically opposed. The United States took no formal position other than restating its desire to renew the MFA based on the earlier protocol.[14]

The essential elements of the EEC proposals were as follows:

- relate the growth of imports from low-cost countries to the trend in domestic consumption;
- globalize the quotas;
- preferential treatment of the smaller LDCs;
- reduced quota growth rates for "sensitive products"; and
- access of LDC markets to DC exports of textile and apparel.

In addition, the EEC proposed that the next MFA include a statement whereby reexports could be charged to the original country.

Naturally, the proposals made by the exporting countries were a light year away from those presented by the EEC. Whereas the EEC proposal would turn the MFA into a highly restrictive trade mechanism, the LDC proposal's would, if implemented in their totality, make the MFA a much more liberalized instrument. The essence of the LDC proposals was as follows:

- restriction of the use of the minimum viable production (MVP) provision of the MFA;
- clarification of the concept of market disruption and introduction of a formal set of "clear-cut and objective" criteria for market disruption;
- implementation of adjustment measures by the importing countries;
- reaffirmation of special treatment for new entrants, small suppliers, and exporters of cotton textiles;
- progressive liberalization of trade in textiles;
- enhanced role of the Textile Surveillance Body; and
- elimination of the "reasonable-departures" provision

Given the wide gap between the EEC and LDC positions, it was assumed that either the entire MFA would collapse or some major concessions by each of the parties would have to be granted. In the event that the MFA died, the only recourse would be unilateral action based on Article XIX, an alternative clearly not in the best interest of the EEC. It could, however, be in the interest of the smaller LDCs, in that under Article XIX it would be very difficult to prove market disruption. Moreover, any unilateral action by the EEC would induce rather harsh retaliation by the major textile suppliers. In summary, a collapse of the MFA would only serve the interests of the smaller LDCs. The large suppliers as well as the EEC each had strong incentives to continue the discussion. Consequently the bargaining began.

The Negotiating Process and Outcome

Between the July meetings and those scheduled for late September, the United States found itself in the reluctant position of mediator between the protectionist EEC and the LDCs. To help the United States in its mediation role, the Congressional Textile Caucus, at a hearing on 28 July 1981, made it known to the administration that a new MFA must not be like previous agreements that worked to the disadvantage of the U.S. industry.[15] The resolution of caucus urged that the United States adopt a global approach to import restraints as its negotiating position on renewal of the MFA, replacing the numerical quota-growth requirement with a guideline such as "related to domestic market conditions," elimination of all flexibility provisions except to take into account statistical aberrations, and in certain circumstances, permission for negative quota growth.

Despite the position of the caucus, the administration was maintaining an open position with respect to renewal of the MFA. While in Jakarta in late August, Ambassador Brock was quoted as saying that "some kind of agreement is better than none at all . . . we [the United States] will play a leadership role to make sure that we get one."[16] Later Brock said that the United States had "suggested that the negotiations should begin by seeing if these concerns can be addressed by the existing agreement, including the present protocol of extension."[17] It was clear prior to the September meetings that the United States was not going to support either the EEC position or that of the domestic industry. In fact, on 14 September Brock remarked that the administration could continue to "live with" the existing MFA.[18]

In an attempt to move the negotiating process along, the United States at the third Textile Committee meeting, held in Geneva 21-26 September, presented what appeared to be a middle-ground proposal. In effect, it floated a draft protocol that noted that an "unsatisfactory situation" existed in the textile industry as a result of a decline in consumption in the DCs and "the growing impact of a very large quota and market shares for imports of sensitive products from a few sources." Further that "countries having small markets, an exceptionally high level of imports, and a correspondingly low level of domestic production" are particularly exposed to the threat of low-priced imports from LDCs. Of even greater significance is the fact that the draft protocol ruled out reductions in base levels, global quotas, and negative growth.[19]

Peter Murphy, U.S. negotiator, was quoted as saying at the meetings, "We are going to have to insist that . . . the commitment to reduce trade barriers and liberalize trade in textiles applies to both developed and developing countries." Moreover, "We are not seeking reductions or negative growth rates from any of our trading partners. We believe, however, all participants should be aware of the implications and ramifications of any actions such as reductions or negative growth rates on other participants in this arrangement . . . including the U.S."[20]

Despite the hope expressed by Murphy that the draft protocol would bridge the gap between the two extreme positions, neither Horst Krenzler, the chief negotiator for the EEC, nor his counterpart Felipe Jaramillo was willing to budge. Krenzler rejected both the demands of the group of twenty-three LDCs for fewer restrictions and the U.S. draft protocol, each for a different reason. With respect to the LDC position, he declared: "The Community can in no circumstances preside over and indeed orchestrate the systematic dismantling of its textile and clothing industry over the lifetime of the future MFA."[21]

In response to LDC demands that restrictions follow upon proof of market disruption, he was equally adamant: "It has been our experience that by the time such evidence is sufficiently convincing, the Community's industry has received a further body blow in terms of lost jobs, diminished share of the market, and company closures."[22]

In regard to the U.S. draft protocol, Krenzler commented that he was unable to agree "for the moment" because EEC members were still negotiating among themselves. In retrospect, it would be accurate to say that the hard line taken by the EEC at the September meetings prevented the U.S. proposal for an extension of MFA II from getting a serious hearing. Even more harmful, the apparent stalemate left the administration open to continued domestic pressure from the Textile Caucus.

Prior to the November Textile Committee meetings, on 27 October the EEC foreign ministers met for the fourth time since the EEC commission's April proposals to bridge the gap between its two major blocs and to arrive at a common position regarding extension of the MFA. Despite the warnings of EEC Industrial Affairs Commissioner Etienne Davignon that failure to come up with a united front in Geneva would lead to a breakdown of the MFA and to the "worst of all possible outcomes," the meeting broke without achieving unity.[23] The main sticking point was the dispute between the "free traders" (West Germany, Denmark, and the Netherlands) and the "protectionists" (France, Italy, and the United Kingdom) over the rate of growth of imports. The "free traders" argued for a 6 percent growth rate; the "protectionists," for a much smaller growth rate or even a substantial cutback. To make matters worse, the United Kingdom continued to insist on the inclusion of a "recession clause," which would permit tighter import restrictions in the event of a sharp decline in consumption resulting from extremely poor economic conditions.

At the start of the last official meeting of the GATT Textile Committee (18 November-22 December), the EEC introduced two negotiating points as part of its proposal: a "surge mechanism," and a provision to regulate restraint levels in the "dominant" supplier countries, particularly in the area of "outward processing."[24] The "surge mechanism" would not operate for restraints below a certain threshold, measured in terms of percentage of total imports. Jaramillo rejected the mechanism there and on 30 November, when it appeared in an EEC-sponsored draft protocol. The United States, for its part, did not see the need to place the "surge mechanism" in the new MFA.[25]

While the negotiations in Geneva were continuing at a snail's pace, the U.S. textile and apparel industry was mounting an offensive against the U.S. draft protocol presented in September. The domestic pressure came from a number of sources, the most devastating from Congressman Carroll Campbell (R.-S.C.), who promised "significant" opposition to a foreign aid authorization measure "strongly supported by the Administration" unless a firmer commitment to the domestic textile industry was forthcoming. Less presumptuously, Shelley Appleton, ILGWU, testified before the House Ways and Means Trade Subcommittee that the U.S. proposal submitted in September fell "far short" of the Textile-Apparel Steering Group's desire to strengthen the textile import restraints.[26]

In response to industry pressure by way of the Textile Caucus, White House Chief of Staff James Baker III in a formal reply to Campbell and to Senator Strom Thurmond promised in December: "This Administration will make every effort to satisfactorily conclude an MFA that will allow us to relate total import growth to the growth in the domestic textile and apparel market. The President authorized me to reaffirm that we shall work to achieve that goal."[27]

In effect speaking on behalf of the president, Baker instructed the U.S. negotiators in Geneva to "strengthen" their proposal, that is, to move toward the EEC position.[28] Despite the disclaimer made by

Murphy, the stage was set for a U.S. capitulation. By coming closer to the EEC position, the United States provided the breakthrough that was necessary to avoid a collapse of the MFA.

The compromise amendments put together by GATT Secretary-General Arthur Dunkel, EEC negotiator Krenzler, and U.S. negotiator Murphy, stated inter alia that bilateral agreements between producers and consumers would allow the latter to react to "sharp and substantial inputs from suppliers that have been consistently under utilized" but that "full and qualifiable compensations" should be paid to both parties in such cases. This resolved one of the main sticking points in the earlier negotiations.[29]

The EEC also appeared to be making some concessions, although very few. At a meeting of the Textile Committee on 10 December Krenzler announced that on the question of the "surge mechanism" the EEC was prepared to set a level below which a limitation could not be fixed. It would be based on 1980 trade figures, so there could be no use of the mechanism based on later figures. Regarding outward processing, another bone of contention between the EEC and the LDCs, Krenzler was prepared to draw a distinction between a dominant supplier and the outward-processing concept.[30] Elimination of the linkage between dominant suppliers and the outward-processing concept made Mexico, Brazil, Colombia, Hong Kong, and India drop their objections to the EEC position.[31]

On 22 December a compromise agreement was signed by all the parties but it pleased no one. Yet, it could be said with some certainty that without President Reagan's order (and domestic industry pressure) to "strengthen" the U.S. position, no compromise would have been possible. At the close of the session Murphy announced that the United States "will not seek reduction in existing levels of trade". In fact, "We strongly believe such reductions to be contrary to the spirit of this arrangement."[32]

The Europeans were far less magnanimous. As far as the EEC was concerned, adoption of the new protocol marked the end of the first, multilateral stage of the process. The second stage is the bilaterals, and the EEC considers the two stages very much linked. In fact, at the final session, Krenzler said, "If it proves impossible to conclude satisfactory new bilateral agreements," the ECC "shall be unable to continue to participate in the MFA. The Community will examine the situation and reassess its position concerning the MFA in the early Autumn of next year."[33]

The key to the compromise and the remaining bone of contention between the EEC and the exporters was and is cutbacks, an issue addressed very vaguely in paragraph six of the protocol, which reads:

The Committee noted the important role of and the good will expressed by certain exporting participants now predominant in the exporting of textile products in all three fibers covered by the Arrangement in finding and contributing to mutually acceptable solutions to particular problems relative to particularly large restraint levels arising out of the application of the Arrangement as extended by the Protocol.[34]

The LDCs interpret this paragraph as not permitting cutbacks; the EEC, as permitting cutbacks.

On 25 February 1982 the EEC trade ministers agreed to ratify the new MFA but said that in the bilateral negotiations, the EEC would allow no more than an overall increase of 1 percent in imports per year over the 1980 figures, and that the average annual cutback from the so-called dominant suppliers would be 10 percent during the 1983-86 period. Under MFA III the EEC has concluded bilateral agreements with twenty-four exporting countries, each containing a far more detailed product coverage and a more limited quota growth rate. For the most sensitive product categories, primarily from the Asian suppliers, the growth rate stipulated ranges from 0.1 percent to 1.5 percent. For the less sensitive categories, the agreed quotas have prescribed growth rates of less than 6 percent. With these new bilaterals the EEC has made it clear that it cannot live with a 6 percent growth rate.[35]

MFA III, as the product of repeated refinements, is the most protectionist MFA to date. Under it, future bilaterals will be allowed to limit the aggregate growth rate of imports to the growth of the domestic market, defined as per capita comsumption of textiles and apparel (estimated by the industry to be 1.5 percent. For the first time, an MFA allows for the globalization of quotas[36] and attempts to continue preferential treatment of smaller LDCs at the expense of the NICs. MFA III's immediate impact will be felt by Hong Kong, Taiwan, and South Korea, who together furnished 53 percent of total U.S. restricted textile and apparel imports in 1981. Under the recently completed bilateral agreements with one of these large exporters, items bound by specific limits have been limited to growth rates between 0.5 percent and 2.0 percent per annum. Smaller exporters, on the other hand, have been allowed growth rates exceeding 6 percent.

Conclusions and Implications

On 22 December 1981 delegates from fifty nations signed a paper that appears to bind their countries to an "orderly" and "equitable" regulation of international trade in textile and apparel products. After almost a year of negotiations, could any signatory nation declare itself a winner? Very simply, no one knows. The Protocol Extending the

Arrangement Regarding International Trade in Textiles appears to appease all sides, yet no side was appeased. As it stands the document is so vague (intentionally) that any interpretation is possible. Is that the lesson of this negotiation? Must such an agreement be so vaguely worded that all parties perceive success? For example, paragraph 10 allows importing countries to restrict imports from an exporter in a particular category if the exporter, after not filling the quota in the past, begins to fill it. If such an action is taken, the importing country must "compensate" the exporter. History reminds us that one of the reasons GATT Article XIX is used so rarely is that it requires compensation. It is therefore unlikely that compensation would be forthcoming in this case either.

Paragraph 6 continues the mockery. Although it does not refer to "reasonable departures," it is being interpreted by the EEC as if it does permit cutbacks in textile and apparel imports from major suppliers. In other words, paragraph 6 is the $500 version of the $1.00 "reasonable-departures" clause of MFA II.

The EEC appears to play the major villain in this trading game, but the United States is not as moderate as one is led to believe. Although it does not interpret the protocol in as protectionist terms as does the EEC, it has made a commitment to limit the growth of major suppliers by reducing flexibility in the bilateral agreement. In fact, according to paragraph 9, the Unites States is legally entitled in "exceptional cases" to lower growth rates in a "mutually acceptable" agreement.

Clearly MFA III is a far cry from the original MFA of 1974. Given its very protectionist spirit, why was it signed? Very simply, it was signed because it was perceived as a second-best solution, far better than no solution. In fact, this is the major conclusion drawn from this case study.

If it is perceived that a trade arrangement such as the MFA is in the best interest of both exporters and importers a compromise solution is possible. A restatement of this proposition would go as follows: If the demise of a trade contract would impose greater costs than would a compromise, the latter is clearly to be preferred. Despite the polemics of the EEC regarding no compromise, the cost in terms of retaliation and of enforcement, even retaliation from only the United States, was too high.

The threat of economic warfare between the United States and the EEC if the MFA were allowed to die also played a role in convincing the United States to side with the protectionists. Had the MFA died and had EEC begun to restrict imports of textiles and apparel, Congress would probably have followed suit. In that event, given the recession and high unemployment, the U.S. bill could very well have included quotas not only on textiles and apparel but also on many other manufactured goods, in effect triggering a world trade war with few winners.

Two other lessons can be drawn from this case study. First, the importance for LDCs to unite, and second, the importance of domestic pressure groups. Although the LDCs won only a few points, they did so by uniting around a common platform. Prior to this MFA negotiation, no such unity was visible. With respect to the second point, the power of the domestic industry lobby should never be underestimated. Pressure on the administration by producers, labor, and their representatives in Congress was very effective. This was not a generalized but a specific pressure: a threat to kill the administration's foreign aid authorization bill. History proves that such a threat can be effectively utilized, i.e. the multilateral trade negotiations and the resulting Carter "White Paper."

References

Aggarwal, Vinod K. 1983. "The Unraveling of the Multi-Fiber Arrangement, 1981." *International Organization* 37 (Autumn): 618-45.

COMITEXTIL. 1980. "Position of the Community Textile Industry Regarding the Arrangement on International Trade in Wool, Cotton and Man-Made Textiles Which Expires on 31, December 1981." Bulletin 80.4, pp. 1-12.

———. 1981. "Results of the MFA III Negotiations." Bulletin, 81.6, pp. 2-15.

Dolan, Michael B. 1983. "European Restructuring and Import Policies for a Textile Industry in Crisis." *International Organization* 37 (Autumn): 583-617.

The Economist. 1981. "The Ten's Textile Tangle." 14 November, p. 61.

General Agreement on Tariffs and Trade. Textile Committee. 1981b. *Arrangement Regarding International Trade in Textiles*. Proposals by developing countries, the European Communities, Hungary and a Statement by the United States. 14-20 July.

———. 1981c. *Report of the Meeting of the Committee Held on 7-8 May 1981*. 22 June.

———. 1981a. *Protocol Extending the Arrangement Regarding International Trade in Textiles*. 23 December.

Glismann, Hans-Hinrich, Dean Spinanger, Joseph Pelzman, and Martin Wolf. 1982. *Trade, Protection and Employment in Textiles*. London: Trade Policy Research Center.

Hwa, Hsung Bee. 1981. "The Fraying Fabric of the MFA." *Asean Business Quarterly* 5: 7-10, 31.

Journal of Commerce. 1981a. "U.S. Stance on Textiles Reaffirmed." 15 September.

———. 1981b. "Reagan Hedging Campaign Vows on Textile Import Restrictions." 1 September.

———. 1981c. "U.S. Will Attempt to Reconcile International Row Over Textiles." 21 August, p. 23B.

Pelzman, Joseph. 1983. "The Multifiber Arrangement and Its Effects on the Profit Performance of the U.S. Textile Industry." Paper presented at NBER Conference on the Structure and Evolution of Recent U.S. Trade Policy. 3-4 December.

———. 1982. "The Textile Industry." In *The Internationalization of the American Economy*, ed. J. Michael Finger and Thomas D. Willett. *The Annals of the American Academy of Political and Social Science* 460: 92-100.

———. 1980. *The Competitiveness of the U.S. Textile Industry*. Columbia: University of South Carolina, College of Business Administration.

New York Times. 1981. "51 Nations Reach Pact on Textiles." 23 December, pp. D1, D4.

U.S. Department of Commerce. 1979. International Trade Administration. "Administration Textile Program" (news release).

U.S. Import Weekly. 1982. "EC Ratification of MFA Final Barring Unsuccessful Bilaterals." 3 March, pp. 508-9.

———. 1981a. "Multifiber Pact Talks Appear Close to Conclusion, Though Deadline Past." 23 December, pp. 287-88.

———. 1981b. "EC Foreign Ministers Fail to Agree on Common MFA Negotiating Stance." 4 November, pp. 121-22.

———. 1981c. "U.S. Move to Extend MFA Rejected, Next Session Set." 30 September, pp. A11-A14.

———. 1981d. "EC Foreign Ministers Fail to Reach Accord on MFA Negotiating Stance." 1 July.

———. 1981e. "EC Commission Urges Greater U.S. Import Share in Renegotiated MFA." 15 April, pp. A3-A5.

U.S. International Trade Commission. 1978. *The History and Current Status of the Multifiber Arrangement*. Washington, D.C.: Government Printing Office.

Wall Street Journal. 1981. "U.S. Moves Closer to European Position in World Textile Talks." 15 December, p. 35.

Women's Wear Daily. 1981. "EEC Seen Divided on Issue of Bilaterals." 28 October, p. 2.

Notes

1. An extreme example of this is the Philippines, which has negotiated specific limits on all textile and apparel items in order to assure market access. A cynical interpretation of the Philippine move would argue that the Philippines is merely trying to acquire quota rents.
2. For more details see U.S. International Trade Commission (1978).
3. Overtures by the United States to initiate Japanese style OMAs with Hong Kong proved unsuccessful.
4. The text of the MFA can be found in U.S. International Trade Commission (1978), Appendix A.
5. By *equitable* the authors meant that it provided for a small but guaranteed 6 percent expansion in the exports of LDCs. The authors considered it "orderly" in that developed country producers would not be subjected to competition at prices "substantially below" their own. The program,

however, was not only disorderly in that it precluded price competition but also inequitable in that it denied market access to efficient producers.

6. The growth rates are determined from imports measured in millions of equivalent square yards. The growth rate within product group was very different from the average growth rates. For an economic analysis of the impact of the MFA on the U.S. textile industry, see Pelzman (1983).

7. U.S. Department of Commerce (1979).

8. COMITEXTIL (1980).

9. Hsung Bee Hwa (1981).

10. One should note that within Asia, trade in textile and apparel represents less than 5 percent of total intra-Asian trade. In part this is caused by extreme specialization and by high nontariff barriers.

11. General Agreement on Tariffs and Trade. Textile Committee (1981c).

12. *U.S. Import Weekly,* 15 April 1981.

13. Ibid., 1 July 1981.

14. General Agreement on Tariffs and Trade. Textile Committee (1981b).

15. Congressional Textile Caucus Resolution, 28 July 1981, Mimeographed, in a letter to Ambassador Brock from Congressman Ken Holland (D-SC, chairman, Textile Caucus). A list of 107 congressional supporters and cosigners was attached to stress the wide acceptance of this resolution.

16. *Journal of Commerce,* 21 August 1981, p. 23B.

17. Ibid., 1 September 1981.

18. Ibid., 15 September 1981. It should be noted, however, that the administration's position in September varied drastically from that taken by candidate Reagan just a year earlier. In September 1980 Reagan informed Senator Strom Thurmond (R-S.C.) in a letter: "The MFA . . . needs to be strengthened by relating import growth from all sources to domestic growth. I shall work to achieve that goal." Ibid., 1 September 1981.

19. *U.S. Import Weekly,* 30, September 1981.

20. Ibid., p. A13.

21. Ibid., p. A12.

22. Ibid.

23. Ibid., 4, November 1981, p. 121; *Women's Wear Daily,* 28, October 1981; *Economist,* 14 November 1981. The consequences of failure was to rely on GATT Article XIX, which would be far too difficult to apply and would bring on retaliation from many LDCs.

24. *U.S. Import Weekly,* 9, December 1981, p. 242.

25. Ibid., p. 242.

26. Statement by Shelley Appleton 14 December 1981, Mimeographed.

27. Letter from James Baker III to Senator Thurmond and Congressman Campbell, 11 December 1981, Mimeographed.

28. From a statement made by Peter Murphy, 14 December 1981, one would gather that the U.S. position was not completely tilting toward the EEC. In fact, Murphy was quoted as saying that although the new instructions sent by Washington would lead to a "strengthening" of the U.S. proposal made in September, the move "doesn't mean embracing all the concepts presented . . . by other importing nations." Yet, he also noted that the EEC "could win us over on some . . . points," namely, "the question of surge" and "the question of dominance." *Wall Street Journal,* 15 December 1981, p. 35.

29. *U.S. Import Weekly,* 23 December 1981, p. 288.
30. Ibid.
31. Ibid.
32. *New York Times.* 23 December 1981.
33. COMITEXTIL (1981), p. 12.
34. General Agreement in Tariffs and Trade. Textile Committee. (1981a), p. 5.
35. *U.S. Import Weekly,* 3 March 1982, p. 508.
36. European globalization was in effect under MFA II, although some would argue in violation of the spirit of the MFA.

7

The World Administrative Radio Conference 1979 Negotiations: Toward More Equitable Sharing of the Global Radio Resources

Barbara A. Fliess

The radio frequency spectrum is a recent focus of the South's overall drive for a global redistribution of resources. The issues are monopolization of communication technology and services by the North, the existing imbalance in the international flow of information, and the so-called communications gap between North and South. The debate over the New World Information Order (NWIO) is less well known than the debate over the New International Economic Order (NIEO). Developing countries (LDCs), in particular the nonaligned nations, put forward ideas that led to the declaration by UNESCO and the United Nations General Assembly in 1978 of a "new, more just and more efficient world information and communication order."[1] Related initiatives have found their way into the forums of the International Telecommunication Union (ITU), the UN specialized telecommunications agency in Geneva that every twenty years convenes a general World Administrative Radio Conference (WARC) to review the international radio communication regulations. Thus, unlike some other North-South encounters discussed here such as the U.N. Committee of the Whole (COW) or the Integrated Commodities Program (ICP), radio issues are not a product of the NIEO pressures of the 1970s but are a permanent and growing feature of the current era, with pressures ever increasing in the future.

Between WARCs global and regional administrative conferences amend the radio regulations with respect to specific services, such as broadcasting, maritime, or space services.[2] How the radio resource is to be divided among different services in the absence of an international market for spectrum, and among countries at different stages of development is the focus of ITU negotiations. The safety of lives, air and sea traffic, internal and national security, the flow of public and private information, and economic production of goods and services are all dependent on spectrum usage. Users around the world share frequencies in terms of geography, time, and signal power. The range of usable spectrum depends on technology and economics. Implicit in ITU documents is the concept that the radio frequency spectrum is a global, natural but scarce resource. Unlike nonrenewable resources, it cannot be used up, but it can become congested.

Newcomers at the International Telecommunications Union

Trends in ITU membership have closely followed the general pattern at the UN. Until the late 1950s, the organization was a club of the North. With developing countries joining after gaining independence, membership had grown to 129 nations by 1965. Not only did subsequent conferencing become more complex, due to technological advances, diversification of services, and more participants, but the presence of an expanding LDC grouping made itself felt in nontraditional demands voiced at ITU meetings. Perceptions differed among participants as to what the meetings were supposed to be all about.

Advanced industrial countries already enjoy a sophisticated telecommunications infrastructure. Accordingly, their radio spectrum requirements reflect the implementation of ever more advanced technologies that offer their people a variety of national and international private and public communications services and that sustain national security structures. Still preoccupied with catching up in the creation and application of a basic communications capability along with educational, social, and economic development, LDCs share an interest in narrowing the existing North-South radio communications gap as reflected in radio spectrum allocation patterns. Over the past two decades, the thrust of their demands has followed two lines. Although telecommunications technology is an essential ingredient of the development process, the promotion of communications facilities and services has never ranked on the agenda of assistance programs as high as food or health care. It was natural that LDCs would come to the ITU forums with demands for technical and financial aid for their communications systems. Furthermore, in view of the finiteness of the radio spectrum and geostationary orbit, growing congestion in certain frequencies, and prospects of future congestion in orbit space, LDCs also began to criticize and challenge the traditional evolutionary first-come, first-served ITU procedures, for the notification and registration of frequency and orbital slot assignments.[3] Watching the mushrooming communications technology industry in the North, they fear that when they themselves have acquired the technological means to use the radio resource more extensively, there will be no spectrum available to them. The current unequal distribution of radio frequencies among the services of the North and the South, and the South's demand for a more equitable reallocation have been summarized best in a statement Sudanese Minister Ali Shummo made in 1977: "You [the industrial nations] have 10 percent of the population and 90 percent of the spectrum, and we [the LDCs] have 90 percent of the population and 10 percent of the spectrum. We want our share."[4] According to the Third World, its communications underdevelopment will persist unless certain principles embedded in the ITU regime, and established and defended by the North, are changed, foremost the registration rule. Many LDCs favor some sort of detailed planning involving a priori allotment of frequencies and orbit space that would guarantee each country entry rights.

ITU conferences preceding the World Administrative Conference of 1979 (hereafter WARC 79) became more and more politicized as LDCs sought to make the international radiocommunications regime more responsive to their own distinct needs. They perceived the negotiating process as a struggle to obtain equitable present and future access to the radio resource from those countries whose services dominated it. ITU decisions are governed by the one-nation, one-vote rule, and participation opened up the opportunity for LDCs to exercise substantial influence if they succeeded in becoming organized as a bloc around shared demands for major reforms. What colored the expectations of many advanced industrial countries in regard to the WARC 79 encounter was the observation that at several preceding ITU conferences, the LDCs had managed to advance some of their objectives.

When ITU first-timers at the 1965 Montreux Plenipotentiary Conference demanded the setting up of a special ITU technical assistance fund to help them develop their domestic communications system, and the creation of a new ITU body to deal exclusively with assistance matters, strong opposition by industrial countries, most notably the United States, prevented the adoption of such schemes by the conference. A resubmission of the proposals at the 1973 Malaga-Torremolinos Plenipotentiary Conference was more successful, and a special fund for technical cooperation was set up. Industrial countries, however, insisted that contributions be voluntary,[5] and rejected a proposal that the International Frequency Regulation Board (IFRB) be given authority to allocate to individual countries orbit slots for communications satellites. Displeased by the domination of the meeting by the concerns of LDCs, the U.S. delegation charged that the conference "spent an inordinate time on issues that had little to do with the role of ITU in furthering international telecommunications."[6] Under the leadership of the United States, which as the major international communications power is a key actor in ITU negotiations, the North wishes to preserve the technical character of the negotiations, but LDCs want them to address also the economic and social aspects of the resource management.

In 1971 a WARC for Space Services was held in Geneva to deal with the rapid developments in the use of geostationary satellites for radio communications, which required new international agreements on the use of orbital positions and associated frequency channels. Although the traditional evolutionary notice and recording policy preferred by the industrial countries was maintained, a resolution and a recommendation providing for equal rights of access to the resource and a denial of any permanent acquisition of rights by first-comers took into account LDC interests. Concerned about getting their fair share in the satellite business and unenthusiastic about satellite broadcasting by one country into another without the recipient's prior consent—a highly politicized issue in debates at the UN Committee on Peaceful Use of Outer Space—LDCs also successfully lobbied that a mandate be given for a future WARC to plan the Broadcasting Satellite Service (BSS) in the 12 GHz band.[7]

Three years later an attack launched by a Third World group led by Algeria on the first-come, first-served principle caused a World Maritime Radio Conference to adopt procedures according to which future allotments of HF radio-telephone coastal stations were to enjoy the same priority as older ones, and all countries, regardless of whether they had maritime interests or not, were given the opportunity to obtain channels for stations. The United States received the lion's share of the allotment, but its delegation believed it was not enough and took a reservation—until then a rare move for the United States in ITU negotiations.[8]

A WARC for the planning of the BSS in the 12 GHz band was convened in 1977 in accordance with the 1971 resolution. At this conference a United States proposal for evolutionary planning according to the first-come, first-served rule was rejected. With the backing of European countries, LDCs pushed through a priori planning for Regions 1 and 3 that apportioned several hundred television broadcasting channels among the regions' administrations.[9] The support for an

LDCish plan by the Europeans, who wished to proceed with terrestrial microwave systems at the same frequencies allocated to BSS, and the ongoing debate at the UN on international broadcasting without prior consent of the receiving country contributed to this outcome.[10] The United States managed to persuade other countries of Region 2 to defer similar planning until a 1983 regional conference and to adopt an interim scheme.[11] Because international agreements on satellite broadcasting are likely to impose controls on the international flow of information, the United States, as the key defender of the principle of free flow of information, prefers to have no international agreement at all.[12] For LDCs, on the other hand, the free flow is equivalent to one-way flow from North to South. They recognize the value of BSS for their economic development but are reluctant to accept its implementation without securing some form of control over its application.

WARC 79: The Changed Negotiation Environment

WARC 79 was to update and redesign as necessary the ITU's Radio Regulations, including the Table of Frequency allocations among user services. Any channeling plans drawn up simultaneously with the frequency allocations by the last general WARC in 1959 were excluded from the agenda; instead, WARC 79 could schedule future conferences for this purpose.[13] Attended by many more delegations than WARC 59, the conference had only ten weeks for negotiations rather than the eighteen weeks its predecessor had for a less complex agenda. And new was the general background rhetoric of the NWIO, the more focused Third World call for equitable access to the radio resource, and the South's voting power at WARC.

The conference had been scheduled far in advance by the 1973 Plenipotentiary Conference. Conference details, including its agenda, were drawn up in several meetings of the ITU Administrative Council. None of the participants at WARC 79 had to persuade one another to come to the negotiating table. Each administration was genuinely interested in a review and revision of regulations and allocations. Although objectives undoubtedly would differ, all administrations shared a stake in a successful conclusion of the conference, i.e. a final agreement that served national interests and was acceptable to the administrations involved. Despite the one-nation, one-vote rule, there has been a high emphasis at the ITU on consensus agreements, resorting to voting only when consensus cannot be arrived at. The management of the radio resource is a prime example of global interdependence. The absence of multilaterally agreed-upon and respected rules coordinating and controlling the use of airwaves would bring havoc to most international and even national communications.

Given the complexity of the bargaining encounter and the fact that much of the discussion would concern highly technical issues and require detailed work and decisions affecting the next twenty years, careful homework by individual administrations on opening strategies and positions at WARC was a sine qua non. The conference was to begin in September 1979, and January of that year was set as the deadline for submitting for consideration at WARC proposals to change, delete, or reaffirm the 1959 WARC provisions. ITU would translate and distribute them in advance to all participants. As early as 1974 individual administrations launched domestic preparations for negotiations that were being hailed as the most demanding ones ever undertaken in the radiocommunications field.

The Adversary Image

The preparatory phase for WARC 79 saw mutual mistrust high in both camps. The scores made by LDCs at other ITU conferences put many industrial countries on alert. The NIEO and later on the NWIO had been launched at the UN. WARC 79 closely followed the 1979 NAM (nonaligned movement) meeting in Havana, whose resolutions did little to alleviate the North's dread of a confrontation. The South feared that the technically superior industrial nations would outwit them in preparations and negotiations. As Christopher Nacimento, a Guyanan minister of telecommunications affairs put it, countries such as the United States "will be represented by vast teams of engineers, specialists, communications lawyers, the technology manufacturers lobbying for their interests." Third World countries could not match these resources and would be "disenfranchised."[14]

The Campaign of the Communications-Rich Nations. Much international attention focused on the preparations of the United States,[15] the most prominent Western communications and space power and a vocal opponent of the NWIO concept. U.S. government agencies, private industry, and other interest groups spent four years hammering out specific WARC proposals. Some broad conference objectives, which most industrial countries shared, were established early; they emphasized incremental adjustments to spectrum allocations and regulatory revisions as opposed to radical changes; the protection of maximum flexibility and adaptability to changing national needs; and the strengthening of the ITU as the implementor of WARC decisions to promote the continuation of an efficient and equitable use of the radio resource.[16] The United States was also eager to avoid a repetition of its isolation at the 1977 BSS WARC, but it firmly maintained that WARC was a technical forum and no place for debate on general political issues, be they East-West or North-South. As G.O. Robinson, the head of the U.S. delegation put it, "We'd rather not see all of this political dialogue spill over into ITU. We have other forums—the UN's Outer Space Committee, UNESCO—for very generalized debate about international inequity and justice, and things that are good and true."[17]

During the preparation period there was intensive internal lobbying, and many countries, especially the United States and Canada, carried their draft proposals for WARC 79 into foreign capitals. For example, starting in 1977 U.S. experts involved in the preparations and diplomatic missions abroad concluded talks with more than fifty countries.[18] In a sense the negotiating process began at an informal level years before WARC formally opened. The aim was to sell ideas about revisions of spectrum allocations and regulations, to gain insight into foreign positions, to coordinate, and to prevent clashes ahead of WARC. Important in the North's preparations was also the emphasis on technical competence as the principal criterion for the choice of delegates for WARC. "It is sometimes overlooked that our basic strength lies in presenting solid, technically sound, fully supported documentation for basic US positions," said the U.S. delegation head.[19] Although LDCs also sent technical experts to WARC, industrial countries sent more. The United States committed unique support equipment to the offices of its delegation that was not shared with other delegations.[20] The strategy was to use technical power to countervail those who would control the votes at the conference.

The Campaign of the Communications-Poor Nations. In light of events at ITU conferences leading up to WARC 79, the North's expectations that the conference would turn into a political showdown were reinforced by the Western media. Western countries started pre-WARC consultations and informal circulation of proposals early and tended to be best informed about those originating within their own ranks. In late 1978 U.S. Senator Harrison Schmitt, a member of the Senate Communications Subcommittee, openly criticized the administration for seeking bilateral talks mainly with "traditional allies" instead of those who commanded the majority of votes at WARC. He also warned that suggestions that the United States "take a reservation to objectionable frequency assignments" or even withdraw from the ITU were not "realistic alternatives" because too much depended on international communications to refuse to comply with WARC decisions.[21]

Little information was available in industrial countries on specific LDC positions for WARC 79, and most speculation remained based on rumors, even after the ITU had begun to circulate country proposals. The reason was simple. Whereas the United States by the end of 1978 was "by far the most advanced and better prepared for WARC than any other nation,"[22] most Third World administrations had yet to draw up their proposals. Scarce competent personnel and technical expertise rendered the necessary preparations a real headache for them. The majority had too few competent people for too much work, and could not afford to engage in intensive bilateral consultation in the fashion of the North because to do so required considerable financial and human resources.

NAM's initiative to coordinate some of the preparatory work of its members was launched late and confined itself to general principles of more equitable spectrum distribution. Working on the formulation of a joint stance at WARC, some member-country experts met in May 1979 in Yaoundé, Cameroon, under Indian chairmanship, and adopted a number of WARC proposals, including one for a future conference to plan satellite services. On the one hand, the meeting was regarded by observers as an indication that these nations prepared collectively for the conference.[23] On the other hand, the picture that emerged from still incomplete LDC proposals circulated by the ITU after January 1979 highlighted the diversity of national priorities within the Third World as well as North-South differences.

The difficulties and frustrations experienced by many LDCs in preparing for WARC 79 was no secret to the North. The ITU and its agencies provided assistance, especially to LDCs, by holding regional seminars on technical issues in Africa, Asia, and Latin America in early 1979. The two-week sessions, which the United States and other industrial countries attended as observers,[24] were well attended by Third World representatives because the ITU underwrote their expenses. Many countries came to WARC better prepared than might otherwise have been the case. Also, in November 1978 a special groundwork session sponsored by the ITU was held in Geneva. Many participants used the occasion to exchange views on proposals and get general feedback. For instance, the United States found that its idea of interservice sharing of spectrum bands to conserve space was not well received by LDCs and some European countries.[25] And on the final day Colombia and other equatorial nations reasserted in a political statement that equatorial states have sovereign rights to the geostationary orbit space above them.[26] Going back to the so-called Bogotá Declaration signed in 1976 by these countries, the claim had reappeared in the

1977 ESS WARC and in one of the regional preparatory sessions. It was certain to be brought up at WARC. Another long-standing controversial issue that observers in the West expected to be raised at WARC related to Third World and Soviet demands at other UN forums for international rules that would oblige nations operating sensing satellites for the gathering of information on crops, soil, and resource conditions to seek prior consent from countries being sensed.[27] Debate on the issue at WARC could negatively affect proposals by industrial countries for more spectrum allocation for earth satellite sensing services. And finally, LDCs were expected to express their dissatisfaction about the ITU's spectrum and orbit registration principle.

U.S. officials and observers worried that the U.S. concentration on technical preparedness for WARC was aimed at the wrong conference and suggested that to induce LDCs to concentrate on technical rather than political matters, the United States should demonstrate more understanding of their concerns. For instance, Senator Schmitt strongly recommended that "if those nations in the Third World need assistance to prepare for WARC, the U.S. should provide that assistance as part of the quid pro quo in WARC negotiations."[27] Others thought that a modest U.S. aid program announced at the 1978 UNESCO conference to assist LDCs in telecommunications development was already gesture enough of good will.[28]

In general throughout the period of preparation, communication between North and South left much to be desired. There were contacts among interest groups, such as national and regional telecommunications organizations, across borders. Intergovernmental communication was particularly poor between the United States and many LDCs (the Europeans have better contacts among NAM members). U.S. bilateral talks with LDCs, particularly in Africa, picked up significantly only after domestic critics pointed to their rarity.[29] Some of the visits were poorly planned; in one case, U.S. officials returned from Senegal's capital without having consulted with, or even learned about, the existence of the communications arm of the Organization of African Unity (OAU).[30] Exchanges of views with LDCs during the late stage of preparations was further handicapped by conflict between Canada and the United States over some of their WARC proposals, which consumed much domestic attention at that point.

Structure of the WARC Encounter

Traditional North-South inequalities were reflected not only in the amount of time and resources invested in preparations but also in the number of proposals submitted to WARC 79. They typically ranged from over 200 to 1,000 per country by industrial countries and from none to 200 by LDCs.[31] The latter were often also much less detailed. Other disparities related to participation in the negotiations themselves. The 15,000 submitted proposals were not rank ordered; each was to receive equal treatment. Many individual LDC proposals of minor international but major national concern were therefore put on an equal footing with others. The result was a greatly enhanced workload for all participants, and countries with smaller delegations were thus at a disadvantage. Of the 142 delegations, 102 were from the Third World (72 percent), but only 857 (51 percent) of delegates were from the South.[32]

The structure of the conference proceedings further reinforced North-South differences. Following the inaugural meeting, participants immediately split up into nine committees,[33] which were further broken down into about 120 working groups and subgroups. Most negotiating took place in these groups. Various articles of the Radio Regulations or parts of the Frequency Table and the relevant submitted negotiating proposals were assigned to the groups. Preliminary decisions taken there were then sent to the committee level and the plenary for amendment and final approval. If proposals on certain provisions required consideration in more than one committee, it was a matter for the committee chairperson to coordinate.[34]

The subgroup structure diffused the strength of the smaller delegations of the South. Although it did not prevent the occurrence of disputes, it helped limit opportunities for heated debate at a collective level. Linkages and trade-offs among issues debated in different groups also were more difficult to achieve. For example, as Committee 5 was plodding through its frequency reallocation agenda, individual Third World representatives repeatedly sought to bring into the discussions their views on the need for radical changes in the regulatory mechanism for frequency assignments, and to link that issue with the ongoing decisions on concrete spectrum redistribution among services. The chairperson then usually intervened by pointing out that regulatory questions fell under the negotiating mandate of a different committee.

Many delegations from LDCs were also unable to participate fully in the bargaining process at all working levels. They had to focus their involvement on the major committees and vote on other matters only at the final stage.[35] Even in key committees, such as Committee 5, complaints arose during WARC 79 from delegations that wished to present their proposals in working groups but were handicapped in doing so by overlapping session schedules.

From the beginning the negotiations operated under heavy time pressures. The ITU budget for WARC 79 was rigid, and costs of continuation beyond the ten-week schedule would have been great and probably also would have added financial burdens for all participants. Taking into account the preparatory work and prior circulation of proposals, albeit incomplete in the case of most nations, the schedule did not allow delegates to waste time on lengthy introductory proceedings. Getting down to business was the motto, but there was also a shared feeling that WARC was not a place for hasty decision making.[36]

A four-day delay of the opening of the conference, which eventually extended WARC by another week, until 6 December 1979, added pressure on the pace of negotiations and heightened awareness of the time crunch. Wrangling between North and South over the conference chairman and disputes over controversial issues later on themselves might have been much more prolonged without these time constraints. Still, by mid-October WARC turned into a day-and-evening marathon, without letup. The pace of accomplishment was slower than many had expected, and there were worries that WARC would not manage to complete its task.[37] The second plenary meeting of sixteen was not held until the seventh week (November 8), when enough drafted agreements had accumulated in committees to render the beginning of final readings and approvals worthwhile.

Time constraints and deadlines had several effects on the conduct of the negotiations, the negotiating process, and the outcome. Pressure was high on delegates—especially from LDCs, who sought to propose amendments in committee or plenary after they could not attend working-group meetings—to keep their statements short and even refrain from having their views taken into account. During the second plenary, a proposal that had not yet been fully discussed in committee pending definition of a term was withdrawn by the Canadian delegate to save time and avoid long discussion in committee. Soviet, Mexican, and Argentine delegates urged the plenary not to engage in protracted debates over the wording of texts but to arrive at a quick decision so as to allow the editorial committee to brush up the version of the Final Acts.[38] Plenaries turned into uneventful gatherings with hardly any substantial decision taking. Any significant change in one provision might have required the modification of other documents and would have added to the time crunch. The end of WARC was characterized by a rush to settle many outstanding issues.

If during committee negotiations delegates had different views on issues that did not concern most of the other delegates present, they were often encouraged by the chairperson to consult informally with a view to reaching a solution outside the meeting. Informal consultations on subjects of importance to delegates from different nations were held prior to the opening of their formal discussion in committee, and ad hoc groups were formally set up to deal with contentious issues. Their proliferation was not welcomed by many Third World delegations because they had difficulties in assigning participants to them.

The time constraint was partially responsible for the number of footnotes in the Final Acts compared with documents adopted by the preceding radio administrative conferences. Time was too short to deal effectively with so many conflicting interests. Also, many controversial or complex issues were deferred for further study by ITU or follow-up at one of the many future conferences decided upon at WARC. (Three world and seven regional conferences were recommended for the 1980s.) The postponements averted much potential escalation of conflicts between LDCs and industrial countries over space service or HF broadcasting planning, and allowed less controversial issues to be settled without delay.

The Negotiations: An Overview

WARC 79 did not turn into a North-South battlefield. Politics of conflict provided the setting for its opening; a spirit of compromise and cooperation marked its end. The conference was characterized by ten weeks of intensive negotiations in which technically oriented discussions won out over political debates. National interests and priorities were given ascendancy over the collective ones seen in polarized North-South negotiations in other international forums. Most opening positions were made by individual nations. Joint proposals originated almost exclusively within the Third World but were few in number. Coalitions that were formed during negotiations were flexible and often comprised delegates from both camps. And finally, the overall agreement hammered out reflected an incremental adjustment process rather than a radical overhaul of the international radiocommunications system. The Final Acts of WARC 79, a thousand-page international treaty containing virtually hundreds of coordinated decisions, contained something for everyone.[39] Most of the negotiated agreements were highly technical in nature, some concerned noncontroversial issues, but others were the outcome of lengthy bargaining over conflicting priorities. Ranging from political and ideological feuds to differences over principles underlying the management of spectrum assignments and conflicting radio frequency allocation demands, they distinctly portrayed the new reality created by the participation and aspirations of Third World nations.

New Order Challenges Old Order: The Chairmanship Dispute

In retrospect, one is tempted to downplay the importance of the few political and ideological showdowns at WARC 79. After all, it turned out to be a success. Nevertheless, the dispute over the conference chairmanship was a significant event. It featured the North-South confrontation politics that the North wished to avoid, and it influenced the psychological climate of the conference. Occurring at the very outset, the dispute threatened the conference with failure even before it had officially started. Once resolved, it set a precedential accommodation and cooperation process that guided many of the subsequent negotiating encounters.

ITU conferences had always chosen their chairmen by consensus,[40] and most delegates from industrial countries came to Geneva believing their informal selection of the head of the New Zealand delegation would be acceptable to all. But when ITU Secretary-General Mili of Tunisia presented the name at the heads of delegations meeting, NAM representatives countered with Mr. Srirangan of India as their preference. So began difficult negotiations that delayed the conference opening for almost a week. The United States-led Western bloc opposed the NAM nominee, proposing instead a series of alternative, usually pro-Western candidates. The NAM group stood firm on the grounds that the Havana conference of NAM had decided that the chairman of WARC should come from its ranks.[41] It even rejected a Swiss, Henry Kieffer.

For the first time the ITU was faced with the possibility of a vote for a conference chairman. It was obvious that the LDCs had enough votes to win, and the domination of WARC 79 by what appeared at first sight to be a solid bloc of the South was the worst scenario industrial countries could think of. A middle-of-the-road solution was found after several days of stalemate when both sides settled for a compromise chairman, Robert Severini of Argentina, which was a more moderate NAM country. A candidate of neither side, he was proposed by a group of Latin American delegates and accepted by consensus. For the West, the deal was sweetened in that Kieffer was accepted as conference vice-chairman and overall coordinator of the three key committees, 4, 5, and 6.

Selection of the committee chairman took place in a more conciliatory atmosphere. The choice of Mohamed Harbi of Algeria, a little-known man (who turned out to be highly competent), as chairman of Committee 5 caused few misgivings on the part of the North, with the exception of the U.S. delegation.

Although most WARC 79 decisions were to take place at the working group and committee levels, the conference chairmanship had considerable symbolic value for a group of LDCs that came to WARC frustrated with its technical preparations. Only once before, at the specialized WARC on Aeronautical Mobile Services, had a non-Western delegate chaired an ITU conference,[42] and the success at WARC 79 could be interpreted by the South as a small step in the direction of NWIO. For the North, it marked a break with tradition, but perhaps equally important was that the consensus rule had survived the political test. The dispute further demonstrated that in a technically sterile negotiating context, the North's technical expertise was no asset, and unity on the part of the South worked well. What distinguished the multilateral negotiations at WARC after the consensus selection of a chairman from those dragging on in other international forums throughout the 1970s was not the relative absence of conflicts of interest—WARC probably had to accommodate many more than most other negotiations—but the relatively weak cohesiveness of the South as one party at the negotiating tables. The LDCs found no mechanism to coordinate national interests and objectives into a shopping list backed in concert. They were generally unwilling to engage with industrial countries in trade-offs across issues, but they were also reluctant to trade off among themselves. Morocco had sought to furnish all LDCs with "memory aids" for organized collective action by asking the ITU General Secretariat to include all the recommendations made at preparatory conferences of NAM in the working documents published for the conference.[43] The recommendation was never followed up, and NAM meetings held during WARC were unable to sustain a unified stand.

Other Political Tests of Strength

A number of political skirmishes at WARC 79 did not relate to North-South divisions. These typically involved small groups of delegations and arose during the examination of credentials in Committee 2 and in Committee 7, which dealt with administrative matters not falling under the work of other committees.

East-West relations were remarkably good throughout the conference. Political differences that did erupt concerned mainly nontechnical issues. In one instance the Soviet Union, joined by several of its Eastern European allies, Cuba, and Nicaragua, strongly argued against acceptance of the credentials of the Kampuchean delegation, but support by China, the United States, and Thailand in favor of their acceptance led to a positive decision by the conference. A challenge by the Soviet Union and East Germany regarding the legitimacy of several delegates residing in West Berlin to act as representatives of West Germany sparked another dispute. The Soviet delegate backed his position by quoting from the 1971 Quatripartite Agreement, but the United States, West Germany, and the United Kingdom countered with a similar quotation from a different passage of the same document. The conference accepted the view of the West but granted the East a note for the record of its position.[44] A bilateral U.S.-Soviet political test of strength occurred in Committee 7 over a Soviet proposal to have the international call signs of Lithuania, Latvia, and Estonia in the old WARC treaty read "USSR" in the new one. Although the U.S. delegate was instructed to oppose this change in U.S. nonrecognition of the Soviet annexation of these countries, he found himself isolated as WARC adopted the change.[45]

A lengthier negotiation on international call signs assignments pitted North Korea against South Korea. South Korea resisted a demand by North Korea that it had over half of a call sign series, HLA-HMZ, that had been assigned to the Republic of Korea since 1959 but before partition had been assigned to Korea. Both countries used the series but only South Korea had call signs registered with the ITU. Bilateral talks outside the conference failed and both countries raised the issue in Committee 7 by accusing the other of distorting data and being unwilling to compromise. After it was offered an additional new series of call signs, South Korea came around to conceding in principle the HMA-HMZ portion to North Korea, seeking still to keep the transition period as lenient as possible. Britain proposed that because call signs that did not correspond to the new separation of the series could not be expected to occur overnight, a footnote should be added to the changed allocation that would recognize the need for an orderly transition and allow South Korea's registered call signs in the HMA-HMZ portion to be removed gradually and without specific time constraints. Siding with North Korea, the Soviet Union and other countries supported the British proposal in principle but demanded a clear time limit for the entire changeover. Subsequent negotiations on a definite date saw Britain proposing 1986 and Algeria suggesting 1982, reflecting the preference of North Korea and its supporters. Both dates, especially Algeria's, were regarded as too short by South Korea.

Cameroon intervened by proposing 1984 as a compromise. In secret ballot voting, the footnote amended with this date was endorsed by the conference as an integral part of the equal division of the call signs series and acceptable to both Koreas.[46]

Secret ballot voting also figured highly in the delicate management of Arab-Israeli tensions surfacing here and there during the frequency reallocation negotiations. The administrations involved exchanged politically assertive statements and counter statements in the final protocol.[47]

Principles and Procedures: Equity North, Equity South

A central focus of the debate at WARC 79 was on the principles and procedures underlying the assignment of radio spectrum frequencies and orbital slots. Of the two areas that involved long negotiations and attracted many participants, one concerned the adequacy of existing regulatory procedures governing registration of frequency assignments for satellite services and the use of the geostationary orbit in providing equitable access on a nondiscriminatory basis. The other area related to LDC requests for preferential access to HF bands for their fixed services.

Many LDCs complained at WARC 79 that the first-come, first-served assignment of satellite frequencies and orbit use served the interests of advanced communications powers but not their own. They considered a detailed, negotiated plan alloting specific frequency channels and geostationary orbit slots to every country independent of its current needs and usage capability as the only means to guarantee every nation equitable access—now and in the future, when more countries would enter the satellite communications age. Advanced industrial countries, most notably the United States, strongly defended the soundness and equity of the existing evolutionary assignment procedures. They countered that allotment schemes of the kind favored by the LDCs would waste spectrum and freeze technology that would, and could, on technical grounds, secure access for every country even in the long run.

Another request shared by many LDCs was to get more access to HF (3-30 MHz) bands. LDCs rely heavily on these bands for basic national (e.g. rural communications networks) and international communications via fixed links. Their use requires relatively little investment compared to bands in higher radio spectrum regions. Thanks to technological innovations, the fixed service in industrial countries has been increasingly channeled via satellite or microwave traffic in higher spectrum bands (VHF, UHF, SHF). Transmission there is better in quality and more reliable but cannot yet be afforded by the majority of LDCs for economic and technological reasons. Losing interest in HF fixed service allocations, many industrial countries instead sought increased allocations there for other services, such as international broadcasting, maritime, or amateur service, whose requirements were often outgrowing existing allocations. The problem was that these requirements could be accommodated only by displacing fixed service in already congested HF frequency bands, and therefore conflicted with LDC priorities. Industrial countries generally acknowledged the importance of the fixed service to LDCs and stressed, as France and the Soviet Union did, that they sought only a "reasonable" reduction of fixed service bands, or suggested, as the United Kingdom did, compensatory allocations for this service on a secondary basis. Among Third World proposals, Uganda and Cameroon in very general terms asked industrial countries to pack in their HF assignments so as to reserve large portions of these bands for countries with scarce resources and immense needs for low-cost communications. Morocco asked industrial countries to refrain from registering HF frequencies for a period of five years and to give to LDCs all the frequencies registered on their behalf that they no longer used.[48] The North saw a greater threat in an Algerian call for HF fixed (and mobile) service bands to be divided 70:30 in favor of the Third World.[49]

The Negotiation Process

Industrial countries wished to avoid debate on political generalities during the negotiations. No single nation so far had been denied through the ITU access to spectrum and orbit, they said. Third World delegates said current rapid satellite-system developments in the North would fill the limited orbit space before most LDCs were in a position to use it. Except for India,[50] none of them could, however, back this concern with concrete evidence; most of it was oriented toward the future. For the same reason, hypotheses by industrial countries that preemption would not happen were also less than persuasive. Another problem for challengers of the existing assignment procedures was that despite agreement among several influential countries that a future specialized WARC should undertake detailed planning for space services, they disagreed as to which space services in which bands should be included. China proposed that only new allocations made at WARC for the fixed satellite service (FSS) below 10 GHz should be planned in this way. India insisted that the FSS, and the feederlinks for the BSS in some economically and technically attractive bands, 4/6 and 11/14 GHz, be included. The most ambitious proposal of all, embracing all space services throughout the entire spectrum, came from Iraq. A modest proposal, confining planning to the BSS feederlinks at 12 GHz was also presented by the Soviet Union.[51]

The matter was further complicated. Equatorial countries—Colombia, Congo, Ecuador, Gabon, Kenya, Somalia, Uganda, and Zaire— jointly called for a future WARC to adopt specific regulations rather than assignment plans. This would guarantee equitable access to the geostationary orbit by all countries and give LDCs in particular preferential treatment. It would also take into account a "prior-consent" condition for the use of orbital positions above equatorial states.[52] The emphasis here was on the condition. It essentially amounted to legitimizing the claims of a would-be geostationary OPEC,[53] and conflicted with notions of compensatory allotment, such as Morocco's proposal that at least one position in the geostationary orbit be reserved for each country.

It became clear during the discussion that the idea of space service planning could not be disposed of with a wink. The Canadian, French, and Australian delegates therefore initiated a search for a compromise among the different parties. Alternatives to space service planning were proposed, among them, improvement of existing technical coordination procedures, including simplification of the process of obtaining assignments, and assistance by the IFRB to individual nations in special need.[54] The key to a viable solution, however, was that nobody seriously objected to the convening of a future Space WARC to deal with the matter. What industrial countries, and foremost the United States, did seek to prevent, though, was a specific mandate for the conference to engage in LDCish planning. The proponents of planning predominantly favored detailed, country-by-country, a priori planning in the manner of the 1977 BSS WARC. Industrial countries, including European countries that in 1977 the BSS assignment scheme, insisted on broader terms of reference for the Space WARC, i.e. consideration of a wide range of possible solutions to the issue of access guarantee. The equatorial country group was not initially enthusiastic about the planning idea but together with LDC "planners" worked out an acceptable accommodation of their interests. According to a draft resolution introduced by Algeria, the future WARC would take place in two sessions, the first of which would "establish principles, technical parameters and criteria for the planning of the orbit and frequency assignments for space services . . . taking into account relevant aspects of the particular geographic situation of equatorial countries."[55]

The Algerian resolution still smacked too much of a priori planning to delegates from industrial countries such as the United States, who also objected to the recognition of the equatorial claims in the text. India subsequently submitted a broader version that gained more acceptance and provided the basis for the final resolution put together during multilateral consultations in which fifteen of the most vocal delegates, a majority of them from LDCs, participated. It called for a Space WARC to be convened no later than 1984 to consider a variety of unspecified approaches to ensure equitable access to geostationary orbit and frequency bands allocated to space services. The text made no reference to equatorial countries, mentioning only "the geographic situation of particular countries."[56] Because the Indian resolution was worded vaguely enough to permit flexible interpretations, planners, antiplanners, and equatorial states could all claim some success. The United States could not resist reemphasizing its understanding of the planning aspect of the resolution to be broad, and attached a special statement; a spokesman for an African group said he expected the future WARC to engage in a priori planning.[57]

At the eleventh hour of WARC 79, in plenary, the equatorial states, led by Colombia, also decided to make explicit their interpretation of the text in one of two protocol statements they submitted on the sovereignty issue. The move reopened the dispute between eight equatorial countries and twenty-three Western nations under U.S. and British leadership. The former wished to clarify that the resolution's reference to the special geographic situation implied also recognition of that of the equatorial states relative to the orbit above them. The statement itself was submitted in the form of a counterstatement, which normally precludes further response. In reality, there had been no prior reservation to which it could have served as a reply. The only one at which it could have been targeted was itself a counterreservation made by the Western group to an earlier protocol statement in which the equatorial states had reaffirmed their sovereignty rights in general terms only. The Western group not only challenged the legality of this move, including its submission after the deadline for reservations, but also reproached the authors for deliberately trying to prevent counterstatements to their claim by other countries. The dispute was resolved finally by a compromise initiated by Conference Chairman Severini. The plenary accepted the statement by Colombia and its allies but allowed the Western group to add another statement repudiating its content.[58] The group of equatorial country delegates was rhetorically strong at WARC but failed to win international recognition of its claims. In practical terms, its members have little effective power to protect their interests. They simply do not have the means to prevent the parking of satellites in orbit above them.

In the HF fixed service controversy, which came to center on the Algerian proposal, the delegates of the United States, Canada, the United Kingdom, France, Australia, and other countries rejected the proposal, as it stood, as a matter of principle. In informal and formal negotiations, they showed understanding for the radio communications needs of the LDCs. They simultaneously launched a campaign pinpointing and highlighting for others whatever technical weaknesses they could find in Algeria's scheme, and they searched for a technical solution to a problem with political undertones. They managed to persuade Algeria's chief of delegation Bouhired in long informal talks that amendments to the existing allocation regulations could help LDCs meet their fixed service requirements. Together with him, they drafted a special cleanup procedure to remove all inactive radio station assignments from the Frequency Table in the HF fixed service bands within a year, thus freeing many frequencies for reassignment.[59] To render the deal even more acceptable, industrial countries also gave their blessing to another general resolution urging minimum industrial and maximum LDC use of IFRB resources to give LDCs more assistance in securing access to HF bands for fixed service, and ensuring protection of their assignments from harmful interference. The final compromise arrangement did not negatively effect the interests of the North.[60]

Frequency Reallocations: A Juggling Exercise in Multilateral Accommodation of Conflicting Priorities

Frequency band distributions among various user services involved clashes of interests in Committee 5 on questions of how much allocation should be granted to which service, and where on the spectrum. Most international radio communications services operate at frequencies between 10 kHz and 40 GHz, with some forty services being allocated certain bands within which to operate. Technical breakthroughs originating in the North provide new communications capabilities gradually extending the upper margin of the usable spectrum. The higher the frequencies, the less intensive their use, and working groups reviewing fewer requests for this part of the spectrum proceeded relatively quickly and without many controversies.

There was a strong unwillingness on the part of LDCs to sacrifice HF fixed service allocations in order to meet requests by many industrial countries for allocations, either on an exclusive or a shared basis, to other services. One of the areas in which it was particularly difficult to reach agreement was international broadcasting. At one extreme stood the United States, which wanted to extend existing HF bands for shortwave broadcasting by almost 50 percent to accommodate the growing demands of its broadcasting services, such as Voice of America, Radio Free Europe, and Radio Liberty. European and Asian nations tended to accept a more moderate increase. At the other extreme stood the Soviet Union, which did not ask for any increase, and many Latin American countries, including Brazil, which opposed extensions on the grounds that they needed the bands in question primarily for their fixed services and deemed existing HF broadcasting allocations adequate. Significant also was the view shared by a group of influential Third World representatives—from Algeria, Nigeria, Syria, Afghanistan, India, Brazil—and China, Yugoslavia, and the Soviet Union, that a future WARC for HF broadcasting services should convene to establish a worldwide detailed assignment plan. Most of these countries wanted such a conference regardless of whether WARC 79 decided to extend the HF broadcasting bands or not. Committee 5 agreed that an ad hoc group should deal with the HF broadcasting question. Negotiations revealed a strong desire by LDCs, especially by Brazil and other Latin American countries, not to tie acceptance of the planning of HF bands for broadcasting and of the draft terms of reference of the ad hoc group to acceptance of requests for an expansion of existing bands. Such a linkage was actively sought by many Western countries in an attempt to influence WARC decisions on HF broadcasting allocations.

The conference finally decided that a future specialized WARC be held.[61] As with the Space WARC, scope and character were kept open. The conference also settled for a 33 percent increase in HF broadcasting allocations. Support by numerous African delegates of the West's request for allocations contributed to this outcome. Countries such as Kenya backed their position with the argument that in large countries with underdeveloped communications structures, HF broadcasting was often the only way to reach dispersed populations. However, their position appeared also rooted in a desire to combat cultural domination resulting from foreign broadcasting services originating from countries such as the United States.[62] Furthermore, the reallocation decision was not a signal for an unconditional go-ahead. According to a footnote to the Frequency Table, broadcasting operations in the new bands can begin only after the fixed service has been satisfactorily transferred by affected nations to other bands; the time limits are 1994 for the one band allocated to the HF broadcasting service below 10 MHz, and 1989 for the bands above 10 GHz.[63] It was a compromise among LDCs and the Soviet Union, which naturally preferred a drawn-out period and countries like the United States, the United Kingdom, and Canada, which pressed for a short transition period.

Still, Western countries decried the inadequacy of additional broadcasting allocations at this WARC. A future WARC adopting any allotment plan conceived by Eastern Europeans and LDCs would leave the West with fewer HF broadcasting channels. Furthermore, LDC determination to defend existing fixed service allocations below 10 MHz narrowly defeated proposals for a worldwide expansion of crowded broadcasting bands at 6 and 7 MHz. At this, the United States, four Western European countries, Saudi Arabia, and two LDCs made a joint reservation in the final protocol to protect their rights to their HF broadcasting services if the future conference failed to make adequate arrangements for international broadcasting allocations.[64] Left undefined was what was meant by *adequate*. Similar but separate reservations were made by West Germany, Austria, Iran, Pakistan, and other nations.

In general, pressure from LDCs prevented major reallocations of bands below 10 MHz from fixed service to other services. Band sharing with maritime and land mobile services was stepped up, but these allocations tended to be on a secondary basis. A significant band reallocation from fixed service to broadcasting, maritime mobile, and amateur services took place between 10 MHz and 30 MHz, accompanied by conditions as to transferring services and scheduling. The HF allocations were among the most difficult to negotiate and at the end of WARC 79 were far from settled. About twenty reservations were made on them, many expressing the concern of a Third World country that it might not be able, due to technical and economic reasons, to transfer displaced fixed service to new bands.[65]

Industrial countries made many initiatives to adopt new technical standards. Measures to enhance the efficient use of the radio spectrum and reduce congestion and harmful interference were often not carried and were resisted by LDCs. The countries with advanced communications technology may have escaped Third World blame for costs associated with such mandatory technical readaptations. LDCs lack the investment resources, technical equipment, and often the expertise to implement such techniques. WARC 1979 deferred a good part of these initiatives for further study by the ITU and reconsideration at future conferences.

In the GHz region of the radio spectrum, the major controversial issue was space services, and more specifically, the frequencies to be allocated to the FSS and BSS links. Demand originated from both the North and the South. Communications satellite services are growing among the Third World, enabling LDCs to communicate over vast distances with remote areas, often by skipping the step of setting up costly traditional ground systems first. Apart from military satellite systems, INTERSPUTNIK and especially INTELSAT, with more than a hundred member countries as indirect or direct users, are the dominant commercial FSS operating internationally.

Prior to WARC 1979, INTELSAT had extensively lobbied member nations to publicize its acute frequency shortage. At WARC, parties easily agreed upon the extension of the 6 GHz band for BSS uplinks, but preferences differed sharply for bands accommodating downlink requirements. In line with INTELSAT recommendations, most LDCs favored the 3.4-3.7 GHz and the 4.5-4.8 GHz bands. INTELSAT was already operating in the bands adjacent to the former. A previous WARC had allocated the latter band to FSS but hardly any satellite system operated there in 1979. Both bands were heavily used by important radiolocation, fixed and mobile systems that the United States, NATO, and other Western nations maintained for military purposes. Radiolocation could cause serious interference to satellite terminals there, but any constraints on radiolocation were unacceptable for these countries, especially for the United States. An LDC grouping led by India, which also cared about its own domestic FSS plans, nevertheless commanded a majority of votes in favor of downgrading this service in the 3.4-3.6 GHz band to status secondary to FSS, which would be the prime user. The United States subsequently threatened not to implement the new FSS frequencies at home, not to provide protection to the service from the radars, and even to use its influence as a major shareholder in INTELSAT to block implementation of the FSS allocations.[66]

The U.S. position led to a search for a compromise solution. West Germany initiated an idea for a footnote to the Frequency Table that would allow Region 2 and Region 3 countries to maintain the primary status of radiolocation in the 3 GHz band but would urge all nations to phase out this service by 1985 and to take all practical steps afterward to protect the FSS in this band.[67] This solution did not find unanimous support, and in committee India criticized its provisions as being too lax. Backed by Algeria, Iran, Afghanistan, and Ecuador, India put forward a mandatory 1990 deadline for a worldwide downgrading of radiolocation in the band. Despite protests by the United States, Japan, and Brazil that the date was too close, Committee 5 decided in favor of the Indian amendment. The United States then moved to implement one of its threats by placing before the committee a special footnote barring the 3 GHz FSS allocation in the United States. To underline its opposition, it also included in the footnote the 4.5-4.8 GHz band.[68] The footnote, whose exemption of the 4.5-4.8 GHz band was also sought by several NATO allies,[69] would severely limit the use of both bands by the FSS in general and INTELSAT in particular.

Jamaica led fifteen LDCs from all regions along with INTELSAT representatives and parties involved in the feud to form an ad hoc group on the last working day of Committee 5 to overcome the impasse. Hours of talks long after the committee had completed its work, and intensive lobbying by the U.S. and its European allies against the mandatory deadline finally led to another compromise. Written by the LDC group[70] and introduced by Jamaica in one of the last plenaries, the proposal traded deletion of the Indian amendment for deletion of the restrictive footnote. The 3.4-3.6 GHz band was allocated on a worldwide, primary basis to FSS downlinks, but Region 2 and Region 3 nations could retain the primary status of radiolocation. The FSS was also added to the 4.5-4.8 GHz band, except in the United Kingdom, the Netherlands, Belgium, and Norway. In a special declaration, the United States, Canada, Australia, Belgium, the United Kingdom, and the Netherlands pledged not to withhold support for the implementation of the FSS in both bands, and to make reasonable efforts to accommodate the FSS.[71] As in the initial compromise, all nations were urged to cease radiolocation operations in these bands by 1985. After other LDCs realized that FSS was better off with this compromise than without and lined up behind the proposal, and after the United States and other signatories of the special declaration declared it a binding treaty, India relented.[72] The United States and its allies got their way in avoiding an obligatory time frame for adjustment of radiolocation. The compromise, like many others at WARC, bought time for nations, in this case for several industrial nations, to adjust their operations to a WARC decision gradually.

Another compromise had to be worked out in negotiations on additional radio frequencies within the existing FSS bands usable for feederlinks for the BSS. Most NAM countries, led again by India,[73] wanted the 14.5-15.35 GHz band for BSS feederlinks. The Soviet Union initially favored a band around 13 GHz. Some Western European delegates liked 10.7-11.7 GHz, and many Region 2 countries, including the United States and Brazil, the 17.3-18.1 GHz band. The United States and some Western European countries operated defense communications in the upper parts of the 14.4-15.35 GHz band, and the Soviet Union operated other important services there. In the initial search for a working group under Committee 5 for an accommodation of the divergent views, the Soviet Union and India each proposed a compromise solution. In both, countries had the option of choosing between two bands, one being the 17.3-18.1 GHz band, according to their own technical and other considerations. The Soviets proposed a second option of 10.7-11.7 GHz; and India, the band preferred by most LDCs. As expected, the Indian proposal was endorsed by the majority of delegates. The United States and the Soviet Union, however, would not guarantee coordination or protection of BSS feederlinks in regard to other existing services in the 14.5-15.35 GHz band.[74]

After stalemate, an ad hoc group was instructed to work on a solution. Although everybody favored a uniform allocation worldwide as the best solution from the standpoint of efficient spectrum use, this proved unrealistic. Informal consultations among twenty-eight delegates, most of them from LDCS,[75] produced a preliminary agreement that sacrificed the worldwide allocation objective to some extent but had something for everybody. A unanimous agreement to provide two or more optional frequency bands for the feederlinks constituted the basic formula. In Regions 2 and 3, the band allocated the BSS feederlinks on an exclusive basis would be 17.3-18.1 GHz, and 14.0-14.5 GHz would also be available. Besides 10.7-11.7 GHz and 17.3-18.1 GHz exclusively allocated in Region 1, a band around 14.5 GHz would be available for Malta and countries outside Europe. Across regions, and especially within Region 1, delegates still argued which frequencies around 14.5 GHz should go to feederlinks on an exclusive basis and which frequencies on a basis of sharing in coordination with BSS. INTELSAT, which operated FSS uplinks in the 14.0-14.5 GHz band, had plans for major service increases there within the next decade. Several countries had substantial investments in FSS uplinks in earth stations and equipment. The FSS networks required wide bandwidth, and reduction would force INTELSAT to operate in uneconomical ways. Japan and Australia suggested sharing in the 14.2-14.5 GHz band only, but Venezuela, Cameroon, and Sudan strongly argued for coordination, with FSS in the entire 14.0-14.5 GHz. Norway and West Germany still sought to persuade other delegates to give up the 14 GHz band idea and instead concentrate on the 10.7-11.7 GHz and/or the 17.3-18.1 GHz bands. In a final vote LDCs carried, the ovewhelming majority favoring 14.0-14.5 GHz for feederlinks on a coordinated basis, and 14.5-14.8 GHz on an exclusive basis.

Despite the fact that Committee 5 had accepted these allocations almost unanimously, Sudan in plenary sought a further modification: an extension of the 14.5-14.8 GHz exclusive allocation for BSS feederlinks by another 100 MHz to a total of 400 MHz. It argued that the bandwidth after all was not enough to meet the projected requirements for Region 1 in accordance with the 1977 BSS plan, and asked that either 14.45-14.85 or 14.5-14.9 GHz be allocated exclusively. Its delegate emphasized that African countries were concerned about the rapidly growing use of frequencies in the 14.0-14.5 GHz band by the FSS. The first-come, first-served assignment policy would enable the FSS to occupy most of these frequencies and preempt access to orbital positions for satellites before African countries were in a position to implement their BSS plans.[76] The proposed extension was strongly backed by Iran, Kenya, Nigeria, and Algeria. The United States rejected any FSS feederlink allocation above 14.8 GHz because of military communications services there, and was supported by Canada, France, West Germany, Switzerland, and Brazil. The request by the African group was defeated in two plenary votes by a small majority.[77]

Other, smaller skirmishes at WARC 79 involved spectrum sharing in satellite service bands. Still far from using satellite services as intensively as the North, the Third World in general saw no special need for it to be given exclusive allocations without coordination with terrestrial services. Many wished to add fixed and mobile services on a primary basis in these bands in the Table, or "additional allocation" footnotes permitting only individual countries listed to operate terrestrial services in certain satellite service bands as well. Footnotes introduced by LDCs at the end often included a long list of countries. It often annoyed industrial countries, which wished to keep satellite services as free as possible from constraints coordination upon interservice interference problems, and reductions in the spectrum available for their use. WARC saw many votes on footnoting specific bands, and on terrestrial service sharing on a primary or secondary basis. Countries, whose national interests were not involved in a proposed footnote, often did not vote. LDCs requesting an additional footnote or inclusion in existing ones usually were not backed by their peers against the North. Had voting occurred solely along political lines, industrial countries would not have succeeded in repeatedly persuading the conference to delete footnotes drafted in working groups, to downgrade to secondary status fixed service allocations originally sought by LDCs on a primary basis, or to attach other constraints on the use of bands by services other than satellite.[78] Often, the priorities of LDCs themselves diverged sharply on these issues. The party with the factually better backed arguments usually prevailed. In one instance, Brazil, Argentina, Guatemala, and Sudan joined forces with the United

States and France in protecting UHF bands exclusively allocated to meteorological aids and satellite service against fixed service. Other LDCs, together with Eastern bloc nations, requested fixed service inclusion in the same bands on a primary basis, and had succeeded in having a working group approve this allocation. In committee, Brazil strongly objected to the decision, pointing out to other LDCs that a majority of the service stations of the World Meterological Organization (WMO) World Watch Program and Global Observation System operated in these bands. The reminder that this service was needed especially in the Southern Hemisphere and benefited all countries contributed to the eventual overturn of the previous working group decision.[79]

Alignments and Bargaining on Intraregional Issues

Issues raised at WARC 79 were often regional. Some were general, others specific; on some, agreement was not difficult; on others, bargaining was lengthy; some involved the particular preferences of a group of LDCs; others gave rise to coalitions of LDCs and industrial countries. Decisions were reached at WARC on all issues, but as elsewhere "moral final" settlements will have to be made in the future.

According to joint or individual proposals from several African countries, the existing ITU division of the world into three regions no longer adequately meets the requirements of LDC's, particularly those in Africa. In view of the different priorities accorded to communications services in Europe and Africa,[80] they proposed that Region 1 be subdivided and a separate African region set up. Africans believed that living under the shadow of Europe hampered the development of their own communications systems. The discussion never really got off the ground. Only Nigeria and Kenya strongly favored immediate creation of an African region. The Europeans, an IFRB representative who was consulted, and most other delegates preferred first to undertake a more careful study. Even such a strong proponent of Third World interests at WARC as Algeria was reluctant to go ahead with a revision. Part of the reason is the proximity of North African countries to Europe. Regardless of the ITU region in which they would find themselves, they would still have to coordinate frequency use with the Europeans.[81] An ad hoc group of representatives from all parts of Region 1 consequently drafted a resolution, later adopted, that instructed the ITU International Radio Consultative Committee to study a possible revision of the regional frequency arrangement and its implications.[82]

In the frequency reallocation negotiations, African countries successfully concentrated their bargaining efforts on defending existing allocations for services that they regarded vital to their national telecommunications development plans against the Europeans, who wished to extend other services into these bands.[83] Again, negotiated packages consisting of Table allocations accompanied by footnotes proved to be a useful mechanism for accommodating divergent intraregional priorities.

Two key actors in an intraregional conflict over satellite service in the 12 GHz band in Region 2 were the United States and Canada. U.S.-Canadian differences related to the 1977 BSS interim plan in which the fixed and the broadcasting satellite service was to share the 12 GHz band until a regional administrative radio conference in 1983. Both countries sought an extension of the band for space services in order to meet their domestic commercial needs. However, the United States also proposed a separation of the frequencies for the two services, with FSS to operate in the 11.7-12.2 GHz band and BSS to move into the 12.2-12.7 GHz band, which was being used at the time by terrestrial services. The United States tried to sell this formula as ensuring the availability of sufficient orbital positions and spectrum to permit all countries in the region to meet their current and anticipated satellite service needs for years to come. If both types of satellites use the same band, satellites in one service must be separated by a considerable distance from those in the other to avoid interference.

In reality, the United States wished to have BSS move also because it was engaged in extensive development planning for domestic FSS in the lower band. Canada objected to the separation because it was interested in developing a hybrid satellite system that would use a single frequency band for both services. It therefore preferred no change until at least the 1983 conference. This was not to the liking of the United States, which also feared that if both space services continued to share the same band, that conference might decide to subject not only BSS but also FSS to the detailed assignment planning the United States resented so much.

Bilateral talks prior to WARC 79 had failed to resolve the dispute between the United States and Canada, but both countries had successfully lobbied for allies among the Latin Americans. Argentina, Venezuela, and Mexico sided with Canada, and Chile and Brazil with the United States. Canada's status quo stance was supported by some Latin Americans, not because of a shared interest in hybrid satellites per se but because they were worried that the U.S. scheme would allow it to quickly exploit the 12 GHz band for its national interest before an equitable allotment plan could protect their future interests.[84]

The outcome of lengthy private and formal negotiations at WARC, in which neither the United States nor Canada could muster sufficient support to isolate the other, was a compromise incorporating inputs from all parties with a stake in the issue. A deal was first struck among the United States, Canada, and Brazil that accepted the U.S. proposition but gave hybrid satellite systems limited access to both separate bands. Other Latin American delegates then initiated a further modification that reserved a middle segment of 11.7-12.7 GHz for continued use by both satellite services until the 1983 conference would make a final decision.[85]

Several other controversies within Region 2 were settled with less satisfaction to constituent countries. Among them were disagreements between the United States and Canada over spectrum allocations for competing services at border regions—often explosive issues where neighborly relations are disharmonious to begin with.

Telecommunications Aid

The gap in economic and telecommunications development between rich and poor countries figured prominently in all plenary speeches of Third World delegates, and accompanied in one context or another all LDC proposals at WARC 79. Discussions on development assistance at this conference, however, were very different from North-South confrontations other negotiating forums have seen.

ITU's primary job is to administer development funds from other agencies, largely from the United Nations Development Program (UNDP). The voluntary ITU fund, contributed to mainly by the Scandinavia, Europe, and Japan, is so small as to be almost not worth mentioning.[86] LDCs at WARC 79 pressed neither for its enlargement nor for the setting up of any other mandatory assistance schemes. Whatever new and increased multilateral technical assistance they sought, they focused neither on one single grand scheme nor on bombarding the North with provocative political arguments. Rather, they identified a multitude of specific issues under ITU's jurisdiction.

As the years 1965, 1971, and 1982 show, LDCs have singled out the ITU Plenipotentiary Conferences, dealing with the administrative and financial side of the regime, as their favorite target for development aid. At WARC 79, a more equitable North-South spectrum distribution was a more important priority for them. Spectrum and orbit rights were scarce resources that would then be safe from preemption by the technically and economically superior North. But there was also competition for these resources within the South itself, and subgroups with different interests and needs sought special assistance at WARC. Serious dispute over aid were also dampened by the willingness of industrial countries to consider proposals as long as they were WARC-related and not targeted at their wallets. As a result there was at least some constructive search for provisions geared toward the development needs of LDCs. Much of it involved informal talks outside regular meetings. Development assistance was not a separate item on WARC's agenda.

What the North "conceded" to the South is contained in fifteen resolutions and recommendations in the Final Acts. The LDCs did most of the drafting; the industrial countries did the editing to ensure that the wording was consistent with their view that the ITU not be involved in North-South wholesale reallocations of either radio frequencies or wealth. Nothing in content here challenged the old world communications and economic order. Some African and Asian delegates jointly sponsored a resolution that recognized that many LDCs could not afford the modern telecommunications that could promote integrated rural development, and that urged all countries to strengthen technical assistance and actively participate in ITU studies in this area. At the initiative of Chile, Ecuador, Colombia, and Nigeria another resolution called on ITU members to support the union's technical cooperation with LDCs in maritime communications development. It also requested the secretary-general to seek the collaboration of forums such as the United States Conference on Trade and Development (UNCTAD) in technically advising LDCs, and of the UNDP and other sources for financial assistance. Cameroon, supported by others, sponsored a technology transfer resolution, urging more technical assistance and telecommunications technology transfer across the board.[87]

One frequently heard LDC statement was that without technical infrastructure and frequency management capabilities, developing countries would be unable to understand frequency management matters or fulfill their obligations and responsibilities under the Radio Regulations; they are too poor and existing bilateral aid is too scarce. Again, many resolutions were drafted and approved to strengthen ITU activities that assist Third World countries with problems, but none set up financial arrangements or was designed to make governments pledge financial support. For instance, Algeria's resolution that the ITU organize meetings to design management structures suitable for LDCs was adopted, but it recommended simply that LDCs use money from existing unspecified international sources for their participation at such meetings and for subsequent implementation of the structures.[88] WARC 79 distributed no single communications aid package for LDCs with financing commitments by the North. Instead, plenaries adopted provisions with significant support by industrial countries, and without much debate—impressive looking in quantity but often vague, and unlikely to make a real, immediate dent in the North-South communications gap.

The overall negotiating climate of WARC 79 undoubtedly was helped by the absence of confrontation over development assistance issues. Nor were there many instances where technical assistance provisions played a major role in influencing compromises. Development assistance could have been strategically used by the North to offer the South or particular LDC groups a carrot to reduce resistance to its spectrum allocation priorities. LDCs challenged—and sometimes succeeded in blocking—the North's allocation goals on the grounds that its sophisticated technology made it easier for the North to locate its services in other parts of the spectrum than technically disadvantaged countries could.[89] Technical underdevelopment thus was an excuse for having LDC preferences prevail.

LDCs themselves could have demanded a reimbursement by the North of their own adjustment costs, but this strategy did not appear at WARC 79. LDCs' lack of technical capabilities did come up in the debate on proposals to allocate spectrum to experimental projects dealing with futuristic high-technology services. It was used in rejecting a U.S. proposal for accommodation of a solar power satellite project. To defeat it, LDCs pointed to interference with their own services that would impose difficult readjustments to environmental and health effects, and to unequal advantages because only the United States would have the technical capacity to utilize the power source.[90] WARC finally merely recommended that ITU study the matter further.

The negative decision on this request could become a precedent for future LDC pressure to control the use of advanced technology to which the majority of countries in the world do not have access. Advanced industrial countries could then be forced to forgo use of such technologies themselves unless they make them available to LDCs as well, directly or indirectly through benefit sharing. The unexpected acceptance by the conference without political debate of U.S. proposals for new frequency allocations for both passive and active remote satellite sensing services has been attributed to the U.S. policy of making sensing data collected by LANDSAT available to other countries.[91] The United States came to WARC with about fifty requests on this subject, and all were approved with only minor modifications.

Conclusion

WARC 79 was hailed as a success by all delegations. There was general relief that despite differences international agreement had been reached on many important issues. As Mohamed Harbi, the Algerian chairman of Committee 5, put it afterward, "ITU is stronger. I talked to many delegates, and they did not expect the results we have achieved. We were pessimistic before the conference. But the result is in balance between developed and developing countries."[92] Many participants lauded not only the cooperation among countries but also the support and impartiality of conference chairman Severini and the entire ITU staff.

Resolving conflict at WARC 79 saw delegates from LDCs and industrial countries actively joining forces. The rule was to satisfy under given technical and spectrum constraints as many allocation requests by countries as possible. Because not all could be accommodated, the strategy was to persuade the unaccommodated delegations to accept the decisions. The bottom line for many was to preserve existing radio station operations.

Alignments at WARC 79 were surprisingly flexible across issues. Bloc voting by the South was not prevalent. One reason for this was the diffused structure of the negotiations. Another was differing national communications needs and priorities because of physical size (e.g. small or large country) or the level of communications development (e.g. Brazil and India are more advanced than others in satellite communications). The result was competition and conflicts among LDCs as well as between them and industrial countries. The most cohesive LDC grouping was the equatorial states, but they were not the most influential among participants at the conference.

The outcome of the WARC 79 negotiations was a plan for incremental change of the radio communications regime. Although LDCs wanted more fundamental reforms, their proposals often lacked persuasiveness. Cast in more general language, they often lacked technical explanations and details that industrial countries provided in support of their propositions. For example, Algeria's proposal for a substantial reallocation of HF fixed service bands in favor of the Third World offered no suggestion as to how further to divide the LDC share among individual countries.

Technical expertise in detail and argument counted. A technical allocation arrangement cannot be drawn up on the basis of political arguments. Technical judgment rather than rhetoric gave a delegation's recommendations credibility in conflictful situations. The LDC focus on many but moderate requests rather than any single, radical one was a more fruitful strategy in that it led at least to some provisions as cornerstones on which to build in the future.

Committees made decisions by majority voting as well as by acclamation. Majority decisions were reaffirmed very often on a consensus basis in plenaries. In the case where a decision had been taken by a majority vote in committee, delegations on the losing side could still reserve their right to raise the issue again in plenary. Here was potential for more extensive lobbying and group pressure politics, and the chances for overturning the decision were heightened. A significant number of countries attempted thus to amend or change decisions taken in committee. On the other hand, time pressure made overworked participants reluctant to accept new debate on decisions they had themselves accepted or did not much care about. The press actually predicted a political North-South showdown to occur at the late stage of WARC 79. In reality, it had occurred at the very beginning. In plenaries, much of the time was spent debating the wording of the final treaty text.

There was not enough time in ten weeks to produce complex new regulations. The conference dealt with very detailed technicalities. The great amount of material to be handled made innovation difficult. The negotiating process, on the other hand, was facilitated by parceling out parts of the old treaty to working groups—it is easier to negotiate a compromise with a limited number of delegates than with an entire plenary assembly. Also helpful and deliberately encouraged were the informal negotiations going on outside the meetings. And finally, without years of preparation for the conference, WARC would have failed in carrying out its task.

The flexibility institutionalized in the ITU regime aided the process of negotiating specifics, and was crucial to rewriting the Frequency Table. Specific reallocations often were packaged with other provisions, such as transition and timing rules. Most changes were phased in over a number of years. This made the "loss" or costs of relocating specific services or changing operation standards look less threatening and unacceptable. The Final Acts of WARC 79 themselves came into force only in January 1982.

Footnotes to the Frequency Table allowing additional or alternative allocations were another instrument serving factions or minorities, and they were extensively used. The drawback of nonuniform allocations is that the objective of optimum use of the spectrum was often neglected. As in the management of a corporation, the goal becomes to satisfy rather than to optimize. On the other hand, whether problems of coordination or harmful interference will actually occur depends on whether countries will use the footnoted frequencies and how intensively. Many such additions and exceptions were sought at WARC only to accommodate projected future demand.

Compliance with majority decisions on allocations and other matters could also be avoided through specific reservations in the Final Acts. The drawback for the deviant country is that its use of frequencies in a way other than agreed upon at the ITU is not protected by that body from interference from legitimate services.

Although there was general satisfaction with the overall agreement hammered out at WARC 79, individual countries expressed unhappiness over inadequate allocations for some services, as well as over some other issues. A total of fifty-one reservations involving eighty-one countries, and thirty-two counterreservations from sixty-three countries were made on specific WARC decisions. The United States alone filed eight reservations, although most of its proposals for WARC were approved in one way or another.[93]

Negotiated agreements can often be reached only with ambiguous provisions that gloss over basic differences between parties. WARC was no exception. Eighty-seven resolutions and ninety recommendations were adopted by the conference. Resolutions were a favorite means for dealing with unfinished conflicts or avoiding major disputes at the conference. Many resolutions, catering to the wishes of LDCs, were couched deliberately in ambiguous language. Regulatory agencies such as the ITU like to define terms and principles precisely. *Equitable access* was invoked repeatedly during WARC 79 discussions, by the North as well as by the South, and it appears in the Final Acts. However, because its meaning is a political hot potato, it is left without definition.

Resolutions on some controversial issues were referred for further study by the ITU or reconsideration by future conferences. The large number of future specialized regional and world administrative radio conferences agreed upon at WARC 79 has been viewed as one of the most significant outcomes.[94] As some delegates warned, however, many Third World administrations will have difficulties preparing for such a heavy schedule. Many pressures originating within the Third World for substantial change in international radiocommunications management were deferred in this manner. When the first session of the planned Space WARC was finally held in August 1985, the industrial countries had to agree to a compromise formula to ward off unabating LDC demands for a tight planning regime to allocate geostationary positions and frequencies for satellites. The details of the prelimnary agreement—a mixed regime involving some orbital slots for LDCs—will be the focus of negotiation at another special conference in 1988.

There may be other factors that helped to keep conflict at WARC 79 at a more manageable level than in other international forums. The ITU's overall jurisdiction is technical and more circumscribed than that of other international forums that also deal with telecommunications matters, such as UNESCO and the UN Committee on Peaceful Use of Outer Space. Because these are available for political debate on principles of communications, they constitute an alternative pressure point for LDCs. Furthermore, within the ITU regime itself, the agendas of pleni-potentiary meetings are more political and less technical than those of WARCs.

ITU's long history of institutionalized negotiations and the existence in the 1959 treaty of a framework for proposals for WARC 79 made radical overhaul difficult. The Final Acts included certain new provisions and more resolutions, reservations, and footnotes than the ones they replaced, but they also included parts of the old agreement. Furthermore, if comprehensive conferences in general accomplish less, the operation of the consensus rule in a forum with expanded membership probably reinforced this tendency at WARC 79. On the other hand, it enhanced the climate of cooperation at the conference.

An issue that is likely to surface at the ITU and may involve a serious North-South dispute concerns the next general WARC. There appears to be a growing sentiment on the part of influential industrial countries such as the United States that the general WARC has become much too cumbersome and that its work can and should be taken over by smaller ITU units. The likely scenario here is a radical reform: the North as the driving force, and the South as the defender of the status quo.

Notes

1. Quoted and discussed in International Commission for the Studies of Communication Problems, *Many Voices, One World* (Paris, UNESCO, 1980), pp. 38-39. For an excellent summary of the changes the proponents of the "new order" demand, see M. Masmoudi, "The New World Information Order," *Journal of Communication* 29, (Spring 1979):172-85.
2. Region 1 includes Europe, Africa, the Middle East, and the Soviet Union; Region 2, the Americas; and Region 3, Asia and Oceania.
3. Frequencies already assigned to a radio station have priority in the process of notification and registration with the International Frequency Registration Board of the ITU and enjoy protection from interference from latecomers.

4. *Science,* 11 August 1978, p. 514. The statement was made at a 1977 Washington meeting of the International Institute of Communication.
5. The United States opposed the scheme, and has not contributed to the fund that since has remained a meager enterprise.
6. Quoted in George A. Codding, Jr., "The New Nations and the International Telecommunication Union: Some Policy Implications for the Future," in *Proceedings of the Sixth Annual Telecommunications Policy Research Conference,* ed. H. S. Dordick (Lexington, Mass.: Heath, 1979), p. 366.
7. G. A. Codding, Jr., and A. M. Rutkowski, *The International Telecommunication Union in a Changing World* (Washington, D.C.: Artech House, 1982), pp. 47-48.
8. Ibid., p. 49. A reservation indicates that a country is not bound on a decision in the Final Acts. Prior to WARC 79 there had hardly ever been a reservation on ITU decisions by the United States.
9. *Broadcasting,* 1 January 1979, p. 51.
10. Codding and Rutkowski, *The International Telecommunication Union in a Changing World,* pp. 48-49.
11. For details on the interim plan, see, for example, *Aviation Week and Space Technology,* 10 September 1979, pp. 75-77.
12. P. L. Laskin, "Legal Strategies for Advancing Information Flow," in *The Control of the Direct Broadcast Satellite,* The Aspen Institute for Humanistic Studies Series on Communications (Palo Alto, Calif., 1974), p. 59.
13. For the WARC 1979 agenda, see International Telecommunication Union World Administrative Radio Conference (Geneva, 1979; hereinafter WARC 1979), Document No. 1-E, 29 September 1978.
14. Quoted in *Broadcasting,* 1 January 1979, p. 52.
15. The United States is the front runner in communications technology and application. According to one estimate, together with the Soviet Union it used 50 percent of the spectrum. M. Porat, "Communications Policy in an Information Society," in *Communications for Tomorrow: Perspectives for the 1980s;* ed. Glenn Robinson (New York: Praeger, 1978). The superpowers had much to lose at WARC 79 because they are the biggest users of spectrum for domestic and international communications, including space intelligence and other military applications. Combined, they use 25 percent of the shortwave broadcasting spectrum. G. Kroloff and S. Cohen, *The New World Information Order,* report to the U.S. Senate Committee on Foreign Relations, November 1977, p. 11.
16. For a presentation of these objectives as incorporated in the U.S. proposals for WARC 79, see WARC 79, Document No. 40-E, 31 January 1979.
17. Quoted in *Broadcasting,* 1 January 1979, p. 50.
18. In 1977 the U.S. State Department sought information on the positions of other governments at WARC 1979. Requests for information were cabled to U.S. embassies, but the results were not satisfactory, partly because embassy personnel lacked the expertise to discuss the subject with foreign officials, partly because many Third World countries had yet to develop their proposals.
19. Quoted in *Broadcasting,* 19 April 1979, p. 64.
20. Among the equipment was a computer that helped the U.S. delegation keep track of developments at WARC 79 by furnishing daily printouts.

There were also communication links with the State Department that allowed consultations with government agency and industry representatives. *Broadcasting*, 17 September 1979, p. 39. It is estimated that the State Department spent about $1 million in preparing for WARC, excluding the expenses of other government agencies or private industry involved. U.S. Congress, Office of Technology Assessment, *Radiofrequency Use and Management*, p. 519.

21. *Broadcasting*, 26 June 1978, p. 72.
22. K. Schaefer, foreign affairs adviser to the Federal Communications Commission, quoted in *Broadcasting*, 11 December 1978, p. 77.
23. For example, a NAM committee of experts since early 1977 had been preparing the Action Program for Cooperation among Broadcasting Organizations of LDCs. The committee consisted of Afghanistan, India, Jordan, Korea (DR), Malaysia, Algeria, Guinea, Kenya, Nigeria, Tanzania, Togo, Tunisia, Zaire, Zambia, Cuba, Panama, Peru, and Yugoslavia. For details, see *Intermedia* (February 1978): 22-23. For an overview of proposals emerging from NAM country meetings, see *WARC 79: Development Communications Strategies*, report to USAID prepared by the Academy for Educational Development, AID/atr-C-1131, No. 47 (Washington, D.C., March 1979).
24. Canada and the United States also sent their successive draft proposals to all ITU members. B. Segal, *The 1979 World Administrative Radio Conference: International Negotiations and Canadian Telecommunications Policy* (Ottawa: Government of Canada, Department of Communications, 1980), p. 1.
25. A major problem in selling the idea to others pertained to the sharing aspect of spectrum use by HF services. LDCs reacted coolly to sharing, arguing that they used HF for domestic communications, and that few of them had the sophisticated know-how and equipment needed to implement sharing. European countries also were not enthusiastic. In view of their proximity to one another and their lack of landmass, sharing would require complicated multilateral agreements among themselves, e.g. on border-area coordination.
26. For an overview of the issues involved, see E. Ambrosetti, "The Relevance of Remote Satellite Sensing," *Journal of International Law and Politics* 12 (Winter 1980): 569-98.
27. Senator Harrison Schmitt, "A Plea for Preparedness for the 1979 World Administrative Radio Conference," *Communications News* (August 1978): 47. For the U.S. domestic debate on what was expected to be raised by LDCs at WARC 79, see *Science*, 11 August 1978, pp. 513-14.
28. Quoted in *Broadcasting*, 17 September 1979, p. 40. According to Curtis White, a Washington-based communications attorney who was a consultant for African countries for WARC 79, the modest AID project was a "plus" for the United States. Ibid.
29. D. E. Honig, a U.S. delegate to WARC 79, believed that the bilateral talks with the Africans might have been held too late to be fruitful, but in general he considered the many bilateral talks U.S. officials held a strong point in U.S. diplomatic preparations for WARC. D. E. Honig, "Lessons for the 1999 WARC," *Journal of Communication* 30 (Spring 1980): 54.
30. Communicated by a U.S. communications lawyer. Some of these meetings

with LDC countries were useful in the eyes of U.S. officials. U.S. lobbying for U.S. proposals reportedly brought the Senegalese delegation to WARC 79 with specific instructions to support U.S. proposals on remote satellite sensing.

31. B. Segal, "International Negotiations on Telecommunications," *Intermedia* 8 (November 1980): 26. The United States came to WARC 79 with over 2,000 proposals, technical support papers, and background papers on technical issues as well as political issues that possibly could be raised there by LDCs.

32. Honig, "Lessons for the 1999 WARC," p. 56. Eighty-seven countries had fewer than ten delegates; thirty-nine had between twenty-one and thirty (e.g. China, Argentina, Nigera, Saudia Arabia); and eight had more than thirty (e.g. France, the United Kingdom, the United States, Canada, Germany). Segal, "International Negotiations on Telecommunications," p. 24. Fourteen ITU members did not send delegations to WARC: Bahamas, Bahrain, Barbados, Burma, Comoros, Equatorial Guinea, Laos, Mauritius, Sao Tomé and Principe, South Africa, Surinam, Tongo, Trinidad and Tobago, Vietnam.

33. Steering Committee 1 met usually once a week on matters related to conference proceedings; no agenda or minutes were published. Committee 2 examined the credentials of delegations. Committee 3 dealt with the conference budget and related issues. Committee 4 considered technical regulations, e.g. technical characteristics of services, designation of emissions, etc. Committee 5 was responsible for spectrum reallocations and general regulations. Committee 6, the regulatory procedure committee, considered proposals concerning the coordination, notification, and registration of frequency assignments and the activities of the IFRB. Committee 7 dealt with general administrative matters, among others the program of future conferences. Committee 8, the restructure committee, considered proposals concerning rearrangements of the Radio Regulations layout. Committee 9, the editorial committee went over the texts approved by other committees and submitted them to plenaries in edited form and translated into three languages. There were few or no controversial issues raised in Committees 1, 3, 8, and 9.

34. WARC 79, *Structure of the World Administrative Radio Conference,* Doc. No. 159-E (Geneva, 1979). More than 80 percent of the proposals submitted to WARC 79 fell under Committee 5. WARC 79, *Summary Record of the First Meeting of Committee 5, September 27, 1979,* Doc. No. 197-E.

35. Segal, *The 1979 World Administrative Radio Conference,* p. 13.

36. The delegate of Costa Rica in a statement at the inaugural meeting warned LDCs especially against pushing for quick decisions, although he also emphasized that the "old order" was responsible for LDC underdevelopment in telecommunications. He suggested that if the ten weeks proved insufficient to produce definite agreements, further sessions might be convened similar to the Law of the Sea conferences. WARC 79, *Minutes of the First Plenary Meeting, Annex 7, September 27, 1979,* Doc. No. 196-E.

37. See *Broadcasting,* 29 October 1979, p. 29; *Washington Post,* 16 November 1979, p. E2.

38. WARC 79, *Minutes of the Second Plenary Meeting, November 8, 1979,* Doc. No. 788-E, pp. 3, 13.

39. International Telecommunication Union, *Final Acts of the World Administrative Radio Conference, Geneva 1979* (Geneva: ITU, 1980). Hereinafter *Final Acts.*

40. The selection of a chairman for a conference without a host government follows unwritten ITU procedures in which the ITU secretary-general holds unofficial consultations to arrive at a person acceptable to the delegations. If the person is then approved at the first heads-of-delegations meeting convened just prior to the inaugural gathering for the preparation of the first day's agenda, the person is accepted by the conference by acclamation. Codding and Rutkowski, *The International Telecommunication Union,* p. 74.

41. See *New York Times,* 25 September 1979, p. D6.

42. It was the Indian delegate Srirangan.

43. WARC 79, Doc. No. 140-E, 4 September 1979, p. 1.

44. E.g. WARC 79, *Summary Record of the Second Meeting of Committee 2, November 15, 1979, Annexes,* Doc. No. 725-E. See also *Report of the Chairman of the U.S. Delegation to the World Administrative Radio Conference of the ITU, to the Secretary of State,* TD Serial No. 116 (Washington, D.C.: Department of State, Office of International Communications Policy, 1980), p. 21.

45. *Report of the Chairman of the U.S. Delegation,* p. 83.

46. For the search for a compromise, see WARC 79, Doc. No. 141-E, Addendum 1, 12 November 1979; WARC 79, Doc. No. 387-E (Rev. 1), Addendum 1, 13 November 1979; WARC 79, *Summary Records of the 21st Meeting of Committee 7, November 23, 1979,* Doc. No. 924-E; WARC 79, *Summary Records of the 22nd Meeting of Committee 7, November 24, 1979,* Doc. No. 925-E; WARC 79, *Summary Records of the 23rd Meeting of Committee 7, November 24, 1979,* Doc. No. 963-E; WARC 79, *Summary Records of the 27th Meeting of Committee 7, November 27, 1979,* Doc. No. 967-E; WARC 79, *Summary Records of the 29th Meeting of Committee 7, November 29, 1979,* Doc. No. 969-E.

47. WARC 79, *Final Protocol, December 3, 1979,* Doc. No. 942-E. The efforts were to defend and deny, respectively, Israel's access to frequency bands used by its neighbors.

48. WARC 79: Uganda, Doc. No. 75-E, 23 July 1979; Cameroon, Doc. No. 120-E, 18 June 1979; Morocco, Doc. No. 140-E, 4 September 1979.

49. WARC 79, Doc. No. 119-E, 18 June 1979.

50. According to Reports, India was encountering difficulties in advanced coordination between its domestic system INSAT and Indonesia's PALAPA. G. O. Robinson, "Regulating International Airwaves: The 1979 WARC," *Virginia Journal of International Law* 21 (Fall 1980): 45.

51. WARC 79: China, Doc. No. 78-E, 18 September 1979; India, Doc. No. 93-E, 13 October 1979; Iraq, Doc. No. 359-E, 25 October 1979; Soviet Union, Doc. No. 63A-E, 26 February 1979.

52. WARC 79, *Draft Resolution on the Use of the Geostationary Orbit,* Doc. No. 400-E, 29 October 1979.

53. A statement by Uganda in its proposals made it very clear: "The geosta-

tionary orbit like other natural resources, such as oil, is an important national resource which must be guarded jealously by every equatorial state which, by virtue of its own natural location and positioning on the surface of the earth, finds itself owning the resource." WARC 79, Doc. No. 75-E, Addendum 1, 27 August 1979.

54. See, for example, Australia. WARC 79, *Use of the Geostationary Orbit— Regulatory Principles*, Doc. No. 356-E, 25 October 1979.

55. *Report of the Chairman of the U.S. Delegation to the World Administrative Radio Conference of the ITU, to the Secretary of State*, p. 75.

56. The countries were Afghanistan, China, Ecuador, India, Argentina, Iraq, Columbia, Kenya, Somalia, Nigeria, Canada, France, the United States, the United Kingdom, the USSR. WARC 79, *Final Report of Ad Hoc Group 2 of Committee 6, November 15, 1979*, Doc. No. 678-E, p. 1 and Annex 1. Resolution BP relating to the use of the geostationary-satellite orbit and to the planning of space services utilizing it. *Final Acts*, p. 744.

57. "The U.S. holds that the words 'planned' and 'planning' in the draft Resolution must be interpreted in a broad and flexible sense. With this interpretation of planning and with the obligation to consider a variety of alternative approaches to the use of the orbit-spectrum resource by space services, the next space conference can lead to the full realization of the objective of equitable access to the resource that the U.S. has always supported." WARC 79, *Summary Record of Part 2 of the 10th Meeting of Committee 6*, Doc. No. 864-E, 6 November 1979, Annex 1. In contrast, Chist Samuel Butler stated in a press interview, "What we are getting is equal access. These resources will no longer be [allocated] on the basis of first come, first served." That, according to Butler, was a big gain for the LDCs. *Broadcasting*, 10 December 1979, p. 82.

58. WARC 79, *Final Protocol, No. 79*, Doc. No. 945-E, 4 December 1979, and Corrigendum No. 1 to Doc. No. 945-E, 5 December 1979; WARC 79, *Minutes of the 16th Plenary Meeting, December 5, 1979*, Doc. No. 980-E.

59. The IFRB was to send a list of all HF assignments in bands allocated to fixed service to each country by 1980. The countries then had one year's time to review entries, delete unused ones, reclassify them according to the extent of use, etc. *Final Acts*, Annex to Resolution CT, procedure for reviewing entries in the master register in frequency bands allocated to the fixed service between 3000 kHz and 27 500 kHz, pp. 757-58. The process has been considerably delayed.

60. This was the opinion expressed in *Report of the Chairman of the U.S. Delegation to the World Administrative Radio Conference of the ITU, to the Secretary of State*, p. 72.

61. *Final Acts*, Resolution DI, relating to the convening of a World Administrative Radio Conference for the planning of the HF bands allocated to the broadcasting service, pp. 831-32.

62. Honig, "Lessons for the 1999 WARC," p. 50.

63. *Final Acts*, Resolution CV, relating to the implementation of the change in allocations in the bands between 4000 kHz and 27 500 kHz, pp. 750-55. Also footnote 3510A, p. 81.

64. WARC 79, *Final Protocol*, Doc. No. 942-E, 3 December 1979. Joint protocol statement No. 36 by Saudi Arabia, Cyprus, Spain, the United States, Greece, the United Kingdom, Northern Ireland, Sri Lanka, and Zambia.

65. Ibid.; WARC 79, *Final Protocol,* Doc. No. 945-E, 4 December 1979. Statements 11, 15, 21, 23, 26, 41, and 66 were reservations of LDCs, most of them Latin American countries, on fixed and/or mobile services. They usually stated that the country might be unable to satisfy its demands for these services with the reduced allocations, and it consequently reserved the right to continue operations in old bands.

66. *Report of the Chairman of the U.S. Delegation to the World Administrative Radio Conference of the ITU, to the Secretary of State,* pp. 48-49.

67. WARC 79, *27th and 28th Reports of Working Group 5D to Committee 5, November 16, 1979,* Doc. No. 722-E, p. 1.

68. WARC 79, *Summary Record of the 20th Meeting of Committee 5, November 21, 1979,* Doc. No. 955-E, pp. 2, 4.

69. A NATO meeting held in late October to make sure that the allies would join in supporting the U.S. position reportedly upset the United States because the backing was not immediately forthcoming.

70. The countries were Brazil, Jamaica, Iran, Nigeria, Ecuador, Mexico, Chile, Kenya, Cameroon, Guayana, Sudan, Fiji, Singapore, Ivory Coast, Thailand, and Argentina. WARC 79, Doc. No. 880-E (Rev. 1), 30 November 1979.

71. Ibid., Annex 3.

72. WARC 79, *Minutes of the 11th Plenary Meeting, November 30, 1979,* Doc. No. 975-E, pp. 9-10.

73. India was one of the few LDCs that accompanied detailed background information and technical evaluations of options of allocations such as in the case of feeder links. E.g. WARC 79, Doc. No. 83-E, 10 October 1979, Addendum 2.

74. See WARC 79, *26th Report of Working Group 5D to Committee 5, November 16, 1979,* Doc. No. 711-E.

75. For a list of countries composing the ad hoc group, see WARC 79, Doc. No. 954-E, 20 November 1979, p. 10.

76. WARC 79, *Minutes of the 11th Plenary Meeting, November 20, 1979,* Doc. No. 975-E, pp. 15-16.

77. WARC 79, *Minutes of the 12th Plenary Meeting, December 1, 1979, Doc. No. 976-E, pp. 5-6.*

78. *See WARC 79, Summary Record of the 13th Meeting of Committee 5, November 14, 1979,* Doc. No. 947-E, pp. 104; WARC 79, *Summary Record of the 18th Meeting of Committee 5, November 20, 1979,* Doc. No. 953-E, p. 5.

79. See WARC 79, *Summary Record of the 15th Meeting of Committee 5, November 16, 1979,* Doc. No. 949-E, pp. 5-6.

80. WARC 79, *Summary Record of the 2nd Meeting of Committee 5, October 1, 1979,* Doc. No. 207-E, pp. 2-5.

81. Honig, "Lessons for the 1999 WARC," p. 50.

82. *Final Acts,* Resolution AE, relating to the division of the world into regions for the purpose of allocating frequency bands, p. 785.

83. For instance, African countries do not have much use for relatively short-distance radio communications services (land-mobile), which the Europeans wanted and recommended to receive additional allocations in the UHF bands. The Africans managed to retain broadcasting allocations up to 950 MHz, which they use for national broadcasting. *Broadcasting,* 17 Decem-

ber 1979, p. 48; *Aviation Week and Space Technology,* 10 September 1979, pp. 76-77.

84. See Robinson, "Regulating International Airwaves," p. 26.
85. Ibid.
86. The fund amounted to less than one-tenth of the total resources devoted to technical assistance in which the ITU is involved. Codding and Rutkowski, *The International Telecommunication Union,* p. 293.
87. *Final Acts,* Resolution CX, relating to the role of telecommunications in integrated rural development, p. 765; Resolution CE, relating to technical cooperation with the developing countries in maritime telecommunications, p. 811; and Resolution DG, relating to transfer of technology, p. 763.
88. WARC 79, *Note from the Chairman of Working Group 6B to Committee 6. Resolution Relating to the Development of National Radio Frequency Management, October 29, 1979,* Doc. No. 397-E.
89. The cost of implementing spectrum reallocation decisions derives from transmittor and receiver modifications or replacement, training of technicians in the use of more spectrum-efficient techniques, etc. The LDC argument was that the industrial countries could adjust better because of their technological advantage. Honig, "Lessons for the 1999 WARC," p. 51. The unwillingness by LDCs to make trade-offs with industrial countries was often backed by the argument that the advanced industrial countries had the technology to find some other solution. Richard E. Shrum of the Office of International Communication Policy, the Department of State, called this "a constant source of exasperation" in North-South relations at WARC. R.E. Shrum, "A Non-Technical Overview of the 1979 WARC," in *WARC 1979: Radio Regulations and Final Protocol. Hearing before the Senate Committee on Foreign Relations, May 18, 1982* (Washington, D.C.: Government Printing Office, 1982).
90. WARC 79, Doc. No. 976-E, p. 17; *Washington Post,* 20 November 1979, pp. D7, D8.
91. Robinson, "Regulating International Airwaves," p. 18.
92. Quoted in *Broadcasting,* 17 December 1979, p. 59. for the congratulatory statements of individual delegates see WARC 79, *Minutes of the 15th Plenary Meeting, December 4, 1979,* Doc. No. 979-E. For the statements made by the secretary-general, and chairmen of the administrative council and of the conference, see WARC 79, *Signature of the Final Acts and Closure of the Conference, December 6, 1979,* Doc. No. 981-E.
93. The WARC treaty has in the meantime also been approved by the U.S. Congress but has not yet been signed by the president of the United States. State Department officials stress that the United States is abiding by its provisions.
94. The timing and priority sequencing of the conferences was itself a matter of negotiating and debate.

8

Negotiating the Lomé Conventions: A Little Is Preferable to Nothing

John Ravenhill

"The Lomé Convention . . . represents the only serious attempt to give real impetus to the new international economic order."[1]

"Lomé has indeed become a symbol of international cooperation. Virtually the sole beacon in an otherwise dark and unlit sea, strewn with unfulfilled hopes."[2]

Ten years after the signing of the first Lomé Convention, few observers of North-South relations would give credence to the claim in its preamble that a "new model for relations between developed and developing states" had been established "on the basis of complete equality between partners." Results of cooperation under the convention have been disappointing, not least to the participants themselves. Yet although the hyperbolic content of the above quotations may easily be dismissed, the negotiation of three successive Lomé Conventions does stand in marked contrast to the general absence of agreements in other areas of North-South relations. More than half the membership of the United Nations is linked by these arrangements between the now twelve-member European Economic Community (EEC) and sixty-six members of the African, Caribbean, and Pacific (ACP) Group.[3]

Are there, then, lessons to be learned from the Lomé experience that might be applied to other North-South negotiations? Any attempt to draw such conclusions must first explicitly acknowledge that the Lomé relationship differs on one or more crucial dimensions from all of the other negotiations examined in this volume. Above all, Lomé is, of course, a "regional" arrangement between the EEC on the one hand, and the former colonies of its member states and other sub-Saharan African countries of "comparable economic structure" on the other.

The relative poverty and lack of an industrial base of the countries of the ACP Group give it a greater homogeneity than the wider Group of 77 (although differences in cultural background and economic structure of the ACP Group have played a significant role in impeding group solidarity). That the relationship includes only one of the world's major industrialized trading blocs undoubtedly has made negotiations less complex: there are few ambiguities about how the costs of any concessions made to the Southern parties to the relationship will be shared. Because only "one" Northern party is involved, the convention is the EEC's *own* development policy—which itself provides an incentive for its maintenance because the member states are able to point to the "concrete achievements" of Lomé in resisting demands from the South in other negotiating forums.

Unlike other North-South negotiations, a Northern international bureaucracy is a significant party to the Lomé relationship. The Commission of the European Communities has its own organizational interests in ensuring a successful outcome to the negotiations. It not only has played the role of a "partial" mediator between the ACP and the member states of the EEC but, at times, has been a significant "initiator," Negotiations between the commission and the EEC member states have been as important in determining the outcome of some issues as have the formal talks between the ACP and the EEC.

Lomé also differs from some of the other negotiations examined in this volume in that the convention ranges across a variety of issue areas. With provisions for cooperation in the fields of trade, industrial development, stabilization of export earnings from commodities, agricultural development, aid, minerals development, and more recently, investment promotion and protection, Lomé is truly a microcosm of the global North-South dialogue. Although this eclecticism potentially considerably complicates the negotiations, it also increases the opportunities for issue linkage for mutually beneficial trade-offs.

A final distinguishing feature of the Lomé negotiations is that they have been subject to an internally imposed deadline. In all three cases the negotiations were for the renewal of existing arrangements as well as for their extension into new areas of cooperation. Failure to have reached agreement before the deadline would have led to at least the suspension of the flow of benefits from existing areas of cooperation. That the initial Lomé negotiations were themselves subject to this constraint is often overlooked. Here the key factors were the expiration of the second Yaoundé Convention at the end of January 1975, the termination of the Commonwealth Sugar Agreement in the same year, and the potential loss of privileged access for Commonwealth countries to the British market.

The principle focus of this paper is on the negotiation of the second and third Lomé Conventions. The demands put forward by the various parties to these negotiations and the effect that these had on the process of negotiations cannot be fully understood, however, without placing them in the context of the events leading to the conclusion of the Lomé I agreement.[4] Lomé I went into effect on 24 June 1975, Lomé II became operative on its expiry in 1980, and Lomé III in 1985.

The Lomé I Negotiations

The success of the African, Caribbean, and Pacific states in forging a negotiating coalition and in achieving many of their principal demands in the Lomé I talks surprised everyone, including themselves. Long divided by cultural heritage, a factor that exacerbated mutual suspicions, anglophone and francophone African states were able for the first time since their independence to reach agreement on a joint approach to relations with the EEC. With this historical divide bridged, it was natural to include the Commonwealth countries of the Caribbean and the Pacific in the negotiating group; however, the extent to which African countries proved willing to jeopardize agreement with the EEC in order to achieve a successful outcome to the talks on access for their partners' sugar exports to the enlarged EEC market was itself unexpected.

Underlying ACP unity was a negotiating platform containing four core principles. These were nonreciprocity in trade and tariff concessions; free and assured access to European markets for ACP exports; a guarantee of stable, equitable, and remunerative earnings in European markets from their principal exports; and the exclusion from a future convention of provisions that would impede cooperation among ACP states. The reciprocity issue was, at the time, the one to which greatest symbolic importance was attached. European insistence on reciprocal tariff concessions from African countries under the Yaoundé Conventions, the abortive Lagos Agreement, and the Arusha Agreements had long rankled not only the weaker parties in the relationship but also Europe's trading rivals, most notably the United States. The EEC originally justified the requirement for reciprocity as necessary to comply with provisions in the General Agreement on Tariffs and Trust (GATT) for the establishment of free trade areas. With the addition of GATT's Part IV in 1965, however, the introduction of Generalized

System of Preferences (GSP) schemes in 1971, an insistence on reciprocity was anachronistic. Although the principle became a bargaining chip in the negotiations (primarily, however, between France and Britain within the EEC's Council of Ministers), it was one whose maintenance would have been as costly—at least in terms of international embarrassment and possible retaliation from the United States—as its abandonment. Reverse preferences were of little significance in maintaining European advantages in ACP markets compared to traditional trading, currency, and cultural links.

Similarly, the other key principles in the ACP platform could be met without significant domestic cost to European member states. Eligibility for membership in the ACP Group had been defined by the EEC as early as Britain's first application for membership as dependent on economic weakness: only countries of "comparable economic structure" to those associated with the EEC under the Yaoundé Conventions were to be considered for similar arrangements. The more developed Commonwealth countries of Asia were deemed to be "nonassociable." The principle, if not the practice, of free access for ACP exports to the European market accordingly could be granted without significant risks to European interests—and these would in any event be protected by excluding competitive agriculture products and by the inclusion of a safeguard clause. Ultimately Europe could—and would—rely on its economic muscle to extract voluntary export restraints from ACP states whose (minuscule) exports of manufactured products were judged to have caused difficulty for European industry.

Agreeing to refrain from obstructing ACP efforts at regional cooperation was a principle that was easily acceptable. Indeed, European aid for regional projects in ACP countries offered lucrative opportunities for European construction companies. Of the major ACP demands in the negotiations, only the principle of stable, equitable, and remunerative export earnings remained. And, this indeed proved to be the most difficult area of the negotiations. That a successful outcome emerged was primarily the result of two factors: innovative proposals, put forward by the Commission of the European Communities before the negotiations began with the ACP, for the establishment of a scheme to stabilize the earnings of associated states from commodity exports to the EEC (which eventually became the STABEX scheme); and the extraordinary developments in the world sugar market in 1973-75 that enabled a coalition to be forged between Commonwealth cane producers and importers on the one hand and European beet growers on the other.

A number of factors favored a successful outcome to the negotiations. It is impossible, of course, to weigh their respective contributions to shaping the eventual outcome, for each undoubtedly played some role.

1. Britain's decision to renegotiate its terms of membership in the EEC and its willingness to use the ACP as a pawn in this game. Negotiating a satisfactory arrangement for the Commonwealth ACP states, especially for Commonwealth sugar exporters, became a litmus test in London of EEC respect for British interests—at least, that is, until Commonwealth sugar producers were perceived in 1974 to be attempting to hold British consumers to ransom.

2. The bureaucratic interests of the European Commission. With the evolution of the association arrangements from the Treaty of Rome to the second Yaoundé Convention, including the expansion of the European Development Fund (EDF), the Directorate-General of the Commission charged with administering the Development Cooperation program grew in size and influence. Although a limited program of assistance for nonassociated states was begun in the early 1970s, the *raison d'etre* of the Development Directorate remained the "special relationship" with associated states. The European Commission, then, had direct organizational interests not only in maintaining the supranational development policy of the EEC *qua* EEC vis-à-vis the existing associates but also in its extension to the developing Commonwealth and to other eligible countries. This would inevitably require a significant increase in the resources of the EDF and, the commission hoped, a larger share of the member states' total aid budget to be channeled through EEC institutions (ultimately, the commission hoped, as part of the EEC's own budget rather than the existing arrangement of direct contributions from member states).

In the Lomé I negotiations, the commission's authority to propose publicly a program to the EEC Council of Ministers was utilized creatively to lay the foundations for a package of measures that encouraged the participation both of the existing associates and of the associables. Included within the commission's memorandum were a recommendation that reciprocity not be required in future trade relations, and the first outline of the proposed STABEX scheme. This was seen as a means of compensating existing associates for having to share their tariff preferences with the associables and, it would primarily benefit African countries, as a factor to offset the potential advantages to the Caribbean and Pacific states of access to the EEC market for their sugar exports on terms similar to those of the Commonwealth Sugar Agreement. The commission also recommended that the real value of aid to existing associates be maintained. In publishing the proposals, the commission created a situation from which it would have been embarrassing for the council members to retreat, e.g. by insisting on reciprocity, and pieced together a package that facilitated the reconciliation of the differences between associates and associables and their coming together in the ACP Group.

3. A propitious external environment. The Lomé I negotiations opened in October 1973, coinciding with OPEC's initial success. In this heady atmosphere of Southern cartel power, member states of the EEC were confronted with new concerns over the security of supply of raw materials. Relations with traditional suppliers would be particularly important if, as the commission reminded the member states, the EEC was not to become dependent on other industrialized countries whose interests would not necessarily always coincide with its. For those member states traditionally less sympathetic to the EEC's regionally oriented development policies, Africa gained a new significance. The importance of the new European concern with security of supply should not be overstated, however. It was insufficient for the ACP Group to succeed in its attempt to link the prices for its commodity exports in European markets to prices paid for manufactured imports from the EEC.

The second development in the external environment that was significantly to affect the negotiations was the rise in the world market price of sugar in 1973-74. Access for the cane sugar exports of Caribbean and Pacific countries to their traditional British market was the most contentious issue in the negotiations in that it was the one in which there was the most direct clash of interests between EEC and ACP producers. Whereas the EEC had aimed at self-sufficiency in sugar supplies under the Common Agricultural Policy (CAP), Britain had traditionally held back domestic beet production so as to provide a market for Commonwealth cane growers. By 1971 high domestic prices had encouraged production within the EEC to such an extent that a surplus was produced roughly equivalent to the level of British imports from the Commonwealth. Beet producers not surprisingly saw Britain's accession to the EEC as providing a market for this surplus, yet to have excluded Commonwealth sugar from the enlarged European market would have reneged on one of the major commitments made to Britain in its act of accession to the EEC. Accordingly, the commission proposed that domestic sugar production be restrained in order to accommodate ACP imports. This provoked strident opposition from the EEC beet lobby, backed by the governments of France, Germany, Belgium, and Italy, and precipitated the worst crisis within the EEC since the French nonparticipation of the mid-1960s.

The problem was (temporarily) resolved by extraordinary developments in the world sugar market. With an unprecedented coincidence
of poor harvests among major beet and cane produceis, the world
market price rose to record levels in 1974, Britain and Italy both faced
sugar shortages as traditional suppliers reneged on their long-term
commitments to exploit the higher world market price. In these circumstances the commission was able to formulate new proposals that,
however, shortsighted, were able to satisfy all interested parties: the
EEC would agree to import approximately the same quantities of sugar
traditionally supplied by the ACP states to Britain and, at the same
time, domestic production was to be increased. ACP states not only
had succeeded in maintaining access to their traditional market and
thereby breached one of the fundamental principles of the Common
Agricultural Policy but also had received a guarantee of prices "within
the range prevailing in the Community" for their sugar exports.[5]

Opening Positions in the Lomé II and Lomé III Negotiations

There are two important features of the outcome of the bargaining
process in the first Lomé Convention that were to play a significant role
in the negotiations for its successors. The first was the formula adopted
for the exchange of concessions. In essence this was the acceptance by
the EEC of the principle of nonreciprocity in the material exchanges in
return for the participation of the ACP in the convention. There was
little in the convention that the larger EEC member states would not
have been able to achieve through bilateral relations; at best the
convention had a facilitating role in maintaining the access of European
business to ACP markets and resources. Nonreciprocity became translated into an ACP unwillingness to pursue issues of mutual interest.
This inevitably weakened the position of the group in the relationship
because it had already given up its principal bargaining resource, a
threat of nonparticipation in the agreement. The enshrinement of
nonreciprocity had the repercussion that the only significant concession available to the ACP in future negotiations was to reduce its own
demands. With the ACP largely playing the role of *demandeurs,* many
of the most important negotiations for successor conventions inevitably were to take place between the donors—the EEC member states.
    The second dimension to have a profound impact on subsequent
negotiations was a divergent interpretation between the ACP and the
EEC of the nature of the agreement reached. ACP states had entered
the negotiations aspiring to pursue what I have termed a strategy of
"collective clientelism."[6] This I characterize as an attempt to capitalize

on their historical ties with the EEC in order to construct a particularistic and exclusive relationship that would provide the group with benefits not available to other developing countries. This strategy can be perceived as primarily a defensive reaction designed to enhance security in the face of two threats. The first derived from the inroads that the more advanced LDCs of Latin America and Asia were making into ACP traditional markets in Europe; African countries in particular were experiencing an erosion of their share of EEC markets for tropical products to the benefit of Brazil, Malaysia, and Indonesia. A second threat came from the actions of the EEC itself. This had two dimensions. One was the danger of future exclusion of ACP exports from the European market as a result of the extension of the EEC's Common Agricultural Policy; here the sugar exports of Commonwealth countries provide the most important example, and exports of beef and of fresh fruits and vegetables were also of concern to some ACP states. Second, the nascent industrialization efforts of some ACP states via the export of labor-intensive manufactures were threatened by the emergence of the new protectionism; in an era in which the nondiscrimination norm of the postwar trade regime was increasingly sacrificed by major industrial countries to the goal of protecting their domestic interests, having a patron appeared to offer significant advantages.

The ACP Group's expectation was that the EEC as collective patron would accept a form of generalized obligation to protect ACP interests; they looked to the "spirit" of Lomé as a guarantee that the EEC would not always employ its superior economic strength to prevail in the event of a clash of interests.[7] Clientelism offered the weaker parties to the agreement an opportunity to claim special advantages on account of their weakness—this being employed, for instance, to ridicule the idea that their activities might pose a threat to the interests of the stronger party.

Despite expressing some reservations—at a meeting in Lagos, two weeks after the negotiations for Lomé I had been concluded—regarding the terms of the agreement (particularly those relating to the access of ACP agricultural exports to the EEC market, and the absence of guarantees of stable and remunerative prices for their primary product exports), the ACP Group appeared to believe that for the most part its strategy of collective clientelism had been successful. In particular, it was encouraged that the EEC made great play in its own publicity materials of its contractual obligations under the convention, and of the equality of the partnership. While itself placing great emphasis on the EEC's contractual obligations, the group hoped that where the convention fell short of ACP aspirations the EEC would interpret its provisions in a creative manner consistent with the "spirit" of Lomé. In other words, the provisions of the convention should be "bent" when this would be favorable to the ACP. In the months succeeding the entry into force of the agreement, however, it became clear that the EEC's perceptions of its commitments and obligations under the convention differed radically from those of the ACP.

Rather than accepting a "generalized" commitment to ACP interests, EEC spokesmen argued that the contractual nature of the relationship necessitated a legalistic interpretation that strictly limited EEC responsibilities to those laid down in the convention. Where there was a conflict between EEC domestic interests and those of the ACP, e.g. over access for ACP agricultural exports to the EEC market, the Commission of the European Communities—responsible for the day-to-day implementation of the convention—applied the letter of the convention rather than its spirit. Nor did the EEC appear to be willing to safeguard ACP interests against those of third parties—the extension of the EEC's Generalized System of Preferences continued to erode the preferential tariff margins enjoyed by the ACP. In addition to its perceptions of a niggardly attitude on the part of the EEC, the ACP Group was angered by the manner in which the relationship was administered; the much-vaunted equality of the partnership was undermined by the commission's unilateral interpretation of the convention's provisions, the absence of ACP participation in key decisions (e.g. on the financing of aid projects), and the high-handed and sometimes paternalistic style of EEC representatives.

A sense of having been betrayed shaped the proposals made by the ACP for subsequent conventions. Because the EEC had failed to interpret the first convention in the "spirit" of Lomé, future agreements would have to include new contractual principles that would leave the EEC no discretionary latitude of interpretation. Accordingly, the ACP opening position in both the Lomé II and the Lomé III negotiations included a number of broad demands of principle that, if adopted, would have significantly extended EEC obligations. These include *total* free access for ACP exports to the EEC market; abolition of the safeguard clause; abolition of thresholds and repayment obligations in the STABEX scheme; indexation of STABEX receipts in order to guarantee ACP import capacity; and indexation of aid flows in order to maintain their real value. (The opening positions of the respective parties in both the Lomé II and Lomé III negotiations, and the eventual outcome of the negotiations are listed in the appendix to this chapter.)

Negotiation on the basis of broad principles appeared to offer two further advantages to the ACP Group. Because the demands did not deal with specific concessions—where potential problems of trade-offs between the interests of individual ACP states might arise—they were seen as conducive to the maintenance of ACP group unity. Also, the negotiating platform was convenient in that it did not require major preparatory and supportive work by overextended ACP bureaucracies, e.g. it was easier to demand total free access to the EEC market for all ACP exports than to isolate particular problem areas and make a detailed case for each product using trade data. This highlights one of the difficulties faced by the ACP Group in the negotiations: the lack of detailed technical information on the issues under discussion.

Although the ACP Group had established a secretariat in 1976, insufficient funds were provided for it to play a major supporting role in the negotiations. A number of ACP governments—most notably some francophone African states—were extremely suspicious of the secretariat, whose dominant personalities and intellects came from the Caribbean. Unlike the Commission of the European Communities, the ACP secretariat was not permitted to propose publicly initiatives for the group. And, again in contrast to the commission, the secretariat had no formal role in the negotiations. Whereas the commission was responsible for conducting the detailed negotiations for the Europeans, the ACP Group entrusted this task to its ambassadors in Brussels—itself symptomatic of the preoccupation of the ACP states with jealously guarding their sovereignty.

Staff morale in the secretariat was low; the group entered the Lomé III negotiations without having finalized its negotiating position—in part because key members of the secretariat were in open revolt against the lame-duck secretary-general. Budgetary contributions went unpaid! The secretariat's financial problems eventually were eased, somewhat ironically, by a grant from the European Development Fund. With a staff of only a dozen experts, the secretariat was overwhelmed by the mountain of paper that emerged in the course of the negotiations (in contrast, the commission's Directorate-General for Development employs over two hundred professionals). To cope with the extra workload in the negotiations, the secretariat even had to "borrow" secretaries from the commission. The secretariat simply was unable to undertake the detailed work necessary to give essential statistical and technical support to the ACP case, a weakness that was to be exploited by the EEC in its insistence on negotiation on a case-by-case basis.

A number of background reports were commissioned by the ACP

Group from outside experts (some financed by the Commonwealth Secretariat and the United Nations Conference on Trade and Development, UNCTAD) for the Lomé II and Lomé III negotiations. In both cases, however, the consultants were appointed too late for their submissions to be used in formulating group positions. The principal purpose of the reports, which arrived after the negotiations were under way, became a justification of the *political* positions that the group had already adopted in the negotiations. Many were of dubious utility, reading more like academic studies than briefs for negotiators. The secretariat was further handicapped in that it lacked its own data bank and thus was almost completely dependent on the EEC for statistical information on the implementation of the conventions.

In retrospect, the opening position of the ACP Group in the negotiations—with its emphasis on principles—at least in part redounded against the group's interests. It offered the EEC an opportunity to appear as the reasonable party in the talks: EEC negotiators were able to claim that although the abstract principles demanded by the ACP Group were unacceptable, they were perfectly willing to discuss problem areas on a case-by-case basis. Further, the negotiating platform at times served to undermine rather than to maintain ACP unity. Quite simply, the demands were not credible to many members of the group. However much they might have believed that the demands were justified, the experience of ongoing negotiations with the EEC during the implementation of Lomé I had convinced many ACP governments that the EEC would not accept an extension of the relationship along the lines that the group had proposed. As a consequence, the ACP Group entered the negotiations with little faith that its major demands could or would be realized. By demanding sweeping changes in the relationship in its opening position, the group also left itself in a situation where its fallback position inevitably would be a long way removed from its opening stance. Immediately it found itself on the defensive, a factor that contributed to the demoralization of the group during the course of the negotiations.[8]

In contrast to the ACP demands for a major extension of the relationship,[9] the favorite phrase used by the EEC in its approach to the Lomé II talks was the "consolidation of existing arrangements"; it appeared in the commission's proposals to the EEC Council of Ministers, the council's response, and in the speech made at the opening of the negotiations by the president of the council. The latter noted that the talks would be concerned with adjustments and improvements, "not with sweeping changes." The commission, charged with the day-to-day conduct of the talks, had sought and received a conservative negotiating mandate from the council. In its memorandum to the council, the commission placed emphasis on what it perceived as the unique features of the Lomé arrangements: the interlinking of various instruments of development cooperation; the contractual nature of the convention and the security that this provided to the ACP; the equality of the Lomé partnership; and the latitude given to ACP countries to decide which developmental models they wished to follow. During the course of the negotiations the ACP Group was frequently to be reminded of these features. Because the Lomé "experiment" was still relatively new and was being conducted at a time when progress in the North-South dialogue was labored, and global economic crisis had reduced the possibilities open to the EEC, the commission asserted that it would be "rash to attempt to take a further major step forward so soon and in such difficult circumstances."[10]

Although there was general agreement within the EEC that the arrangements of proven worth in the convention should be maintained, member states rejected any significant extension of EEC obligations along the lines proposed by the ACP Group, being well aware that concessions would be certain to encourage additional demands from its partners in the convention. Proposals of the ACP Group were perceived as inevitably imposing substantial costs in a variety of domains. The most obvious was monetary; in a period of recession there was little enthusiasm among the member states for any major extension of the aid relationship. A second type of cost would have been the damage caused to domestic EEC interests, especially in the agricultural sector, if demands of the ACP Group for total free access for its exports were granted. Third, the EEC wished to avoid any commitment within the Lomé relationship that might have been seized upon by the Group of 77 as setting a precedent for concessions in the global North-South dialogue. An obvious example was the ACP demand to have STABEX benefits index-linked to prices for imported manufactured goods. Similarly, the EEC director-general for development in the Lomé III negotiations noted that the Mediterranean countries of the EEC had rejected further trade concessions to the ACP Group "not because of the ACP but because of the precedent that would be created vis-a-vis far more formidable competitors."[11] Finally, and contrary to the aspirations of a collective clientelist strategy for an exclusive relationship, the EEC wished to avoid any measures, e.g. guaranteeing the preferential tariff margins enjoyed by the ACP Group that would have tied its hands in its relations with other LDCs.

EEC negotiators were well aware of how the balance of bargaining power in the relationship had shifted with the successful negotiation of

Lomé I. At the core of the EEC's approach to the negotiations was the belief that the weakness of the ACP Group was such that no major concessions were necessary in order to force agreement to a new convention. Whereas the ACP Group in 1973-75 had been able to exploit the desire of an anxious suitor to conclude an agreement, the EEC's bargaining hand had been transformed in the renegotiations. A convention was already in place with a package of arrangements that provided not inconsiderable benefits to the ACP Group, financial flows that the group would have found difficult to forgo. In the intervening years, the ACP Group's bargaining hand had been further weakened by developments in the international economy, OPEC's success had redounded to the disadvantage of most ACP states, which were faced wtih soaring fuel bills and declining markets for their primary product exports as a result of recession in the West. Commodity power had proven illusory: the world sugar price had collapsed to one-quarter of the level prevailing in February 1975. Meanwhile, the optimism that had prevailed at the time of the initial negotiations regarding the realization of New International Economic Order (NIEO) goals in global forums disappeared in the disillusionment following the failure of the Conference on International Economic Cooperation (CIEC). Because other countries had failed to come forward with concessional arrangements for LDCs along the lines of Lomé, the EEC was able to fall back on the argument that the convention represented the best deal available.

Having constructed a package that EEC negotiators believed offered a sufficient incentive to induce all ACP states to participate, the EEC felt able to pursue its own interests in the Lomé II and Lomé III negotiations. Besides attempting to minimize the costs of the convention through resisting ACP demands, the European approach had three principal dimensions: minimization of the negative impact of the relationship on European domestic interests; the promotion of European business interests in ACP states; and an attempt to impose greater conditionality on the ACP states in their use of aid provided under the convention. Interwoven with the last two dimensions in particular was an attempt by the Commission of the European Communities to expand its powers at the expense of the member states. Negotiations between the member states and the commission, therefore, were as important in determining the outcome of many of its proposals as were talks with the ACP.

On the first dimension, the commission proposed the insertion of a new convention of provisions relating to abnormal competitive practices such as dumping and export subsidies, and the establishment of an obligation for all parties to the convention to engage in consultations in the trade sphere in order that potential difficulties arising from the disruption of the European market by ACP exports might be avoided.

In the area of promoting European interests in ACP states, the principal initiatives were a scheme to facilitate the maintenance of ACP exports of minerals to the European market (which was to become known by its French acronym, SYSMIN, and contrasted with ACP demands for minerals to be included within the existing STABEX scheme); additional funding for the promotion of mining exploration and development in ACP states; a proposal for reciprocal investment promotion and protection agreements, and the establishment of an EEC-backed investment guarantee scheme; and the conclusion of bilateral fishing agreements between the EEC and ACP states.

On the third dimension, the EEC sought to retreat from the rhetoric of the first convention, which emphasized the equality of the partners in the relationship and the contractual obligations of the EEC. These attributes of the convention reflected the heady atmosphere of cartel power and of Southern demands for the creation of a New International Economic Order that prevailed during the negotiation of the first convention. Their most concrete manifestation was the STABEX scheme, under which the EEC was contractually obliged to provide transfers when ACP states' earnings from their exports of various agricultural commodities to the EEC fell below the average level for the previous four years. During the negotiation of the first convention, the EEC, in deference to ACP countries' sensitivities over their sovereignty, dropped its initial demand that STABEX transfers be conditional on the signature of an agreement on their ultimate employment. Two developments angered the EEC during the implementation of the first convention: its obligations to provide transfers under the scheme to the Amin regime despite the human rights abuses in Uganda; and the use of transfers by a number of recipients for purposes other than those for which they were intended, e.g. the purchase of vehicles for security forces.[12]

To resolve these problems, the EEC community made two proposals. The first was to insert a human rights clause in the convention. It would make reference to Articles 3 and 5 of the UN's Universal Declaration on Human Rights, and could be employed to justify suspension of aid to offending regimes. The second was to require that the granting of a STABEX transfer be dependent on prior agreement as to its use between the European commission and the ACP recipient. Neither of these items was resolved to the satisfaction of the commission during the negotiation of Lomé II, and both were resurrected for the subsequent round of talks.

A more fundamental initiative on the conditionality dimension was put forward by the European commission for the Lomé III talks. Again, it was partly a reflection of the change in the conventional wisdom of international aid agencies since the negotiation of Lomé I. The new commissioner for development, Edgard Pisani, proposed a dramatic reorientation of European aid away from its traditional focus on infrastructure and prestige projects that, Pisani admitted, had too frequently led to the construction of "cathedrals in the sand." The new priority, put forward in a 1982 communication from the commission to the EEC Council of Ministers, would be to aid recipient countries in their pursuit of self-reliant development strategies and, in particular, to help them achieve self-sufficiency in food production. To ensure that EEC aid would be utilized for these purposes, the memorandum proposed a middle road between the "rigid conditionality imposed by financing bodies and the irresponsibility of non-conditionality." This was to be achieved through "a political dialogue" with recipient governments "concerning the effectiveness of the policies which they ask the Community to support and the relevance of such policies in terms of the general objectives of the Community's development policy."[13] To meet the financial requirements of the new policy, the commission proposed that the share of member states' aid channeled through the EEC should be increased, and repeated its long-standing request that funding of the European Development Fund be part of the EEC regular budget.

In both sets of negotiations resistance to some of the commission's proposals came both from the ACP Group and from among the member states. Having established the principle of nonreciprocity in the Lomé I agreement, the ACP Group was extremely reluctant to pursue issues of benefit to the EEC—even where there were prospects of mutual benefit. A principal reason was its unwillingness to allow the convention to impinge on its freedom of action, a stance that was ironic at a time when it was attempting to introduce new principles into the convention in order to tie the EEC's hands. An unfortunate consequence from the perspective of the ACP Group as a group was that this encouraged individual member states to break ranks, e.g. to sign bilateral fishing agreements, and the potential bargaining leverage of these resources was lost to the group.

Human rights was a particularly sensitive issue, given its centrality to issues of ACP sovereignty. There was no place in a commercial convention for this issue, according to the ACP Group. Reference to the UN's Declaration on Human Rights was rejected on the grounds that all ACP states were UN members and respected their obligations under the treaty.[14] Similarly, references to dumping and export subsidies were deemed unnecessary because the EEC could utilize GATT complaint procedures in the event that difficulties arose. Proposals for mandatory consultations in the trade sphere were perceived as a European attempt to introduce voluntary export restraints by way of the back door. Proposals for investment guarantees received a similar negative response, the ACP Group arguing that its introduction for its closest trading partners would send the wrong signals to other parties and, in any event, would be contrary to the position of the Group of 77 in the global dialogue.

By far the most serious threat to ACP interests, however, was perceived as coming from the commission's proposals in the Lomé III negotiations for policy dialogue. These were to have the effect, whether intended or not, of placing the ACP Group on the defensive for the entire talks. ACP states perceived "policy dialogue" as an attempt to undermine the nominal equality of the relationship, in essence to remove all that had been achieved in the first Lomé talks. Policy dialogue, by increasing the conditionality attached to the aid under the convention, would infringe directly on ACP sovereignty and lead to a situation where ACP development strategies were dictated from outside. As a counter to these proposals, the ACP Group put forward the proposition that its "acquired rights" under previous conventions should not be subject to renegotiation.[15]

ACP resistance to many of the commission's proposals was assisted by the lukewarm support with which they were greeted by key EEC member states. This was particularly true where the proposals would have had the effect of extending EEC competence at the expense of that of the member states. The proposed investment guarantee scheme, for instance, although gaining the support of smaller member states, was opposed by the "Big Three"—France, Germany, and Britain—on the grounds that adequate national schemes were already in existence. Insertion of a human rights clause, although strongly backed by Britain and the Netherlands, received only halfhearted support from other member states, which perceived it as an unnecessary obstacle to a successful conclusion of the negotiations. And, according to one commentator, the commission's proposals for policy dialogue were greeted with some bemusement by member states, who found the arguments excessively academic.[16] For some, there was a more practical ground for resisting the new development priorities:

whereas European construction companies had been significant beneficiaries of the projects financed by previous European Development
Funds, a far smaller proportion of the future fund would be likely to
find its way back to Europe if emphasis was to be placed on promoting
self-reliant agriculture. Again, the member states found the proposals
to be introducing unnecessary "political" difficulties into the negotiations, and the commission was eventually instructed to backtrack from
its initial ideas on policy dialogue.

Process and Strategies

Both renegotiations of the Lomé Convention were required, under
the terms of the previous conventions, to begin eighteen months before
their expiration dates—the ultimate deadline for the negotiators. Beginning the talks so long in advance caused a number of problems. In
the Lomé II negotiations, the talks began merely thirty months after
most of the provisions of the first convention had become operational.
Consequently, there had been little opportunity to assess the impact
that the convention would have on commercial relations between the
EEC and the ACP Group (by the time that the talks opened, for
example, only 10 percent of the aid funds provided by the convention
had been disbursed). In the Lomé III talks, the opening negotiating
session occurred before either side had formalized its detailed positions. Probably most important, the lengthy period set aside for the
negotiations ensured that there would be months of preliminary skir-
mishing and stalemate before both parties began serious negotiation of
the issues. This tendency was reinforced by the emphasis on principles
in the ACP Group's opening positions.

Day-to-day negotiations were the responsibility of the Commission
of the European Communities and the ACP Committee of Ambassadors (the Brussels-based representatives of the ACP states). In both
sets of negotiations, subcommittees were established that covered the
principal areas of the convention: trade cooperation; customs cooperation; STABEX and mineral products; industrial cooperation and fish-
eries; financial and technical cooperation; regional cooperation; the
problems of the least developed, landlocked, and island countries;
legal and institutional matters; and agricultural cooperation (a new area
proposed by the ACP Group in the Lomé II talks). Division of the
subject matter for the talks into functional areas to be negotiated by
specialists in the field (usually the head of divisions within the commission and the ambassadors of the ACP states most concerned with
particular issues) follows the prescription to "fractionate" that is

favored by some theorists of negotiation. At times it did have the advantage that the momentum of the negotiations was sustained in that it proved possible to reach agreement on relatively noncontroversial issues such as the convention's institutions. Yet interaction in the negotiating subcommittees frequently produced stalemate, and in the Lomé II negotiations in particular tended to further exacerbate the sour atmosphere in which the talks were enveloped.

A number of factors contributed to this outcome. The negotiating subcommittees were often a continuation of specialist groups that had been established during the course of the first convention to examine areas in which problems had arisen. In many cases, therefore, the groups were looking once again at problems that had been on the agenda for some years, problems where the position of the parties had differed markedly in large part over alternative interpretations of EEC obligations under the convention, problems that had not been resolved. The resurrection of the old issues, especially the ACP Group's demands for various absolute principles to be recognized in the new convention, served not to promote serious discussion but to provoke comments along the lines of "Your proposals are not serious: We have told you repeatedly that this is impossible." Little attempt was made to address the points made by the other party in a constructive manner.

A second problem was that although the subcommittees were divided into various technical and functional areas, the subject matter frequently was not technical but political. Demands made by the ACP Group were not for incremental changes justified according to consensual knowledge but for the acceptance of new principles to underlie the various regimes.[17] This was freely admitted by the ACP ambassadors. In the customs subcommittee in the Lomé II negotiations, for example, the ACP spokesman asserted that the group was seeking a "political commitment" by the EEC.

Finally, the process through which ACP Group positions were arrived at tended to undermine any advantage that was derived from negotiating in specialized subcommittees. As in the wider global dialogue, the talks took place between two coalitions that often had difficulty in forging their respective positions in intracoalition bargaining. Once a common position had been reached, there was little latitude for movement in bargaining with the other party. Progress in the talks in the subcommittees frequently was thwarted when either the commission or the ACP Committee of Ambassadors claimed that it lacked a mandate to negotiate on the points raised by the other. This was compounded by the structure of the negotiations, which were conducted at two levels. In addition to the meetings between the commission and the ACP committee, a number of negotiating sessions were scheduled for the ACP-EEC Council of Ministers, which comprised ministers from the home governments of the parties to the convention. Because these large-scale conferences were grandiose affairs that attracted the attention of not only the governments concerned but the international media, the natural tendency was for any concession by the parties to be left to these meetings. This was particularly true of the EEC, which saw the ministerial sessions as a means of driving a wedge between the ACP ambassadors and their home governments in an attempt to persuade them to define a narrower negotiating mandate for the ambassadors.

In both sets of negotiations, stalemate followed the initial presentation of opening positions, a situation that was broken only when the ACP retreated from its demands of principle. During this period the two parties attempted to forge crosscutting coalitions by going outside the formal negotiating process to appeal directly to governments in the national capitals.

For the ACP Group, the nature of its demands of principle in combination with its rejection of the European initiatives generally precluded successful pursuit of this tactic. It had also lost its principal European supporters since the negotiations for Lomé I. The liberal Dutch government had been defeated at the polls. The Labour government in Britain, having achieved what it perceived as a favorable arrangement for Commonwealth sugar producers, had reverted to its position of emphasizing that the EEC development policy should be more globalist in its outlook. Its inclination to oppose any major extension of the privileged treatment afforded the ACP Group was reinforced by its economic difficulties and desire to minimize British obligations to EEC budgets. The advent of the Thatcher government during the final stages of the Lomé II negotiations certainly did not help the ACP cause. France, meanwhile, appeared more concerned to reinforce bilateral relations between Paris and the francophone group than to underwrite a general improvement in the position of the ACP Group as a whole. While the ACP Group had little success in building transnational alliances in the negotiations, individual ACP states fared somewhat better in forging coalitions with their traditional protectors in the pursuit of fairly modest, country-specific objectives, e.g. Botswana gained British support for its attempts to modify the beef protocol, and Senegal won French backing for an increase in the duty-free quota provided for ACP tomato exports.

European efforts at dividing the ACP Group were more successful. One reason was the lack of faith of many ACP countries in the group's own negotiating position. Rather than serving as a rallying point, the demands of principle tended to divide the group. The EEC encouraged this by attempting to bypass the institutionalized channels of the negotiating process by going directly to heads of state in ACP countries and arguing that the positions being advanced by the Brussels-based ambassadors and ACP secretariat were extreme, and unrepresentative of the true interests and opinions of ACP governments. This tactic was facilitated by the generally poor communications that existed between ACP representatives in Brussels and their national capitals, a cause of the lack of coordination that frequently appears to occur in the North-South dialogue between domestically based and foreign-based representatives of Third World governments.

European divisive tactics were facilitated in that coalition maintenance proved more difficult for the ACP Group in the renewal talks than in the negotiations for the first convention. In the initial negotiations, the symbolic importance attached to ACP unity had facilitated a joint negotiating stance that had imposed minimal costs on individual ACP states (with the partial exception of some francophone countries that had to swallow their pride and accept the principle of nonreciprocity in trade relations with the EEC). In renewing the conventions, coalition maintenance was more difficult in that many of the issues involved questions of intragroup distribution of benefits, ACP states were well aware that the EEC, having succeeded in constructing a package that contained something for all members of the group in order to attract their signature to the initial convention, was unwilling to commit significant additional sums. In this situation, intra-ACP Group bargaining assumed the characteristics of a zero-sum game; logrolling became more difficult. Unity was already strained by the imbalances in the distribution of aid under the convention. Once the negotiations began to focus on specific proposals whose costs and benefits for individual states could easily be assessed, the fragility of the coalition was exposed. There was a reluctance on the part of many states to support the group's proposals for new initiatives that would have required a significant volume of resources, e.g. Nigeria's proposal in the Lomé II negotiations for a fund for industrial cooperation, for fear that such projects would impinge on existing financial flows.

Moreover, the structure of the relationship assisted the EEC in the pursuit of a divide and rule strategy: as a clientelist relationship, Lomé resembles Galtung's concept of a "feudal interaction structure." For the most part, the ACP Group *as a group* lacks an institutionalized role in the implementation of the convention, which occurs primarily on a bilateral basis between the European commission and ACP national governments.[18] This has hampered ACP efforts to institutionalize its grouping, one of its principal problems being a lack of credibility even among its own members. Beyond its colonial origins and periodical negotiations with the EEC, the group has no logical *raison d'etre* and, indeed, typically does not act as a group in other negotiating forums. Membership is scattered around the globe; for the regional groupings the most salient economic actors are not other members of the ACP Group and, in the case of the Caribbean and Pacific countries, not even the EEC. Consequently, ACP countries have not been willing to provide the necessary resources to build up the group's institutions.

Problems in maintaining its coalition limited the tactics available to the ACP Group in the talks. In any case, given the asymmetry of the Lomé relationship, it was scarcely surprising that warnings should predominate over threats in the tactics of the weaker party. In the best of circumstances, threats by the weaker party are barely credible; in these talks they were made even less so by the lack of unity within the ACP Group. Although ACP representatives made reference to the interdependence of the parties and, in particular, to their role as raw material suppliers, no attempt was made to exert leverage over the EEC in the negotiations by threatening to cut off commodity exports. Given the weakness of most ACP economies and their urgent need for export earnings, this was hardly surprising. Only one ACP state in the Lomé II negotiations appeared to be well placed to make a threat of this nature: Nigeria, on account of its oil exports. Yet although Nigeria threatened the use of its oil weapon at the time of the negotiations in an attempt to force Britain to make concessions on the transition to majority rule in Rhodesia/Zimbabwe, it declined to make such threats in support of the ACP Group.

Despite the talk of interdependence, the ACP Group had little success in mobilizing national resources in support of the group's bargaining position. Individual ACP states were more inclined to break rank and use their national resources to construct bilateral arrangements with the EEC. Furthermore, fractionation of the negotiations into subgroups had the effect of making it more difficult for the ACP Group to engage in issue-linkage by mobilizing its resources in one area in support of its demands elsewhere.

Threats to the interests of the EEC ran the risk of jeopardizing the benefits arising from bilateral relations with the member states, which, for many ACP countries, were more significant than those derived from the convention itself. The only EEC interest that the ACP Group might threaten was the bureaucratic interest of EEC institutions, particularly the Directorate-General VIII of the commission, in the convention's survival. Accordingly, the most telling threat—or, at least, tactical bluff—in the ACP Group's arsenal was its ability to refuse to sign a new treaty. An adjunct of this tactic was the capacity of the group to delay a final settlement in the hope of securing an improved EEC offer. This latter ploy was given added weight by the desire of the French government in both sets of negotiations to gain the plaudits for a successful conclusion of a new convention while France held the chair of the EEC Council of Ministers. Ultimately, the credibility of the threat would be undermined by ACP fears of a curtailment of the flow of benefits if a new convention was not signed before the expiry of its predecessor. As Zartman noted in the context of the Yaoundé negotiations, the least developed are least able to gamble.[19] That the Europeans were well aware of this was apparent to the Pisani memorandum, which, in proposing a convention of unlimited duration, argued that as a result of its renegotiation every five years "unnecessary confrontations are caused, when everyone knows from the outset that the Convention will be renewed in one form or another."[20]

ACP countries attempted to capitalize on their comparative weakness in a number of ways. They continually emphasized that any extension of the relationship would not impose significant costs on the EEC, arguing that the group was ill equipped to take advantage of tariff concessions and unlimited free access for its exports. They attempted to play on the EEC's sense of moral obligation by reminding it of how poorly the economies of the ACP states had fared since the signature of the first convention and of the EEC's special responsibilities for the ACP Group arising out of the "spirit" of Lomé. Similarly, they noted the EEC's failure to meet its obligations in North-South relations, particularly its promise to devote 0.7 percent of its GNP to foreign aid, and argued that this was all the more reason for the EEC to make an extra effort within the Lomé context. Another favorite tactic was to exploit the statements of senior EEC officials, particularly, in the Lomé II talks, those of then-Commissioner for Development Claude Cheysson, which had admitted the inadequacies of the existing Lomé arrangements. Cheysson, for instance, had argued at one time that STABEX was incomplete because it failed to cover the real value of ACP export earnings, and had stated that the provisions for industrial cooperation "lacked operational content." Warnings were given of the damage to the EEC's international reputation should the negotiations break down (a matter of some ambiguity, given the less than enthusiastic reception that the Group of 77 had given to Lomé when it was first signed). Finally, the ACP engaged in tactics of "coercive deficiency," issuing dire predictions of the consequences for their economies and populations should the negotiations fail to bring significant new benefits.[21]

Choice of tactics by the EEC was dictated primarily by its desire to minimize the cost of the relationship. The principal strategy was to put pressure on the ACP Group in order to force a quick capitulation, thereby playing on ACP fears of an interruption to the flow of benefits from the convention. An early ploy, designed to limit the scope of discussions, was to seek to confine the negotiations to a narrow and restricted timetable, in the Lomé II negotiations initially set at six months. As one ACP spokesman noted, given the size and diverse structure of the ACP Group, and the range of issues involved, the proposed timetable would have been totally infeasible without unconditional surrender to the EEC position. Having failed with this tactic, the ECC adopted others, with the intention of maximizing the leverage gained from the time constraint: it delayed announcing its position on important issues until the last moment (the most notable example being the size of the aid package for the successor conventions—which was not put forward until what was scheduled to be the last ministerial meeting); and it demanded that the ACP Group provide extensive detail in support of its claims (here the EEC was safe in the knowledge that in most instances the group had neither the staff nor the data to respond effectively in the short time available to such requests).

Many of the initial ACP proposals were rejected on the grounds that they were "not serious," "demagogic," or "in total conflict with the Community's legal basis."[22] At times, particularly during the Lomé II talks, it appeared that the commission had as its intention the humiliation of the ACP ambassadors. ACP demands for the acceptance of new principles in the convention were dismissed out of hand; in a paternalistic manner the EEC warned that pursuit of these "extreme" objectives endangered the existing pattern of cooperation in the convention. ACP negotiators were frequently reminded of the depressed state of the economics of the member states, of the unfavorable international environment, and of the lack of public support for further aid initiatives.[23] The EEC was "doing its best" for the ACP Group at a time when it was engaged in "more important negotiations" over its own budgetary difficulties and the EEC's enlargement (Greece during the Lomé II negotiations; Spain and Portugal during Lomé III). The inability of the EEC to offer better terms to ACP states than those enjoyed by its own producers was put forward as a constraint on EEC freedom of decision making; the Europeans also argued that acceptance of ACP demands would require EEC to abandon its concern for the less favored developing countries while giving further benefits to the "already privileged" ACP Group, an attempt to capitalize on the sensitivities of the relationship between the ACP and the wider Group of 77. Meanwhile, some commission initiatives, e.g. provision of investment guarantees, were characterized as being primarily to the benefit of the ACP Group rather than of EEC interests.

By far the favorite EEC tactic, however, was to remind the ACP of the achievements of the existing Lomé arrangements and to contrast this with the lack of progress in the global North-South dialogue. As the chairman of the ACP Committee of Ambassadors noted at the end of the Lomé II negotiations, "The absence of measures by the developed countries, far from evoking a positive and dynamic response from Europe, were seen and used as arguments against the ACP cause."[24] At the same time, however, the EEC was careful to argue that Lomé could be only a minor contribution to ACP development needs, and therefore could not fulfill all of the aspirations that the ACP Group had expressed for it. Rather perversely, the EEC used the argument that the contractual nature of the convention itself justified limitations on the implementation of the provisions; Lomé was a "concrete" relationship with accompanying obligations and was contrasted by representatives of the EEC with the noncommittal promises made by the EEC in global forums.

In both sets of negotiations the first eight months were characterized by stalemate. Progress came only when the ACP Group fell back from its demands of principle to accept the formula put forward by the EEC: incremental change from a case-by-case consideration of problem areas. The ACP Group's retreat from its original position was quite precipitous, placing the group on the defensive in the talks and contributing to an erosion of morale. Yet, in both sets of negotiations—in what has apparently become part of the ritual of the Lomé talks—the ACP walked out of what was scheduled to be the last ministerial meeting in protest at the amount of the EEC's aid offer for the new convention. In large part this was a response in the manner in which the EEC presented the aid offer (*montant*). This was kept by the EEC to the last negotiating session in the realization that an earlier presentation would inevitably give the ACP Group somewhat greater bargaining leverage to exert in support of an aid increase.

Inevitably, the *montant* was the subject of difficult negotiations between the member states. In both sets of negotiations the British government was insistent on limiting its contribution to European funds: in the first, it was joined by the French Treasury, which had significantly increased its bilateral commitments; in the second, by the

Bonn government. After such difficult internal negotiations, the aid offer was presented to the ACP as a nonnegotiable item. In both rounds of talks, the ACP Group responded by rejecting the original offer and leaving the talks—a ploy that won it an increase of 500 million European Currency Units (Ecu) in the Lomé II talks, and 400 million Ecu in the most recent negotiations. In the meantime the EEC had attempted to force the hand of the ACP Group. First, it emphasized the time constraint and the possible disruption to the flow of benefits. Second, it attempted once again to maneuver outside the formal negotiating structure in order to divide the ACP states. In the Lomé II talks, for instance, Commissioner for Development Cheysson was dispatched on a tour of ACP capitals to persuade ACP home governments of the reasonable nature of the EEC offer and of the dangers of disruption of the flow of benefits that would accompany a breakdown in the relationship.

With the ACP Group's reluctantly accepting the EEC aid offer as the best deal available at the time, negotiations came to an end—despite many issues left unresolved in both sets of talks. In some cases, e.g. the ACP Group's proposals in the Lomé II negotiations for the establishment of a Fund for Industrial Cooperation, the convention mandated the creation of a special expert committee to examine the matter. Similarly, in the Lomé III negotiations, the ACP request for additional commodity agreements for EEC purchases of specific quantities of its exports at guaranteed prices was quietly buried in a committee established to monitor trade in these products but that lacked any powers.

An Evaluation

Were the Lomé negotiations successful? An answer depends on the criteria employed to define success. Alternatives include (a) the reaching of an agreement—a minimalist approach; (b) whether the parties achieved their stated goals—although this approach assumes that these were not bargaining chips but targets that the parties believed could be achieved; (c) whether the negotiations actually reached agreement where this might reasonably have been expected to have been feasible; (d) whether the negotiations "improve or at least not damage the relationship between the parties";[25] and (e) whether learning has occurred in the relationship.

From the minimalist perspective the negotiations ended successfully in twice renewing the convention. Existing benefits were maintained and, indeed, the areas of cooperation were extended to provide additional benefits to the parties. Agreement fell far short of the parties' stated goals, but, as noted above, at least as far as the majority of the ACP Group was concerned, there was little expectation that the group's opening negotiating position would be realized. For the ACP Group, there was marginally improved access for some of its products, slight improvements to the rules of origin and the safeguard clause, lower thresholds for eligibility for STABEX transfers, improved product coverage and more favorable repayment terms, a new scheme (SYSMIN) to help minerals exporters, and the new Center for Agricultural Cooperation. Additional resources were provided for financial and technical cooperation in the new conventions, although these did not maintain the value of real per capita aid that had been achieved under Lomé I. And the opportunity costs of the convention were minimal—because reciprocity was not required in most matters, few constraints were placed on ACP freedom of action.

From the European perspective, the negotiations were also perceived as successful. The outcomes were tactial victories for the EEC in that they were much closer to its opening positions than those of the ACP Group. Although the EEC paid most, it moved least—and the additional cost of the new conventions was not great in terms of its total budget, the aid allocations of individual member states, or the constraints placed on European policy toward other LDCs. As in all clientelist relationships, the convention involved an exchange of nonequivalent resources, the principal benefit to the EEC as a whole being the maintenance of Lomé as the showpiece of its development policy. Although the commission had failed to realize most of the proposals set out in its initial negotiating positions, these were largely secondary objectives in the talks, the first priority being one of damage limitation in the sense of resisting ACP demands for more sweeping changes.

If, however, one evaluates success in terms of whether negotiations "improve or at least not damage the relationship between the parites," the outcome is less clear-cut, This was particularly true of the Lomé II negotiations, which ended in an atmosphere of disillusionment and considerable bitterness. Both parties attached appendices to the convention containing unilateral declarations of their understanding of key issues and, in the case of the ACP Group, its disappointment at the results reached. In one sense, both parties were losers in that the talks probably damaged the much-vaunted partnership. Any lingering hopes that Lomé would indeed serve as a model for a new international economic order were crushed by the negotiations. In their outcome, and the manner in which they were conducted, the Lomé II talks tarnished the image of an equal partnership, and did little to dispel criticisms that Lomé is essentially a neocolonial arrangement.

There are two principal explanations for the atmosphere in which the talks were conducted and concluded. The first is the fundamental disagreement between the two parties regarding the nature of the obligations that the EEC had assumed in its role as collective patron. Conflict and bitterness were inevitable as the ACP Group discovered, first, that the EEC did not share its interpretation of European obligations, and second, that the group was unable to impose its own definition of the obligations on the EEC. But additional—largely avoidable—bitterness also arose from the manner in which the negotiations were conducted. In part this derived from the ACP Group's opening position, with its insistence on establishing new principles in the relationship. This served to exasperate further EEC officials, already frustrated that the ACP Group expected the EEC to go beyond what were perceived as generous contractual provisions in the relationship. In addition, however, some EEC officials displayed a marked lack of sensitivity toward the formal equality of the partnership, the symbolic importance of maintaining ACP solidarity, in short, toward "issues of recognition, of dignity, of acceptance, of rights and justice," which, as Zartman and Berman note, "may be more important than the actual disposition of a material good,"[26] Rather than following the advice of Fisher and Ury to separate the people from the problem, the Lomé II talks allowed personalities to become problems,[27] The bitterness that accompanied the initial talks precluded joint approaches to the identification and solution of problems; the negotiations were perceived as an arena in which it was necessary to score political points. There is little doubt that the outcome of the talks could have been reached more efficiently, with less damage inflicted on the "spirit" of the relationship.

Could the substantive outcome of the negotiations have been different? Probably not—to any significant degree. Given the unfavorable international economic climate, the asymmetry of power between the two negotiating groups, and the unwillingness of the EEC to agree to significant extensions of the relationship, the ACP Group could at best have expected to realize incremental improvements to the convention. The outcome inevitably would have been disappointing for the weaker parties; their problem was that the low-cost concessions in the Lomé relationship had been exhausted, and the EEC simply did not perceive the ACP Group to be of sufficient significance among its present or future economic partners to allow the group to tie its hands in economic policy-making.

On both the ACP and EEC sides, however, there were perceptions that the ACP Group could have achieved more. ACP representatives believed tht their failure to do so was largely the product of a lack of unity in the group. From this perspective, too many ACP states perceived the relationship as one in which the ACP would outline its aspirations and Europe would indicate what it could afford to give, which, as the chairman of the ACP Committee of Ambassadors pointed out, was "an approach that should not be confused with negotiations,"[28] According to this perception, the ACP Group had failed to capitalize on its bargaining strength in the negotiations. But where the ACP strength lay, at a time when most of the group faced severe economic difficulties and were particularly vulnerable to a curtailment of the benefits provided by the convention, was not spelled out by the more militant ACP representatives.

More realistic was the view expressed by European negotiators that the ACP Group would have had greater success if less time had been wasted on the demands of principle and more energy given to promoting those cases in which hardship caused by restrictions in the convention could have been demonstrated. The ACP negotiating hand was further weakened by the group's unwillingness to consider proposals put forward by the EEC, and which may have been in the mutual interest in the long term (e.g. some form of guarantee for European investments). By tersely dismissing all European initiatives in the Lomé II negotiations, the ACP Group inevitably came to the table empty handed.

Gains from the pursuit of better tactics by the ACP Group at best would have been marginal—if for no other reason than some of the principal issues were decided not by talks between the ACP Group and the EEC but within the EEC itself. This was true of the size of the aid offer but also, for example, of the commission's proposals in the Lomé III talks for improved access to the European market for ACP agricultural exports (which were vetoed by France and Italy). With the absence of progress in the areas of trade and industrial cooperation, financial and technical cooperation became the most significant element in the relationship. Although the ACP Group was able to negotiate a third convention whose 294 articles stood in marked contrast to the 94 articles of the Lomé I agreement and extended the relationship into new areas of cooperation, this was a hollow victory without the resources to finance the extended shopping list. Here the negotiations on the *montant* within the EEC were decisive.

Meanwhile, lack of unity among the Europeans ensured that they were unsuccessful in implementing some of the proposals put forward in their opening positions. Because the major concern was to resist ACP demands, however, lack of unity was less important to obtaining their principal objective than it was to the ACP Group. Still, difficulties in formulating group positions caused problems in that, once internal agreement had been reached, proposals were presented to the ACP Group as nonnegotiable. This, not surprisingly, contributed to the reluctance of the ACP to pursue issues of potential mutual interest.

Some learning did occur, nevertheless. The Lomé III negotiations were conducted in a less hostile atmosphere. In part this can be attributed to the resignation of the ACP Group to the fact that the relationship would inevitably fall short of its original aspirations for collective clientelism. The group was less inclined to concentrate on abstract principles and retreated at an earlier stage from its opening position to negotiate on a case-by-case basis. There was a greater willingness to consider issues of mutual interest, e.g. provisions relating to investment guarantees. The commission also adopted a more conciliatory stance, displaying greater awareness of ACP sensitivities. In the Lomé II negotiations (in sharp contrast to the initial convention) its memorandum to the EEC Council of Ministers requesting a mandate contained very little of interest to the ACP Group. In the Lomé III memorandum, however, there were a number of sweeteners to encourage the ACP Group to accept the idea of policy dialogue, for instance, proposals for increased financial assistance, and for improved access for the group's agricultural products. While these major initiatives were lost in the council, the commission did move during the negotiations toward the removal of a number of the features of the convention that had been particularly irksome to the ACP Group, e.g. more flexibility in the derogation procedures for the rules of origin, and in the calculation of STABEX transfers where there has been significant fluctuations in the value of an ACP state's currency.

Lomé may, then, be judged to have been a qualified success although falling far short of the high aspirations expressed at the time of its initial signing. This returns us to the question of why the negotiations were successful and what lessons may be learned from them.

In an otherwise insightful essay on North-South negotiations, Rothstein asserted that the Lomé negotiations were successful because they "focused on practical reforms and reflected relatively objective calculations of felt national interest; conflicts over principles were avoided and the inflated objectives and the rigidities of group-versus-group confrontations were avoided."[29] The analysis of the Lomé negotiations presented above clearly undermines Rothstein's argument. Principles have played an important part in the Lomé negotiations. Similarly, the politics of forgoing group positions has frequently led to the same inflexibility and stalemate that have characterized the global North-South dialogue.

What was different about the Lomé I negotiations, however, was that the principle to which the ACP Group attached the greatest symbolic importance—nonreciprocity—was one to which the EEC could agree because it incurred no significant cost in doing so. Subsequently, the principles demanded by the ACP Group in its opening positions were to have the same effects as in other global negotiations: stalemate and an atmosphere of bitterness. But, by then, the original convention was in place and providing a flow of much-needed resources to the ACP. Here two other factors came into play: the deadline imposed by the expiration of the convention with consequent possible termination of benefits; and the economic weakness of the ACP states, which made them more vulnerable to a disruption of these flows than more advanced LDCs would have been. As a consequence, ACP states were willing both to retreat from their original demands of principle and to accept partial agreements, secure in the knowledge that the convention would be open to renegotiation again after three years, at which time they could expect to realize further incremental gains.

Finally, it was important that Lomé was the EEC's *own* development policy. To have failed to have renegotiated the convention after it had received so much publicity in 1975 would have been embarrassing to say the least. The role of the Commission of the European Communities in administering the convention gave a significant Northern bureaucracy important organizational interests in the renewal and extension of the relationship—the European Development Fund has become the second-largest item in EEC expenditure behind the CAP, but in excess of the finance provided to the Regional and Social Funds. The Development Directorate now enjoys a budget in excess of that of the aid agencies of medium-sized donors such as Sweden.

Any attempt to draw lessons from the Lomé negotiations for other components of the North-South dialogue must always bear in mind the unique characteristics of the relationship outlined at the beginning of this chapter. This caveat notwithstanding, the following hypotheses can be put forward, which may or may not be a correct interpretation of the Lomé experience or have validity in the wider North-South context but at least may be worthy of further investigation:

1. Negotiations are more likely to be successful where there are marked asymmetries between the parties, especially when their economic structures are primarily complementary rather than competitive.[30]
2. Regional negotiations have more chance of success in the North-

South dialogue than does global bargaining.[31] This is particularly the case where the parties have historical ties and long experience in dealing with each other.

3. Successful negotiations are more likely when the parties are attempting to renew an existing agreement that all parties perceive as bringing some benefits (even if, as in the Lomé case, the benefits might be unequal or nonequivalent).

4. Negotiating deadlines encourage brinkmanship but ultimately facilitate the reaching of agreements, especially when the time constraint is reinforced by the fear of loss of benefits from existing arrangements.

5. North-South negotiations will be subject to a "foot-in-the-door" effect. Each time an agreement is renegotiated, Northern parties inevitably will be subject to pressure to make additional concessions. Although change may only be incremental, the benefits accruing to Southern countries will tend to increase over time.[32]

6. Lack of issue-specific expertise will lead Southern states to adopt maximal opening positions. Rather than serving to unite the group, demands of principle and confrontational positions will be divisive in circumstances where the demands are not perceived as credible, and demoralizing in that the South has to move furthest from its opening position in order to reach a formula for serious negotiations that can produce a settlement. Maximal opening positions may also obstruct the realization of change (albeit incremental).

7. Southern groupings are handicapped by their lack of institutionalization, and by the absence of an adequate secretariat able to supply technical information. There is a need for a "Southern OECD." As collective goods theory would predict, however, a viable Southern secretariat will be established only if it is financed disproportionately by more wealthy members of the Group of 77.

8. Fractioning of negotiations into functional and/or technical subcommittees will not improve the prospects for a successful outcome where one or more of the parties perceives the problem to be primarily "political" in nature. Uncertainly and lack of consensus on technical knowledge will produce stalemate in North-South negotiations.

9. Southern countries will tend to dismiss Northern proposals even when these are ostensibly for projects for mutual benefit because (a) they are suspicious of Northern intentions, and (b) they jealously guard their sovereignty—projects for "mutual" benefit are perceived as infringing upon their freedom to act. Lack of attention to mutual benefit inevitably weakens the Southern negotiating hand.

10. Even if Southern countries pursued a more effective negotiating strategy, only incremental gains can be expected to be realized in situations where industrialized countries oppose the introduction

of new principles and norms into regimes. Improved tactics will be insufficient to overcome fundamental disparities in issue-specific power.

11. Negotiations are more likely to have a successful outcome when there is a Northern bureaucracy with significant organizational interests of its own in negotiating or maintaining an agreement.

12. Concessions are made by the party with the lowest tolerance for breakdown.

13. In areas where the opportunity costs of agreement are close to zero, an unsatisfactory agreement will be accepted by the South as long as it contains sufficient concessions for Southern negotiators to save face. A little is truly perferable to nothing at all.

Notes

Research on which this chapter is based was initially funded by the Institute for the Study of World Politics, and the University of California, Berkeley. Its revision was facilitated by a research grant from the University of Sydney.

1. Preamble to the resolution of the EEC-ACP Parliamentary Conference in Luxembourg of 29 September 1978, quoted in "Report on the Negotiations for a New Lomé Convention" (Broeksz Report), *European Parliament Working Documents* No. 487/78 (Luxembourg. 1 December 1978), p. 48.

2. Rabbi L. Namaliu, president of the ACP Council of Ministers, *Courier* 89 (January-February 1985): 4.

3. The original 46 ACP states: Bahamas, Barbados, Botswana, Burundi, Cameroon, Central African Republic, Chad, Congo, Dahomey (Benin), Equatorial Guinea, Ethiopia, Fiji, Gabon, Gambia, Ghana, Guinea, Guinea-Bissau, Grenada, Guyana, Ivory Coast, Jamaica, Kenya, Lesotho, Liberia, Madagascar, Malawi, Mali, Mauritania, Mauritius, Niger, Nigeria, Rwanda, Senegal, Sierra Leone, Somalia, Sudan, Swaziland, Tanzania, Togo, Tonga, Trinidad and Tobago, Uganda, Upper Volta, Western Samoa, Zaire, and Zambia. During the period of application of the first convention thirteen additional states acceded: Surinam, Seychelles, Comoros, Djibouti, Solomon Islands, Sao Tomé and Principe, Cape Verde, Papua New Guinea, Tuvalu, Dominica, Saint Lucia, Kiribati, Saint Vincent and Grenadines. During the second convention, Vanuatu, Zimbabwe, Belize, Antigua and Barbuda, and St. Christopher and Nevis joined the ACP Group; Greece acceded to the convention as the tenth EEC member state on 8 October 1981. Mozambique and Angola joined the third convention.

4. For additional discussion of the Lomé I negotiations see I. William Zartman, "Europe and Africa: Decolonization or Dependency?" *Foreign Affairs* 54 (January 1976): 325-43; Isebill V. Gruhn, "The Lomé Convention: Inching Towards Interdependence," *International Organization* 30 (Spring 1976): 241-62.

5. On the extraordinary developments in the sugar market and their importance for Lomé I, see Carole Webb, "Mr. Cube versus Monsieur Beet: The Politics of Sugar in the European Communities," in *Policy Making in*

the European Communities, ed. Helen Wallace, William Wallace, and Carole Webb (London: Wiley, 1977), pp. 197-225.

6. John Ravenhill, *Collective Clientelism: The Lomé Conventions and North-South Relations* (New York: Columbia University Press, 1985).

7. For the importance of "generalized exchange" in clientelist relations, see S.N. Eisenstadt and Luis Roniger, "The Study of Patron-Client Relations and Recent Developments in Sociological Theory," in *Political Clientelism, Patronage and Development* ed. S.N. Eisenstadt and Rene Lemarchand (Beverly Hills, Calif.: Sage Publications, 1981), pp. 274-75.

8. Some learning did occur, however. Although many of the principles demanded in the Lomé II negotiations were revived at the start of the Lomé III talks, this appeared to be more of a ritualistic formula than a serious statement of the group's intent. Having made a token gesture toward the principles, the group moved more rapidly than had been the case in the Lomé II talks toward the less acrimonious discussion of particular cases.

9. In his statement to the opening session of the talks for Lomé II, for instance, the chairman of the ACP Council of Ministers noted:

> Although the Lomé Convention represented a positive step forward in its time, the ACP have never considered it as history's terminal station.
>
> Today our sole purpose here is to seek to make with you, our partners, another significant step . . . these arrangements cannot be regarded as a mere holding operation limited to the rearrangement, adaptation, or adjustment of the Lomé Convention.
>
> The ACP is not interested in a purely cosmetic exercise. We reject any such approach and see grave danger and little benefit for any of the contracting parties deriving from it.
>
> We of the ACP have come to seek to negotiate for the eighties, a new Convention which must represent a significant step forward as Lomé did in 1975.

"Statement by the President of the Council of ACP Ministers on the Occasion of the Opening of the Negotiations of the Successor Arrangements to the Lomé Convention," ACP/340/71/Rev. 2 (Brussels: ACP Group, 24 July 1978), pp. 8-9.

10. Commission of the European Communities, "Commission Memorandum on the Future ACP-EEC Negotiations for the Renewal of the Lomé Convention," COM(78) 47 final (Strasburg: 15 February 1978), p. 5.

11. Dieter Frisch, "Lomé III: Living Through Difficult Negotiations," *Courier* 89 (January-February 1985): 19.

12. For further details of the STABEX scheme, see John Ravenhill, "What Is to Be Done for Third World Commodity Exporters? An Evaluation of the STABEX Scheme," *International Organization* 38 (Summer 1984): 537-74; Ravenhill, *Collective Clientelism,* ch. 3.

13. Commission of the European Communities, "Memorandum on the Community's Development Policy," *Bulletin of the European Communities,* Supplement 5/82 (1982), p. 16.

14. On the narrow definition of human rights pursued by the EEC in the Lomé II talks, see Ronald I. Meltzer, "International Human Rights and Develop-

ment: Evolving Conceptions and Their Application to Relations between the European Community and the African-Caribbean-Pacific States" in *Human Rights and Development in Africa* ed. Claude E. Welch, Jr., and Ronald I. Meltzer (Albany: State University of New York Press, 1984), pp. 208-25.

15. "The ACP concept of acquired rights is therefore the principle that whatever advances or achievements we have made in ideas, formulations, or procedures in Lomé I and Lomé II should at least be maintained in the successor Convention." Speech of the president of the ACP Council of Ministers at the opening of the Lomé III negotiations.

16. Christopher Stevens, "The Renegotiation of the Convention" in *Europe, Africa and Lomé III,* ed. Robert Boardman, Timothy M. Shaw, and Panayotis Soldatos (Washington, D.C.: University Press of America, 1985), p. 68.

17. On the importance of consensual knowledge for collaboration, see Ernst B. Haas, "Why Collaborate? Issue-Linkage and International Regimes," *World Politics* 32 (April 1980): 357-405.

18. Ravenhill, *Collective Clientelism,* ch. 9.

19. I. William Zartman, *The Politics of Trade Negotiations Between Africa and the European Economic Community* (Princeton: Princeton University Press, 1971).

20. 'Commission of the European Communities, "Memorandum of the Community's Development Policy," p. 20.

21. On the concept of coercive deficiency see I. William Zartman "The Analysis of Negotiation," in *The 50% Solution,* ed. I. William Zartman (New York: Doubleday, 1976), p. 54 and Thomas Schelling, *Strategy of Conflict* (Cambridge: Harvard University Press, 1960).

22. Edwin W. Carrington (deputy secretary-general of the ACP secretariat), "How Lomé I Became Lomé II" (Paper presented at the University of Antwerp, February 1980).

23. "I should like you to remember the international climate, the state of the North-South dialogue, paralysed by the egoism of the great powers, lack of imagination and an absence of will, and which, from the failure of UNCTAD in Belgrade to the drastic cuts in IDA resources, piled disappointment on bitterness. . . . It is worth remembering that the first Lomé Convention was signed by a Community at the height of its economic and commercial power, that the second Convention was established in 1979 by a Europe which thought it could see the light at the end of the tunnel, following the first oil crisis, but which did not know that there was another crisis approaching. We all know what economic and monetary disorder has reigned since then." (Gaston Thorn [president of the Commission of the European Communities] quoted in *Courier* 89 [January-February 1985]: 9-10.)

24. Donald B. Rainford, "Lomé II: 'An Improvement', But It Is Hoped That the Spirit of Partnership Will Be 'Rekindled.' " *Courier* 58 (November 1979): 25.

25. Roger Fisher and William Ury, *Getting to Yes* (Boston: Houghton Mifflin, 1981), p. 4.

26. I. William Zartman and Maureen R. Berman, *The Practical Negotiator* (New Haven: Yale University Press, 1982), p.84.

27. Fisher and Ury, *Getting to Yes,* ch. 2.
28. Rainford, "Lombé II," p. 24.
29. Robert L. Rothstein, "Is the North-South Dialogue Worth Saving?" *Third World Quarterly* 6 (January 1984): 172.
30. Opposed to this hypothesis is the alternative: successful North-South negotiations will take place only where the parties are relatively evenly balanced such that reciprocity and mutually beneficial trade-offs are possible within a particular issue area. This alternative hypothesis places emphasis, in Keohane's terms, on "strategic" reciprocity: the exchange of similar items of equivalent value. As the Lomé negotiations demonstrate, however, reciprocity need not necessarily take the form of equal exchange, or the exchange of equivalents. A strict interpretation of the alternative hypothesis would also deny the possibility of issue linkage for mutually beneficial trade-offs. In the Lomé relationship, the paradox for the ACP Group is that its weakness is its strength but ultimately its weakness: it was only on account of its comparative weakness that the EEC was willing to enter into a contractual relationship with the ACP Group in the first place; its weakness, however, means that it is not a sufficiently significant economic partner for the EEC to enable it to extend the relationship in the manner that it desires. See Robert O. Keohane, "Reciprocity in International Relations," *International Organization* 40, No. 1 (winter 1986): 1-28.
31. As Geoffrey Barraclough argues, regional negotiations will become more attractive to LDCs in the absence of progress in global forums. "The Struggle for the Third World," *New York Review of Books,* 9 November 1978, p. 54. This is not to argue necessarily that such negotiations will be any easier. Regional negotiations cannot necessarily be equated with more narrow, functional negotiations; as in the case of the Lomé negotiations, their scope may be so wide that they appear to be a microcosm of the global dialogue. Regional negotiations also are not necessarily more harmonious than their global counterparts; in an age of continuous negotiations over North-South issues, the same representatives may find themselves facing each other in various forums simultaneously. Bitterness in one forum spills over very easily into others. In this context it is interesting to note that representatives of the EEC complained that ACP negotiators from the Caribbean were to blame for the bitterness of the Lomé II negotiations, for they had insisted that serious attention be given to the claim in the convention's preamble that Lomé should serve as a "model" for the new international economic order. Caribbean negotiators, it was asserted, particularly in contrast with those from francophone Africa, failed to "understand" the EEC and the "nature" of the Lomé relationship.
32. The EEC response to the "foot-in-the-door" effect was to propose that the future Lomé arrangements should take the form of a framework that will be of indefinite duration.

APPENDIX
PRINCIPAL AREAS OF NEGOTIATION

A. Commercial Cooperation

Status Quo	ACP Opening Position	EEC Opening Position	Outcome
1. *Access for ACP Exports* (Lomé II & III)			
Free access for "authentic" ACP exports other than agricultural products included in the CAP.	Access to the EC market for *all* ACP exports free of duties, levies, and quantity restrictions.	Maintenance of existing arrangements with case-by-case consideration of problematic items.	Lomé II: Marginal improvement in access for five agricultural products: marginal improvements in beef, banana, and rum protocols. Lomé III: specific time limit for EEC to respond to ACP requests for improved access for individual products.
2. *Rules of Origin* (Lomé II & III)			
Detailed regulations requiring local processing sufficient to produce change of tariff classification, and/or specific local value-added requirement (normally 50% +).	Reduction in the value-added requirement for originating status to 25%.	Maintenance of existing arrangements that protect ACP efforts at "authentic" industrialization. Review "concrete" problems on a case-by-case basis.	Lomé II: More liberal derogation procedures. Lomé III: Derogations to be granted where local value added is at least 60%. Longer derogation periods.

3. *Safeguard Clause* (Lomé II & III)			
EEC member state may resort to safeguard measures if "serious disturbance" in sector of economy.	Exemption of ACP exports from safeguard arrangements.	Safeguard must be maintained to guarantee access provisions. Amenable to a "less brutal" implementation.	Lomé II: New arrangements/preconditions for imposition of safeguard is such action deemed necessary by EEC. Lomé III: New annex specifies required consultation procedures.
4. *Maintenance of ACP Tariff Preferences (Lomé II & III)*			
ACP exports, subject to CAP are guaranteed more favorable treatment than that applied to MFN suppliers. Other products enter duty free.	No erosion of ACP tariff preferences without compensation.	EEC cannot allow ACP to dictate its foreign commercial policy. ACP receives compensation through other areas of the convention's "privileged relationship."	No change.
5. *Commodity Agreements (Lomé III)*			
Special purchase arrangements for specific quantities of ACP sugar and beef exports. ACP exporters receive prices approximating those paid to EEC producers.	Extension of commodity agreements to all principal ACP agricultural exports, with EEC to guarantee price and market shares.	Problem of unstable earnings from commodity exports covered by STABEX. ACP loss of market shares caused by its lack of competitiveness.	No additional commodity agreements.

B. Industrial Cooperation

Status Quo	ACP Opening Position	EEC Opening Position	Outcome
1. *Financing* (Lomé II) No separate provision: financing of industrial cooperation occurs through EDF and European Investment Bank (EIB).	Creation of a special fund for industrial development to be jointly managed by the ACP and EEC.	Unity of EDF must be maintained.	Consultative Group established to investigate sources of financing for ACP industrial development.
2. *Restructuring/Consultations* (Lomé II) No provision.	Active encouragement to be given to restructuring in the EEC to make way for ACP manufacturers.	Mandatory consultations in the industrial domain to be held to improve information flow regarding ACP exports.	Voluntary consultations to be held between interested parties.
3. *Investment Guarantees* (Lomé II) No provision.	Opposed.	Necessity for some (unspecified) action to promote and protect EEC investments in ACP states.	Mandatory extension to all EEC member states of terms of bilateral investment treaties between an ACP state and EEC country.

4. Investment Promotion (Lomé III)

Status Quo	ACP Opening Position	EEC Opening Position	Outcome
Commitment to encourage investment that accords with the development priorities of ACP states.	EEC should take necessary measures to encourage private-sector involvement in ACP Group.	Special accords for the promotion and protection of EEC investment.	New statement recognizing the importance of the private sector to ACP development, the need for fair and equitable treatment for investors and for a predictable and secure investment climate. Joint study to be conducted on measures to facilitate increased private investment flows.

C. Stabex

Status Quo	ACP Opening Position	EEC Opening Position	Outcome
1. Product/Market Coverage (Lomé II & III) Earnings from exports of 33 agricultural products plus iron ore to the EEC. Coverage for exports of these products to all markets for designated countries for which EEC traditionally not principal market.	Coverage for all exports (including services) regardless of market.	Willing to examine additional products on a case-by-case basis. System cannot include minerals because (a) cost; (b) "artificial" export prices in minerals transactions; (c) possibility for manipulation by MNCs; (d) more extensive system would duplicate the IMF's Compensatory Financ-	Lomé II: Product coverage widened to 43 agricultural products plus iron ore. No coverage of services. New scheme—SYSMIN—to provide loans to maintain production and export of 7 minerals to the EEC. Iron to be transferred from STABEX to SYSMIN at end of Lomé II.

Status Quo	ACP Opening Position	EEC Opening Position	Outcome
		ing Facility. STABEX is part of the "privileged" relations between the ACP Group and EEC: the latter is not responsible for all ACP external trade.	Lomé III: Extension of the system to 48 agricultural products. No coverage for tourism or other services. SYSMIN not extended to compensate for export earnings losses in minerals sector.
2. Calculation of transfers (Lomé II and III) Shortfall on nominal trend in export earnings.	Indexation of receipts to guarantee import capacity and to compensate for deteriorating terms of trade.	Principle of indexation unacceptable.	Lomé II: Existing arrangements maintained. One % "statistical adjustment" to transfers.
3. Thresholds (Lomé II and III) "Dependency" and "fluctuation" thresholds must be met before eligible for transfer.	Abolition of thresholds.	Thresholds necessary to enable system to concentrate on significant problems.	Lomé II: Reduction in thresholds from 2.5% to 2% for least developed, landlocked and island; from 7.5 to 6.5% for others. Lomé III: Further 0.5% reduction in all thresholds.

4. *Repayment* (Lomé II and III) Required (except for designated "least developed" countries) when quantity of exports at least equals reference level.	Abolition of repayment requirement.	Would undermine idea of STABEX as a trade instrument not an aid source.	Lomé II: More liberal and flexible system for repayment. Lomé III: No change.
5. *Utilization of Transfers* (Lomé II and III) ACP states must inform commission of how transfers utilized.	ACP Group has sovereignty over use of transfers from STABEX	Transfers to be used in pursuit of the system's objectives.	Lomé II: Vague and largely meaningless clause on utilization of transfers. Lomé III: ACP Group must "communicate substantial information" on proposed use of transfer before transfer agreement is signed. ACP Group required to notify commission of use made of transfer within 12 months. Failure to provide notification may lead to suspension of future transfers.

D. Financial and Technical Cooperation

Status Quo	ACP Opening Position	EEC Opening Position	Outcome
1. *Specialized Funds* (Lomé II)			
No special funds: all projects financed from EDF.	Special funds to be created for regional development, commercial promotion, transport and communications, the least developed ACP states, exceptional aid, and industrial cooperation.	Unity of EDF must be maintained.	No special funds created.
(Lomé III)	Special fund for transport and communications		No change.
2. *Management* (Lomé II and III)			
Projects to be drawn up by ACP Group in consultation with EEC. EEC responsible for financing decisions. ACP states responsible for execution of projects.	Joint management of aid procedures, including financing decisions.	Joint management already practiced for all important decisions. EEC is a bilateral donor not a multilateral institution.	EEC retains control of the financing decisions. Greater ACP participation in tendering procedures etc.
	Improvement and acceleration of management procedures.		Time limits introduced for various stages of administrative decision
3. *Maintenance of real value of aid* (Lomé II)			
No provision.	Maintenance of the real value of aid by periodic adjustments during course of convention.	Opposed.	Not implemented.

4. Reference to EEC's global commitments (Lomé II)	No reference.	EEC must respect its international commitments, i.e. 0.7% GNP in ODA pledge.	Lomé is a concrete reflection of the EEC respect for its commitments.	No reference in convention.
5. Untying of Aid (Lomé II)	Aid tied to purchases in EEC or ACP Group other than in "exceptional" cases authorized by EEC.	Complete untying of aid.	Will consider only on a case-by-case basis.	Provision for consideration on a case-by-case basis.
6. Political requirements/objectives (Lomé II)	Aid to contribute to the economic and social development of ACP states by correcting structural imbalances. No reference to ACP states' policies.	Exclusion of all political considerations from aid question.	Insertion of statement that aid to be directed toward meeting basic human needs.	No reference to basic needs.
(Lomé III)		Opposed to any infringement of ACP sovereignty, the imposition of conditionality, or the erosion of the group's "acquired rights" under the convention.	Need for "policy dialogue" to ensure that there is consistency between the activities financed by European aid and the policies pursued by ACP governments. Priority to be given to food sector strategies.	New chapters in the convention dealing with the objectives, principles, and instruments of cooperation. No specific reference to policy dialogue. Provisions for program aid and aid for maintenance/rehabilitation to enable pursuit of sectoral approach if agreed by ACP Group and EEC.

Status Quo	ACP Opening Position	EEC Opening Position	Outcome
7. Access to European Food Surpluses (Lomé II & III)			
Not included in convention.	Guaranteed access through multiyear subsidized contracts.	Not amenable to inclusion in convention.	Consideration to be given to requests on a case-by-case basis.
8. Volume of EDF			
European currency units 3,390 million (Ecu) for duration of Lomé I.	Maintenance of real value of aid, taking into account the following criteria: correction for erosion of purchasing power 1975-85; preservation of real value of transfers to Yaoundé associates; increase in number of ACP states and their populations; the privileged and exemplary character of the Lomé relationship; erosion of ACP commercial preferences; needs of the least developed, landlocked, and island countries; extension of STABEX; new fields of cooperation; and evolution of the GNP of the EEC. Total requested for Lomé II was 10.8 billion Ecu. A similar sum was requested for Lomé III.	Lomé II: 5,107 million Ecu. Lomé III: 8,100 million Ecu.	Lomé II: 5,607 million Ecu.—a decrease in real aid per capita from the Lomé I figure. Lomé III: 8,500 million Ecu.—roughly maintaining the real value of the EDF.

E. Human Rights
(Lomé II & III)

Status Quo	ACP Opening Position	EEC Opening Position	Outcome
No reference to human rights.	ACP Group opposed to reference to human rights because all members belong to UN and respect its Declaration on Human Rights. EEC in no position to lecture ACP on this issue, given its treatment of migrant workers, its relations with South Africa, and the situation in Northern Ireland.	Reference to UN Declaration on Human Rights to be inserted in convention. Aid other than humanitarian relief to be suspended for countries where there is a "serious and continued violation of fundamental human rights."	Lomé II: No reference Lomé III: Reference in treaty's preamble to adherence to the principles of the UN Charter and to the parties' "faith in fundamental human rights." Annex I affirms the parties' commitment to eliminate all forms of discrimination and proclaims their "determination to work effectively for the eradication of apartheid which constitutes a violation of human rights and affront to human dignity."

F. Cultural Cooperation
(Lomé III)

Status Quo	ACP Opening Position	EEC Opening Position	Outcome
No separate chapter.	A new chapter on cultural and social cooperation that would include references to the rights of ACP migrant workers and students in the EEC states; the undertaking of an inventory of ACP cultural artifacts held by the EEC with view to their eventual return.	Not opposed to cooperation in the cultural field. But reference to ACP artifacts in the EEC unacceptable. Situation of migrants and students a matter for bilateral negotiations.	New Title VIII devoted to cultural and social cooperation concerned primarily with use of aid to develop human resources. No reference to ACP artifacts. Joint declaration on ACP migrant workers and students in Annex IX to convention commits parties to respect international law and to refrain from discrimination. ACP states to take "the necessary measures to discourage irregular immigration of their nationals into the Community."

9

Debt Negotiations and the North-South Dialogue, 1974-1980

Chandra Hardy

The focus of this chapter is the treatment of the debt problem of the developing countries in the context of the North-South dialogue over the period 1974-80. A study that traced the earlier history of the debt negotiations that have taken place between developing countries and their Western creditors would illuminate the substance of the argument, but the emphasis here is on the negotiations process—the factors influencing the negotiations and how the process in turn influenced the outcome of the negotiations.

The debate on Third World debt has a long history and it is far from over. However, the period 1974-80 was chosen because beginning in 1974 the LDC position on debt became more clearly defined and specific proposals were placed before the UN General Assembly. Discussions and negotiations took place on these proposals and the North's counterproposals in a variety of places over the next six years. Also during this period, we can identify specific outcomes in regard to the treatment of the debt problem of the poorest countries and the conduct of future debt renegotiations. In short, the period offers a set of concrete proposals and outcomes on the debt issue to examine and evaluate.

Debt has long been a staple in North-South discussions and has been viewed from quite different perspectives by the two parties. For developing countries, the debt issue could not be separated from the issue of the adequacy of the level of resources available for development, for debt is the result of the distribution and terms of past levels of capital flows, and debt servicing is a claim on current resources. However, the preference of the North has been to keep the issue of resource transfers and debt-servicing quite separate.

Early History

Almost as soon as they were established in 1947, it became clear that the World Bank and the International Monetary Fund (IMF) were not well suited to meeting the financing needs of the developing countries. The bank was set up to mobilize and on-lend funds at market rates of interest to enable countries to pay for capital goods imports. But the developing countries needed money to build the human, physical, and administrative infrastructure for development; the benefits of such investments were far in the future and they were not self-liquidating. They could not earn the foreign exchange required to repay conventional loans in convertible currencies. In short, the developing countries needed grants.

In 1949 the developing countries proposed the establishment of a UN fund for economic development that would make low-interest loans for a variety of development purposes. During the 1950s the view that there were investments important to development that could not be financed entirely on a loan basis gained wide acceptability, and this led to increasing support in the UN for the establishment of a special UN fund for economic development (SUNFED) that would make annual grants of $3 billion to developing countries. This idea was not favored by the United States and as the president of the World Bank, Eugene Black, admitted frankly, the creation of the International Development Association (IDA; the bank's soft-loan affiliate) was "really an idea to offset the surge to SUNFED."

The Emergence of Debt Problems

The claims on IDA greatly exceeded the resources available. Consequently, access to IDA was restricted to the low-income countries and even so met only a small part of their needs. This meant that the bulk of the capital flows to the developing countries was at or near market terms. Also, by 1950 a major source of funds was suppliers' credits guaranteed by the creditor governments as part of the postwar-recovery, export-promotion effort, and by the mid-1950s several developing countries were experiencing debt-servicing difficulties. Indeed, the origin of the Paris Club is the 1956 request by Argentina for a multilateral meeting of its creditors.

In 1964 Raoul Prebisch, the first secretary general of the United Nations Conference on Trade and Development (UNCTAD), drew attention to the growing burden of debt and the inadequacy of the procedures for debt rescheduling. At that time three countries (Brazil, Argentina, and Turkey) had already rescheduled their debts *five* times at creditor club meetings. Ideally, he said, there should be no debt problem. The level of external assistance should be geared to a country's development needs and the terms of the debt should be geared to the country's debt-servicing capacity, and "if debt restructuring is required, it should not be divorced from a country's development program." But for another decade the role of the developing countries was limited to conducting what was essentially an international monologue to no apparent effect despite the endorsement of their view in the 1969 report of the prestigious Pearson Commission. The commission, consisting of six Northerners and two Southerners, recommended that (1) debt relief operations avoid the need for repeated reschedulings, and (2) debt relief be considered a legitimate form of development assistance. The report had no success in changing attitudes to debt relief.

The Beginning of the Dialogue

In May 1974 the UN General Assembly convened its Sixth Special Session, which signaled a major turning point in North-South relations. In previous sessions the General Assembly had considered·threats to world peace. Now for the first time economic conditions in the developing countries were recognized as an issue of global concern and security. The session ended with adoption of the resolution and program of action on the establishment of a New International Economic Order (NIEO).

Later that same year (December 1974), the General Assembly met again in the Seventh Special Session and agreed on a resolution containing the Charter of Economic Rights and Duties of States. The proposals of the developing countries had gained global attention. They could no longer be ignored by the North, but negotiations were hard come by. Instead, various position papers were commissioned and the literature on indebtedness mushroomed as both sides sought to define their positions better.

The Lima Declaration of March 1975 followed, and then the Manila Declaration of February 1976, which spelled out the Group of 77 position on debt:

(1) Debt relief should be provided by bilateral creditors and donors in the form of waivers or postponement of interest payments and/or amortization, cancellation of principal, etc., of official debt to developing countries seeking such relief. In that framework, the least developed, the developing landlocked and the developing island countries should have their official debts cancelled.

(2) Multilateral development finance institutions should provide programme assistance to each developing country in institutions.

(3) Agreement should be reached to consolidate commercial debts of interested developing countries and to reschedule payments over a period of at least 25 years. The consolidation of commercial debts and the rescheduling of payments would require the establishment of suitable financial arrangements or machinery which might include, inter alia, a multilateral financial institution, such as a fund or a bank, designed to fund the short-term debts of interested developing countries.

The proposals were placed on the agenda at UNCTAD IV in Nairobi in 1976 and were strongly resisted by the creditor countries that wished to preserve the traditional case-by-case approach to debt crises and that wished to maintain a distinction between debt relief and development assistance. The Nairobi meeting ended with no agreement on debt.

The CIEC Negotiations

Debt then emerged as a major issue at the Conference on International Economic Cooperation (CIEC), which had been organized at the suggestion of France and began in December 1975. Representatives from twenty-seven countries—nineteen developing and eight developed—took part. Its stated objective was to examine issues in the areas of energy, raw materials, development, and finance, and the stated intention was that the CIEC would lead to concrete proposals for an equitable and comprehensive program for international economic cooperation including agreements, decisions, commitments, and recommendations.

The participants met several times over the next eighteen months, and in the course of the discussions the North tabled a response to the LDC debt proposals in the form of the U.S.-EEC proposals that (a) defined measures to prevent debt crises from arising; (b) laid out the features for the improvement of creditor club operations; and (c) suggested procedures to maximize assistance to low-income countries. The Group of 8 proposal advocated distinguishing between acute debt crises and longer-term structural problems. In the former case the traditional creditor-club mechanism should be used; in the latter case, the World Bank was to examine the country's economic situation and requirements in detail prior to convening a meeting of the aid donors if warranted. If the donor countries perceive long-term difficulties, "they would to the best of their abilities enhance assistance efforts in response to the debtor country demonstrating a willingness to take corrective measures."

The Group of 19 simply resubmitted their proposals that would have debt and resource transfers "considered in an integrated manner against the background of internationally accepted targets and socio-economic objectives and priorities of the debtor countries."

In June 1977 CIEC ended with no agreement on debt, but in the course of the discussion some important divisions in the ranks surfaced. Mexico and Brazil expressed reservations about the Group of 19 proposal on commercial debt. Mexico said that for countries relying primarily on world financial markets, solutions to the problems of indebtedness were to be found in the normal working of these markets. These statements caused great confusion, and later Mexico forcefully indicated that although its own interests were somewhat different, it nevertheless stood firmly in favor of the Group of 19 proposal.

Sweden and several other European countries somewhat supported the Group of 19 proposals on official debt. Sweden said that the multilateral institutions should play a larger role in the resolution of debt problems, and that the creditor countries should provide additional ODA to the poorest countries by granting debt relief or by taking equivalent measures (e.g. untied program aid). And by December 1977 Sweden, Canada, Switzerland, and the Netherlands announced that they were canceling all ODA (Official Development Assistance) debts of the poorest countries.

After the failure of CIEC, attention shifted to the upcoming UNCTAD meeting in Geneva. The developing countries pressed successfully for a high-level meeting in the spring of 1978 with debt as the sole item on the agenda. Three expert groups met in 1977-78 to prepare for the meeting, and in the course of their discussions there was a noticeable shift in positions. The Group of 77 backed away somewhat from the call for generalized debt cancellation; the emphasis was on the debt of the poorest countries and on seeking agreement on guidelines as to the conduct of future debt negotiations. With regard to the debt of the poorest countries, the Group of 77 allowed that conversion to grants, a reorganization of existing debt on IDA terms, and untied programs aid were alternative options to consider. Several Group B countries that had canceled debts to the poorest countries urged others to follow suit, but the U.K. delegation allowed that the case against retroactive conversion of loans to the poorest countries to grants was really very weak.

The 1978 Debt Ministerial Meeting

Against this background and the need to have some success on at least one item on the North-South agenda, much was expected from the March ministerial meeting, which was attended by forty ministers and deputy ministers from developed and developing countries. At the beginning of the week both sides rehearsed their well-known official positions, but the divergence within the groups and the possible areas for compromise were equally well known. The U.S. delegate, Under-Secretary of State for Economic Affairs Richard Cooper, was scheduled to speak later in the week. It seemed to this observer that both sides believed that if there was to be an end to the impasse, it had to come from the United States, but in his public statement Cooper did not reveal any flexibility on the debt issue.

What happened next is indicative of the role of personalities in these negotiations. Dame Judith Hart, the minister for overseas development in the United Kingdom, held marathon meetings with both groups, which caucused and sat through the night drafting and redrafting. The result one morning was Resolution 165 on retroactive terms regarding adjustment and guidelines for the conduct of future debt negotiations (see chapter appendix for Annex 1).

Resolution 165 is loosely worded and not binding, and did not amount to much in terms of the amount of debt relief provided, but agreement on it was nevertheless a major accomplishment. It represented international recognition that the issues of resource transfers and debt relief could not be separated, at least in the case of the poorest countries, and it established criteria for improving the mechanisms for the conduct of future debt negotiations.

The Winding Down of Negotiations

Resolution 165 in effect took the issue of debt cancellation off the North-South agenda. The Group of 77 on several occasions thereafter drew attention to the fact that creditor countries were interpreting the resolution as they saw fit. In practice, although some countries had canceled all ODA debts to the poorest countries or adjusted the terms, other creditors were providing debt relief for a limited period and to a limited group of countries. The Group of 77 calls for compliance with the spirit of Resolution 165 had no impact. The focus of the negotiations then shifted to seeking ways to make the following four concepts operational:

a. International consideration of the debt problem of a developing country would be initiated only at the specific request of the debtor country concerned.
b. Such consideration would take place in an appropriate multilateral framework consisting of the interested parties, and with the help as appropriate of relevant international institutions to ensure timely action, taking into account the nature of the problem, which may vary from acute balance-of-payments difficulties requiring immedi-

ate action to longer-term situations relating to structural, financial, and transfer or resources problems requiring appropriate longer-term measures.

c. International action, once agreed by the interested parties, would take due account of the country's economic and financial situation and performance, and of its development prospects and capabilities and of external factors, bearing in mind internationally agreed objectives for the development of developing countries.

d. Debt reorganization would protect the interests of both debtors and creditors equitably in the context of international economic cooperation.

There was no disagreement in principle on concepts (a) and (d), which said that debt reorganization can be initiated only at the request of debtors and that creditors and debtors should be treated equitably. The disagreement centered on concepts (c) and (b), on the nature of the debt problem and on the appropriate multilateral framework. Group B maintained there were two types of debt problems: acute, for which there was the Paris Club; and structural, for which there were the Consultative Aid Groups. The Group of 77 argued that in practice these distinctions could not be made because debt problems had both short- and long-term features. The Group of 77 also wanted to establish an independent debt commission that would replace the Paris Club and exercise an oversight on the role of the World Bank and the IMF in debt negotiations.

The search for agreement continued at UNCTAD V in May 1979 in Manila. Several members of Group B believed that the distinction between short-term and long-term debt problems was too sharp, and wondered whether the World Bank and the IMF could not become a focal contact point for debtors. Group B requested an informal meeting with bank and IMF staff. The chairman explained that they were trying to improve on the guidelines, specifically in regard to analysis of short- and long-term debt problems and improvements in the operation of the creditor-club mechanism. The author participated in this meeting and made suggestions for the dissemination of information on Paris Club operations; expanded coverage of the eligible debt; an independent chairperson for the meetings; and some flexibility so the debtors could stretch out repayment periods to avoid repeated reschedulings. But conscious of our role as observers, staff avoided comment on the distinction between short- and long-term problems, and suggested that the subject be referred to the World Bank and IMF.

Despite much goodwill and great effort to reach agreement, both sides agreed that their problems were political, not technical. So the negotiations dragged on until September 1980, when the Group of 77 gave up on the call for an independent debt commission and both parties agreed to refer to the heads of the World Bank and the IMF the problem of making the agreed guidelines operational.

Evaluating the Process of Negotiations

In reviewing the history of the debt negotiations, four factors stand out as having exercised a major influence on the process and the outcome. These were the ways the negotiations came about, attitudes toward debt relief, the preparation of the arguments submitted, and the political context of the negotiations.

How the Negotiations Began

The shift in global economic power to the oil exporters in 1974 and their political solidarity with the rest of the Group of 77 enabled the developing countries to exert pressure in the United Nations for negotiations on reforms of the working of the international economic system. This was significant for two reasons. First, the North agreed to these negotiations very reluctantly and only because it was politically difficult to do otherwise, but the North did not accept the reality of the Group of 77 as a negotiating partner. It was expected that the OPEC cartel would break up and that Group of 77 solidarity would evaporate under the impact of oil price hikes or more ancient divisions. Second, although debt was only one of the agenda items for reform, at the North's insistence the debt negotiations took place independently of trade and other financial matters. This meant that the North did not recognize the extent of the interdependence of the global economy and the impact of LDC debt problems on its own prospects for economic recovery. It also meant that there was no scope for trade-offs in the debt negotiations. By contrast, if the two parties met now, their perceptions of the economic dimensions of the problem would be much less divergent, although their political difference might be the same.

Attitudes toward Debt Relief

The Group of 77 steadfastly maintained the link between the debt and resource-transfer issues and the need for equitable treatment of debtors. One of the unwritten rules of the Paris Club is that a debtor must seek an equivalent amount of debt relief from all its other creditors. But there was no similar nondiscrimination rule that required the creditors treat all debtors equally. Unfortunately, although the Group of 77 was emphasizing the economic argument for reform, it had little to offer Group B by way of inducement either by showing the economic gains to the North of providing debt relief or its potential loss from failing to do so.

Group B, on the other hand, saw little economic merit in the Group of 77 case and disliked the threat of the loss of power implicit in its proposals. The negotiations were thus seen by Group B as a zero-sum game. The Group of 77 position was characterized as "demands for much from those who have nothing" or as a "statement of their rights and our obligations." And because Group B saw no economic gain (and some possible cost) in providing debt relief, its strategy was to stall the negotiations in the hope that they would lose all momentum. In the words of some commentators, "Group B tried to talk the subject to death," and its objective was to prevent any change in existing procedures that would minimize its political advantage.

The Arguments Submitted

The quality of the dialogue was generally poor. The Group of 77 generally berated the North for failing to meet the 0.7 percent of GNP target for ODA, and cited the inadequacy of the size of drawings under IMF facilities and the austerity of IMF stabilization conditions, all of which, it was argued, adversely affected achievement of the Group of 77's growth and social objectives.

The principal points in the reply of Group B were

1. that the poor did not have a debt problem but a poverty problem;
2. that the middle-income countries from time to time had liquidity problems and that the mechanisms in place for dealing with them could be improved but were basically adequate; and
3. that generalized debt relief would benefit past heavy borrowers, penalize creditworthy borrowers (which presumably would not get debt relief), and would amount to untied program aid. In other words, generalized debt relief would diminish the creditors' control over the disposition of their aid resources and over the debtors.

Having stated the premise that debt and resource transfers were separate issues, Group B then used another important argument, namely, that the provision of debt relief would somehow compromise or tarnish the principle that debtors had an obligation to repay their debts.

The link between debt relief and development assistance seemed so axiomatic to the Group of 77 that it failed to provide theoretical arguments or case studies in support of its view. It relied on rhetoric that became more heated, repetitive, and boring. It never submitted, for example, supporting documents such as the Pearson Commission report, the UN study on the balance of payments adjustment process in developing countries, or any World Bank study, although frequent references were made to Robert McNamara's speeches on the need for more ODA.

The Group of 77 also never attempted to refute the argument of Group B that the provision of debt relief would weaken the *principle* that borrowers need to honor their debt obligations. Group B's argument was not logical and the Group of 77 might have argued, for example, that without in any way diminishing the borrower's obligations in incurred debts, two important qualifications to the principle could be made. One, that creditors that make bad loans should bear losses because that is the risk creditors take in making loans, and two, that attempts by creditors to impose onerous conditions on debtor countries have had a long record of failure and in the end have proved even more costly to the creditors. The Group of 77 might have cited the consequences of the efforts of the Allies to extract reparation payments from Germany after World War I, and the defaults by Britain and France on their U.S. debts in the 1930s on the grounds that their obligations to their people exceeded those to their creditors.

The bulk of the preparatory work for the Group of 77 was done by UNCTAD, and these remarks are not meant to be critical of UNCTAD. The staff of the Money and Finance Directorate led by Mr. G. Arsenis worked to the limits of exhaustion, but debt was for them only *one* of the items on the money and finance agenda and UNCTAD is a small institution. A Third World secretariat adequately staffed might have done better, but its task would in any case have been extremely difficult because conventional wisdom over this period supported Group B's position.

Studies prepared by the Organization for Economic Cooperation and Development (OECD), which acted as Group B's secretariat, and official reports of the World Bank supported the view that the debt problem was neither general nor unmanageable. Another body of opinion held that the developing countries were wasting their political capital asking for debt relief when they should have been asking for more ODA. The prime minister of Jamaica (Michael Manley), seeking help for his country's debt difficulties, was told that Jamaica and other developing countries did not have a debt problem; that what developing countries needed was more debts.

The response of Group B at higher policy levels is adequately summarized in remarks by Richard Cooper, under secretary of state for economic affairs before the U.S. Senate in 1978. Cooper noted that some of the proposals of the developing countries for reform of the international economic system were helpful, but "some of the developing countries' proposals would violate fundamental principles of the existing world economic system, and it is impossible, therefore, for us to accept them in their present form. I have in mind the forgiveness of official or private debt (which would destroy the basis of international credit)." Later in his testimony Cooper observed, "Many developing countries, however, view the debt issue from a different perspective. . . . Some low-income developing countries view debt relief as a means of supplementing what they consider to be inadequate flows of development assistance. Their emphasis is not on whether or not individual countries have the capacity to service debt, but on the proposition that the failure to meet development targets justifies the need for debt relief."

Cooper also commented that (a) few developing countries are interested in relief on commercial debt; (b) developing countries have focused North-South discussions on relief for the official concessional debt of the low-income countries; (c) most of the pressure for generalized debt relief is coming from a few countries that would benefit most from current developing country proposals; (d) for a large number of other low-income countries, the issue has developed political importance far beyond its economic significance; and (e) higher-income countries interested in maintaining their access to capital markets have repeatedly emphasized that they are not interested in debt relief.

A contrasting view was offered by UNCTAD Secretary General Gamani Corea in a speech to Swiss bankers. He stated that the Group of 77 had essentially two proposals: (a) that the official debt of the low-income countries, that is the debt arising out of past aid, be rescheduled or in the same way given relief, as a way of increasing aid to them; and (b) that the commercial debt (particularly important to the middle-income countries) should be refinanced so that the debt portfolio is better structured. And on a prescient note, Corea added, "One has to draw attention to the need for action to prevent panic in financial markets."

The Politics of the Dialogue

North-South negotiations are not simply about economic issues. This was also the case with the debt negotiations. The bulk of the debt is owed to the five major creditor countries (the United States, the United Kingdom, Germany, France, and Japan), and this is true for oil, nonoil, low-income, and middle-income developing countries. As the principal sources of external financing, the major creditor countries exercise enormous control over the developing countries. Although foreign savings (capital flows) finance only a small part of the level of investment in developing countries, that part often represents the difference between growth and stagnation because foreign savings enable countries to finance a higher level of investment than they could with domestic savings alone.

In the debt negotiations the developing countries were trying to reduce the control exercised by the creditors, hence the acrimony and confrontational attitude. But the issue of control was never directly addressed; it was only alluded to in the discussions of IMF stabilization programs that had become a prerequisite of Paris Club meetings and in the explicit request that debt restructuring take into account the debtor's development objective.

Political considerations also played a role within the two groups. Group B was very divided. The smaller creditors wanted to negotiate, and to indicate that they have some sympathy for the Group of 77 position, Canada, Sweden, the Netherlands, and Switzerland announced after CIEC that they were canceling their debts to the low-income countries. Australia, New Zealand, and Finland announced that their loans to this group had always been on a grant basis. The United Kingdom was not only in favor of retroactive terms adjustment but supported a larger role for the World Bank and the IMF in the operations of the creditor club meetings. Japan and Germany were silent. France wanted to preserve its role as a convener of Paris Club meetings. The United States, the largest creditor, was the most adamant in resisting changes and emphasizing the need to maintain a group position. The United States also effectively used the fact that the public stance of the middle-income market borrowers in going along with the Group of 77 position was at odds with their private stance. The negotiations were usually chaired by France, but the United States used its power to obstruct efforts to reach accommodations.

The division in the Group of 77 related to the treatment of commercial debt. For most of this period, the large Latin American borrowers enjoyed easy access to commercial bank loans at low interest rates. These countries and their bankers were locked in a scorpion's dance and were publicly saying the same thing—there was no mention of debt difficulties or the possibility of difficulties that could not be handled by the market. Yet, Mexico was proposing in another less public forum, a World Bank-IMF development committee, what became known as the Mexican proposal for a new source of longer-term commercial loans to the middle-income developing countries.

The Group of 77 failed to deal with this division in its ranks. Analysis of the debt and balance of payments problems of the major market borrowers would have gone a long way toward weakening the perception of Group B that the negotiations had more political than economic significance. The Group of 77 also failed to capitalize on the fact that the fastest growing trade during the 1970s was South-South trade. The newly industrializing countries (NICs) were looking for new markets and trade concessions in other developing countries to counter the slow growth of trade with the North, but the Group of 77 was unable to devise any increased bargaining strength from this development.

Who and Where

It is difficult to gauge the significance of who were the negotiators and where the negotiations took place, but both factors may have had some impact on the outcome. The negotiators for Group B were bureaucrats, who are never predisposed to innovation. Their forte seems to be to protect the status quo, and this they did effectively and with greater cohesion and confidence as the negotiations dragged on because the principals did not change much.

The Group of 77 was handicapped by the fact that its chief negotiators tended to be from the poorest countries, thus lending credence to the view of demands from those who have nothing. The rotation of the chairmanship of the group did not make for continuity. It was also not helpful that the negotiators represented countries that had never experienced a Paris Club rescheduling. This was not altogether surprising, for by 1980 only sixteen developing countries had even been to the Paris Club, and this number did not include Venenzuela, Sri Lanka, India, or Pakistan.

The negotiations took place in Paris (CIEC) and mainly at UNCTAD meetings. This reflected the preference of the Group of 77 for a forum in which it would have a greater political advantage, but it had two disadvantages. First, the group had to rely on officials from constituent countries' foreign ministries on what was largely a financial matter, whereas if the negotiations had taken place in the international financial institutions, the representatives would have been from the economic ministries. Second, the UN forum revealed a tendency to search for consensus in drafting proposals. The technique of smaller expert groups was used, but it was not as effective as in the Law of the Sea negotiations because of the insufficient expertise of the negotiators and their inability to depart from the consensus rule.

Assessing the Outcome

Were the negotiations a succes or a failure? Against the background of the North's lack of motivation to negotiate and the divergence in the opening positions of the two parties, the negotiations have to be viewed as a modest success. At the CIEC in 1977 the North provided $1 billion of grant aid to the poorest countries. It was stated that this should not be viewed as debt relief but rather as an "earnest of the seriousness with which the donors view the resource problem of the poorest countries." However, the adoption of Resolution 165 eliminated the distinction between debt relief and resource transfers for the poorest countries, and the measures taken to implement the resolution—including cancellation, retroactive terms adjustment, etc.—provided debt relief on about $6 billion out of a total debt of the low-income countries of $50 billion (1979). The agreement on criteria for the conduct of future debt negotiations was an important agreement on principles, even though agreements reached at UNCTAD are not binding on the World Bank and IMF.

If, however, the negotiations are viewed against the background of the growing debt burden of the developing countries, its adverse impact on their development, the costliness of repeated reschedulings in various forums, and the risks LDC debt problems pose to the structure of international credit markets, then they have to be viewed as a failure. It is difficult to avoid the conclusion that the interests of the world community would have been better served had the LDC proposals in the Manila Declaration (see above) been adopted.

This review also suggests that a different set of actions on the part of the South might have produced a more desirable outcome even in the face of the obstacles presented by the North. The South rested its case on the moral argument. The Group of 77 expected the North to see the justice of its case and to act. This represented a poor reading of history. The moral argument is never very convincing in political circles. Britain's post-World War II appeals to the United States for a loan based on its stalwart defense of democracy and subsequent suffering fell on deaf ears. The argument that the loan would be used to buy U.S. goods and stimulate U.S. economic growth was more effective. This does not mean that the moral argument is wrong, simply that it is never enough. In the course of the negotiations, the Group of 77 rhetoric should have been reduced and the case should have been gains for both sides.

In presenting arguments, the Group of 77 might have been more successful if the negotiators had been financial experts. For this reason, it might have tried on a least one occasion to move the negotiations to the international financial institutions (as desired by the North) and tested whether a change of location and the participation of financial experts would have produced different results. At any rate, the group would have benefited from the assistance of a Third World secretariat in preparing more analytical and factually based arguments, and the negotiators needed to be able to call on technical experts at the negotiating table. The latter role could not be filled by UNCTAD without compromising its role as a global body.

Cooper's remarks suggest that the South's confrontational attitude and weak argumentation had a greater impact on policymakers in the North than they should have. In this the South has only itself to blame.

Irrespective of the negotiating forum, some flexibility needed to be given to the Group of 77 negotiators to depart from the unanimity rule. It does not diminish the group's political solidarity to recognize that some economic reforms are of greater interest to some developing countries than others. Small expert groups should be able to prepare proposals that have the support of the majority and that safeguard the interests of the minority. The search for proposals satisfying every single member (of both groups) produced a stalemate, polarized attitudes, and prevented efforts to work on compromises.

The Group of 77 was the politically weaker partner in the negotiations, but it was not as weak as it believed itself to be, and the group did not make great efforts to increase its political bargaining power. This could have been done by (a) forming alliances with Group B supporters, and (b) extracting support from the NICs who needed the cooperation of the group in other areas. Even when trade-offs were not possible with the North this should not have prevented trade-offs from occurring within the South.

As an observer at these negotiations, the author was struck by the poor quality of the information available to both parties and the need for research on *global* economic issues. The studies prepared by the OECD and other agencies looked at the debt in excruciating detail. It was expressed as a ratio of everything for which there were data; it was deflate by numerous indices and so on to show that all was well. The weakness of these studies is that the debt was looked at in isolation, not in its national and global economic context.

The lack of political will in the North to negotiate major reforms needed to improve the working of the global economy cannot be underestimated. And even where there is willingness, Northern negotiators face difficulties from a political system that sets a premium on reducing short-run costs, not on maximizing the long-term gains to be derived from accommodating the demands of the developing countries. But Northern intransigence is no excuse for Southern incompetence.

There are substantive disagreements on many North-South issues, but in regard to debt the South had the better case. The negotiating process was itself an obstacle to progress. It was therefore up to the South to improve its argumentation, to adopt a flexible stance to better the procedures, and to make greater efforts to mobilize political support for its view. The South's capacity to negotiate with the North will also increase through South-South cooperation.

Appendix

11 March 1978

TRADE AND DEVELOPMENT BOARD
Third (ministerial) part of the ninth special session
Geneva, 6 March 1978

*Debt and Development Problems of Developing Countries
Resolution Adopted by the Board, on March 11, 1978**

The Trade and Development Board,

Recalling Conference Resolution 94 (IV) on the debt problems of developing countries, and Board Decision 149 (XVI),

Recording with appreciation the valuable contribution by the reports of the Intergovernmental Group of Experts in analysing the debt problems of developing countries and the Report of the Meeting of Multilateral and Bilateral Financial and Technical Assistance Institutions with Representatives of the Least Developed Countries (TD/B/681 and Add. 1),

Noting the pledge given by developed countries to respond promptly and constructively, in a multilateral framework, to individual requests from developing countries with debt servicing difficulties, in particular least developed and most seriously affected among these countries,

Recognizing the importance of features which could provide guidance in future operations relating to debt problems as a basis for dealing flexibly with individual cases,

Recalling further the commitments made internationally by developed donor countries to increase the volume and improve the quality of their official development assistance,

Aware that means to resolve these problems are one of the urgent tasks before the international community,

Agreed to the following decision:

A.

1. Members of the Board considered a number of proposals made by developing and developed market economy countries.

2. The Board recognizes that many poorer developing countries, particularly the least developed among them, face serious development problems and in some instances serious debt service difficulties.

3. The Board notes with interest the suggestions made by the Secretary-General of UNCTAD about an adjustment of terms of past bilateral official development assistance (ODA) in order to bring them into line with the currently prevailing softer terms.

4. Developed donor countries will seek to adopt measures for such an adjustment of terms of past bilateral ODA, or other equivalent measures, as a means of improving the net ODA flows in order to enhance the development efforts of those developing countries in the light of internationally agreed objectives and conclusions on aid.

5. Upon undertaking such measures, each developed donor country will determine the distribution and the net flows involved within the context of its own aid policy.

6. In such a way, the net flows of ODA in appropriate forms and on highly concessional terms should be improved for the recipients.

7. The Board recommends that the fifth session of the Conference should review measures taken in pursuance of the above.

B.

1. In accordance with resolution 94 (IV), the Board has reviewed the intensive work carried on within UNCTAD and other international fora on the identification of those features of past situations which could provide guidance for future operations relating to debt problems of interested developing countries.

2. Notes with appreciation the contributions made by the Group of 77 (TD/B/670, Annex II) and by some Group B members (TD/B/L.498).

3. Common to the varying approaches in this work are certain basic concepts which include, *inter alia:*
   (i) International consideration of the debt problem of a developing country would be initiated only at the specific request of the debtor country concerned.

(ii) Such consideration would take place in an appropriate multilateral framework consisting of the interested parties, and with the help as appropriate of relevant international institutions to ensure timely action, taking into account the nature of the problem which may vary from acute balance-of-payments difficulties requiring immediate action to longer-term situations relating to structural, financial and transfer of resources problems requiring appropriate longer-term measures.

(iii) International action, once agreed by the interested parties, would take due account of the country's economic and financial situation and performance, and of its development prospects and capabilities and of external factors, and bearing in mind internationally agreed objectives for the development of developing countries

(iv) Debt reorganization would protect the interest of both debtors and creditors equitably in the context of international economic cooperation.

4. The Board requests the Secretary-General of UNCTAD to convene a meeting of an Intergovernmental Group of Experts to recommend to the tenth special session of the Board prior to the fifth session of the Conference detailed features for future operations relating to debt problems of interested developing countries taking into account the above-mentioned concepts and in the light of proposals made on this issue.

References

Chandra S. Hardy. *Rescheduling Developing Country Debts, 1956-1981: Lessons and Recommendations, Monograph, no. 15,* June 1982, Overseas Development Council, Washington, D.C.

Mason and Asher. *The World Bank Since Bretton Woods,* 1973, Washington, D.C., The Brookings Institute.

R. Prebisch. *Towards a New Trade Policy for Development,* Report of the Secretary General, UNCTAD 1964, New York, United Nations.

Partners in Development. Report of the Pearson Commission on International Development, 1969, New York, Praeger.

Department of State. *Proposals Submitted by the G19 on the Problems of Indebtedness of Developing Countires,* 16 September 1976.

———. *CIEC Discussions on Debt,* 23 October 1976.

Richard N. Cooper. *Testimony Before the Sub-Committee on Foreign Economic Policy,* U. S. Senate, February 1978.

Gamani Corea. *Convergent and Divergent Approaches to the North-South Dialogue,* Aussenwirtschaft, June 1977, Zurich.

Additional Reference

United Nations Conference on Trade and Development, Debt Problems of the Developing Countries. TD/B/545, Geneva, 1975.

————. *Selected Issues Relating to the Establishment of Common Norms in the Future Debt Reorganizations.* TD/AC.2/9, 31 October 1977.

————. *Agreement on Features to Guide the handling of Future Debt Problems of Developing Countries.* TAD/INF/1201 29, Geneva, September 1980.

Conclusions: Importance of North-South Negotiations

I. William Zartman

Reduced to the basics, the lessons of these encounters are painfully simple and obvious. In cases when agreement was reached, someone devised an alternative that was better for both sides than the status quo, and, cutting through the fog of poor information and conflictual perceptions, convinced the other parties that this was so. Where there was no agreement, this did not take place. When it did take place, it did so because at least one party was initially willing to search for alternatives rather than dismiss anything but the status quo—or to take the maximalist alternative offered by the other side as the only alternative to the status quo. Sometimes it was the North that led this creative search, sometimes the South, and in most cases both parties did benefit—or could have benefited—from third-party mediators' leading the search. In the successful cases, all joined in the search for mutually beneficial alternatives in the end, and—almost definitionally—there was no case in which all joined in which did not end in a successful agreement.

The cases show that the nominal sign of success was a pretty good indicator of real success, that is, that parties were indeed better off when the settlement emerged. However, this should not be read to indicate that the settlement terms were or were not the best available alternative to the status quo. Although nothing can prove that better alternatives could have been negotiated, neither does agreement on one set of terms prove that better (or worse) agreements were not possible.[1] By looking at the record, analysts can identify the elements that made for a successful outcome and can suggest others that could have made for a more successful outcome if that were possible. The fundamental questions remain the same: How to induce parties to search for a better alternative to the status quo, and how to help them find it. These questions can be answered in several ways.

Problems and Constraints

To begin with the negative, the two greatest problems that have bedeviled most cases of North-South negotiations are confrontations and technical ignorance. The two are related. Unprepared for a well-grounded technical debate on past and future effects of various measures, and predispositionally unconvinced of the usefulness of a search for common benefits, the parties launch into ideological statements identifying universal causes and assigning blame. Because constructive dialogue appears unpromising, the other side responds in kind. Ignorance (which some would call, rather, an absolute conviction that basic effects are so evident that further technical details are unnecessary) breeds confrontationism, and confrontationism (which some would call simply a basic need to put responsibility where it belongs) breeds disregard for technical information.

North and South both share the blame for the *confrontation* and the counterproductive atmosphere it creates.[2] Yet, the behavior is not perverse; each confronts for a purpose, no matter how one-sided. The South, feeling wronged and aggressed after years of exploitation, acts aggressively. Like many revisionists, the Group of 77 believes that it cannot get the North's attention without some strong language. Once begun, strong language becomes a habit; if it is successful, it proves its worth, and if it is not successful—as is more frequently the case—it proves its need. Broadly, the North's attitude has been one of disinterest; it tends to regard the whole set of issues as one big diversion forced on it by the South. Again and again, the North has sought to talk the problem to death, frequently by drowning it in technical reiterations. Confronted with confrontationism, the North could either respond in kind or could produce a raft of technical data that confirmed its case and refuted the other's rather than looking for constructive innovations, thus perpetuating the confrontation on a different level. In most encounters, each side spent much time within its own fortress, using its chosen weapons to defend its own positions and shoot at its opponent's.

The classical paradox on which negotiation is built is contained in the Toughness Dilemma:[3] The tougher (more unyielding) a party acts, the greater its chances for an agreement lose to its positions but the greater the chances for no agreement at all, whereas the softer (more yielding) a party acts, the greater the chances for an agreement but the less the chances for a favorable one. Negotiations theorists have spent much effort in trying to resolve this paradox, often by introducing intervening variables such as time and stature. Thus, one finding is that negotiators should be tough to demand and soften to reward. While this does not resolve the problem of when to shift, it does indicate that confrontation is to be expected as an initial approach but that parties are also expected to move at some point to a more flexible and creative behavior to construct a mutually satisfactory agreement. This first, basic lesson still has to be learned by many negotiators of both the North and the South.

The cases also show that unrelieved toughness is not merely a personal failing but frequently an organized characteristic. Both politicians and technicians have professional reasons to be unyielding and confrontational, although both also have cause to be flexible and creative. As a bureaucrat, the technician is ordered to provide data and repeat arguments, holding the line, although as an expert, the technician can also attack the subject as a problem to be solved, in cooperation with others if necessary. The accounts of the debt, Lomé, IPC, IWA, and COW negotiations all point to technicians in a bureaucratic role thwarting creative agreements. Similarly, politicians have appeared in negotiations to repeat confrontationist rhetoric, in the absence of any technical grasp of the subject, but they have also had the power to make the necessary innovations and compromises when the bureaucrats got stuck. By their presence or their absence, politicians played a negative role in the Lomé, COW, IWA, WARC, and IPC negotiations. Although North-South negotiators are sometimes advised to concentrate on one role or the other, the cases studied here seem to show clearly that better advice would be to use the two roles constructively. Politicians need to be kept informed of conditions and possibilities and need to realize when the time for confrontation has passed. They need to look for—and instruct their supporting technicians to look for—creative potentialities, which can be won only with the other party's agreement, or else their countries will be stuck with the unimproved status quo. Technicians need to be told that merit points can be gained by creative problem-solving as well as for holding the line, and need to develop innovative uses of data, as technicians did successfully in WARC, Law of the Sea, and Lomé.

Another answer to the Toughness Dilemma depends on sequences and structures. Assuming one begins with toughness, sometimes that toughness leads to softness, if the responding party needs an agreement, whereas sometimes it leads to countertoughness and then deadlock. It all depends on the initiator and on the power relations between the parties. The cases bring some further insights. In two instances— MFA and Lomé—toughness was pursued by the North and it led to

Southern softness and a final agreement. In four other cases toughness backfired, leading either to breakdown or to an agreement by the others to go ahead anyhow. In two of these cases—IPC and COW—the toughness was wielded by the South, causing the North to dig in its heels and grant at most only symbolic concessions. In one case—IWA—it was wielded by the North in hopes of the same response as in MFA and Lomé, but it evoked only countertoughness from the South in the end. In one case—Law of the Sea—it was the United States under Reagan that tried to tough it out, giving it its chance to modify the resultant agreement among the other parties. Adding up the experiences, it can be seen that unyielding confrontationism (COW) is simply unproductive, and that holding firm on a one-sided compromise can work to produce an agreement only when it is done by the stronger side—i.e. the side with less to lose in breakdown—and when the weaker side is not prepared to live with its loses (MFA and Lomé but not IWA, and not IPC). Of course, this analysis reduces these encounters to a single-move dynamic, but it does indicate that cooperation and coalition is a better strategy for the South than confrontation, once initial positions have been declared, and that both sides get a better deal when the North offers to meet the South even a quarter of the way rather than not meeting it at all.

North and South are also both at fault in not developing a full information base for creative negotiations, as already noted. Each side finds enough *information* to buttress its position on many occasions, often at a very ideological level, and goes no further. As a result, parties often never even get to talking about the same aspects of the subject. In the debt negotiations the parties traded rhetoric, in COW they traded blame, in neither nor in Lomé were they in possession of the techincal information that would have allowed the trade-offs that creative agreements are made of. Furthermore, in the IPC and IWA negotiations, the information the parties did have was conflicting and so they could not agree of the value of various outcomes; instead of trying to find a common and more reliable data base, the parties merely defended their own data, even though one set—and maybe both—was bound to be wrong. The debt discussions brought out a further problem that was typical of many other cases: proposed solutions tended to be two-edged swords, punishing the conscientious payers while bringing relief to the egregiously overindebted. As a result, the parties argued opposite sides of the same solution, rather than searching for technical solutions that would separate the two effects. Thus, parties often not only lacked information but also failed to use it to attract the other party's cooperation, engage its interest, and induce its agreement.

There are many positive examples of information development in the North-South cases. The years of UNCLOS were simply seminars in conditions and implications of deep-sea technology, and the negotiations dragged on to a large extent because parties first had to learn what they were talking about and where their interests lay. Particularly successful were the joint efforts to build a common data base, which brought the parties together as problem solvers. Briefings offered by the Quaker-Methodist Neptune Group for both Northern and Southern delegations helped fill this need.[4] The Nyhart MIT computer model for comparing the economic performance of various seabed mining formulas was used by many delegations to test their proposals, and when implications became clearer, proposals were modified accordingly. In the Lomé II negotiations, the sugar company of Tate & Lyle advised both the British and the Caribbeans, with positive results. WARC 1979 was successful in part because of careful technical and political preparation before the meeting, through regional seminars by the International Telecommunications Union (ITU), intensive bilateral consultations by the United States and a special effort of the National Aeronautics and Space Agency (NASA) on satellite communications, and discussions in the Non-Aligned Movement (NAM).

It is in the interest of all parties to develop the best informational base possible for their negotiations, and this is particularly true for North-South economic negotiations that need to replace emotional confrontation with clear charts for the future. Better information will not eliminate all conflict (it may heighten some, while reducing others), but it will turn debate onto more factual levels. In the exercise of persuasion, the need for threats and promises, with their attendant implications of coercion and interference, can be reduced when future effects can be agreed to and predications or warnings shared. Parties can turn to a common attack on the problem rather than on each other's positions. This aspect can be enhanced if information sources are shared, background studies are jointly sponsored or prepared by independent agencies, open technical briefing sessions are offered by third parties, and independent expert groups are used to provide technical maps of the terrain and to develop a consensual information base for negotiations.

Beyond technical information needed to master the subject, parties need to develop better knowledge about their own interests and the positions and interests of the other parties. To parties with trouble finding time to prepare their own positions, it may sound like perfection to be asked to learn about the other party's interests and positions as well, yet both are required for a successful pursuit of one's own interest. Studies of the two most successful cases—UNCLOS and WARC—point out the high degree to which preparation and shared information helped create a better understanding of needs and positions and contributed to a favorable outcome. Indeed, the studies indicate that negotiations in the two cases began with a shared sense of unresolved problems, were accomplished by constructing packages of shared benefits, and arrived at an outcome that was close to Pareto optimality. Obvious as it may seem, but rare in practice, this kind of accomplishment is possible only when parties have a firm grasp of their own interests and a good understanding of what matters to the others as well.

Problem Solving and Timing

The basis for any agreement is a *formula,* a conscious attempt to arrive at a joint definition of the problem and the solution and to combine relevant portions of both parties' positions into a common justification of terms of trade.[5] The notion of a formula covers a number of advantages that need to be highlighted for a successful negotiation. Although the formula of one side can be adopted to the exclusion of the other's, the notion generally brings out the nature of negotiation as a process of coming together rather than prevailing. Many of the North-South encounters to date have failed to reach agreement because they represent a clash between basic notions of redistributive justice ("to those that have not it shall be given") and equity justice ("to those that have it shall be given"), with each side holding out for its victory. The UN Committee of the Whole foundered on this conflict; the Lomé Convention succeeded because it found its formula for agreement, whose compromise nature is attested by the attendant debate over its real degree of success. Negotiation should be a positive-sum process, not a matter of victory and defeat. This means that each party receives something for its agreement, and finds a place for its desiderata in the framework of agreement. The agreement must be fair to both sides, and although each side naturally seeks a formula that is closest to its own positions, each must make an effort to broaden that position to include something for the other party to make its agreement worthwhile. An invitation to find a common solution to a common problem is the beginning of a search for a jointly satisfactory formula. It can begin with an examination of the other party's position for weakness, not in an effort to discredit it but rather in an attempt to complement it with positions that will remedy its deficiencies. The specifics of this general approach will of course vary with the different matters under discussion.

These characteristics were hard to find in the cases, and their absence limited the satisfaction of even successful agreements. The Law of the Sea negotiations are a unique, almost-textbook case of building formulas. Negotiations began when the opening formula of "extended underwater national resource jurisdiction in exchange for narrow territorial sea plus rights of passage" became understood. Discussions then proceeded to devise formulas for the various issue areas covered in the negotiations. The most crucial of them was the imaginative bridging of the competing redistributive and equity formulas for deep-sea mining; an innovative parallel banking system, in which a private firm choosing a site also deposits an equivalent site with the international authorities for development, that overcame the conflict between the redistributive demands for a supranational Enterprise monopoly and the equity demands for free enterprise competition. This conflict emerged unscathed in the debt, wheat and commodities, and Committee of the Whole negotiations, none of which found a formula to reconcile equity and redistribution.

In between success and failure were less innovative formulas, some of which permitted important progress on implementing details nonetheless. WARC and Lomé negotiations found their point of equilibrium in an agreement to seek only improvements on the previous conventions (WARC 1959; Lomé I), a mandate carried out with more imagination and creativity in WARC 1979 than in Lomé II (or indeed Lomé III, in 1984). Textile negotiations operated through clear parameters but combined them in ambiguous or conservative fashions, resulting in restrictive, unsatisfying agreements. MFA's formula, the elements of which were inherited from past textile arrangements, concerned market expansion and market disruption but focused on the latter at the expense of the former.

Finding mutually agreeable formulas is a creative process, and so the ways of going about it are infinite. Combining and bridging competing proposals is one way that has been noted. Another involves finding proposals that go less far in the desired direction than the other party might wish but that are nonetheless better than the status quo. The land between reality and perfection is strewn with measures that can improve one side's lot without being offensive to the other side. The challenge is to find them. This is what happened in the MFA, Lomé, WARC, and UNCLOS negotiations, and is the key to their outcome. It is precisely what did not happen in the wheat negotiations, where in the end the South felt that the proposal was not better than the status quo and turned it down. In the IPC, COW, and debt negotiations not enough time was spent on alternative formulas, and if any were found, not enough time was spent on emphasizing their attractiveness to the other side.

Related to the creation of a formula is the provision of trade-offs. Although global negotiations may be so broad that the balance sheet is hard to keep track of, excessively narrow topics provide little chance for trade-offs in encounters where one side is short of items to trade. Because negotiation is less a matter of making a decision than of putting together a package of counterbalancing payoffs and establishing the terms of trade among them, in order to make a positive decision possible, an array of items is necessary to provide the basis for agreement. Issues need to be disarticulated to provide trade-offs, and in the process to overcome intransigence over large problems. Fractioning and packaging are necessary steps in the construction of an attractive agreement and in the provision of material for exchanges and compensations. Admittedly, as in any human interactions, trade-offs are a matter of perception; Nicolson's famous confrontation between the Warrior, who negotiates only to win, and the Shopkeeper, who negotiates to strike a deal, remains a standoff as long as the Warrior sees it as a contest of will and principle rather than a search for a trade-off of price for quantity.[6] But perception is theoretically vulnerable to effective persuasion and the skillful use of side payments, both items that return the discussion to trade-offs.

The fact is, as the studies show, that North-South negotiators have been characteristically uninterested in developing trade-offs that could be used to buy the other side's agreement to their proposals, and so have lost the round. Almost every one of the case studies makes a major point of the unexploited possibilities of trade-offs, inducements, benefit sharing, compensations on details, and even procedural institutional concessions to make changes appear less threatening that dragged down the search for a productive agreement. The reasons that this should be so often go back to earlier points about confrontation and ignorance. Parties became hung up on general principles and righteous feelings, they were overwhelmed by the complexity and uncertainty of the subject, they thought that the other side did not deserve inducements and compensation, they believed the opponent had nothing to trade off, they saw trade-offs as leading to increased demands, and they believed that the adversary would be unresponsive to inducements. These are mirror-image perceptions, applicable to both sides on most occasions, and usually neither side put them to the test. The only exception was the Conferences on the Law of the Sea. The basic trade-off came early—coastal control over resources in a broad exclusive economic zone (EEZ) and a modified archipelago concept for the South in exchange for transit rights through straits and archipelagic waters and a narow territorial sea limit for the North—and others followed down to the Reagan coda, the only point at which they were not successful. North-South negotiators would do well to learn the lessons of UNCLOS.

Other than the crucial shift from tactics of toughness to tactics of softness, the two important elements of *timing* concern the initiation and conclusion of negotiations. It is insightful but not surprising to note that the most successful negotiations began either upon the expiry of a previous round of agreements or upon the crystallization of a shared perception of a recognized problem (and, at best, a recognized solution as well). These conditions are, after all, two different ways of providing a formula—either through an existing framework of reference or through a consensus on the nature of the problem. MFA, Lomé, and WARC fall in the first category, UNCLOS in the second.

Haas further breaks down the latter into three conditions propitious for the creation of new regimes: new consensus on goals, new possibilities opened by new knowledge, and new power configurations.[7] UNCLOS (and Lomé I, in 1974) included aspects of the first two, but for the most part these conditions have been elusive. Indeed, it has been the source of frustration for the South that no consensus of new goals has developed, to the point where this might be considered an effect rather than a cause, refocusing analysis on the second and third conditions. WARC is a good example of propitiousness caused by new technology but it stands (with UNCLOS) as a rare case. In an age of technological change this may be surprising, and it is most likely that there are technological changes that could be used to further new creative agreements if the parties were only to devote some energy to exploring them. Lomé tries to favor such developments through aid to production and diversification, but in both Lomé and MFA negotiations technological changes in industrialization brought problems rather than breakthroughs.

Similarly, changes in power joined changes in technology to bring about UNCLOS as well as WARC, as countries gained both the technical ability and the political will to make disruptive changes in their "occupation" of sea, seabed, and radiowaves, just as political changes brought about the pre-Lomé Yaoundé agreements between Europe and its newly sovereign former colonies. But the great illusion of North-South negotiations, which gave rise to the encounters but then betrayed its initiators, was the perception, momentarily shared, that Southern power had increased. It is probably true that major regime changes only follow power changes, and it is certainly true that negotiators banking on an illusion will end up in front of the choice between massive confrontation and disillusion, a nutshell history of the early North-South negotiations. Because a search for broad triggers of North-South negotiations reveals conditions that turn out to be usually absent or ambiguous, consideration should focus instead on smaller effects.

Formal or even informal triggers are not enough to define propitiousness. An agreement may expire or a sense of the problem develop just at a moment that is quite unhelpful for finding new solutions. Such was the case for IPC and Lomé, and even for IWA and COW, ripeness was a fickle thing. Because North-South negotiations are primarily economic, ripeness depends to a large extent on variations in price and quantity and their effects on supply and demand. Commodity agreements tend to arise under the shadow of low prices, present, impending, or recent. Yet, price considerations of the moment proved to be an unstable peg on which to hang IPC, IWA, and Lomé negotiations. Other elements of cost-benefit calculation also come into play: the benefit the parties got out of the expiring agreement; their projections of benefits and other economic conditions into the future. In the absence of consensus these have tended to favor uncertainty, continuity, and conservatism, not innovative creations. In sum, the experience on initial timing suggests that the elements of major regime change are generally not present, and that more short-term components of cost-benefit calculations have ambiguous effects on the outcomes, favoring small rather than large change in most cases.

Negotiations end when the parties have reached the best possible agreement, so concluding time is important and is usually facilitated by the presence of a firm (but not rigid), realistic deadline—the time by which an agreement becomes necessary and continued disagreement more costly. Often deadlines are inherent in the proceedings: when there is an agreement to be renewed, the expiration of the current agreement gives the deadline. In its absence, particularly in asymmetrical situations where only one side believes that "things can't go on like this," deadlines may have to be created. The most frequent tactic is to announce a target deadline or to use other forums as a pacer, such as citing the need to report to the coming UN session; neither is very effective. Pro forma deadlines can be cast aside with impunity because they do not contain the basic ingredient of a real deadline—automatic application of sanctions or the worsening of both parties' conditions.

Deadlines imposed *by* the parties all suffer from this weakness to some extent, for parties can usually remove what they impose, whereas deadlines imposed *on* the parties—either by the problem or by an outside agency—have a greater chance of being real, for the sanction is independent of the parties to whom it applies. The nature of North-South problems is not helpful in this regard, in that it usually makes inherent sanctions a long-term rather than a sudden, immediate matter. This is another reason that Southerners have felt obliged to raise a confrontational tone: to give some urgency to the process of finding solutions.

Other than expiry deadlines (in the case of MFA and Lomé), examples of deadlines in North-South negotiations have come primarily in the negative. Although much of the length of the Law of the Sea Conferences was a healthy exercise in learning, the negotiations suffered badly from the lack of a deadline: they could go on seemingly forever with impunity. COW, like UNCLOS, passed deadlines provided by UN General Assembly sessions without a murmur. The procedural and substantive aspects of deadlines must coincide; if even an effective deadline is too early, leaving too little time for the real working out of problems, parties will meet it only symbolically, without any effect on the substance of their conflict, or else they will start preparing for it negatively, by shifting their behavior from a search for agreement to an attempt to pin blame for breakdown on the other party. WARC 79 was budgeted for ten weeks and extended one more; appropriately, the budget and the agenda ran out at the same time. COW met one deadline with a meaningless, token statement. Yet, deadline is a crucial element in reaching an agreement. The very nature of negotiation is such that parties will continue to try to improve terms if they are under no constraint to wrap up an agreement.

There are three elements that can be put to greater use in building deadlines into North-South negotiations, each with its strengths and weaknesses. One is the *unilateral deadline*. Although the threat of one side to impose some sort of sanctions if agreement is not reached is a form of ultimatum, it is not as harmful to the negotiating atmosphere as ultimata that aim at a specific (substantive) agreement. Nevertheless, the threatening party is in an awkward and thereby somewhat ineffective position: it must enforce its deadline impartially but it must also (for other reasons) try to take advantage of it to make the best deal. Generally, a threat to withdraw or a threat to go it alone is the preferred form of a unilateral deadline. Each must be credible, but the threatening party must also credibly commit itself to negotiate fairly if the procedural deadline is respected.

Second is the use of *scheduled political change* in a negotiating country as a deadline. In this case, the deadline is externally or impartially imposed; it works directly on one party but there needs to be an even greater awareness among other parties of its effects. Countries with regular democratic elections risk government changes that could affect negotiations. If a favorable government is in power, future elections serve above all as a deadline for the other parties who wish to get an agreement. In calculating the deadline, it is important to count in the time required for ratification as well, when necessary, lest one administration's agreement be turned down by a new legislature. Although individual circumstances may vary, it is generally wrong to hope for better results after the election and more appropriate to aim for a conclusion of the agreement under the administration of the government that entered into the negotiations.

Third, other *North-South encounters* can be used as deadlines and played against each other. Some North-South negotiations have failed because (or at least at the same time as) parts of their agenda were picked up by concurrent encounters and enacted there. Lomé II negotiations competed with UNCTAD (United Nations Conference on Trade and Development) V in 1979, and UNCTAD and CIEC (Conference on International Economic Cooperation) competed with the Tokyo Round of GATT negotiations. More helpfully, the International Wheat Agreement negotiations were paced by the GATT Round. The result has been a patchwork of partial measures, to be sure, but nevertheless a record of uneven progress to complement a more wholly negative record of some encounters. North-South negotiations then became a pacer that provided deadlines for other forums. Because a deadline is essentially a juxtaposition of alternative courses and their consequences, the possibility of scheduling competitive alternatives needs to be more closely examined by policymakers.

The inability of unsuccessful North-South encounters to set and meet deadlines is symptomatic of their characteristic asymmetry, in that one side can hold out while the other feels the pinch. It often takes a procedural artifice—expiry, threats to withhold signature, external events, competitive opportunities—to restore some equality by putting both parties before a time limit by which they must find agreeable terms. Of course, the deadline can then be used tactically and by both sides; the three Lomé negotiations all contain examples of such use by both North and South to shape the final agreement.

In sum, the cases tell clearly that one way to improve North-South negotiations is simply to utilize to the fullest the opportunities offered by the negotiation process. This includes efforts to overcome an atmosphere and tactics of confrontation, better attention to the diagnostic phase of negotiation and the development of information, a conscious search for formulas that create positive-sum outcomes, and an exploitation of the possibilities offered by timing and ripeness in the beginning, middle, and end of the process.

Incrementalism

The attack on the old economic order began as global revisionism, and as global revisionism it has failed. It has already been suggested that it failed because the power base for total change is not present: power has not passed from North to South, the perception of power in the oil price rises of the 1970s has been a bubble burst, and the residue is still only negative power (the power to withhold signature), procedural power (the power to provoke an encounter), and disruptive power (the power to cause default). Indeed, were North-South negotiations only a power play, they could be dismissed as not only unimportant but even uninteresting, given the asymmetrical context. But they are a response to need that will not go away. They should not be seen as a game between two sides, where nothing happens when there is no meeting, but as working groups concerned with a problem that persists whether there is a session or not.

The debate on globalism is well known and need not be pursued here. The arguments are mirror images of each other: those in favor of seismic change argue that the economic order is a whole and needs total redesigning lest unchanged parts keep the new parts from working, against which those in favor of glacial movement argue that the whole works well and to toss it out would be to leap into the unknown. Yet there is room in the middle, and it is in the nature of negotiation to find it. Many of the characteristics of that process already discussed support the search for less than global change. Problem solving, retreat from confrontation, formulas that satisfy both sides, all favor partial changes rather than massive revision. Perhaps the broadest argument for such partial changes is that they are the best possible. If even partial changes are hard to agree on, global change—as the record shows—is impossible. Revolutionaries may prefer to let things get so bad that the only alternative is total reordering, but economics lends itself badly to that kind of process.

The advantage of gradual change is that it removes the threatening aspects of globalism from agreement and allows the parties to test their solutions and get used to them. The challenge for North-South negotiators lies not in avoiding piecemeal change but in improving it. Incrementalism was the order of the day in the Lomé and WARC negotiations, to everyone's satisfaction in the latter case and to the South's dismay in the former. Yet it was more the limited degree of Lomé incrementalism than the incrementalism itself that caused the dismay; African states believed that the amount of improvement over the previous agreement did not even keep up with changes in their own fortunes. There was not enough incrementalism! The MFA is an interesting case of successive incrementalisms, whatever its shortcomings may be: limited-party Orderly Marketing Arrangements (OMAs) developed into a Short Term Arrangement (STA) and then a Long Term Arrangement (LTA) for cotton, and then expanded to cover other products in the Multifiber Arrangement. Incremental change was rejected by the South in the IWA negotiations, in hopes of a better deal; incrementalism as an approach was also rejected in the IPC and COW negotiations, and the South retired, its honor intact but its hands empty. The previous lessons of the encounters could have been played back onto many of the cases to make a better deal possible, but in general the broad conclusion is that partial improvements are the surest and most feasible road to a new order.

Most discussion of incrementalism concerns piecemeal measures. The procedural aspects of the same concept are less frequently explored, although they are a common part of negotiation and have sometimes played a crucial role in the cases studied. Instead of looking for agreement only on those topics where it is possible, negotiators may also seek agreement among those parties willing to agree, and leave the rest outside. Obviously, parties in any number will not do; they must be numerous enough or important enough in weight to matter, and to form a pole of attraction for those remaining outside. But if the purpose of the negotiation becomes an agreement among most instead of all parties, tactics and implications change considerably. The purpose of such negotiations becomes agreement only among those who can agree but also isolation of the recalcitrants, to be brought in at a later date. Because recalcitrants no longer block agreement, the price that they can extract for later adhesion drops. At the same time, the agreement in operation may allay some of their fears and make their later accession easier.

In seeking such partial agreement, it is important to resist the temptation to turn the outcome against the recalcitrant or to use it to reinforce existing camps and divisions. This is an obvious temptation and difficulty that would worsen rather than improve the chances of later change and broader agreement. To the contrary, the partial agreement should seek to build on crosscutting cleavages, bringing in additional items and interests if necessary to break up broad existing coalitions. To be sure, such tactics will lead to struggles over marginal members between the signatory majority and the isolated recalcitrants, but North-South negotiations are already the scene of such struggles before agreement is reached. Partial agreement should not be an initial goal of negotiations but one that can be adopted during their course when unanimity appears unlikely; in the event, it may serve as a threat position that can actually help the last chances of unanimity.

Participant incrementalism is particularly appropriate for asymmetrical multiparty conflicts if some of the stronger parties find an interest in joining a coalition with the weak that maximizes their power, and it has been used in occasion in North-South negotiations, notably in the UNCLOS and the Yaoundé and Lomé treaties.[8] Once begun, it leaves the minority with a number of different strategies to choose within two general options, either to *A*ccommodate or to *B*argain.[9] The A options are Accede and Abide. The recalcitrant can join the agreement at a later moment according to its original terms, as countries join the Nuclear Non-Proliferation Treaty, or abide by it without formal accession, much as the United States does to the Universal Declaration of Human Rights. In both cases, the outsider joins the provisions of the negotiated settlement without change. In this procedure, the terms of the agreement have been set by the majority, and the minority accommodates to them later on, without exacting anything (in treaty terms) for the signature.

The B options are more numerous. In bargaining a new relationship, the minority can try to Buy In, Buy Out, or Buy Off the majority. In the first strategy, the minority can seek to join the agreement but bargain its accession against new concessions that preserve the nature of the agreement but give the new members a special place in it. Buying In is what Britain did in joining the European Communities, at the price of some special provisions.

In the second strategy, the minority can Buy Out the majority by negotiating a new agreement between the two groups of parties, offering a new universal agreement if the majority will dissolve its own former agreement; universality is bargained against changes in the nature of the agreement, an outcome sometimes possible only when both sides have crystallized their positions. Buying Out was the tactic of the English-speaking nonassociates of the Yaoundé Agreements (1963-74) between largely French-speaking Africa and the EEC when they refused to accede to a new association agreement but instead demanded a new relationship as the price of their agreement to what became the Lomé Accords.

The third strategy is the most hostile type of relations, consisting of minority attempts to woo away members of the majority from their agreement and into a counteragreement with the minority. Carried to an extreme, Buying Off could lead to two competing agreements and a disorderly economic arrangement. More likely, however, the competitive order would lead to new attempts to bargain a universal agreement from the newly elaborated positions of strength. Early relations between the European Common Market (EEC) and the European Free Trade Area (EFTA) might stand as an example.

Some of these strategies are now used within North-South negotiations, particularly as an encounter moves toward agreement. Buying In was the tactic of the U.S. delegation led by Leigh Ratiner at the last UNCLOS session, and it failed for related reasons: lack of domestic support and lack of a perceived commitment to success (discussed below). Buying Off perpetuated the premeeting stalemate at the CIEC. They are also used in the reverse of the commonly held notions of majority and minority: in the Yaoundé and Lomé negotiations, in the International Wheat Agreement, and in the Multifiber Agreement, it was the North that established the terms and left the South with the option of accommodating or bargaining. Various strategies were picked within the two options. In current conditions of asymmetry—as this review of A and B options seeks to suggest—partiality is a better road to universality. Partial agreements can provide stepping-stones to universal agreements by creating new negotiating conditions that help equalize power.

Incrementalism means making progress by stages. *Structural incrementalism,* in which the steps reflect incremental shifts in power relations, is often typical of political decolonization and has been analyzed in this connection. Such studies have produce conclusions that could be taken to heart in North-South economic relations: structural imbalance was the occasion for active but tacit (informal) bargaining, whereas structural balance with interlocking interests was the occasion for direct bargaining. In other words, in decolonization, the two sides negotiated informally from positions of inequality until they finally reached a power balance; then they held a formal session to negotiate the terms on which power would shift from one side to the other; and then they continued to negotiate informally within the new power relation. Carried over to economic negotiations, this implies that agreements should be flexible and allow for future evolution. It also implies that a long program of preparation is needed before formal restructuring sessions can be envisaged, involving occasions—both governmentally and privately organized—to exchange views and understand each other's interest. Problem-solving exercises—study, not negotiation, sessions—can be particularly useful in turning government delegations' attention from refuting each other's positions to joining in a common, diversified attack on a problem.[10]

The one basic lesson of studies of structural incrementalism is that bargaining takes place after structural changes—changes in power relations—have taken place, and not as a means of making them take place. But negotiations need not aim at all or nothing, or await the moment when a total reversal of roles is possible. Smaller changes can be ratified by negotiation, giving parties the opportunity to work together—including working for new changes—in the new relation. Because power is participation,[11] structural changes merely concern the ability to take part in substantive decisions. Just as structural change need not be total, so all parties cannot be expected to accede to full participation at once. New participants from the South—New Industrialized Countries (NICs), OPEC members, group interest representatives—can work for institutionalized roles at moments when their fortunes are most favorable (which does not seem to be at this moment for many NICs or OPEC members, to be sure). It should be remembered that unlike political decolonization, the goal of economic negotiations is not power transfer but power sharing (broader participation). If this sounds like a Northern strategy of cooptation, it should also be remembered that Western civilization has generally coopted the challenger by adopting the challenger's goals. Refusing access offered to a few parties because others continue to be excluded merely prolongs problems instead of moving them by steps toward a solution.

Procedures and Mechanics

In addition to processual improvements, there are improvements that can be made in the procedural mechanics to facilitate North-South negotiations. The cases hold abundant lessons. When parties do not feel equally constrained to negotiate, when power or aims are out of balance, or when trust is elusive, a *mediator* is especially useful. Mediators make communication possible when it breaks down; they think up new formulas for agreement when the parties run out of ideas; they can add side payments when it becomes otherwise hard to come up with a positive sum; they become the vehicle of trust when the parties do not trust each other; and they can provide some pressure to move the parties to agreement. In a large multilateral negotiation, mediation may come from an individual delegate (a role played by Tommy Koh of Singapore in UNCLOS negotiations) or from an international organization, such as the Commission for the European Communities in the Lomé and Yaoundé negotiations. In these cases, some of the mediator's powers are limited; small states and international organizations composed of state members—or even more so, private organizations—have few resources for side payments and little other than moral leverage over states, but they can provide communication, formulas, and trust.[12]

There are two types of mediators: partial and impartial. Impartial mediators are hard to find, although again in international economic negotiations international organization secretariats are particularly well placed to play the role, and the need for technical information and expertise as the basis for trust indicates the direction in which to develop. Partial mediators are equally possible (contrary to common misperceptions) and may be all that can be found in the North-South context, but they have a special role. Partial mediators are expected to "deliver" the party to whom they are partial, as they bring together the two sides to make up an agreement. The role thus requires leverage as well as expertise. The Commission for the European Communities and the Commonwealth Secretariat are bodies that have worked well as mediators, although neither was impartial by its very position and both related well to the stronger side. In the case of the COW and the International Commodities and Wheat negotiations, mediators might have been able to salvage the negotiations.

Mediators work between sides; negotiations can also be carried on more productively when the monolithic unity of the sides is broken up. As it stands, the sides are too large and diverse at the same time to provide the basis for a meaningful position, creating pressure to find acceptable outcomes at the level of the least common denominator or rhetoric. This was particularly the problem for global negotiations such as CIEC and COW. The nature of large international negotiations as parliamentary diplomacy means that the arena is occupied by two political parties, each putting greater emphasis on internal solidarity rather than on accommodation, and therefore each serving as a veto bloc. That nature is inappropriate to the encounter, which is not one of finding alternating governmental majorities but, rather, one of problem solving and formulation. Two alternatives can be suggested: coalition and representation.

Coalition formation breaks down monolithic sides into smaller pieces, with the parties or small groups of parties free to seek out common or complementary interests in the other camp. Common interests permit consensus, complementary interests allow trade-offs. In this way, asymmetry can be attenuated. To be sure, coalition building may lead to the creation of new sides, but it is more likely to yield a series of crosscutting and interlocking ties and agreements that make a final outcome more likely and a final collapse more costly to already partially agreeing parties. Coalition building among groups of interests (littoral states, landlocked states, straits states) was used with great success in the UNCLOS, to the point where observers have pointed out that it was scarcely a (typical) North-South negotiation. The success of crosscutting coalescing would be to reduce the North-South—i.e. confrontational—elements of international economic bargaining.

Representation—the other alternative to plenary confrontation—assumes fixed interest groups, to the point where enough trust and commonality is developed for one member to be able to act as the spokesperson for the group. In some circumstances, representation can go hand in hand with coalition building, for representatives can talk with each other to build interlocking ties. To the extent that the represented groups are large and inflexible, however, representation is an alternative to coalition because the chances for formation of new groups and interrelations and of belonging to several interest groups are reduced. The UNCLOS developed some representational activities in its small drafting groups; Cancún, although scarcely a paragon of accomplishment, was a half-step toward representation, for, although participants spoke only for themselves, they were chosen on the basis of representational criteria.

To be effective, representation must obey a number of conditions. It must be truly representative, with links back to the plenary group and the units represented, and not simply be an elite group of the powerful acting irresponsibly. It must include members who have the qualifications of those they represent, and not simply those acting as formal representatives but without interests and experiences in common with affected members. At the same time, representations should be the hyphen between their constituents' specific sovereign interests and broad universal consensus, neither the strict veto-wielding defender of every detail of the former nor the architect of a structure that is either the meaningless lowest common denominator or an imposed creation removed from those who will implement it. Each of these conditions is illustrated in the negative in one or more North-South encounters, and few are illustrated in the positive outside of the UNCLOS. Yet they constitute an attainable package that will help negotiations out of the stifling unanimity requirements of the Group of 77 and the Northern Group B, and they are endorsed not only by experience but also by a group as experienced in cohesion and negotiation as the Commonwealth.

One of the most important procedural innovations discussed in connection with North-South negotiations is the provision of a Southern *secretariat,* comparable to OECD for the North or to the Commission for the European Communities. Such a secretariat is frequently mentioned as a source of the technical information often lacking to Southern delegations and as a liaison and coordination group for the disparate Southern delegations. Many bodies are now available to play parts of this role but they are all hampered by aspects of their nature, leaving the need still unfilled. The Commonwealth Secretariat has provided valuable services in Lomé discussions and in its study of North-South negotiations in general, yet its membership is both North and South but only a part of each. UNCTAD is often considered the Southern body correspondent to the World Bank and the IMF, but it is a universal UN organization, a venue for negotiations as well as a corporate body, and it has interests of its own that hamper its role as a secretariat (as seen in the IPC negotiations and others). Other UN organs suffer from the same limitations, as seen in the operations of the FAO and the World Food Conference in the IWA negotiations. The role is open for casting, and seems to be a useful—almost necessary—part of improved interaction.

Yet there are major problems in the provision of a Southern secretariat. The most important is its effect in reinforcing the closed cohesion and identity of the Group of 77 as a group just at the time when the need and opportunity for crosscutting groups and trade-offs seems most apparent. The Commonwealth report on North-South negotiations improvements, which supports the idea of a Southern secretariat, is nonetheless replete with appeals for a breakdown of the "straitjacket . . . of negotiating processes around the central North-South structure,"[13] and the contradiction between the two ideas is never joined. One might argue that information, like the initial poltical organization, needs its solidarity phase before being able to break down into smaller, crosscutting directions, and that therefore a Southern secretariat, once established, could then create smaller issue-oriented support groups that could join with similar agencies from the North to develop information. This seems overly complicated, or rather this seems to formalize overly the innate complexity of the situation. It also places great emphasis on the very sources of weakness in the South: money to support a secretariat, expertise to staff it, and cooperation to rely on it instead of single-shooting for one's own interest. The experience of the Southern members of the Lomé accords, a microcosm of the larger North-South encounters, is scarcely encouraging, and yet it is from Lomé above all that support should come for the idea of a secretariat.

Because of the Lomé experience, any new Southern secretariat is likely to be self-limiting and its dangers of reinforcing Southern bloc confrontationism are realistically limited. By the same token, its ability to meet the need for a solid informational resource are limited as well. A secretariat is doubtless necessary, but equally so are the other sources of information already discussed, notably the use of private agencies and the development of cooperative North-South efforts to generate information. Greater use can be made of contract studies by private groups (even if they are physically located in the West) or by Northern and Southern university teams cooperating together. Even the Bretton Woods institutions can be asked to make studies of use to the South, as the African governors asked for the succession of reports on accelerated development. Of course, none of these agencies can serve the coordinating function of a secretariat.

A final procedural element often discussed is the selection of *appropriate arenas* for North-South negotiations. To date, each side has held out for arenas where its power is greatest: the South in UN plenary organs, where numbers count; the North in the Bretton Woods institutions or bilaterally, where their weight counts. The choice of arena, however, is more than a choice of venue; it is, rather, a choice of the way in which the international economic order is to be repaired. Global negotiations might take place under World Bank auspices but would more likely imply a UN forum, whereas commodity negotiations would take place among a more restricted group and changes in the World Bank would be discussed in the bank itself. (Perhaps only on trade matters would there be a choice between two agencies, UNCTAD or GATT). Yet this choice too is not necessarily determinant; incremental change took place in a universal meeting such as the WARC, and productive formulation and trade-offs by small groups occurred in a UN conference such as the UNCLOS. In fact, the choice of appropriate arenas may well be secondary in importance to the application of other lessons of the past.

There is another part of the same conclusion that is important. Procedure should serve substance: parties prefer one venue over the other because it is considered more conducive to a productive outcome. But in that case, the chosen arena should prove its worth, or the parties cannot make claims for its selection. If the problems of the world economy are supposedly best handled in the World Bank and the

IMF, then these institutions should show results that satisfy both sides and all (or most) parties. If they are better handled in UNCTAD or global agencies, then it is incumbent on the defenders of the venue to facilitate the results that justify its choice. The proof of the pudding is in the meeting.

Conclusions

Unusually, perhaps, this study has not focused on strategies for the North and strategies for the South but on insights that are applicable, available, and useful to both sides and all parties. That is in the nature of negotiation in its essence, where parties are equal, decisions are unanimous (any party has a veto), and strategies open to one are open to all. While reality is bumpier than such theoretical considerations, they are still basic to the process at its best. Many of the conclusions have pointed to the fact that anything weakening the monolithic rigidity of the two sides is to the good, for it facilitates a joint attack on the problem, a common search for a formula for agreement, a cooperative development of broader information and understanding, a network of trade-offs, a tissue of crosscutting relations, and a positive-sum outcome. In any case, there is enough disparity in reality to keep this goal from ever being attained fully, until a new international economic order itself breaks down the distinctions between North and South. A number of tactics and strategies applicable to both sides have appeared in these studies.

1. Seek to join the other party in an attack on the problem, beginning with a common identification of it, rather than making a confrontational attack on the other party. Look for the appropriate moment to shift from tough demands to more flexible cooperation, and make sure that there are political decisions or decision makers on hand to authorize the shift.
2. Invest in serious preparation for both the technical aspects of the problem and an understanding of one's own interests and of the other party's. Use occasions for joint study and problem-solving exercises to lay the basis for a common approach.
3. Look for a formula for agreement that encompasses the other party's needs as well as the proposer's.
4. Seek items that can be traded off, both among the details of both sides' positions and in their basic elements as well. Build coalitions among parties from both sides with common interests.
5. Use or create realistic deadlines out of such neutral elements as

expiry dates, external events, or competing opportunities to achieve the same goal.

6. Create agreements that are partial, incremental, and flexible when possible, and when total change is not available.
7. Build on an agreement among those parties willing to agree if unanimity is not possible.
8. Provide for mediators, either through secretariat-type organizations or by identifying national representatives who can play the role.
9. Use representatives, drafting groups, and executive committees, and provide them with trust, information, and accountability.
10. Look for ripe moments in the evolution of the problem and of relations among concerned parties, and use them as the basis for negotiations.

Although negotiations analysis seeks to provide an alternative to the merely hortatory aspects of the debate to date, which has made it a dialogue of the deaf, it must admit that better exhortation is necessary and that negotiation depends on effective persuasion, just as negotiation analysis can provide insights into its improvement. One characteristic that appears to be crucial in analysis of past cases is the necessity of a commitment to agree. When parties were committed to finding an outcome agreeable, they could find an agreeable outcome, as in Yaoundé and Lomé negotiations or in UNCLOS until 1981. When the precommitment to agree was absent, negotiations collapsed or became symbolic, as in CIEC or UNCLOS 1982. When an agreed outcome vanishes, parties negotiate for something else—to avoid blame for collapse, or to maintain group solidarity. It is hard to come to a more basic recommendation than that parties should engage in negotiation with a commitment to arrive at an agreement.

Notes

1. Nor, indeed, are we saying that a given encounter was either bound or right to fail but, rather, that the parties were rational in not agreeing to currently offered terms and could have tried to improve on those terms in various ways discussed.
2. See Commonwealth Group of Experts, *The North-South Dialogue: Making It Work* (London: Commonwealth Secretariat, 1983), esp. pp. 7f, 11.
3. See, among others, Otomar J. Bartos, "How Predictable Are Negotiations?" in *The 50% Solution,* ed. I. William Zartman (New York: Doubleday Anchor, 1974; New Haven: Yale University Press, 1986).
4. See Howard Raiffa, *The Art and Science of Negotiation* (Cambridge: Harvard University Press, 1982), ch. 18; James Sebenius, *Negotiating the Law of the Sea* (Cambridge: Harvard University Press, 1984).

5. For fuller discussion of formulation, see I. William Zartman and Maureen Berman, *The Practical Negotiator* (New Haven: Yale University Press, 1982), ch. 4.

6. See Harold Nicolson, *Diplomacy* (New York: Oxford University Press, 1964), pp. 24-27.

7. Ernest B. Haas, "Why Collaborate?" *World Politics* 32 (April 1980): 537-604.

8. Friedheim's study of UNCLOS in this volume was particularly helpful in triggering some of the following ideas. See also James Sebenius, "Negotiation Arithmetic: Adding and Subtracting Issues and Parties," *International Organization* 37, no. 2 (1983): 281-316.

9. There is, of course, also an S Option, Staying Away.

10. On structural incremental bargaining, see Donald Rothchild, "Racial Stratification and Bargaining," in Zartman, ed., *The 50% Solution*.

11. Harold Lasswell and Abraham Kaplan, *Power and Society* (New Haven: Yale University Press, 1950), p. 75.

12. On mediation see Saadia Torval and I. William Zartman, ed., *International Mediation in Theory and Practice* (Boulder: Westview, 1985).

13. Commonwealth Group, *The North-South Dialogue,* p. 15. On the secretariat, see pp. 17, 75.

Index

ACP Group (members of the African, Caribbean, and Pacific Group): ambassadors of, 230, 235; divisiveness in, 231-33; Group of 77 compared to, 214; membership of, 213, 216; secretariat of, 222-23. *See also* Lomé Conventions

Afghanistan and WARC 79, 191, 193

Africa: and EEC markets, 220; hunger crisis in, 127, 141; unity in, 4, 179; and UNCLOS, 96; and WARC 79, 179, 191, 196, 197, 198, 200. *See also* ACP Group

Algeria: and WARC 79, 185, 187, 188-89, 190, 191, 193, 196, 197, 200, 202; and World Maritime Radio Conference (1974), 174

Amersinghe, Hamilton Shirley, 75-76

Appleton, Shelly, 158, 163

Archer group, 100

Argentina: and debt negotiations, 260-61; and WARC 79, 181, 196-97, 198; and wheat negotiations, 124, 143-44

Arrow, Kenneth, 77

Arsenis, G., 268

Arusha Agreements, 215

Australia: and debt negotiations, 270; and WARC 79, 188, 190, 194, 195; and wheat negotiations, 120, 124, 126, 136, 138, 143

Austria and WARC 79, 192

Axelrod, Robert, 79, 83

Baker, James, III, 163-64

Bargaining process: between African and European Communities, 12; and commodity bargaining, 29-39, 42-44; and COW, 51, 62, 63-71; and debt negotiations, 266-71, 274; and determinacy, 5-6; example of issues of concern in, 11-13; hypotheses about, 9-10; and incrementalism, 7-8, 290-94; individual's role in, 69; in large organizatons, 75; and Lomé Conventions, 229-39; and multifiber arrangement, 161-65; need for studies

about, 5-6; phased explanation of, 8; and power, 6-7; and timing, 7; and UNCLOS, 90-101; and UNCTAD, 32-33, 36-38, 42-44; and WARC 79, 175-79, 201; and wheat negotiations, 128-34, 142-46. *See also* Bargaining strategies; Bargaining structure; Success/failure; Timing

Bargaining strategies: and bargaining process, 7; and Lomé Conventions, 229-37; and North-South relations, 299-300; and risk/cost factors, 7-8; and WARC 79, 177, 202-3. *See also* Bargaining process

Bargaining structure: and bargaining process, 6-7; and commodity bargaining, 29-39, 42-44, 36-38; and Lomé Conventions, 229-31; and UNCLOS, 87-90; and WARC 79, 179-82. *See also* Bargaining process

Belgium: and sugar market, 218; and UNCLOS, 74; and WARC 79, 194

Bell, Richard, 121

Berman, Maureen R., 239

Bilateral agreements and multifiber arrangement, 150, 151-54, 155-57, 164, 165

Black, Eugene, 260

Boerma, Addeke H., 118

Bogota Declaration (1976), 179

Botswana and Lomé Conventions, 231

Brazil: and debt negotiations, 260-61, 263; and EEC markets, 220; and multifiber arrangement, 164; and WARC 79, 191, 193, 194, 196-97, 198, 199, 202

Britain. *See* United Kingdom

Brown, Christopher, 28

Butz, Earl, 121

Cameroon and WARC 79, 185, 187, 186, 195

Campbell, Carroll, 163

Canada: and debt negotiations, 263, 270; and WARC 79, 177, 179, 181, 188, 190, 192, 194, 196, 198-99; and wheat negotiations, 116, 120, 124, 136, 137, 143

CAP (Common Agricultural Policy), 120-21, 129, 135, 218, 219, 220, 242
Carter [Jimmy] administration: and commodity bargaining, 33; and wheat negotiations, 121-22, 135, 136, 144
Center for Agricultural Cooperation, 238
CFA (Committee on Food Aid Policies and Programs), 118
Charter of Economic Rights and Duties of States, 261
Cheysson, Claude, 234, 237
Chile: and UNCLOS, 86; and WARC 79, 198, 200
China: and multifiber arrangement, 150; and WARC 79, 185, 187, 191, 197; and wheat negotiations, 128, 146
CIEC (Conference on International Economic Cooperation): and debt negotiations, 262-63, 271, 272; Group of 77 resistance to, 51; and incrementalism, 293; influence on COW of, 49, 50-51; and Lomé Conventions, 225; results of, 12; and wheat negotiations, 119
Coalitions; and Lomé Conventions, 231-33; in North-South relations, 295-96; and UNCLOS, 78-80, 85, 89; and WARC 79, 182, 202
Collective clientelism (Lomé Conventions), 219-21, 224, 232-33, 238, 241
Colombia: and multifiber arrangement, 164; and WARC 79, 178, 188, 189, 200
COMITEXTIL, 158
Commission of the European Communities. See Lomé Conventions
Committee on Food Aid Policies and Programs (CFA), 118
Committee on Peaceful Use of Outer Space (United Nations), 174, 205
Committee of the Whole [United Nations General Assembly]. See COW
Commodity bargaining: autonomy in, 24; and bargaining process, 29-39, 42-44; and bargaining structure, 29-39, 42-44, 36-38; and commodity production/trade, 21-23; and compromises, 29-30, 33, 34-35, 36, 38, 41; developing countries' dependency on, 23; explanations/alternatives in, 39-42; and financing of agreements, 26-27; and Group of 77, 29-39; and Group B (developed countries), 30, 33-34; importance of South in, 38; and IPC origins, 24-29; and learning process, 29; and mediator, 36-37; mistakes in, 33, 40; objectives of, 38-39; OPEC influence on, 34; political context of, 27-28, 32-33, 280; and power, 20, 21, 23, 38; reform of, 42-44; secretary/general's [UNCTAD] role in, 16-19, 20, 24, 26-27, 29, 31, 32, 34, 35, 37, 41; success/failure of, 39-42; and technical expertise, 35, 36-37, 43, 280, 281; themes/variations of debate about, 21-24; and timing, 287; and Toughness Dilemma, 280-81; trade-offs in, 37-38; and trust, 23-24; UNCTAD role in, 16-19, 20, 24, 26-27, 29-39, 41, 43; U.S. role in, 33-34, 36, 39, 40-42; as a zero-sum game, 28. See also Common Fund
Common Agricultural Policy (CAP), 120-21, 129, 135, 218, 219, 220, 242
Common Fund: accomplishments of, 16-18; agreement signed for, 11-12; and compromises, 34-35; and developed countries, 18; as financing mechanism of IPC, 15; AND GROUP OF 77, 18, 20, 21; AND NIEO, 15, 16; purpose of, 15, 16, 26; ratification of, 15, 16; success/failure of, 16-19, 21, 27; UNCTAD role in, 17-19, 20, 21, 26; U.S. view of, 33-34, 41-42; and wheat negotiations, 142, 144
Commonwealth Sugar Agreement (1975), 214, 217
Compromises: in commodity bargaining, 29-30, 33, 34-35, 36, 38, 41; and Common Fund, 34-35; and Lomé Conventions, 244; and multifiber arrangement, 164, 166; and UNCLOS, 84, 108; and WARC 79, 182, 183-84, 188, 189, 194-95, 199, 201, 203, 204; and wheat negotiations, 143
Conference on International Economic Cooperation. See CIEC
Conferences of the Non-Aligned States, 58, 67. See also NAM
Confrontation: in North-South relations, 279-81; at wheat negotiations, 144-45
Congo and WARC 79, 188
Consensus: and COW, 56-57, 65-68; and debt negotiations, 271; and Group of 77, 29-31; and North-South relations, 286;

in UNCLOS, 73, 74, 76, 77, 78, 91, 101, 102-4; and WARC 79, 175-76, 183-84, 203, 205
Cooper, Richard, 264, 768-69, 273
Corea, Gamani, 16, 19, 26, 37, 269. *See also* UNCTAD: secretary-general of
Cotton. *See* Multifiber arrangement
COW (Committee of the Whole [United Nations General Assembly]): agenda items for, 57-58; and bargaining process, 51, 62, 63-71; CIEC influence on, 49, 50-51; and consensus, 56-57, 65-67, 68; creation of, 48, 49-54; decision making in, 56, 64; deliberations of (1978-1979), 54-59; EC views of, 60-61; and formulas, 283; and global negotiations, 12, 59-63; and Group of 77, 51-54, 55-56, 58-60, 61-62, 64, 66-67, 68; and group system of negotiations, 65-66; and incrementalism, 291; industrialized countries' views of, 52-54, 59-60, 64, 66-67, 68-69; lessons learned from, 67-71; and NIEO, 50, 59; and North-South relations, 48-49, 63-64; and OECD, 63; OPEC influence on, 50, 58-59, 65-66, 68, 69; political context of, 280; and power, 65; purpose/mandate of, 12, 49-50, 51, 53-57; resolutions pertaining to, 49-54, 57; and rule changes, 70; success/failure of, 67-68; and technical expertise, 280, 281; and timing, 287, 288; and Toughness Dilemma, 280-81; and trade-offs, 76; and UN system, 48-49, 59; and United Kingdom, 63; U.S. views about, 52-53, 55, 56, 57-58, 60, 61, 62, 70-71
Creditor control, 269-70
Cuba and WARC 79, 185
Cutbacks and multifiber arrangement, 164-65, 166

Davignon, Etienne, 162-63
De Swaan, Abram, 79
Deadlines in North-South relations, 287-89. *See also* Timing
Debt cancellation, 263, 264, 270, 272
Debt negotiations: arguments presented in, 267-68, 272-73; and bargaining process, 266-71, 274; and beginning of the dialogue, 261-62; and CIEC, 262-63, 271, 272; and consensus, 271; and creditor control, 269-70; and debt cancellation, 263, 264, 270, 272; and debt relief, 261-63, 264, 266-68, 272; and debt reorganization, 264-65; and debt servicing, 259, 260-61; early history of, 260; and emergence of debt problems, 260-61; evaluation of, 266-71; factors influencing, 266-71; and formulas, 283; and Group of 8, 262; and Group of 19, 262-63; and Group of 77, 259, 260, 261-62, 263, 264, 265, 266-68, 270-71, 272-73; and Group B, 263, 265, 266-68, 270, 271, 273; and IDA, 260; and IMF, 260, 265-66, 267, 270, 272; and ministerial meeting (1978), 263-64; and moral concerns, 272; outcomes of, 272-74; and Paris Club, 260, 265, 266, 270, 271; political context of, 265-66, 269-71, 273-74; and power, 267, 273; quality of debate about, 267-68, 273; and Resolution 165, 264, 272; and resource transfers, 259, 262-63, 264, 266, 267, 272; role of individual in, 264; success/failure of, 272-74; and technical expertise, 272-73, 280, 281; and Toughness Dilemma, 280-81; and trade-offs, 273; and UNCTAD, 260, 262, 263, 265, 268, 269, 271, 272, 273; winding down of, 264-66; and World Bank, 260, 262, 265-66, 268, 270, 272; as zero-sum game, 267. *See also* name of country
Debt relief, 261-63, 264, 266-68, 272
Debt reorganization, 264-65
Debt servicing, 259, 260-61
Declaration of Human Rights, 226, 228, 292
Denmark and multifiber arrangement, 159, 163
Determinacy, 5-6
Developed countries. *See* name of country
Displacement and wheat negotiations, 138-39
Dunkel, Arthur, 124, 164

East Germany and WARC 79, 185
EC (European Community): and COW, 60-61; and wheat negotiations, 120-21, 122, 123-24, 126, 128-29, 140, 143, 144. *See also* Common Agriculture Policy (CAP); EEC; name of country

Ecuador: and UNCLOS, 86; and WARC 79, 188, 193, 200

EDF (European Development Fund), 217, 222, 227, 229, 242

EEC (European Economic Community): and GATT Tokyo Round (1976), 120-21; and multifiber arrangement, 156-67; and UNCLOS, 102. *See also* Lomé Conventions

Egypt: and multifiber arrangement, 151; and wheat negotiations, 128, 143, 146

Energy issues. *See* OPEC

England. *See* United Kingdom

Engo, Paul, 76

Enterprise preserves, 84, 94, 96, 108, 284

Equity: and ITU, 173-74; and success/failure, 29-30; and UNCLOS, 108; and WARC 79, 175, 179-80, 186-87

Estonia and WARC 79, 185

European aid issue (Lomé Conventions), 227, 228-29, 236-37

European Development Fund (EDF), 217, 222, 227, 229, 242

Evanson Group of Juridical Experts, 80

Extended jurisdiction issue, 86-87, 91-92, 101, 104-5, 107

FAC (Food Aid Convention), 122-23, 126, 129-30, 134-35, 141

FAO (Food and Agriculture Organization International), 115, 118, 119, 130-32, 136

Federal Republic of Germany: and COW, 63; and debt negotiations, 269, 270; and Lomé Conventions, 228; and multifiber arrangement, 159, 163; and sugar market, 218; and UNCLOS, 74; and WARC 79, 185, 192, 193, 195, 196

Finland and debt negotiations, 270

Fisher, Roger, 239

Fixed service allocations, 190-92

Food and Agriculture Organization International. *See* FAO

Food Aid Convention. *See* FAC

Food security issue, 119-20, 126-27, 128-30, 135-37, 142

Formulas in North-South relations, 283-87

Forum tactics, 51-52

France: and debt negotiations, 269, 270; and Lomé Conventions, 228, 231, 234, 236, 240; and multifiber arrangement, 159,

163; organization of CIEC suggested by, 262; and reciprocity issue, 216; and sugar market, 218; and UNCLOS, 74, 105; and WARC 79, 188, 190, 196-97

Free traders/protectionists, 162, 166

Frequency allocations, 175, 186-87, 190-97, 190-98, 201, 203-4

Fund for Industrial Cooperation, 237

Gabon and WARC 79, 188

GATT (General Agreement of Tariffs and Trade): and COW, 51; eighth meeting of (1986), 3; and Lomé Conventions, 228; and reciprocity issue, 215-16; and wheat negotiations, 117, 120-21, 124, 128, 135, 140. *See also* Multifiber arrangement

Generalized System of Preference (GSP), 215-16, 221

Germany. *See* East Germany; EEC; Federal Republic of Germany

Grains Conventions, 129-30

Greece and Lomé Conventions, 235

Group of 8, 262

Group of 19, 262-63

Group of 77: ACP group compared to, 214; and CIEC, 51; and commodity bargaining, 29-39; and Common Fund, 18, 20, 21; and confrontation, 279; and consensus, 29-31; and COW, 51-54, 55-56, 58-60, 61-62, 64, 66-67, 68; and debt negotiations, 63, 259, 260, 261-62, 263, 264, 265, 266-68, 270-71, 272-73; and FAO, 119; Fifth Ministerial Meeting of (1983), 63; and group system of bargaining, 65-66, 131-34, 273; and IPC, 25, 42; leadership of, 40, 131-34, 135-37; and Lomé Conventions, 224, 228, 234, 236; politicalization of issues by, 131-34; and power of, 76; solidarity of, 19, 31-32, 33, 35-36, 38, 40-41, 76, 266, 273; technical understanding of, 131-32, 137-39; and United Nations, 3, 49; and UNCLOS, 77, 79, 82, 83-84, 86-87, 92, 94-98, 100-101; and wheat negotiations, 115, 118, 119, 121, 123, 125-26, 130-34, 137-38. *See also* Commodity bargaining; LDC; NIEO; name of country

Group B (developed countries): and commodity bargaining, 30, 33-34; and debt negotiations, 263, 265, 266-68, 270, 271, 273

Group system of negotiations, 29-32, 43, 65-66, 131-34, 273

GSP (Generalized System of Preference), 215-16

Guatemala and WARC 79, 196-97

Haas, Ernest B., 19, 20, 285

Harbi, Mohamed, 184, 202

Hart, Judith, 264

Hathaway, Dale, 124, 136

Hong Kong and multifiber arrangement, 150, 151, 154, 158-59, 164, 165

Human rights issues, 226, 227-28

IDA (International Development Association), 260

IFAD (International Fund for Agricultural Development), 118

IFRB (International Frequency Regulation Board), 173-74, 190

IMF (International Monetary Fund): and COW, 51; and debt negotiations, 2, 3, 260, 265-66, 267, 270, 272; and wheat negotiations, 126-27, 133, 141

Incrementalism, 7-8, 230, 236, 239, 242, 243-44, 290-94

India: and debt negotiations, 271; and multifiber arrangement, 151, 164; and WARC 79, 187-88, 189, 191, 193, 194-95, 202; and wheat negotiations, 125, 128, 133, 141, 143-44

Individual, role of: in bargaining process, 69; in debt negotiations, 264; in UNCLOS, 76

Indonesia: and EEC markets, 220; and multifiber arrangement, 159

Industrialized countries, views of COW of, 52-54, 59-60, 64, 66-67, 68-69. See also name of country

Information development. See Technical expertise

Integrated Program for Commodities. See IPC

INTELSAT, 193, 194, 195

Inter-Governmental Committee of the World Food Program (WFP), 118

International Agreement on Wheat (London, 1933), 117

International Development Association (IDA), 260

International Economic Conference (Geneva, 1927), 117

International Economic Cooperation, Conference on. See CIEC

International Frequency Regulation Board. See IFRB

International Fund for Agricultural Development (IFAD), 118

International Grains Agreement (IGA), 117, 122

International Monetary Fund. See IMF

International Seabed Authority, 73, 84, 96

International Seabed Resources Agency, 105-6, 108

International Telecommunications Union. See ITU

International Wheat Agreements (1974-1979), 12, 117, 122, 123, 126

International Wheat Council. See IWC

INTERSPUTNIK, 193

IPC (Integrated Program for Commodities): and commodity bargaining, 24-29; as example of global negotiations, 11-12; and Group of 77, 25, 42; and incrementalism, 291; and NIEO, 15; and OPEC, 24; origins/purpose of, 24-29; outcomes of, 16-18; political context of, 280; and regime creation, 19-20, 25-26; and technical expertise, 280, 281; and timing, 287; and Toughness Dilemma, 280-81; and UNCTAD, 24-25, 26, 27-28; and wheat negotiations, 119, 142, 143. See also Common Fund

Iran and WARC 79, 192, 193, 196

Iraq: and WARC 79, 188; and wheat negotiations, 125

Israel and UNCLOS, 102

Italy: and Lomé Conventions, 240; and multifiber arrangement, 159, 163; and sugar market, 218; and UNCLOS, 74

ITU (International Telecommunications Union): complexity of conferencing of, 172; and equity, 173-74; and LDC demands, 172-75, 179; membership in, 172; politicalization of, 173-75; and technical aid/expertise, 173-74, 178, 199, 282; U.S. and, 173-75. See also WARC; WARC 79

IWC (International Wheat Council), 115, 118-20, 138, 140

Jamaica: and debt negotiations, 268; and WARC 79, 194
Japan: commodities import bill in, 23; and commodity bargaining, 33; and COW, 52; and debt negotiations, 269, 270; and multifiber arrangement, 150, 151, 154, 159; and UNCLOS, 74, 105, 106; and WARC 79, 193, 195, 199; and wheat negotiations, 124, 129, 146
Jaramillo, Felipe, 160, 162, 163
Jayakumar, S., 79, 89, 92

Kadane, Joseph, 108-9
Kampuchea and WARC 79, 185
Kennedy Round of GATT, 117, 122, 123
Kenya and WARC 79, 188, 191, 196, 197
Kieffer, Henry, 183
Kissinger, Henry, 39
Koh, Tommy, 76, 79, 89, 92, 294
Korea: and multifiber arrangement, 150, 154, 158-59, 165; and UNCLOS, 74; and WARC 79, 185-86
Krasner, Stephen D., 84
Krenzler, Horst, 160, 162, 164

Lagos Agreement, 215
LANDSAT, 201
Latin America: and debt negotiations, 270; and UNCLOS, 86, 96, 105; and WARC 79, 191
Latvia and WARC 79, 185
Law of the Sea Conferences (mid-1960s), 85
Law of the Sea Treaty. See UNCLOS
LDCs: and ITU, 172-75, 179; and multifiber arrangement 155, 157-67; and WARC 79, 178-79, 186-87. See also Group of 77
Lehman, John, 87, 107
Lessons learned from: commodity bargaining, 29; COW, 67-71; incrementalism, 294; Lomé Conventions 241, 242-44, 213-14; multifiber arrangement, 166-67; North-South relations, 278, 280
Lima Declaration (March 1975), 261
Lithuania and WARC 79, 185
Lomé Conventions: accomplishments/outcomes of, 213, 216-19, 236, 238; and bargaining environment, 238-39; and bargaining process, 229-37; and bargaining strategies/tactics, 229-37, 240; and bargaining structure, 229-31; and CIEC, 225; and coalitions, 231-33; and collective clientelism, 219-21, 224, 232-33, 232, 238; and concessions, 244; and deadlines, 214-15, 242, 243; and European aid issue, 227, 228-29, 236-37; evaluation of, 237-44; and formulas, 283; and Group of 77, 224, 228, 234, 236; and human rights issues, 226, 227-28; and incrementalism, 230, 236, 239, 242, 243-44, 292, 293; issues in, 214, 215-16, 221, 224, 225-29, 236-37; lessons learned from 241, 242-44, 213-14; and ministerial sessions, 231, 236; and *montant*, 236-37, 240; and moral concerns, 234; and NIEO, 225, 226, 238; and North-South relations, 213-15; and OPEC, 218, 225; political context of, 223, 230, 241, 243, 280; and power, 224-25, 233-34, 239, 242; purpose of, 213-14, 236; and reciprocity issue, 215-16, 219, 227, 238, 242; spirit of, 220-21, 234, 239; and STABEX system, 216, 217, 221, 224, 226, 229, 234, 238, 241; and subcommittees, 229-30; success/failure of, 237-44; and SYSMIN, 226, 238; tactics used in, 231-36, 240; and technical expertise, 222, 243, 280, 281, 282; and timing, 214-15, 242, 243, 286, 287, 288, 289; and Toughness Dilemma, 280-81; trade-offs in, 214, 222; and UNCTAD, 223. *See also* Lomé I Convention; Lomé II Convention; Lomé III Convention
Lomé I Convention (1975): and ACP unity, 215; and EEC Council of Ministers, 217; and external environment, 218-19; negotiations at, 215-19; outcomes of, 216-19; and sugar market, 216, 217, 218-19; and United Kingdom, 216, 217, 218-29. *See also* Lomé Conventions
Lomé II Convention (1980); and "consolidation of existing arrangements", 223-24; issues in, 221, 224, 225-28; opening positions in, 219-29. *See also* Lomé Conventions
Lomé III Convention (1985): and collective clientelism, 241; environment of, 241;

opening positions in, 219-29; and policy dialogue, 228, 241. *See also* Lomé Conventions

Long-Term Cotton Textile Arrangement (LTA), 150, 151-54

McCracken Report (OECD), 34
McNamara, Robert, 268
Malaga-Torremolinos Plenipotentiary Conference (ITU, 1973), 173
Malaysia: and EEC markets, 220; and multifiber arrangement, 159
Malta and WARC 79, 195
Manila Declaration (February 1976), 261-62, 272
Manley, Michael, 268
Marei, Sayed, 118
Market disruption (multifiber arrangement), 154, 155-56
Martin, Edwin, 118
Mediators: Commission of the European Communities as, 214; in commodity bargaining, 36-37; in multifiber arrangement, 161-62; in North-South relations, 294-95
Mexico: and debt negotiations, 263, 270; and multifiber arrangement, 164; and WARC 79, 181, 198
Miles, Edward, 89, 92
Montreux Plenipotentiary Conference (ITU, 1965), 173
Moral concerns: and debt negotiations, 272; and Lomé Conventions, 234; at WARC 79, 197; and wheat negotiations, 130, 141, 145
Morocco and WARC 79, 184, 187, 188
Multifiber arrangement (MFA I), 156
Multifiber arrangement (MFA II), 12-13, 150, 156-57
Multifiber arrangements (MFA III): accomplishments/outcomes of, 149, 161-65; Articles of, 155-56; and bargaining environment, 157-61; and bargaining process, 161-65; and bilateral agreements, 156-57, 164, 165; and compromises, 164, 166; conclusions/implications of, 165-67; and cutbacks, 164-65, 166; and EEC, 157-67; and formulas, 283; and free traders/protectionists, 162, 166; and incrementalism, 291, 293; and interna-

tional regulation of textile trade, 150-57; issues in, 157-61; and LDCs, 155, 157-67; lessons learned from, 166-67; and LTA/STA, 150, 151-54; and market disruption, 154, 155-56; and outward processing, 164; purpose of, 154-55; and quotas, 155, 156-57, 158-59, 165, 166-67; and "reasonable departures," 156-57, 158, 166; and recession clause, 159, 163; signing of, 165-66; and surge mechanism, 163, 164; and timing, 286, 288; and Toughness Dilemma, 281. *See also* name of country

Murphy, Peter, 162, 164

Nacimento, Christopher, 176
NAM (non-aligned movement): meetings of, 3, 58, 67; and WARC 79, 176, 178, 183-84, 282
Nandan Group on the rights of the LL/GDS, 80
National Aeronautics and Space Agency (NASA), 282
NATO and WARC 79, 193, 194
Negotiations. *See* Bargaining process; Bargaining strategies; Bargaining structure; Group bargaining system; name of subject of negotiations, e.g. Commodity bargaining
Netherlands: and debt negotiations, 263, 270; and Lomé Conventions, 228, 231; and multifiber arrangement, 159, 163; and WARC 79, 194
New International Economic Order. *See* NIEO
New World Information Order. *See* NWIO
New Zealand: and debt negotiations, 270; and WARC 79, 183
Nicaragua and WARC 79, 185
Nicolson, Harold, 285
NIEO (New International Economic Order): and Common Fund, 15, 16; and COW, 50, 59; creation of, 1-2, 261, 266; and IPC, 15; and Lomé Conventions, 225, 226, 238; and OPEC, 15; Program of Action for, 119; and UNCLOS, 73-74, 82, 84, 91, 92, 93-94, 96, 98, 102, 108; and WARC 79, 171, 175; and wheat negotiations, 119, 133-34
Nigeria: and Lomé Conventions, 232, 233;

and WARC 79, 191, 196, 197, 200; and wheat negotiations, 146

Non-aligned movement. See NAM

North-South relations: and appropriate arenas, 298-99; and bargaining process, 5-13; and bargaining strategies, 299-300; coalitions in, 295-96; conclusions about, 299-300; confrontation in, 279-81; and consensus, 286; formulas in, 283-87; importance of, 278-301; and incrementalism, 290-94; and information development, 281-83; lessons learned from, 278, 280; mediators in, 294-95; need for new approach to, 3-5; and power, 286-87; problem solving in, 283-86; problems/constraints in, 3-5, 279-83; procedures/mechanics in, 294-99; and regime creation, 286-87; representation in, 296-97; secretariats in, 297-98; success/failure in, 1-3, 278, 183, 184; and technical expertise, 279-83; 286; timing in, 286-89; and Toughness Dilemma, 279-81; and trade-offs, 285-86; and zero-sum terms, 3. See also Group system of bargaining; United Nations; name of bargaining, e.g. commodity bargaining, Lomé Conventions

Norway: and COW, 60-62; and WARC 79, 194, 195

NWIO (New World Information Order), 171, 176, 184

Nyhart MIT computer model, 282

ODA (Official Developmental Assistance), 263, 264, 267, 268

OECD (Organization for Economic Cooperation and Development): and COW, 63; and debt negotiations, 268, 273; and wheat negotiations, 128, 129, 142

OMAs (Orderly marketing agreements), 150

OPEC: and COW, 50, 58-59, 65-66, 68, 69; and commodity bargaining, 34; and debt negotiations, 266; and IPC, 24; and Lomé Conventions, 218, 225; and NIEO, 2, 15; and North-South relations, 2; and WARC 79, 188

Organization of African Unity (OAU), 4, 179

Organization for Economic Cooperation and Development. See OECD

Outward processing, 164

Pakistan: and debt negotiations, 271; and WARC 79, 192; and wheat negotiations, 125

Pardo, Arvid, 73, 84, 86, 105, 107

Paris Club and debt negotiations, 260, 265, 266, 270, 271

Paris Conference on International Economic Cooperation. See CIEC

Parliamentary diplomacy and UNCLOS, 75-84, 87-88

Pearson Commission, 261, 268

Peru and UNCLOS, 86

Phased explanation of negotiation process, 8

Philippines and multifiber arrangement, 159

Pisani, Edgard, 227, 234

Plan B of the Third World, 84

Political context of: commodity bargaining, 27-28, 32-33; debt negotiations, 265-66, 269-71, 273-74; Group of 77, 131-34; ITU, 173-75; Lomé Conventions, 223, 230, 241, 243; WARC 79, 177, 184-86, 203, 205

Portugal: and Lomé Conventions, 235; and multifiber arrangement, 151

Power: and commodity bargaining, 20, 21, 23, 38; and COW, 65; and debt negotiations, 267, 273; and Group of 77, 76; and Lomé Conventions, 224-25, 233-34, 239, 242; and negotiation process, 6-7; and North-South relations, 286-87; and wheat negotiations, 145-46

Prebisch, Raoul, 25, 260-61

Private Group on Straits, 80

Quaker-Methodist Neptune Group, 282

Quotas in multifiber arrangement, 155, 156-57, 158-59, 165, 166-67

Radio Free Europe, 191

Radio Liberty, 191

Ratiner, Leign, 293

Ravenhill, John, 143

Reagan [Ronald] administration: and multifiber arrangement, 163-64; proposal for a global economic conference of, 4; and Toughness Dilemma, 281; and UNCLOS, 11, 87, 91, 94-96, 98, 105. See also United States

"Reasonable departures" (multifiber arrangement), 156-57, 158, 166

Recession clause (multifiber arrangement), 159, 163
Reciprocity issue (Lomé Conventions), 215-16, 219, 227, 238, 242
Regime creation, 19-20, 25-26, 33, 40, 43-44, 286-87
Representation in North-South relations, 296-97
Resolution 165, 264, 272
Resource transfers, 259, 262-63, 264, 266, 267, 272
Rhodesia and Lomé Conventions, 233
Richardson, Elliot, 76
Robinson, G. O., 177
Rothstein, Robert L., 143, 241
Rule changes, 70

Saouma, Edward, 119, 131, 132, 136
Satellite boradcasting, 173-75, 178-79, 186-90, 196-97, 198-99, 201
Saudi Arabia and WARC 79, 192
Schmitt, Harrison, 177, 179
Seabed minerals issue, 85-87, 89, 96, 98-101, 104-7
Secretariats, 297-98
Secretary/general [UNCTAD: role in commodity bargaining of, 16-19, 20, 24, 26-27, 29, 31, 32, 34, 35, 37, 41
Senegal: and Lomé Conventions, 231; and WARC 79, 179
Severini, Robert, 183, 189, 202
Short-Term Cotton Textile Arrangement (STA), 150, 151-54
Shummo, Ali, 173
Single Negotiating Text (UNCLOS), 75-76, 83, 92, 94
Small group effectiveness (wheat negotiations), 144
Somalia and WARC 79, 188
South Korea. See Korea
Sovereignty issue (WARC 79), 189-90
Soviet Union: and UNCLOS, 85, 87, 91-92, 94, 96, 102; and WARC 79, 179, 181, 185, 188, 191, 192, 194-95; and wheat negotiations, 116, 118, 121, 124, 128, 129, 134, 135, 146, 138
Spain: and Lomé Conventions, 235; and UNCLOS, 74
Sri Lanka and debt negotiations, 271

STA (Short-Term Cotton Textile Arrangement), 150, 151-54
STABEX system, 216, 217, 221, 224, 226, 229, 234, 238, 241
Stevenson, John, 76
Strategic explanation of negotiation process, 7. See also Bargaining strategies
Structural explanation of negotiation process, 6-7. See also Bargaining structure
Success/failure: of commodity bargaining, 39-42; of Common Fund, 16-19, 21, 27; of COW, 67-68; of debt negotiations, 272-74; and equity, 29-30; of Lomé Conventions, 237-44; of negotiation process, 10-13; of North-South relations, 1-3, 278, 183, 184; of UNCLOS, 104-6; of WARC 79, 183, 202, 204-5; of wheat negotiations, 124-40, 142-43
Sudan and WARC 79, 195-96, 196-97
Sugar market, 216, 217, 218-19, 220, 231
Surge mechanism (multifiber arrangement), 163, 164
Sweden and debt negotiations, 263, 270
Switzerland: and debt negotiations, 263, 270; and UNCLOS, 74; and WARC 79, 196
Syria and WARC 79, 191
SYSMIN, 226, 238

Tactical explanation of negotiation process, 7. See also Bargaining strategies; name of tactic, e.g. Confrontation
Taiwan and multifiber arrangement, 150, 154, 158-59, 165
Tate & Lyle, 282
Taylor, Lance, 16
Technical aid/expertise: and commodity bargaining, 35, 36-37, 43; in debt negotiations, 272-73; and Group of 77, 131-32, 137-39; of ITU, 173-74, 178, 282; and Lomé Conventions, 222, 243; and North-South relations, 286; and UNCLOS, 80; and WARC 79, 176-79, 184, 190, 192, 199-200, 201, 202-3; and wheat negotiations, 131-32, 137-39
Textile Surveillance Body, 155
Thailand: and multifiber arrangement, 159; and WARC 79, 185
Third World. See Group of 77; LDC
Thurmond, Strom, 163
Timing: and negotiation process, 7; in

North-South relations, 286-89; and WARC 79, 181-82; and wheat negotiations, 135

Tollison, Robert D., 37-38

Toughness Dilemma, 279-81, 279-82

Trade management system. *See* multifiber arrangement

Trade-offs: in commodity bargaining, 37-38; and COW, 76; and debt negotiations, 273; in Lomé Conventions, 214, 222; and North-South relations, 285-86; and UNCLOS, 77, 81, 82, 87, 88, 91-92; and WARC 79, 180, 184

Treaty of Rome, 217

Trust and commodity bargaining, 23-24

Tunisia and wheat negotiations, 125

Turkey: and debt negotiations, 260-61; and UNCLOS, 102

Uganda: and Lomé Conventions, 226; and WARC 79, 187, 188

UN. *See* United Nations

UNCLOS (United Nations Conference on the Law of the Sea): and acceptance of Law of the Sea Treaty, 73, 105-6; accomplishments/outcomes of, 76, 77-78, 82, 90, 91, 101-4, 106-8; and African group, 96; agenda issues of, 80-82; analysis of, 106-8; and bargaining process, 90-101; and bargaining structure, 87-90; benefits of, 83-84, 101; causes for negotiations of, 84-87; and coalitions, 78-80, 85, 89; complexity of, 73, 74-75, 80-81, 90, 108; and compromises, 84, 108; and consensus, 73, 74, 76, 77, 78, 91, 101, 102-4; and developed countries, 88-89; and EEC, 102; evaluation of, 83-84; and extended jurisdiction issue, 86-87, 91-92, 101, 104-5, 107; and formulas, 283; and Group of 77, 77, 79, 82, 83-84, 86-87, 92, 94-98, 100-101; and incrementalism, 292, 293; individual's role in, 76; and international equity, 108; and Latin American group, 86, 96, 105; methodological appendix for, 108-10; and NIEO, 73-74, 82, 84, 91, 92, 93-94, 96, 98, 102, 108; North-South dimension in, 11, 83-84, 94, 96; and parliamentary diplomacy, 75-84, 87-88; and Reagan administration, 87, 91, 94-96, 98, 105; and seabed minerals issue, 85-87, 89, 96, 98-101, 104-7; and Single Negotiating Text, 75-76, 83, 92, 94; and special-interest groups, 83, 85-86; success/failure of, 89, 104-6; and technical expertise, 80, 280, 282, 283; and timing, 286, 288; and Toughness Dilemma, 280-81; and trade-offs, 77, 81, 82, 87, 88, 91-92, 286; and U.S., 74, 77, 80-82, 84-85, 86, 87, 91-92, 94-98, 100-101, 102, 104, 105-6. *See also* name of individual country

UNCTAD (United Nations Conference on Trade and Development): and bargaining process, 32-33, 36-38, 42-44; and Common Fund, 17-19, 20, 21, 26; and debt negotiations, 42, 260, 262, 263, 265, 268, 269, 271, 272, 273; and group bargaining system, 29-32, 43; and IPC, 24-25, 26, 27-28; -IV (Nairobi, 1976), 25, 34, 39, 262; leadership of, 40; and Lomé Conventions, 223; members' attitudes about, 31-32; proposals of, 32; and regime creation, 19-20, 33, 40, 43-44; staff of, 28, 30-31, 32; strengths/weaknesses of, 18-19, 30-31, 32, 40-41; -V (Manila, 1979), 3, 34-35, 265; and WARC 79, 200; and wheat negotiations, 117, 119, 122, 123-24, 132-32. *See also* Commodity bargaining; Secretary/general

UNESCO and WARC 79, 171

UNIDO (United Nations Industrial Development Organization), 58

United Kingdom: and commodity bargaining, 33; and COW, 63; and debt negotiations, 263, 264, 269, 270; and Lomé Conventions, 216, 217, 218-19, 228, 231, 236; and multifiber arrangement, 159, 163; and reciprocity issue, 216; and sugar market, 216, 217, 218-19, 231; and UNCLOS, 74; and WARC 79, 185, 187, 189, 190, 192, 194

United Nations, 1-2, 49-54, 59, 62-63, 64, 67-68, 261, 266. *See also* COW; UNCLOS; UNCTAD; name of committee; name of document, e.g., Manila Declaration

United Nations Conference on the Law of the Sea. *See* UNCLOS

United Nations Conference on Trade and Development. *See* UNCTAD

United Nations Development Program, 199

United Nations Industrial Development Organization. *See* UNIDO
United States (U.S.): and bilateral textile agreements, 150, 151-54, 155-57; and chairmanship dispute of WARC 79, 183-84; and commodity bargaining, 33-34, 36, 39, 40-42; and Common Fund, 33-34, 41-42; and COW, 52-53, 55, 56, 57-58, 60, 61, 62, 70-71; and debt negotiations, 269; domestic textile pressures in, 163-64, 167; and frequency allocations, 191, 192, 193-94, 195, 196-97, 201; and information development, 282; and ITU, 173-75; and multifiber arrangements, 150, 151-54, 156, 157-67; and reciprocity issue, 216; and satellite broadcasting, 174-75, 178-79, 186, 188, 189, 196-97, 198-99, 201; and Toughness Dilemma, 281; and UNCLOS, 74, 77, 80-82, 84-85, 86, 87, 91-92, 94-98, 100-101, 102, 104, 105-6; and WARC 79, 174-77, 178-79, 183-84, 185, 186, 188, 189, 190-97, 198-99, 201, 204; and wheat negotiations, 116, 118, 119, 120-27, 128-29, 130, 133, 135, 136, 139, 140, 143, 144; White Paper [Administration Textile Program], 157, 167. *See also* Carter [Jimmy] administration; Ford [Gerald] administration; Reagan [Ronald] administration
Ury, William, 239

Values and negotiation process, 7
Venezuela: and debt negotiations, 271; and WARC 79, 195, 198
Villain, Claude, 124, 136
Voice of America, 191

WARC (World Administrative Radio Conferences), 13, 173-75, 178-79, 184, 191-92
WARC 79 (World Administrative Radio Conference, 1979): adversary image at, 176-79; bargaining environment of, 175-79, 20; and bargaining strategies, 177, 202-3; and bargaining structure, 179-82; chairmanship dispute at, 183-84; and coalitions, 182, 202; committies at, 180-82, 203; and compromises, 182, 183-84, 188, 189, 194-95, 199, 201, 203, 204; conclusions about, 201-5; and con-

sensus, 175-76, 183-84, 203, 205; and equity issue, 175, 179-80, 186-87; Final Acts of, 181, 182-83, 200, 203-4, 205; and formulas, 283; and frequency allocations, 175, 186-87, 190-97, 190-98, 201, 203-4; and international broadcasting, 191-92; and intraregional issues, 197-99; LDC position at, 178-79, 186-87; moral concerns at, 197; and NAM, 176, 178, 183-84; and NIEO, 171, 175; and NWIO, 171, 176, 184; political context of, 177, 184-86, 203, 205, 280; preparations for, 175-79, 203; purpose of, 13, 175, 176; resolutions of, 204; and satellite broadcasting, 178-79, 186-90, 196-97, 198-99, 201; and sovereignty issue, 189-90; success/failure of, 183, 202, 204-5; and technical aid/expertise, 176-79, 184, 190, 192, 199-200, 201, 202-3, 280, 282, 283; and timing, 181-82, 286, 288; and Toughness Dilemma, 280-81; and trade-offs, 180, 184. *See also* ITU; name of country
West Germany. *See* Federal Republic of Germany
WFC (World Food Conference/Council), 115, 118, 119-20, 126, 130, 133-34, 145
WFP (Inter-Govermental Committee of the World Food Program), 118
Wheat Agreements, 136-37
Wheat negotiations: acquisition/relinquishment of reserves, 120-27, 128-29; analysis of, 127-40; and bargaining process, 128-34, 142-46; and CIEC, 119; and compromises, 143; confrontation at, 144-45; and EC, 120; evaluation of, 126, 140-42; and FAO, 115, 118, 119, 130-32; and financing of reserves, 120-27, 128-29, 141; Group of 77 role in, 115, 118, 119, 121, 123, 125-26, 130-34, 137-38; issues in, 120-27; IWC role in, 115, 118-20, 138, 140; and Kennedy Round of GATT, 122, 123; leadership at, 135-37; lessons learned from, 142-46; and market stability, 116-18; misperceptions at, 137, 144; moral concern in, 130, 141, 145; and NIEO, 119, 133-34; prices of, 116-18, 137-38, 140-41; power/dependency at, 145-46; purpose of, 115, 118; and quantity of reserves, 120-27, 128-29; security issue in, 116-20, 126-27, 128-30, 135-37,

142; small group effectiveness at, 144; and Soviet Union, 116, 118, 121, 124, 128, 129, 134, 135, 138, 146; success/failure of, 124-40, 142-43; technical understanding at, 131-32, 137-39; and timing, 135; uncertainty at, 139-40; UNCTAD role in, 119, 122, 123-24, 132-32; and U.S., 116, 118, 119, 120-27, 128-29, 130, 133, 135, 136, 139, 140, 143; and WFC, 115, 118, 119-20, 126, 130, 133-34, 145. *See also* FAC; WTC; name of country

Wheat Trade Convention (WTC), 122, 122-23, 129-30, 133, 138, 139

Willett, Thomas D., 37-38

Williams, Maurice, 136

World Administrative Radio Conference. *See* WARC; WARC 79

World Bank: and debt negotiations, 2, 3, 260, 262, 265-66, 268, 270, 272; and wheat negotiations, 126, 133

World Food Conference/Council. *See* WFC

World Hunger Commission, 135

World Maritime Radio Conference (1974), 174

World Meteorological Organization, 197

WTC (Wheat Trade Convention), 129-30, 133, 138, 139

Yaounde Conventions, 12, 214, 215, 216, 217, 234, 292, 293

Young, Oran R., 75

Yugoslavia: and WARC 79, 191; and wheat negotiations, 125

Zaire and WARC 79, 188

Zartman, I. William, 129, 142, 144, 145, 234, 239

Zimbabwe and Lomé Conventions, 233

Printed in the United States
by Baker & Taylor Publisher Services